YOU DECIDE!

Current Debates in Criminal Justice

YOU DECIDE!

Current Debates in Criminal Justice

Bruce N. Waller

Youngstown State University

Prentice Hall
Upper Saddle River, New Jersey
Columbus, Ohio

Library of Congress Cataloging-in-Publication Data

Waller, Bruce N.
  You decide! : current debates in criminal justice / Bruce N. Waller.—1st ed.
      p. cm.
  Includes bibliographical references.
  ISBN-13: 978-0-205-51410-6 (alk. paper)
  ISBN-10: 0-205-51410-3 (alk. paper)
  1. Criminal justice, Administration of—United States—Popular works.
I. Title.
  KF9223.W255 2009
  345.73'05—dc22

                                                            2008020452

Vice President and Executive Publisher: Vernon Anthony
Acquisitions Editor: Tim Peyton
Editorial Assistant: Alicia Kelly
Media Project Manager: Karen Bretz
Director of Marketing: David Gesell
Marketing Manager: Adam Kloza
Marketing Assistant: Les Roberts
Production Manager: Kathleen Sleys
Creative Director: Jayne Conte
Cover Design: Bruce Kensselaar
Full-Service Project Management/Composition: Kavitha Kuttikan/Integra Software Services
Printer/Binder: Bind Rite, Robbinsville/Command Web

Credits and acknowledgments borrowed from other sources and reproduced, with permission, in this
textbook appear on appropriate page within text.

Pearson Education Ltd., London
Pearson Education Singapore, Pte. Ltd
Pearson Education Canada, Inc.
Pearson Education–Japan
Pearson Education Australia PTY, Limited
Pearson Education North Asia, Ltd., Hong Kong
Pearson Educación de Mexico, S.A. de C.V.
Pearson Education Malaysia, Pte. Ltd.
Pearson Education Upper Saddle River, New Jersey

Prentice Hall
is an imprint of

PEARSON
www.pearsonhighered.com

CC LIBRARY SERVICES
AUSTIN, TX

10 9 8 7 6 5 4 3 2 1
ISBN-13: 978-0-20-551410-6
ISBN-10:   0-20-551410-3

Contents

Preface

This book contains debates on controversial issues that are central to criminal justice. The issues were selected because they raise important criminal justice questions, and because the answers to those questions have not been settled. In every case, I have tried to find the strongest advocate for each side. If for several of the debates you read both sides and still can't reach a decision about who is right, that's not a bad result. If you have already reached a settled conclusion on one of the issues, and the debate unsettles that conclusion, that may be a good result. And if you read both sides of the debate, and recognize that there are strong and interesting arguments on both sides, that may be the best result.

These debates cover a broad spectrum of issues in criminal justice. They start with basic questions about police procedure and methodology: the role of discretion in professional policing and the use of deception in police investigation. Next is the continuing controversy over the role of victims in the criminal justice process, and from there the debates move to controversial questions about criminal trials and dealing with criminal suspects: debates over the widespread use of plea bargaining, the use of jailhouse informants, jury selection, and jury-nullification. The next set of debates deals with treatment of those found guilty of criminal offenses: the restorative vs. retributive models, the use of shaming punishments, mandatory minimum sentencing practices, "selective incapacitation" of repeat offenders (as in "three strikes" laws), supermax prisons and the solitary confinement of prisoners, questions concerning the rights of prisoners, the requirement that sexual offenders register (and the public posting of such registrations), and capital punishment. Juvenile justice issues are examined in the next two debates, and the concluding debate deals with controversies surrounding the Patriot Act. Many of these debates have close connections, and the readings for one may be relevant for others: for example, the debates on shaming punishments, supermax prisons, and prisoners' rights have significant overlap.

The book can be used as the primary text for a course on issues in criminal justice; however, it would also be an ideal accompaniment to introductory criminal justice courses as well as courses in criminal justice ethics, giving students an opportunity to examine a wide range of contemporary issues through the work of outstanding contemporary criminal justice writers. Though there are interconnections among the issues debated, each debate is presented as a stand-alone chapter, so that debates can be examined in any order, and debate topics can be chosen to fit a variety of course designs and interests. Another good use for the book is for paper topics: Examining opposing views on key criminal justice issues and then writing an account of which view is stronger and *why* is an excellent way of pushing deeper into basic issues of criminal justice. The reading selections are by well-regarded contemporary experts, but they were also chosen for their clarity of style and their accessibility to students. The essays are substantive but very readable.

Sincere thanks to many people who helped and encouraged. First, to my colleagues at Youngstown State University, who have given me many useful ideas and valuable references and have constantly stimulated my thinking on these topics. My students at YSU have been a wonderful source of encouragement with their enthusiasm for and insights into the debates discussed here. The amazing efficiency of our departmental administrator, Joan Bevan, makes all my work easier and better: there is no problem she can't solve, and—with the aid of our excellent student worker Hannah Detec—she solves most of them before I'm even aware of them. The librarians at YSU have been amazingly helpful at finding obscure references and articles and misplaced books. I would also like to extend thanks to my reviewers: Gary A. Sokolow, College of the Redwoods; Larry L. Bench, University of Utah; Anthony A. Peguero, Miami University; Kim M. Marino, Marist College; Jeffrey Lane Yates, University of Georgia; Shawna Cleary, University of Central Oklahoma; Stephen R. Wilson, University of Colorado at Boulder; Martha J. Jones, Fort Hayes State University; Mike Carlie, Missouri State University; Susan F. Brinkley, University of Tampa; Ryan Schroeder, University of Louisville; Luis Salinas, University of Houston; Trina L. Hope, University of Oklahoma; and Ken A. Egbo, Edinboro University. Many friends have been very generous in providing suggestions and deepening my understanding of all facets of these issues, including especially Fred Alexander, Nawal Ammar, Luke Lucas, Chris Raver, Jack Raver, Lia Ruttan, and Lauren Schroeder. My editors at Pearson, Dave Repetto and Tim Peyton, have been supportive, instructive, picky, pushy, and cordial throughout: everything editors should be. Thanks also to Kavitha Kuttikan for her superb work in shepherding this book through all the gritty production details. Finally, my greatest debt is to my family—Mary, Russell, and Adam—who provide constant support and profound joy.

Introduction

The story is told of a man of few words, who one Sunday went to church alone because his wife didn't feel well. Upon his return, his wife asked what the preacher's sermon had been about. "Sin," the man replied. His wife pressed on, "What did the preacher say about sin?" "He was against it." It would seem that criminal justice should be almost that uncontroversial. It focuses on two things: crime and justice. Everyone is against the former, and for the latter. But in fact, criminal justice is rich with lively and vigorous debates. Indeed, in a criminal justice history that spans thousands of years, there are probably more criminal justice controversies currently than at any time in the past.

Criminal justice deals with the institutions and agencies that control crime in society: the police enforcement of laws, the arrest of suspected violators, the investigation of criminal acts and the trials of the accused, and the punishment and/or rehabilitation of criminal offenders. Each of those areas generates well-known controversies: How strict and severe should police enforcement be? Should the police make discretionary judgments concerning the enforcement of the laws? Should the police employ deception in investigating crimes? Should criminal charges be handled through plea bargains? Should juveniles be prosecuted as adults? How long should prison sentences be? Under what conditions should offenders be incarcerated? Is the death penalty an appropriate punishment? Many of those issues are comparatively recent in the history of criminal justice: the juvenile justice system developed in the nineteenth century, and before then children were imprisoned and executed with little regard for age. The death penalty was widely used and rarely questioned for many centuries. And questions regarding the proper professional conduct of police officers could hardly arise before the development of a professional police force, another nineteenth-century process.

So there are perhaps more specific criminal justice controversies than ever before; but looking at a deeper level, there are also controversies over fundamental underlying questions. One of the most basic of those deep questions has to do with the relation between individuals and society: to what degree should individual liberties and rights be sacrificed for the security of the community? In despotic, totalitarian, and authoritarian societies, the answer is easy: individual rights and liberties count for nothing against the majesty of the ruler or the good of the state or the commandments of religion. But in a democratic society, the opposite tendency is supposed to prevail. It was Benjamin Franklin who said, "Those who would give up essential liberty to purchase a little temporary safety deserve neither liberty nor safety." We could increase our security—at least temporarily—by allowing the police unlimited access to our private lives; and we could convict more felons if we allowed the police to torture suspects to obtain confessions. But a democratic society, in which the rights and liberties of individuals are held in high regard, cannot make such sacrifices for increased security. The same consideration operates in one of our basic democratic principles of justice: "It is better for 10 guilty to go free than for one innocent to be convicted." Such a principle would be absurd under a monarchy or a totalitarian system, but for a democratic society that prizes the individual liberty of every member, it is a bedrock principle of justice. And many of the specific controversies in criminal justice are shaped by deeper questions about the proper relation between the security of the society and the freedom of the individual.

The tension between individual liberty and community security is one deeply contested issue that shapes our views on specific criminal justice issues; another is the status of criminal offenders in our society. For many centuries, a common punishment for criminals was banishment: the criminal was excluded from the community. Though banishment is not now in common use (though deportation of noncitizens does occur), some contemporary approaches to punishment are almost equivalent: a sentence of life imprisonment without parole, for example. The contrasting view regards offenders as members of the community who must be reformed, and who retain their community ties and rights. Whether we regard miscreants as aliens to be controlled and isolated or as misguided community members to be reclaimed will have a profound effect on many more specific issues: the debate over the restorative justice model, the question of prisoners' rights, the issue of selective incapacitation, and even the debate about the death penalty. The debates in this volume focus on specific issues in criminal justice, but the issues they raise often run very deep; and a strength of the debates included here is that the advocates often touch on those deeper questions.

The debates covered here are serious, and the disputes often run deep. These are debates that sometimes generate more heat than light, as both sides of the controversy defend entrenched positions, regard opposing arguments as personal attacks, and treat opponents as villains driven by unworthy motives. The first step in appreciating the subtleties and depth of these issues is to recognize that there are no *bad* guys in these arguments; rather, there are people who place different levels of emphasis on values and goods that almost all of us share or can at least respect. Advocates of supermax prisons have genuine concerns about the dangers of managing violent offenders who may pose a threat to society, to fellow prisoners, and to prison workers. And those who oppose supermax prisons have genuine concerns about the harsh treatment meted out to those supermax prisoners, the effects of those conditions on prisoners' psychological health and on increased tendencies toward violence, and whether such harsh conditions of imprisonment undermine important societal values. The opposing sides may have substantial differences, and may give differing weights to different values. But if we can start from an appreciation of the legitimate concerns of *both* groups, our debates may be more instructive; at the very least, they will be more cordial.

One of the most tempting argumentative mistakes or fallacies is the *strawman* fallacy: the fallacy of distorting or misrepresenting your opponent's argument in order to make it easier to attack. After all, it's much easier to knock down a strawman than the real thing, and much easier to refute a distorted misrepresentation of a position or argument than the real thing. While it may be fun to knock the stuffings out of a strawman, it won't win you any real victories. And while it may be fun to distort an opposing view and then refute it, that won't win you any real converts. When you give a false account of your opponent's view, your opponent is not likely to be convinced by the refutation of a view she never held in the first place. The other problem with the strawman fallacy is that it keeps you from understanding and appreciating opposing views—views that might (unless you are infallible) be better than your own, or that at least might contain positive elements. A much better policy than strawman distortions is a *principle of charity*: Try to cast opposing views in the strongest possible form. This is important for understanding, appreciating, and learning from views you oppose, and essential if you hope to convince your opponents.

The second argument fallacy that must be avoided—and that, like sin and the strawman fallacy, is also very tempting—is the *ad hominem* fallacy. "Ad hominem" means "to the man," and the *ad hominem* fallacy is the fallacy of trying to refute an argument by attacking the man (or woman) who gave that argument. When someone gives an *argument*, you must look at the argument itself; the *source* of the argument is irrelevant to the *strength* of the argument. An evil person may give an excellent argument, and a virtuous person may give a terrible argument. If I give an *argument*, my argument must stand or fall on its own merits; and whether I am drunk or sober, sincere or hypocritical, vicious or virtuous matters not at all to the quality of my argument. Thus, an advocate of supermax prisons may work for a private prison corporation that operates a supermax facility, and may have a strong financial stake in preserving supermax prisons. Knowing that the person has a special personal financial interest might give you good reason to scrutinize her arguments very carefully; but that is *not* good grounds for rejecting her arguments. The argument must be judged on its merits, not on its source. Suppose you read an argument in favor of supermax prisons; you don't have to know *who* wrote the argument in order to evaluate the quality of the argument. If you discover that the argument was given by a large investor in private supermax facilities, that won't change the argument into a bad one; and if you discover instead that the argument was given by a winner of the Nobel Peace prize, that will not make the argument one degree better. It's still the same argument, whether it was given by a saint or a sinner, by a paragon of virtue or an exemplar of evil. And if you focus on the *source* of an argument rather than on the argument itself, you will cut yourself off from enlightening arguments given by people you don't like (and will be too easily swayed by the arguments of those you *do* like).

That does not mean that *ad hominem* arguments are always wrong or always fallacious. There are many times when *ad hominem* arguments are relevant and valuable. If I ask you for a loan, it will be very valuable for you if someone points out that I'm a deadbeat who never repays his loans. If I ask you to join me for lunch, it will be quite relevant if someone points out that I have the manners of a shark in a feeding frenzy, that I bore my luncheon companions with long stories about my childhood, that I drink heavily during lunch and become loud and obnoxious, and that I always stick my luncheon companions with the check. And when someone *testifies*—for example, when a witness testifies in court, or I *testify* that I truly did see a fleet of extraterrestrial invaders—then *ad hominem* attacks against the source of *testimony* are relevant and important. As Samuel Johnson said:

> Argument is argument. You cannot help paying regard to their arguments, if they are good. If it were testimony you might disregard it. Testimony is like an arrow shot from a long bow; the force of it depends on the strength of the hand that draws it. Argument is like an arrow from a cross-bow, which has equal force though shot by a child.

If you are evaluating *argument*, it doesn't matter whether the source of the argument is a heroin addict, a notorious liar, and a dirty cheat. But when a jail-house informant *testifies*, it is quite legitimate to attack his motives, his character, and his veracity. If the District Attorney has offered the witness a "get out of jail free" deal in exchange for his testimony, that is something that you (as a juror) would want to weigh carefully when evaluating the testimony of that witness. But when considering *arguments*, rather than testimony, the temptation of *ad hominem* fallacy must be avoided. The papers in this volume—and the opposing views of those in your class—are *arguments*, not testimony. Feel free to attack the *arguments themselves*; it's perfectly legitimate to point out that someone has given an argument that doesn't work, that fails to establish the claims it is making. But don't fall into the fallacy of trying to refute an argument by attacking the source of that argument. It's not an effective way to examine arguments; and furthermore, it's not likely to make you many friends.

Probing into the debates on pivotal issues in contemporary criminal justice is fascinating, and for those planning a career in criminal justice it is vitally important: these are among the key issues you must confront for yourself in your professional life. But these are also contentious issues: issues on which people hold views that are deeply felt and in fundamental conflict. To make this a worthwhile rather than a destructive study, it is essential to treat others respectfully, and avoiding *ad hominem* and strawman fallacies is a vital first step in practicing respectful disagreement. Learning how to argue and disagree graciously and honestly and how to appreciate and learn from people with views very different from your own may be just as important as learning the details of these pivotal debates in contemporary criminal justice.

Should the Police Practice Discretion When Enforcing the Law?

Police Should Exercise Discretion in Deciding When to Arrest
  Advocate: John Kleinig, Professor at John Jay College of Criminal
    Justice, City University of New York, and Professor at the Centre for
    Applied Philosophy and Public Ethics of the Australian National
    University; author of many books and articles, including *The Ethics
    of Policing* (New York: Cambridge University Press, 1996).
  Source: "Selective Enforcement and the Rule of Law," *Journal of
    Social Philosophy*, Volume 29, Number 1 (Spring 1998): 117–131.
Police Discretion Has No Place in a Democracy
  Advocate: Jeffrey Reiman, William Fraser McDowell Professor of
    Philosophy at American University; author of many books and
    articles, including *The Rich Get Richer and the Poor Get Prison:
    Ideology, Class, and Criminal Justice*, 8th Edition (Needham, MA:
    Allyn & Bacon, 2007).
  Source: "Against Police Discretion: Reply to John Kleinig," *Journal of
    Social Philosophy*, Volume 29, Number 1 (Spring 1998): 132–142.

When a police officer observes a violation of the law—someone not wearing a
seatbelt or driving 10 miles over the speed limit, or an underage teenager smoking a cigarette, or a middle-aged man eating a sandwich and drinking wine in a
municipal park where no alcoholic beverages are allowed—she has a decision to
make: Should she arrest the lawbreaker? Warn him? Reprimand him severely,
but not arrest him? Ignore the violation? Such decisions are required of police
officers on a regular basis, and the decisions are typically made on their own,
without supervision or public reporting.

As John Kleinig has noted, when a police officer chooses to beat up a homeless person in a dark alley, that is *not* a case of discretionary police behavior; rather, it is a clear *violation* of the rules and regulations that the police officer is under an obligation to follow and uphold. That a police officer may have the power and opportunity to commit such an offense does not make it discretionary. Genuinely *discretionary* police behavior falls within a range of allowed and legitimate choices. Thus, a police officer may have *discretion* over whether to ticket a driver who is exceeding the speed limit by 5 to 15 miles an hour; but giving a speeding ticket to a driver who is within the speed limit would fall outside the range of legitimate discretion.

Most of us have no objection when a police officer exercises her discretion, and chooses not to ticket us for driving 10 miles over the speed limit. But if blacks are routinely ticketed for driving over the speed limit, while similar behavior by whites is ignored, or if a noisy outside suburban party (perhaps involving some underage drinking) is ignored, while a similar party in a less affluent neighborhood draws police sanctions, then the police discretion becomes more troubling. Unfortunately, such discriminatory discretion—against young people, against minority races and ethnic groups, and against people of lower economic status—has occurred: "racial profiling" is the best known example, exemplified by complaints of minority youth that they received a ticket for "driving while black."

▪▪▪ Points to Ponder

- When there are laws that do not enjoy popular support—such as laws against gambling, in a community where gambling is common—police officers often "exercise discretion" and ignore most violations. If you are a police officer in such an area, is it alright to look the other way when a high school chemistry teacher arranges a pool on the Super Bowl? When a local bar owner runs a small bookmaking operation for his customers? Is it alright to accept free drinks from the bar owner who keeps the small book? Football tickets? Super Bowl tickets?
- A major concern of allowing police *discretion* is the possibility that it leaves too much room for police *discrimination* against people (ethnic groups, protesters, gays) they don't like. Are there effective ways of preventing or at least minimizing such discrimination?
- If you favor zero-tolerance policing, does consistency require that you also *oppose* police discretion? That is, is there a basic conflict between zero-tolerance policing and the exercise of police discretion, or are they compatible?
- Jeffrey Reiman argues that laws giving discretion to police would be acceptable *only if* legislators explicitly built such discretion into the law. Would it be possible to write such a law? Could you write a law—for example, a traffic law—that builds in an element of police discretion? *If* it is possible to write such a law, would you consider that law better than our current law, which does not have police discretion built in?

- A key argument between Kleinig and Reiman concerns police professionalism. Both are strong advocates of well-trained, highly professional forces. But while Kleinig sees police discretion as a vital element of such professionalism (on the model of physicians and lawyers), Reiman argues that police discretion would be something entirely different from the discretion of other professionals, and would be *wrong*. Is there an important difference between police discretion and medical discretion?

Selective Enforcement and the Rule of Law

John Kleinig

"Is it justifiable in a free society to allow police officers freedom to determine whether or not to arrest someone when they legally and physically can make the arrest?" This is the question to which Jeffrey Reiman has recently answered an unambiguous "no." It is not the first time that the question has been answered this way, though Reiman's robust defense must once again give pause to those who, like myself, believe that some discretion in this regard ought to be allowable. . . .

Political authority as we now understand it is not primarily goal-oriented, but contractual. It does not authorize those in power to achieve some desirable end by whatever means they consider appropriate, but is a limited *authorization* to secure certain specified ends (as enshrined in law) by means that are limited. That being so, Reiman argues, any discretionary authority that police exercise can be justified in only two ways: either as an explicit grant by citizens or as the conclusion of an argument showing that it would be reasonable to make such a grant. He takes it that there is no basis for believing the former: police are "simply and explicitly authorized to enforce the law that the people's representatives enact, and no more."

Is there any good reason to think that people *should* give police some discretion about whether or not to enforce the law? Reiman offers four reasons for thinking that no good grounds exist for giving them that discretion: (1) it would render the laws "vague and uncertain"; (2) it would effectively give police the power to

John Kleinig. "Selective Enforcement and the Rule of Law," *Journal of Social Philosophy*, Volume 29, Number 1 (Spring 1998): 117–131. Reprinted with permission from Blackwell Publishing Ltd.

amend laws that the people's representatives had passed; (3) it would almost certainly be used discriminatorily; and (4) it would be used coercively as a form of leverage. In what follows I shall attempt to meet the challenge posed by Reiman's arguments, and shall argue that it is reasonable to allow to police a limited discretionary authority in regard to their enforcement of law. . . .

The Rule of Law

As Reiman rightly observes, the idea of "a government of laws, not men" is of ancient pedigree. Not only Plato but also Aristotle was convinced that "the rule of law is preferable to that of any individual." And in liberal democratic regimes, the rule of law has been appealed to as the main bulwark against tyranny. Any theoretical doubts that people have had about its appropriateness have usually been allayed by the spectacle of what happens in societies that have rejected it.

Nevertheless, appeals to the rule of law are neither as transparent nor as compelling as Reiman seems to believe. First of all, there is considerable debate about what is encompassed by the rule of law, and for this reason it can be questioned whether a rule of law excludes the recognition of limited discretionary authority; and second, there is a tension between the rule of law and democratic expectations.

The rule of law is a political ideal. Essentially, it sets forth conditions for government that are intended to preserve the governed from the tyranny of arbitrary power. For some writers this is understood *formalistically*, as requiring no more than the existence of and subscription to fixed and preannounced formal rules, rules that are articulated with sufficient clarity to enable exercises of governmental authority to be predicted with some certainty. But for other writers, the rule of law is interpreted more *substantively* to require that rules promulgated by governmental authority be broadly concordant with a particular conception of human entitlements. Thus "rule of law values"—the separation of powers, equality and formal justice, liberty and notice, substantive fairness, procedural fairness, and efficient administration—are intended to secure citizens not only against arbitrariness but also against oppressive rules.

Reiman does not explicitly join this debate, though he is clearly concerned about both oppression and arbitrariness. He accepts that respect for human freedom and human equality need to be preserved in—indeed, constitute the *raison d'être* for—civil society. It could be that freedom and equality can be protected not only by adherence to the rule of law but also by commitment to a conception of human rights or personal sovereignty, the latter pressed as political demands additional to that of the rule of law. But I think that he implicitly accepts the richer, more substantive view of the rule of law, for he quotes with approval Locke's contention that "*where-ever law ends, tyranny begins*," and that the person who "exceeds the power given him by the law . . . may be opposed, as any other man, who by force invades the right of another." This strongly suggests that Reiman sees the rule of law as securing us not merely against arbitrariness but also against (other?) violations of our rights.

Because of this, Reiman believes that in a free society adherence to the rule of law will preclude the grant of discretionary authority to police. It is only if such authority has been explicitly granted, or if it is reasonable to expect it to be granted, that we may reconcile police discretion with the rule of law. He takes it that the former has not occurred, and believes the latter to be lacking in merit.

Consider now the second issue: the coherence of the rule of law with democratic or contractual processes. Reiman seems to take it for granted that there is an easy fit between the rule of law and its modern expression in liberal democratic society. Yet a little reflection indicates that this is not the case. The rule of law, at least according to Reiman's conception, seems to require that laws be applied exceptionlessly. Democratic and contractarian theories, on the other hand, emphasize the value of the majority will, and that will need not be limited to or even be compatible with the substantive requirements of law. . . .

The seriousness of this potential tension between the rule of law and democratic values is not unrelated to the way in which we construe both the rule of law and democracy. If democracy and the rule of law are both thought of formalistically—as no more than a crude majoritarianism, on the part of one, and a law of rules, on the part of the other—then the tension could be quite significant. But if democratic rule is anchored instead in the values of equality and freedom, and the rule of law is likewise anchored in a the-

ory of human rights, the rule of law may be seen as expressing one of the conditions under which (liberal) democratic aspirations may be realized.

Have people actually withheld discretionary authority from the police? Reiman might have referred to the full enforcement statutes that have been passed in many states. If the people have not spoken, then their representatives certainly have, and they have charged police with responsibility to arrest anyone who violates a law. What more appropriate evidence could we want in a democratically ordered society? Strong as this consideration is, however, I am not entirely convinced that we should take it as our only—or even as decisive—evidence of what the people have chosen.

First of all, a great number of violations are dealt with informally by police, and for the most part their choice not to arrest or summons or cite does not meet with public disapproval. We all know that many of those who are stopped for traffic offenses—such as speeding or having defective tail lights—are let off with a warning rather than a summons, and yet, unless the case is an egregious one, we do not complain. Maybe our failure to protest can be put down to naked self-interest—the recognition of our own propensity to speed or our failure to make regular checks of our car's condition, and the desire that we should be treated leniently if caught. But I think there is rather more to it than that. For we also recognize that people exceed the speed limit or fail to ensure that their car is not in violation of laws relating to its condition for many different reasons, and in some of these cases we would feel that an injustice had been done were a ticket to be issued or the driver arrested. For the most part, we would be more upset were someone who was speeding for a "legitimate" reason to be ticketed than we would be were someone not to be ticketed for a comparable offense for which there were no "legitimating" reasons.

Reiman alludes to the possibility of a public acceptance of discretion, but says that it does not amount to a public grant of authority. In the circumstances which he has in mind—the nonarrest of drug dealers and prostitutes on condition that they become informants—I am at least sympathetic. But this is probably a special case; at least it is a more controversial one. What we might ask is whether the circumstances in which the discretion is exercised are such that the discretion could (though not necessarily will) be sustained in a public forum. In the case of the circumstances under which the services of drug dealers and prostitutes are obtained, I can imagine that there would be a significant division of opinion. But in the cases to which I earlier alluded, in which traffic laws are violated, I think that the argument for publicly defending an exercise of discretion not to arrest or ticket is much stronger.

Second, there is some reason to view full enforcement statutes only as broad statements of purpose and not as rigid requirements. This is not to say that they would be modified if challenged. They are, however, products of a political process, a process that is sometimes best served if statements are made in categorical and unqualified terms. Lending credence to this view is the finding that despite provisions for doing so, full enforcement statutes are rarely enforced and, further, this fact per se brings with it no public outcry. It is only when the discretion is exercised in what seem to be *inappropriately* lenient ways that complaints are heard. Although we are all aware that the police exercise discretion, when it is not felt to be oppressive it is rarely opposed. Furthermore, it is not uncommon for the police to publicize in broad terms the fact that they selectively enforce the law. What generally sticks in people's craw is not less than full enforcement per se, but the discriminatory way in which that is sometimes practiced and the disregard for victims that it sometimes displays.

Third, although legislation sometimes mirrors a social consensus (or at least social majority), it does not always do so. It may be progressive or lag behind social change. There are many reasons for the hiatuses that occur between legislation and social values—some understandable, some reprehensible—and sometimes police are left with the task of making informal adjustments so that social peace may be preserved. Statutes outlawing sodomy, adultery, and fornication may remain on the books for political reasons, yet police would alienate significant sections of their community and generate considerable social turmoil were they to enforce them.

For these reasons, I do not think it unreasonable to argue that the purpose of full enforcement statutes is not so much to require that every law be enforced on every occasion on which it can be, but to place an onus on police to enforce. The difference is important. Those who violate the law know that police have a defeasible obligation to enforce it. Enforcement is not optional; but neither is it mandatory. It is a defeasible obligation on the part of police to investigate law breaking and to take some action with regard to all violations that are called to their attention.

As I noted earlier, there is a sense in which full enforcement statutes are politically necessary. To pass laws and not require that they be enforced or to indicate explicitly that whether or not they will be enforced will be left to the discretion of the police, would be to undermine their force as law. *Even if* it is left to the discretion of police whether or not to enforce the law by means of arrest or summons, the law needs to be magisterially asserted. Otherwise those who break the law will not see their fate as a consequence of their violating the law but only as a matter of negotiation between themselves and the police. Allowing police discretion to enforce the law selectively is not intended to sanction the latter.

Let us now look in more detail at Reiman's four objections.

Vagueness and Uncertainty

Reiman's first claim is that any acceptance of discretion will render the law "vague and uncertain." Why should we think this to be the case? If the law says that the speed limit is 55 mph, and police do not generally ticket people unless they are traveling 10 mph over the speed limit, the law is not thereby rendered vague and uncertain. Nor does it suggest that the

speed limit is really 65 mph and not 55 mph. A person who is traveling at 70 mph will be charged with traveling 15 mph over the speed limit, not 5 mph. And a person who happens to get picked up for traveling at 60 mph cannot complain that he wasn't traveling over 65 mph, and therefore should not have been picked up. Of course, he might wonder why he, of all the people who travel over 55 and under 65 mph, was picked up. But if at 60 mph this person was creating a risk, then there does not seem to be any problem about the police picking him up and not others.

This having been said, it might still be reasonable for us to agree that the police generally wait until people are about 10 mph over the limit before they move in. The reasons here are practical. Our speedometers may be slightly off. The instrumentation used by the police may not be completely accurate. The road may be straight and clear, and visibility good, and no risk may be involved. We may have simply allowed the car to drift above the speed limit, easy to do when one has been driving for a while. It involves a better use of police resources to target those who are more than 10 mph over. And, finally, there may be all sorts of personal reasons why we were traveling above the limit—to get someone to hospital, because we are late picking up the children, we need to get to a bathroom, and so on. Unless there is some special reason to give the law strict liability status, its rigid application in some of these cases would be obnoxious, and would do little to advance the purpose of the law. Laws are not contextless requirements but embedded in social purposes, and although they provide clear guidelines, they are not, or at least should not be, impervious to the social purposes that have informed them. "Overreach" of the law, as Klockars calls it, the working of injustice because laws are expressed too specifically or generally, is correctable by means of discretionary judgments. The correction doesn't make the law vague or uncertain, but allows factors relevant to the law's purpose (both in general and in particular cases) to be incorporated into its enforcement.

Another way of putting this is to say that humans are rational beings, capable of understanding not only the terms of laws (their letter), but also the purposes (or spirit) that led to their promulgation. A person who is "given a break" when traveling at 63 mph, because he was responding to an anxious call from his wife, is not going to go on his way less certain about the law, because he understands not only the letter of the law but also the spirit that infuses it.

Confusion of Powers

Would selective enforcement in effect give police the power to amend the law, and thus subvert the purposes that have made the doctrine of a separation of powers so valuable to sustaining liberal democratic structures? Reiman certainly thinks so, and he is not alone in this. The virtue that informs the doctrine of separation of powers is the dispersal of power and thus a diminished likelihood of its being used tyrannically: "liberty will be best protected if police, judges, and law makers each do what they are mandated to do." Whereas it is the

task of the legislature to make and amend the law, it is the task of the police to enforce it. . .

The discretionary decisions of individual police officers are often "private" and therefore veiled from public scrutiny. This clearly poses a problem, for if police are to be given the power to make discretionary judgments, they need to be accountable for exercises of that power, and that will be very difficult to achieve if their decisions are made out of public view.

But what I think we should conclude from this—and what is to some extent manifest in practice—is that police discretion needs to be much more carefully circumscribed than judicial discretion. We should note what this means and what it doesn't. Since police discretion is private in the sense that much of what police do is unsupervised, this will remain the case whether or not they have the formal power to act in a discretionary manner. So removing, circumscribing, or not granting them the power to make discretionary judgments about whether or not to arrest will have no effect on the visibility of their conduct. The question we must ask then is: Is it better that police not have that formal discretionary power (even though they may privately act as though they do), or that they be granted a formal discretionary power, although one that is circumscribed (even though we may not be able to keep a close eye on how they use it)?

How we answer this question goes to the very heart of our aspirations for policing. If we see the largely paramilitary structure of contemporary policing as necessary or desirable, then, whether or not it is possible to provide better supervision, the denial of discretionary authority will better reflect the discipline of police work. But if we wish to encourage greater professionalism in policing, then the answer will most likely be the grant of discretionary authority, along with efforts to educate police in its wise use.

In addition, we should note that although it may be practically difficult to give the decisions of individual police officers the same kind of scrutiny as the decisions of judges, there is nothing to stop the general practice of police decision making from being publicly reviewed, and nothing to stop certain general kinds of discretionary decisions from being discussed in a public forum. Indeed, there often is such discussion when the assumed discretion is exercised in a way that is thought to be harmful to the legitimate interests of those involved—whether they be citizens who believe that they have been discriminatorily targeted, suspects who feel they have been harshly treated, or victims who consider that their legitimate expectations have not been met. I have no problem with greater publicity in this regard, and indeed would think it highly desirable. . . .

But Reiman, I suspect, would oppose the grant of discretion *even were* there to be such discussion, *even were* it to be generally agreed that some such discretion would be utilitarianly desirable, and *even were* discretionary guidelines to be publicly promulgated. His reason for this would probably be that powers that should be separate would here be conjoined, that the checks and balances so important to preserving a free society would here be compromised. But this assumes a separation of powers that has never existed; nor could it have. Judges are appointed by politicians; police chiefs are appointed by mayors; funding for the judicial and executive branches of government is usually determined by the legislative branch; and so on. The question is not so much: What separation can we achieve? but: What of importance is secured by whatever arrangement that exists? What we want and need is not a complete separation of powers but sufficient separation—sufficient, that is, for independence and strength—so that we can ensure that the values of a free society are nurtured and preserved. I do not see any virtue in the separation of powers *in abstracto*, but only insofar as it is able to safeguard citizens against tyranny. If it is possible to do well (even better) with less than complete separation, then there should be no decisive objection to that being so.

Of course it would be different if police acted as though they had the discretionary authority to add to our current stock of laws. That indeed would make the exercise of discretion tyrannical. But what we have in mind in talking of selective enforcement is a lessening of the grip of law, an easing of the burdens it imposes, and this, provided that, as a result, victims do not go unrequited, should not be seen as an instance of tyranny. Indeed, I am arguing almost the opposite, viz., that a form of tyranny (or certainly harshness) may reside in always applying the law as written in the circumstances as given.

Reiman is correct to identify the issue of police discretion as an area of concern. But the appropriate response, I believe, is not to condemn that discretion as a transgression of proper boundaries, but to bring it into the public domain for monitoring and discussion, as necessary.

What I think should be more worrying from Reiman's perspective is some form of departmentally sanctioned discretion—where, for example, a police chief promulgates as departmental policy a qualification of the law as written. Suppose, for example, the law forbids the possession of marijuana, but the police chief informs members of the department that no action should be taken against those who have less than 1 oz. of marijuana in their possession. Here, it might be argued, the chief exercises a form of discretion that effectively "amends" the law as written. Is *this* justifiable?

Although it may not be legally provided for, I do not see why it should not be morally justifiable, though there are clearly problems if a decision of this kind is cloaked in secrecy. Although a public *announcement* might well send the wrong message, it is not too difficult to see how a police department could justify this way of husbanding its resources.

Davis gives the example of a police department that, in the face of a law prohibiting gambling, promulgates to its members the following rule:

> In the absence of special circumstances, we do not ordinarily arrest for social gambling in the absence of (a) a complaint, (b) a profit from the gambling other than gambling winnings, or (c) extraordinarily high stakes. When we receive a complaint, we ordinarily investigate, but for

first offenders we may break up social gambling without making arrests.

What is going on here? I think it is reasonable to suggest that the legislature did not have as its focus the weekly game of cards played by a group of friends, where only a few dollars change hands over the course of an evening—although there is nothing in the statute to exclude such activities from its purview. With good reason we might also suggest that were the legislature to have attempted to qualify its prohibition so that activities such as these were excluded from its purview, it would have gotten into legislative quicksand. It could not have used the above wording, since it invites inquiries into the meaning of "special circumstances," "extraordinarily," and "ordinarily," and even then is expressed permissively. As Reiman recognizes, human behavior and the circumstances in which it occurs are extraordinarily diverse, and good legislative practice usually involves the drawing of relatively bright lines. My contention is that a police organization that has one ear open to the legislature and one to the community will be able to develop reasonable guidelines for the exercise of discretion.

The foregoing case also touches upon another point that often guides police discretion: the presence or absence of a complaint. Of course, the presence or absence of a complainant is not a decisive feature in deciding whether to go ahead with an arrest, for sometimes victims refuse to lay a complaint for reasons that have nothing to do with the seriousness of a situation. Yet, in the absence of a complaint that would assist in any case for prosecution, arrest may achieve very little. So, although police may have a legally sufficient reason for making an arrest, they may choose not to arrest if the charges are minor and the case will otherwise have a very uncertain future. Scarce resources are expended that might have been more productively used elsewhere.

Discrimination

It is the possibility of using discretion in a discriminatory way that troubles me most. It troubles me, not just because of the *possibility* of discretion being exercised discriminatorily, but because *appeals to discretionary power have often been used* to cloak discrimination. Yet we may wonder whether removal of whatever assumed discretionary competence that police have with regard to arrest will resolve this problem, or even go any way toward alleviating it.

As I indicated earlier, the unsupervised nature of much police work will not change just as a result of some change in policy with respect to arrest/nonarrest. If police deviate from discretionary guidelines by claiming that they are only exercising a discretion they have, they will just as readily claim that they have or do not have legally clear grounds for arrest when they act discriminatorily under a full enforcement policy. The poor and ethnically different will still tend to attract disproportionate attention, and not just because they may be in violation of the law more frequently. For the source of discrimination is not to be found in the power to use discretion but in the disposition to act with

prejudice, and there is probably no greater difficulty involved in showing that guidelines for exercising discretion were ignored than in showing whether legally sufficient grounds for arrest were present.

Once again, to the extent that it is possible, the best counter to poorly or discriminatorily exercised discretion is not to outlaw it but to reeducate its users and to require that, where decisions or patterns develop that appear discriminatory, they be justified. Given the absence of supervision, this will not guarantee anything, but it may function to deter the development of entrenched practices of discrimination. Ultimately, the issue is not one of having or not having full enforcement laws. It is a matter, rather, of police who want to make fair decisions.

Improper Leverage

Reiman is concerned that discretionary authority will be used in a tyrannical fashion. In particular, he is concerned that the additional power that discretion to arrest gives to police beyond their power to arrest enables them to coerce people into doing things that they would otherwise be unwilling to do. In other words, it allows for the tyrannical exercise of power. He instances the cooption of someone as an informant in exchange for nonarrest.

Why does this constitute a tyrannical use of power? Reiman writes that

> if we are not ready to endorse a law requiring all citizens to give the police whatever information they want, then such use of discretion as leverage to get information

amounts to allowing police to exercise a power over some citizens that we would not allow them to exercise over all.

One thing to note about this criticism is that it is leveled at a particular use of discretion, and not at selective enforcement as such. The police officer who allows a speeding motorist to go unsummonsed after a stern reprimand about the dangers of speeding is not exploiting that power to gain something to which he would not otherwise have had access. We could, therefore, forbid police from using their power as leverage without denying them the power to enforce the law selectively.

So why does Reiman use this argument? It seems to me that the importance of the argument is that it gives *some* plausibility to the idea that the power not to arrest might contribute to tyranny. It is necessary to give plausibility to that claim because, at first blush, the power not to arrest those who have done that which would justify arrest appears to be the very antithesis of a *tyrannical* use of power. I am sure that the motorist who gets off with just a warning or reprimand feels relieved rather than oppressed. Tyranny would be involved were the officer to take the view that even though the speed limit was 55 mph, he would ticket people who were traveling only at 50 mph. Or because the color of their car was displeasing to him. Those would be tyrannical police acts. So the additional leverage that a police officer may gain as a result of his discretionary authority is necessary to give some credence to the idea that it is a tyrannical power.

But as far as I know, defenders of police discretion have not argued that police should be able to impose *greater* burdens on others than the law allows. The argument for selective enforcement is always an argument that police should be permitted, in appropriate circumstances, to impose less than a full enforcement policy would dictate.

Maybe a greater burden could be imposed in cases in which informants are coopted. But I do not think it necessary that this should occur. Note that there is a considerable difference between there being a law requiring that we give police whatever information they want, and the choice offered to offenders to avoid arrest by becoming informants. In the first case, the threat of arrest attends the refusal to provide information per se. In the second case, the threat of arrest attends the violation of some other law, but may be removed if a person is willing to provide information. To the person in the latter situation, becoming an informant may represent an acceptable bargain and, if there are no significant victims involved, the arrangement may represent good social value. If the person does not wish to become an informant, then the arrest that follows will be sufficiently justified by the initial offense, and does not need additional support from the refusal to provide information.

Most of us are aware that police frequently gain informants by means such as these. Yet for the most part their use evokes from us no angered or resentful response. Reiman takes our reaction to manifest no more than the lack of respect we have for drug dealers and prostitutes, and our acquiescence in their being treated "in a tyrannical fashion." But I think we need to distinguish two different kinds of case. One is the situation in which the police officer says something like: "If you are prepared to give me a certain piece of information, I won't take you in." The other is where the officer uses arrest as a *continuing threat* in order to have the person become an ongoing informant. In such cases, where the offender might be looking at a few years in prison, and becoming an informant has significant risks and no clear endpoint, the arrangement may well be seriously exploitative of a vulnerable person.

What Reiman establishes, I think, is that the discretion not to arrest can be easily misused, and needs to be monitored. Officers who make use of informants should be required to submit for approval the uses they make of them and the conditions under which they retain their services.

Conclusion

It is important that a free society be governed by rules, not men. But the adherence to rules need not be mechanical, for the rules, apart from curbing governmental arbitrariness, also serve important social purposes beyond themselves. If those wider purposes are not being served, then either the rules should be amended or, if that poses problems, there should be granted to those who administer them the power to make discretionary judgments concerning their application and enforcement. Provided that those who make such judgments can be held accountable for them, it should be possible to secure a greater just freedom than would be the case were no such discretion permitted. ■

Against Police Discretion: Reply to John Kleinig

Jeffrey Reiman

In "Selective Enforcement and the Rule of Law," John Kleinig has presented a powerful rejoinder to my argument that police discretion has no rightful place in a liberal democratic state. He replies to the four reasons which I give for the undesirability of police discretion. Those reasons are: (1) that police

Jeffrey Reiman. "Against Police Discretion: Reply to John Kleinig," *Journal of Social Philosophy*, Volume 29, Number 1 (Spring 1998): 132–142. Reprinted with permission from Blackwell Publishing Ltd.

discretion renders the laws vague and uncertain. Rather than stating forthrightly what will and what will not be permitted, laws subject to discretionary enforcement effectively contain the additional wild-card proviso "if a police officer judges it appropriate ... "; (2) that by adding this proviso, police discretion effectively amends the laws as passed by the people's representatives, and thus usurps the exercise of legislative authority; (3) that police discretionary power is almost certain to be used frequently in ways that discriminate (in effect, if not in intent) against the poor, powerless, and unpopular in our society—undermining the legitimacy of the law where it is most in need of legitimacy; (4) that granting police discretion to decide whether or not to enforce the law gives police officers the ability to use that discretion as leverage over other citizens, say, by threatening arrest if a citizen won't reveal some desired information.

In what follows, I shall start with some general observations about the issues. Then, I shall respond to Kleinig's specific replies to my four reasons for finding police discretion undesirable, and show why I think these replies are unsatisfactory. I shall close with some final comments on the issue, including a further argument against police discretion, namely, that it is incompatible with treating us as citizen-sovereigns of a liberal democratic polity and that it is an affront to our dignity as responsible agents.

General Observations

A large part of my objection to police discretion is that it usurps the legislative authority of the people and their elected representatives. Consequently, if there are laws that the people truly want enforced with discretion, I have no objection if the people through their representatives include express provision for discretion in the law when they enact it. Quite the contrary, that is exactly what I think they should do. It follows that, even where I might agree with Kleinig that discretionary enforcement serves some valuable social aim, my view will be that it is still wrong that that discretion is simply taken by the police as their right. If discretionary enforcement is what the citizens want, then let them say so in the law. They and their elected representatives are the only ones with both the right and the duty to do so. What's more, doing so in the visible arena of the legislature will force open discussion of the proposal. Hence it is irresponsible of the legislature to refrain from providing for discretion in the law when they want it and instead to leave it to police to build it in in the far less visible realm in which they work.

In the essay to which Kleinig is replying, I defined "police discretion" as "the freedom of police officers to decide whether or not to arrest an individual when the conditions that would legally justify that arrest are present and when the officer can make the arrest without sacrificing other equally or more pressing legal duties." Consequently, if the police must prioritize their enforcement activities because of limited resources (so long as this prioritization reflects the choice to enforce other equally or more important laws), I do not count this as discretion for purposes of this discussion. I think in general that the legislature should keep the number of laws down to a number that the police can effectively enforce. If they don't, then the police will have no choice but to prioritize and my objection will be to the irresponsibility of the lawmakers in forcing this on the police rather than making the hard choices for which they were elected. Thus, when, as he does at numerous points, Kleinig justifies police discretion as needed to husband limited resources, my difference with him will not be over what the police do so much as over what the legislature has failed to do.

Because he is a fair-minded fellow, Kleinig has offered me additional ammunition for my argument by pointing out that many states have passed full enforcement statutes charging "police with responsibility to arrest anyone who violates a law." I was content to think that simply passing laws that state categorically that people doing such and such will be arrested, and so forth, was enough to show that the people and their representatives have not given the police discretionary authority. That they have in many cases gone further and expressly mandated full enforcement only strengthens my claim here—for which I thank Kleinig. He, however, takes the fact that there is no public outcry when the police handle violations without arrest as indicating that even explicit full enforcement statutes do not express what the people have chosen. This seems a stretch to me. If the people's representative pass *both* categorical criminal laws calling for arrest *and* laws that insist that those criminal laws

be fully enforced, then it seems that the people have done enough to show their will. That there is little or no public outcry over much selective enforcement nonetheless is better explained as apathy (or perhaps frustration at having twice tried and failed to get the police to enforce the laws), than as indication of yet a different public will than that already twice expressed in the laws. Indeed, that the police and Kleinig think that it is okay to second guess the public in the face of two layers of laws is evidence, in my view, of the way in which police discretion undermines the people's role in a liberal democratic polity.

Kleinig occasionally speaks of the denial of discretionary authority as implying that the police are to apply the law mechanically. And, in the same spirit, he suggests that we will want to grant the police discretionary authority if we would like to "encourage greater professionalism in policing." I think that the use of the term "mechanical" in this context is misleading. As Kleinig himself suggests in his essay, determination of whether legally sufficient grounds for arrest exist is as complex a matter as judging whether or not to arrest when one has the discretionary authority to do so. Police work will always require intelligence and judgment, and denial of discretionary authority is not going to change that. The use of the term "professionalism" is, in my view, even more problematic. Since the opposite of professionalism appears to be amateurism, it's hard to deny that one wants to encourage professionalism in policing. However, traditionally, professionals (doctors, lawyers, and the like) have successfully asserted the right to exercise authority at their discretion and to be accountable only to fellow members of their profession for that exercise. This model has no place in policing. The authority that doctors and lawyers possess is that of *knowledge* (they are authorities *on* health or the law). Such authority is rightly judged by others who are equally authorities in those areas. Police have this sort of authority, they are authorities *on* law and perhaps *on* order as well. However, the authority that police have that Kleinig would have them exercise with discretion is, by contrast, that of *power* (police have authority *over* other citizens, the right to arrest them and use force in the process). Allowing authority of this sort to be exercised with discretion is a dangerous thing even if Kleinig is correct that we should allow it. In any event, we should not be fooled by the positive sound of the term professionalism into thinking it appropriate to treat the authority that police exercise as including discretion in the way that the authority of doctors and lawyers does.

Specific Reasons, Replies, and Responses

I turn now to Kleinig's responses to the four reasons I offered for the undesirability of police discretion. For ease of identification, I shall number the first paragraph in which each of the four reasons is discussed.

(1) In response to my claim that discretion renders the laws vague and uncertain, Kleinig writes:

> If the law says that the speed limit is 55 mph, and police do not

generally ticket people unless they are traveling 10 mph over the speed limit, the law is not thereby rendered vague and uncertain. Nor does it suggest that the speed limit is really 65 mph and not 55 mph. A person who is traveling at 70 mph will be charged with traveling 15 mph over the speed limit, not 5 mph. And a person who happens to get picked up for traveling 60 mph cannot complain that he wasn't traveling over 65 mph, and therefore should not have been picked up.

Now, before responding to Kleinig's claim that this poor fellow cannot complain, consider a different question: What is the *real* speed limit in this example? It seems to be sometimes 65 mph and sometimes 55 mph. Does a driver in this situation get clear guidance about how fast to drive from the legal system, that is, the *whole* legal system from lawmaker to law enforcer? Clearly not. If he drives at 55 mph, he will find everyone passing him in full view of the police. If he drives at 60 mph, he probably won't get a ticket except when some police officer thinks he should. That he cannot complain if this happens makes things worse rather than better. The situation that Kleinig describes is one in which a person is asked to think that he may in fact drive 60 mph *while he has no grounds to complain if he gets penalized for doing so.* This is precisely what police discretion does. It sends a mixed and confusing signal that takes it largely out of the citizen's hands whether he gets penalized or not.

That the citizen can avoid being ticketed by driving 55 mph is no better answer here than that he could avoid being ticketed by not driving at all. Why should he drive at 55 mph, allowing all cars to pass him, when he sees others driving above 55 mph in full view of the police? The law is not just words on a lawbook page or numbers on a speed limit sign. It is a whole system which includes these words and numbers in a real human practice that the citizen confronts as a whole. The speed limit signs tell him one thing and the police practice tells him another. Consequently, his ability to control his fate is weakened by the contradictory and confusing message that he receives from the legal system as a whole.

Can this driver rightly complain? Perhaps not in our discretion-ridden legal system. But, morally speaking, I think he can complain because the legal system failed to do what it was supposed to do. It failed to give him clear guidance about how to avoid getting penalized—just the flaw for which laws are sometimes found unconstitutional because of vagueness. Did this driver have reason to think he was courting a ticket by driving 60 in a 55 mph zone? The answer seems to me to be: yes and no. *Yes*, because he knew that the posted speed limit was 55 mph. *No*, because he didn't know that going five miles over that limit was in fact treated as breaking the law. *Yes and no:* how much more uncertain can the law be than that?

(2) Regarding my claim that police discretion effectively amends the laws that the people's representatives have passed, Kleinig describes a situation in which, though the law prohibits all gambling for money, a police department promulgates a rule among its officers that excludes arresting people for social gambling for moderate stakes. Of this, Kleinig writes:

> What is going on here? I think it is reasonable to suggest that the legislature did not have as its focus the weekly game of cards played by a group of friends, where only a few dollars change hands over the course of an evening—although there is nothing in the statute to exclude such activities from its purview. With good reason we might also suggest that were the legislature to have attempted to qualify its prohibition so that activities such as these were excluded from its purview, it would have got into legislative quicksand.

I don't deny that the police in this example are modifying the legislature's work in a good way, and maybe even in a way that the legislature would have wanted its work modified. But, good or bad, the police are modifying the law. The people's representatives passed a law against gambling, and the police have transformed it into a law against certain kinds of gambling and not against others. The police have taken over a job that is not theirs to take. That a blanket law against gambling is a bad law, I am the first to admit. But it is the people's law, and they will never make better laws if they can leave it to the police to clean up their poor lawmaking. For this reason, we should not so quickly accept that the legislature couldn't have made a law closer to their real intention without getting into "legislative quicksand." Quite the reverse. Trying to spell out just what it is about gambling that makes it the appropriate target of a criminal law would have been a good exercise for the legislature and for the people whose representatives they are. Because police discretion will patch up their incomplete law-making, the people and their representatives are deprived of a valuable exercise in democratic governance and allowed to shirk the responsibility to make good and adequately specific laws. If, instead of covering up for their poor lawmaking, the police enforced the law as the lawmakers wrote it and, say, started arresting well-to-do suburbanites at their weekly gin rummy games, the lawmakers would soon be back at the drawing board trying to make a law that clearly targeted the kind of gambling the people want penalized. The short-term costs to those suburbanites would, in my view, be far outweighed by the benefits of making the lawmakers make the law express the people's real will. And, knowing that the police will not clean up their sloppy work will make the lawmakers more careful in future lawmaking as well.

If the legislature finds that it cannot specify what kind of gambling is illegal, then that is grounds for wondering whether it should be illegal after all—wondering that doesn't occur because the police have patched the law. Moreover, if the legislature cannot specify what kind of gambling is illegal but make a law against it wholesale expecting the police to do the specifying, then they fail to make a law that can guide the citizens in their behavior and thus they fail at what they were elected to do. All of this is covered up— and kept insulated from change—by

police discretion. Some gambling will lead to arrest and other gambling will not, and the distinction between them will be made by the police, not by the people's representatives.

(3) In response to my claim that discretion will be used discriminatorily against the poor, powerless, and unpopular in our society, Kleinig proposes that discretion be limited by guidelines promulgated by police departments. As to whether this will be effective in preventing discrimination, Kleinig contends that it will be no less effective than a full enforcement policy:

> If police deviate from discretionary guidelines by claiming that they are only exercising a discretion they have, they will just as readily claim that they have or do not have legally clear grounds for arrest when they act discriminatorily under a full enforcement policy. . . . For the source of discrimination is not to be found in the power to use discretion but in the disposition to act with prejudice, and there is probably no greater difficulty involved in showing that guidelines for exercising discretion were ignored than in showing whether legally sufficient grounds for arrest were present.

Kleinig's response seems to me to be unsatisfactory on several grounds. First of all, as his account shows, guidelines for discretion place an additional layer of desiderata on top of the determination of whether legally sufficient grounds for arrest are present. Even if it is true that "there is probably no greater difficulty involved in showing that guidelines for exercising discretion were ignored than in showing whether legally sufficient grounds for arrest were present," there is surely greater difficulty in showing that *both* sets of rules were misapplied than in showing that the law alone has been misapplied. At very least, Kleinig's proposal gives the police two levels at which they can deny that they were acting discriminatorily, instead of one. Second, if there were a full enforcement policy, then citizens would come to expect it and they would be able to protest where it was violated, particularly if it were violated in a discriminatory fashion. Under a policy that allows discretion, the citizens have additional grounds for uncertainty about what the police are actually doing, and thus it will be more difficult for them to complain about what appears to be discrimination. And finally, if guidelines for discretion can be formulated that are satisfactory, then they will express the implicit will of the lawmakers and the people who elected them. But, then, the lawmakers should have bitten the bullet and formulated those guidelines themselves as part of the laws they were making, rather than make incomplete laws and let the unelected police fill in the blanks.

(4) I argued that discretion gives police officers a kind of leverage over citizens that can be used tyrannically. What I have in mind here are cases—seen commonly in film and television portrayals of police work—in which the police hold the threat of arrest over some small-time crook as a way of compelling that individual to become an informant. This is clearly a power that police have only when they can refrain from arresting someone who is legitimately subject to arrest.

And it is a power which we would not grant to police over all citizens, since if we wanted that we would pass a law requiring all citizens to give police whatever information the police want. Consequently, police discretion here gives police a special power over some citizens which the lawmakers have not given the police over those citizens and which the lawmakers would not give the police over all citizens.

Against this, Kleinig's reply has three parts. First, he takes it that we could simply forbid the police to use their discretion this way, while leaving the rest of their discretionary authority intact. He does not, however, explain how this would work, and it seems that his earlier observation on the difficulty of controlling police decisions of this sort would work against it. As I said earlier, it seems that outright prohibition of discretion would give citizens the best and clearest weapons against such leverage. For example, imagine a small-time crook who had been "leveraged" into becoming an informant by the threat of arrest not carried out. Suppose that this fellow decides he no longer wants to be an police informant, and the police officer involved decides to arrest him. If there were no discretion allowed, the would-be noninformant could point to earlier cases when the police officer could have but didn't arrest him. This would give him a weapon against continued exploitation. However, as long as discretion is allowed, the police officer will always be able to explain the earlier nonarrests as appropriate discretion. Even if, as Kleinig has suggested, the police officer would always be able to claim that legally sufficient grounds for arrest didn't exist in the earlier case, the fact remains that allowing discretion gives the police two levels of protection of their actions, whereas forbidding discretion leaves them only with one.

Second, Kleinig maintains that the occasional trade of nonarrest for information (as opposed to the continuing threat of arrest to make someone an ongoing informant, which Kleinig admits "may well be seriously exploitative of a vulnerable person") is an acceptable practice. To the individual who has violated a law for which he could be rightly arrested and who is offered nonarrest in return for information, writes Kleinig,

> becoming an informant may represent an acceptable bargain and, if there are no significant victims involved, the arrangement may represent good social value. If the person does not wish to become an informant, then the arrest that follows will be sufficiently justified by the initial offense . . .

But, if the initial offense justified arrest, how was it justified not to arrest him? Did the law say that people who commit this offense will be arrested unless they can provide some "good social value"? Either the legislature which passed the relevant law wanted people to be arrested who violated it, or the legislature wanted the police to be able to use this law sometimes not to arrest but to get information. If the former, then, in not arresting, the police officer violates the wishes of the legislature and the people they represent. If the latter, then the legislature has misled the citizenry by passing a law saying one thing while wishing and expecting something different. Either way, the citizens are swindled out of real democratic control of the agents of their government.

Third, Kleinig makes here a point he makes generally, namely, that discretion is not tyrannical because it amounts to allowing the police, not "to impose *greater* burdens on others than the law allows," but, rather "to impose less than a full enforcement policy would dictate." Naturally, allowing the latter is not as bad as allowing the former, but that doesn't mean that allowing the latter is good. It still modifies undemocratically the laws as made by the people's representatives; it still renders unclear what really is going to be treated as illegal; and it still leaves room for continued leverage against small-time crooks to make them into ongoing informants—which both Kleinig and I regard as exploitation of the vulnerable, but which he thinks and I doubt can be eliminated surgically while leaving police discretion intact.

Concluding Comments

I conclude, now, with a more general observation about the significance of police discretion and its incompatibility with law as an instrument of self-governance by the citizens of a liberal democratic state. In his discussion of the discretionary administration of speed laws, Kleinig refers to the driver let off without a summons as one who has been "given a break." And later, Kleinig adds: "I am sure that the motorist who gets off with just a warning or reprimand feels relieved rather than oppressed." Now, I think that there is something inappropriate in our thinking of the police as "giving us a break"—however natural it is for us to want to get one. What it suggests is that the power to arrest is the police officer's own power and we, his subjects, are relieved that he has shown the mercy not to impose the full force of his power. What's wrong here is that, in a liberal state, the police officer's power belongs to the citizens. It is *our* power, not the police officer's own. Thus, Locke said of the extent of the political authority in a legitimate state, that it is "the joint power of every member of society." And John Rawls has written that, in liberal democratic polities, "political power, which is always coercive power, is the power of the public, that is, of free and equal citizens as a collective body."

We are not to be thankful to the police officer for giving us a break, as if his mercy were a gift to us from him. Rather, his "mercy" is his disobedience of our will as expressed in our laws; he has twisted into his own shape (for however good a reason) a power which we gave him in a shape that we designed. Such mercy (however natural it is to desire it) is an insult to us as citizens of a democracy. If we want speeding laws to be administered mercifully, then it is our business to build mercy into our laws. If we want speeding laws to be administered with discretion, then it is our business to build discretionary authority into our laws. If we make laws, we should expect them to be carried out as we make them. Anything less fails to take us seriously as the sovereign citizen-rulers of a democratic polity.

But discretion is not only an insult to us as citizen-sovereigns of a

liberal democratic state, it is an insult to us as responsible agents. The distinguished philosopher of law, Lon Fuller, catalogued eight features of what he called the "internal morality of law." Among these are that the law be clear enough to guide citizens in choosing how to conduct themselves, and that there be congruence between official action and declared rule. I think that I have shown that discretion undermines both of these features. Interestingly, Fuller thought of these features of law as a morality because he thought of law as a purposive enterprise, one that implicitly treats the people subject to it as responsible agents. He wrote:

> To embark upon the enterprise of subjecting human conduct to the governance of rules involves of necessity a commitment to the view that man is, or can become, a responsible agent, capable of understanding and following rules, and answerable for his defaults.

> Every departure from the principles of the law's inner morality is an affront to man's dignity as a responsible agent.

To the extent that police discretion makes the law unclear and opens a gap between the stated rule and the official actions done in its name, it does not address the citizens as individuals capable of governing themselves in light of public rules. Rather it subjects citizens to an ill-defined and unpredictable police authority in the face of which citizen self-governance is reduced to guessing what the laws will actually mean in the hands of this or that police officer.

In closing, I want to acknowledge the very important fact that instituting a policy of full enforcement will require significant changes in our legal system if this policy is not to bring worse evils than the discretion it is meant to replace. For instance, police often refrain from arresting individuals because they may have to spend a night in jail until they can see a judge and because, even if they are acquitted, they will end up with a damaging arrest record. Consequently, for full enforcement to work, we will have to staff our courts with enough judges so that arrestees can see them in short order, and we will have to eliminate the practice of holding acquitted persons' arrest records against them. Since jailing arrestees because there's no judge around and holding arrest records against acquitted people amount to punishing people who are either presumed or legally innocent, these changes seem long overdue.

The most important change that full enforcement requires, however, is that we reduce dramatically the number and complexity of our criminal laws. And this too seems long overdue. . . . The simple fact is that a free society should have few and clear criminal laws that the police should be expected to enforce wherever they apply.

In short, full enforcement is part of a "package deal." If, as I expect, we can't have the whole package—if we are not about to limit criminal law to a small number of clear statutes or to provide resources for speedy, non-punitive treatment of arrestees, and so on—then Kleinig is right: We should keep police discretion and try to curb its abuses. But, then, we should admit that we have failed to stand up to the full measure of our roles as citizen-sovereigns of a liberal democratic polity. Instead of controlling the exercise of our public power by means of rules we have democratically enacted, we have handed this job over to the police and can only hope that they perform it fairly to the disadvantaged, and mercifully to us all. ∎

⁞⁞⁞ The Continuing Debate

What Is New

Some of the most interesting recent studies of police discretion have focused on how neighborhood/environmental factors influence police discretionary behavior. Studies indicate that in communities of lower economic status, police are more likely to make arrests (rather than give warnings or pursue other alternatives). In addition, police are likely to use greater force in economically disadvantaged neighborhoods. Notice that such studies are not merely finding that more arrests occur in poorer neighborhoods; rather, when confronted with similar offenses, police discretionary behavior results in a greater likelihood of arrest when the offense took place in a poor neighborhood than in a more affluent environment.

Where to Find More

Perhaps the classic paper on police discretion—which brought the issue of police discretion into the open and into debate—is Joseph Goldstein, "Police Discretion

Not to Invoke the Criminal Process," *Yale Law Journal*, Volume 69 (1960): 543–594. Important and influential early studies of the issue by Kenneth Culp Davis are *Discretionary Justice: A Preliminary Inquiry* (Baton Rouge: Louisiana State University Press, 1969), and *Police Discretion* (St. Paul, MN: West, 1975).

Arguments against police discretion are developed by Ronald J. Allen in "The Police and Substantive Rulemaking: Reconciling Principle and Expediency," *University of Pennsylvania Law Review*, Volume 125 (1977): 62–118; and "The Police and Substantive Rulemaking: A Brief Rejoinder," *University of Pennsylvania Law Review*, Volume 125 (1977): 1172–1181.

John Kleinig, editor, *Handled with Discretion: Ethical Issues in Police Decision Making* (Lanham, MD: Rowman & Littlefield, 1996) is an excellent collection of articles (and responses) on the question of police discretion.

A clear examination of issues related to police discretion (particularly its relation to styles of police professional behavior) is Laure Weber Brooks, "Police Discretionary Behavior: A Study of Style," in Roger Dunham and Geoffrey P. Alpert, editors, *Critical Issues in Policing*, 5th Edition (Long Grove, IL: Waveland Press, 2004).

Samuel Walker, *Taming the System: The Control of Discretion in Criminal Justice, 1950–1990* (New York: Oxford University Press, 1993), is a larger examination of police discretion and of attempts to improve police discretionary behavior and avoid discriminatory behavior. M. K. Brown, *Working the Street: Police Discretion and the Dilemmas of Reform* (New York: Russell Sage Foundation, 1981), examines the complex decision-making process confronting police officers in their daily work.

Among the important recent studies of the impact of neighborhood socioeconomic status on the discretionary behavior of police are W. Terrill and M. D. Resig, "Neighborhood Context and Police Use of Force," *Journal of Research in Crime and Delinquency*, Volume 40 (2003): 291–321; K. J. Novak, J. Frank, B. W. Smith, and R. S. Engel, "Revisiting the Decision to Arrest: Comparing Beat and Community Officers," *Crime and Delinquency*, Volume 48 (2002); S. D. Mastrofski, M. D. Reisig, and J. D. McCluskey, "Police Disrespect Toward the Public: An Encounter-Based Analysis," *Criminology*, Volume 40 (2002): 519–552; and Dennis D. Powell, "A Study of Police Discretion in Six Southern Cities," *Journal of Police Science and Administration*, Volume 17, Number 1 (1990): 1–7. Jeffrey Reiman discusses a number of studies in *The Rich Get Richer and the Poor Get Prison: Ideology, Class, and Criminal Justice*, 8th Edition (Needham, MA: Allyn & Bacon, 2007).

Should the Police Use Trickery and Deceit in Investigations and Interrogations?

Some Police Deceit and Trickery Is Legitimate
  Advocate: Christopher Slobogin, Professor of Law and Alumni
    Research Scholar, University of Florida College of Law.
  Source: "Deceit, Pretext, and Trickery: Investigative Lies by the
    Police," *Oregon Law Review*, Volume 76 (Winter 1997).
Lying by Police Should Be Generally Prohibited
  Advocate: Margaret L. Paris, Associate Professor, University of
    Oregon School of Law.
  Source: "Lying to Ourselves," *Oregon Law Review*, Volume 76
    (Winter 1997).

There are some clear boundaries that police investigations are not supposed to cross. For example, police cannot "entrap" suspects into committing a crime: police can set up a sting operation, in which they pose as drug dealers or prostitutes and arrest those who seek them out; but they cannot seek out citizens and entice them into illegal acts. An undercover officer cannot offer a citizen a thousand dollars to make a drug delivery, and then arrest the citizen for drug dealing; in that case, the idea for the criminal act comes from the police, and there is no reason to suppose that the entrapped citizen was eager to become a drug dealer. And of course there are other restrictions: the police cannot legitimately beat a confession out of you, or obtain a confession by threats, or refuse to allow a suspect access to his/her lawyer, or subject the suspect to such severe and prolonged questioning that the suspect becomes psychologically disoriented and physically exhausted. But beyond such obviously coercive measures, the lines governing legitimate police interrogation techniques become rather blurred, and *almost* anything goes. As Jerome H. Skolnick and Richard A. Leo note:

> Contemporary police interrogation is routinely deceptive. As it is taught and practiced today, interrogation is shot through with deception. Police are instructed to, are authorized to—and do—trick, lie, and cajole to elicit so-called "voluntary" confessions.

Among the routine deceptive techniques practiced during interrogation are mis-representation of the seriousness of an offense (a suspect might be told he is being charged with murder, when in fact the crime victim's injuries were not lethal), making false promises to the defendant (such as promises of leniency), and pretending to have evidence (such as fingerprints or the confessions of other members of the group). Are such deceptive techniques legitimate methods of police investigation? Should there be tighter restrictions on police methods of interrogation?

Christopher Slobogin agrees with a general prohibition against lying, but he believes that deception by police—though it causes some serious harms—can be justified as a special exception: lies to publicly identified enemies are legitimate, and criminals are enemies of society. But this requires, Slobogin insists, that the process be public, and that those suspected of criminal behavior recognize that the police view them as enemies. Margaret L. Paris welcomes Slobogin's concern over the proper limits of deceptive police interrogation, but believes that he does not go far enough. Because of the destructive consequences of police deception, Paris would allow deceptive interrogations only in the most extreme and extraordinary circumstances: when such deception is the only possible means of saving lives.

⚏ Points to Ponder

- One recommendation for dealing with the problem of deceptive interrogation techniques is to videotape all interrogation sessions, so that the jury could judge whether confessions were genuine, and a judge could decide whether a confession was obtained under coercive circumstances (and so should not be admitted as evidence). Should videotaping be required? Would that solve the problem?
- In one of the most common forms of deception employed by police interrogators, the interrogator pretends to be deeply concerned for the welfare of the suspect, and tries to convince the suspect—under the guise of concerned friendship—that confession would be of great benefit to the suspect ("the District Attorney would think more kindly of you if you could explain why you were justified in committing the crime and make people understand your situation," etc.). Under Slobogin's model of what counts as acceptable deceptive interrogation, would that sort of deceptive practice be prohibited?

- A common concern about the practice of police deception in interrogation is that it is difficult to prevent the further spread of such deception: If we become accustomed to lying and faking evidence in interrogations, wouldn't that make it too easy to take the next step and actually fabricate evidence (if we're "certain" that this suspect is guilty); or perhaps go from lying to the suspect to lying to a jury during the trial? Is that a realistic concern?
- Paris asserts that "It harms a society when the officers who enforce its laws behave like the worst used car salesmen." Paris does not note any specific harms that are caused to society from such police behavior; would it be possible to list such specific harms?

Deceit, Pretext, and Trickery: Investigative Lies by the Police

Christopher Slobogin

A lie is a statement meant to deceive. Many police, like many other people, lie occasionally, and some police, like some other people, lie routinely and pervasively. Police lie to protect innocent victims, as in hostage situations, and they tell "placebo lies" to assure or placate worried citizens. They tell lies to project nonexistent authority, and they lie to suspects in the hopes of gathering evidence of crime. They also lie under oath, to convict the guilty, protect the guilty, or frame the innocent.

Some of these lies are justifiable. Some are reprehensible. Lying under oath is perjury and thus rarely permissible. On the other hand, lying that is necessary to save a life may not only be acceptable but is generally applauded (even if it constitutes perjury). Most types of police lies are of murkier morality, however. In particular, considerable disagreement exists over the permissibility of lying to suspects as a means of gathering evidence. If the police want to uncover a conspiracy, search a house, or obtain a confession, may they lie in an effort to do so? . . .

The Nature of Investigative Lies and Why They Occur

Of the many varieties of lies police tell, the most prevalent type is probably the lie told to catch a criminal, if only because apprehending perpetrators of crime is a primary job of the police. Of

Christopher Slobogin. "Deceit, Pretext, and Trickery: Investigative Lies by the Police," *Oregon Law Review*, Volume 76 (Winter 1997). Reprinted with permission from the publisher and author.

course, lies to catch criminals can be directed at nonsuspects whom the police believe have useful information. Most, however, are aimed at the suspects themselves and occur in one of three contexts: undercover work, searches and seizures, or interrogation. In each of these three contexts, the following discussion borrows from the sociological literature in exploring the nature and causes of police lies and then briefly reviews the law's (usually accommodating) response to them.

Undercover Work

Undercover work is by definition deceptive. It normally involves outright lies. Typically, an undercover agent gives or presents a fake identity and a fabricated history, denies any involvement with the police, and engages in any number of other lies. For example, an agent might pose as a lover, a prisoner, a priest, or a member of the Mafia; in playing such roles, lying is inevitable and extensive.

Law enforcement's justification for this type of deception is twofold. First, certain types of crime—for instance, so-called "victimless crime," fraud, narcotics sales, organized crime, and terrorism—are considered difficult to detect or prevent through other means. Second, independently from solving a particular crime, undercover agents and informants gather general information about criminal activity and the key figures in it that is thought to be otherwise inaccessible. These objectives have led every major police department to devote significant resources to undercover work by police officers and by "snitches" recruited to work for the police.

The Supreme Court has given wide leeway to this type of deceptive activity. Indeed, even the Warren Court— popularly perceived as the most liberal group of justices in the Court's history on the subject of criminal suspects' rights—expressed a strong aversion to regulating undercover work. The established basis for this stance, found in a number of Court decisions, is that one assumes the risk that one's acquaintances are government agents; any expectation to the contrary is unreasonable and therefore not protected by the Fourth Amendment. Accordingly, as a constitutional matter, police need neither a warrant nor any level of suspicion before engaging in undercover operations. . . .

The message to the police is that, as far as the law is concerned, they have virtual carte blanche to engage in deceptive undercover work.

Searches and Seizures

Lying meant to effectuate a search or a seizure is routine practice for many police officers. Such lies come in at least two varieties. The first involves lying about police authority to conduct the search or seizure. For instance, police may state that they do not need a warrant when they know the law requires they have one, assert they have a warrant when they do not, or state they can get a warrant when in fact they know they cannot. This last ruse, designed to encourage acquiescence from an otherwise unwilling person, is one among many deceitful ways of obtaining consent; police have also been known, for instance, to get motorists to sign a consent form for a car search by misrepresenting the form as a ticket. Finally, the police may simply make up a reason for conducting a search and seizure, such as when they fabricate a traffic violation as a ground for stopping a car.

The second type of lie misrepresents the police's purpose, not the police's authority. These so-called "pretextual" actions arise in a number of contexts. For instance, the police might ask for permission to enter a house for some innocuous purpose (such as investigation of a nonexistent burglary), when their actual intent is to conduct a search of its interior once inside. A similar, extremely common ruse is an effort to get a better look at a car's occupants and contents by stopping the car for a traffic violation, one which is not made up (as described in the preceding paragraph) but which is never or rarely enforced except in pretextual situations. In the same pretextual vein is a lie to get a suspect to "come quietly" rather than risk a violent arrest or a police "suggestion" that a person have a "short chat" with officers, whose real intentions are to seize the individual for a much longer period of time. In all of these situations, the police have the technical legal authority to engage in the act based on consent or some minor violation of the law but are dissembling their purpose.

As with undercover work, the primary police justification for both types of deceptive searches and seizures is their efficacy at catching criminals. According to Jerome Skolnick, a veteran observer of the police, the typical police officer believes that he has "the ability to distinguish between guilt and innocence" and that once he has decided that someone is guilty (or

suspicious), he "ought to be free to employ the techniques of his trade." Skolnick implies that lies to suspects about police authority or purpose are, as far as the police are concerned, "techniques of the trade" that should be fostered rather than criticized.

This assertion is borne out by the observations of sociologists Thomas Barker and David Carter, who also conclude that many police endorse an "end justifies the means" approach to deception. One statement they report seems particularly illuminative on this score. Told that his description of police methods for obtaining consent sounded like "a lot of lies," one officer responded: "It is not police lying; it is an art. After all the criminal has constitutional protection. He can lie through his teeth. Why not us? What is fair is fair."

The sentiment that "it takes a liar to catch a liar" apparently resonates with many police officers. Particularly interesting is the officer's reference to police lying as an "art," which dovetails with Skolnick's observation that police see fabrication as part of their craft. It suggests that, in this investigative context, police do not think they are "lying" at all; they are merely playing a role.

In short, police view deceitful searches and seizures as a professional investigative tool—the moral equivalent to undercover investigation. While courts presumably disagree with this stance when the lies are about police authority (because if the claimed authority did not exist, then the Fourth Amendment is violated), most have put their imprimatur on the much larger category of pretextual searches and seizures. After intimating it would do so on more than one occasion, the Supreme Court itself recently affirmed that the typical pretextual police action does not violate the U.S. Constitution. In Whren v. United States, which explicitly upheld a concededly pretextual traffic stop, the Court stressed that the subjective mental state of the police is irrelevant to Fourth Amendment analysis in most situations. As a result of decisions like these, the police know that as long as they have a legal explanation for their action, any duly limited entry, stop or seizure will usually be considered constitutional regardless of the hidden agenda.

Interrogation

As with undercover work, fabrication in the interrogation context is openly acknowledged by the police today. Indeed, the leading interrogation manual, authored by Inbau, Reid, and Buckley, continues to preach vigorously the merits of deceptive interrogation techniques, despite the Supreme Court's implicit criticism of one of its earlier incarnations in Miranda v. Arizona. The techniques they espouse include: (1) showing fake sympathy for the suspect by becoming his "friend" (e.g., by falsely telling a person suspected of rape that the interrogator himself had "roughed it up" with a girl in an attempt to have intercourse with her); (2) reducing feelings of guilt through lies (e.g., by telling a person suspected of killing his wife that he was not as "lucky" as the interrogator, who had recently been on the verge of seriously harming his nagging wife when the doorbell rang); (3) exaggerating the crime in an effort to prod the suspect into negotiating or in hopes of obtaining a denial which will indirectly inculpate the suspect (e.g., accusing the suspect of stealing $40,000 when only $20,000 was involved); (4) lying that suggests the futility of denying the truth (e.g., statements that sufficient evidence already exists to convict when it does not); and (5) playing one codefendant against another (e.g., leading one to believe the other has confessed when no confession has occurred).

Many other deceptive techniques, somewhat less openly acknowledged, are associated with giving the warnings mandated by Miranda. For instance, police might tell the suspect that "whatever you say may be used for or against you in a court of law," despite the fact that police are extremely unlikely to testify for the defense in any subsequent prosecution. They might also mislead the suspect into believing that only written statements are admissible or that a state-paid attorney will be provided only once the individual is in court.

As with the other investigative lies discussed, the police believe these techniques are necessary to catch criminals, in this situation because of the suspect's natural reluctance to respond to direct questions and the general prohibition on physically coercive interrogation practices. . . .

Which Police Lies Are O.K.?

. . . In recent times, probably the best known treatment of lying and its justification is the work by the moral philosopher Sissela Bok. Because her framework for evaluating deception throws considerable light on the nature and moral viability of police lying, this Article will rely primarily on her work. . . .

Bok's Framework

Bok begins by asserting that lies require a reason. They require a reason because, more so than truth, they have routine deleterious effects on the hearer of the statement, the maker of the statement, and society at large. The duped, she notes, often "feel wronged . . . [and] are wary of new overtures." Their autonomy is also denigrated by the lying, because they have been deprived of the ability "to make choices for themselves according to the most adequate information available." As to the negative effects of lying on those who perpetrate the lie, Bok points out how lying can become an intrinsic part of one's personality: "psychological barriers wear down; lies seem more necessary, less reprehensible; the ability to make moral distinctions can coarsen; the liar's perception of his chances of being caught may warp." Further, others will trust the liar less. Also, "paradoxically, once his word is no longer trusted, he will be left with greatly decreased power—even though a lie often does bring at least a short-term gain in power over those deceived." Finally, lying harms society:

> The veneer of social trust is often thin. As lies spread—by imitation, or in retaliation, or to forestall suspected deception—trust is damaged. Yet trust is a social good to be protected just as much as the air we breathe or the water we drink. When it is damaged, the community as a whole suffers; and when it is destroyed, societies falter and collapse.

. . . Bok next postulates an apparatus for assessing the reasons that might be given for lying. Her principal assertion here is that lies that cannot be justified publicly are not justifiable. Furthermore, she asserts, the "public" which assesses the lie must be composed of "reasonable persons" taken from all walks of life, including "those representing the deceived or others affected by the lie"; this public assessment is particularly important where lying by the government is involved. Finally, she develops three steps these reasonable persons should pursue in assessing the worth of the lie.

First, those who evaluate the lie must "look carefully for any alternatives of a non-deceptive nature available to the liar." They should only begin to consider excuses for a lie after determining that no truthful statement would do.

If no such alternatives present themselves, the second step involves "weighing . . . the moral reasons for and against the lie." Bok identifies four conceivable justifications for lying: (1) preventing harm; (2) producing benefit; (3) fairness, which includes giving people what they deserve, correcting injustice, and simple revenge; and (4) veracity itself, in the sense that telling a lie may protect the truth. However, Bok is very leary of any of these justifications, given the ease with which a liar can manipulate these concepts to justify any lie. Thus, she emphasizes that reasonable persons evaluating a lie should "share the perspective of the deceived and those affected by lies." They should "be much more cautious than those with the optimistic perspective of the liar [and] value veracity and accountability more highly than would individual liars or their apologists."

Third, in evaluating the moral reasons for and against the lie, reasonable persons should be particularly attentive to identifying its potential ill effects on those not directly involved in the lie:

> Under all circumstances, these reasonable persons would need to be very wary because of the great susceptibility of deception to spread, to be abused, and to give rise to even more undesirable practices . . . Spread multiplies the harm resulting from lies; abuse increases the damage for each and every instance. Both spread and abuse result in part from the lack of clear-cut standards as to what is acceptable. In the absence of such standards, instances of deception can and will increase, bringing distrust and thus more deception, loss of personal standards on the part of liars and so yet more deception, imitation by those who witness deception and the rewards it can bring, and once again more deception.

The potential for spread and abuse, Bok writes, is particularly likely when the lies are told by people in power. Thus, she concludes, reasonable persons need to construct the "clearest possible standards and safeguards in order to prevent these [government] liars from drifting into more and more damaging practices—through misunderstanding, carelessness, or abuse."

Bok's Lying Scenarios

. . . Of all lies, Bok finds lies in a crisis to be the most justifiable. The classic crisis, of course, occurs when life is imminently threatened. Telling a lie to prevent such harm is justifiable because little time exists to consider alternatives, the negative effects of the lie are outweighed by the fact that an innocent life will be saved, and those effects are negligible in any event. Lies of this type are so extraordinary that they "would neither be likely to encourage others to lie nor make it much more likely that the person who lied to save a life might come to lie more easily or more often." Whether lies could be told to avert less immediate or less significant harms would depend upon a number of factors, especially whether the use of force is the only alternative. In general, however, Bok resists enlarging this exception without a careful public assessment of the claim of crisis from the perspective of the deceived. Liars making this claim, she cautions, can be counted upon to exaggerate the threat, its immediacy, or its need.

Put in terms of Bok's four possible excuses for lies, lying in a crisis is best seen as a way of preventing harm and to a lesser extent as a means of producing benefit. In contrast, Bok says that the claim that lying to liars is permissible derives primarily from a fairness or "just deserts" excuse. As Bok says, to justify lying simply because the recipient is a liar "would be to make oneself entirely dependent on the character deficiencies in others, and to stoop always to the lowest common denominator in reciprocating lies for lies." Further, of course, we may be wrong about when someone is lying. For this reason, lying to people we think are liars is "likely to invite vast increases in actual deception and to escalate the seriousness of lies told in retaliation, . . . a notion [that] would not stand up well under the test of publicity."

Lying to a liar might also be grounded on the veracity excuse to the extent lying is meant to reveal the mendacity of the recipient of the lie. Here again, Bok agrees with St. Augustine, who stated that "mendacity is best rebutted, not imitated." Truthful alternatives generally exist for exposing a lie. Even if there are none, the damage caused to the character of the liar and society at large by routinely lying to people thought to be liars outweighs the veracity excuse.

The claim that lying to enemies is justifiable is closely related to the previous two types of claims. An enemy often precipitates crises and will often lie to win. In terms of excuses, lying to an enemy might both prevent harm and promote fairness. While Bok is more hospitable to this claim, she again argues for caution. Both the fairness and prevention of harm excuses are, in her mind, very prone to abuse.

As Bok notes, the fairness excuse takes on added allure here because not only is an enemy usually a liar but he is also perceived as bad—outside the "social contract" as Bok puts it—and thus arguably less worthy of truthfulness. Yet, as Bok points out, the identification of enemies, like the identification of liars, is a treacherous task, easily tainted by bias and prejudice. Further, many liars invoking this excuse tend to avoid the public scrutiny necessary to justify the lie. For

these people, "paranoia governs them to such an extent that they imagine that the public itself constitutes the conspiracy they combat."

Lying to enemies to prevent harm raises the same types of concerns. To the liar, enemies are too readily perceived. Furthermore, even when enemies are clearly identified, lies to them may be heard by and can deceive friends as well, with a consequent serious loss of trust when the deception is unveiled. In particular, Bok points out that "when a government is known to practice deception, the results are self-defeating and erosive." Here she quotes Hannah Arendt, the astute observer of totalitarian states, who argues that government deceit over the long run results in "the absolute refusal to believe in the truth of anything, no matter how well it may be established." Eventually, it destroys "the sense by which we take our bearings in the real world."

Bok does concede, consistent with the discussion on lies in a crisis, that "whenever it is right to resist an assault or a threat by force, it must then be allowable to do so by guile." Thus, says Bok, deceiving a kidnapper may be justifiable when deceiving enemies in business is not.

Moreover, in a passage that has direct implications for police lying, Bok is willing to countenance lying to an enemy in one nonemergency situation: when a public declaration of hostilities against the alleged enemy is made. She reasons that:

> Such open declarations lessen the probability of error and of purely personal spite, so long as they are open to questioning and

requests for accountability . . . The more openly and clearly the adversaries, such as criminals, can be pinpointed, and the more justifiable, therefore, the criteria for regarding them as hostile, the more excusable will it be to lie to them if honesty is of no avail.

She goes on to say:

If the designation of a foe is open, as in a declaration of war, deception is likely to be expected on all sides. While it can hardly be said to be consented to, it is at least known and often acquiesced in. But the more secret the choice and pursuit of foes, the more corruptible the entire process, as all the secret police systems of the world testify. There is, then, no public control over who counts as an adversary nor over what can be done to him. The categories of enemies swell, and their treatment grows increasingly inhumane.

Even with such an open declaration, however, Bok worries that the public will be swept up by the mere fact that hostilities have been declared and not remain reasonable and objective in evaluating whether lying is permissible. Because such declarations do not "lessen the possibility of joint discrimination by members of a group or society [they] ought therefore to function only in combination with a strong protection of civil rights."

Bok and the Police

Overall, Bok makes a provocative case against lying in most instances. Except for lying in imminent crises and lying to publicly declared enemies, most lying is to be avoided. Unfortunately, Bok only fleetingly reflects on the applicability of these conclusions to lying by the police. . . . Nonetheless, her analysis is rich in implications for police deceit, and in particular investigative lying. . . .

First, we must inquire into whether the reasons for Bok's general injunction against lying make sense in the law enforcement context. Bok's premise that lying should generally be avoided is based on the assertion that deceit harms the dupe, the liar, and society. That assertion tends to be borne out by social science research indicating that in many situations trust is crucial to one's own sense of self-worth and the formation of relationships. But does investigative lying by the police produce these three harms to any significant extent?

Very likely it does, even when one focuses solely on investigative lying that is viewed as necessary because truthful, noncoercive alternatives are not available. First, almost by definition, deception during undercover operations, searches and seizures, and interrogation diminishes the dignity and autonomy of the dupe. In each of these situations, the dupe will be making decisions about whether to disclose embarrassing or incriminating knowledge or whether to allow access to private areas while lacking information that is potentially highly relevant to such decisions (e.g., the identity or motives of the liar or the scope of one's rights).

To a Kantian, this fact alone might justify a ban or substantial limitations on investigative lying. To one of a more utilitarian bent, however, greater harm from investigative lying will

probably need to be identified to outweigh the benefit that comes from
deceitful police work that is necessary
(i.e., for which there is no truthful,
noncoercive alternative). In other
words, the assessment of costs associated with investigative lying must
focus on the second and third potential harms Bok identifies—those
inflicted on the liars (in this case the
police) and on society at large.

The latter costs are likely to be the
heaviest. There is no doubt, for
instance, that the deceit connected
with covert investigation can undermine trust in government not only in
those who are targets of the deceit but
among those duped by it. Typically,
undercover work is relegated to the
underworld and is rarely exposed to
the rest of us. When it is, however, the
feeling of betrayal can be significant.
For example, when citizens of a mid-
size midwestern community discovered that a local executive had been an
undercover spy for an FBI investigation of his company, many were outraged. As a reverend stated in
explaining the reactions of his congre-
gation to the news:

> The biggest feeling here right
> now is a sense of being violated.
> It's as though I became a good
> friend of your family, came over
> to your house all the time, then
> started rifling through your
> drawers . . . It's not an intruder,
> though. It's someone who's
> trusted—by a company and by an
> entire community.

A member of the same church condemned the federal government with
the words "they're about as under-
handed as anybody."

Knowledge of undercover work
not only undermines trust in government but can be deeply inimical to a
democratic society. Carried to its "Big
Brother" extreme, as it has been in
some countries, government snooping
chills speech, association, and the general openness of society. Although the
possibility that one's acquaintance is a
government agent is a risk the
Supreme Court tells us we must
assume, empirical research strongly
suggests that it is not a risk most people want to assume.

Just as clear is the sense of
betrayal, as well as outright hostility,
on the part of those subjected to pretextual police actions, reactions which
again lead to antipathy not only
toward police but also the government
they represent. Perhaps one of the
most damning examples of this phenomenon is the fact that African
Americans in Los Angeles and other
urban areas cynically joke about the
"offense" of "driving while black." As
one court bluntly described the inherent risk of pretextual actions:

> Some police officers will use the
> pretext of traffic violations or other
> minor infractions to harass mem-
> bers of groups identified by factors
> that are totally impermissible as
> a basis for law enforcement activity
> —factors such as race or ethnic ori-
> gin, or simply appearances that
> some police officers do not like,
> such as young men with long hair,
> heavy jewelry, and flashy clothing.

The belief that police lie during
interrogation can also have harmful
effects. As several commentators have
pointed out, betrayal in the interrogation room might not only taint the

police and society generally but also undermines the effectiveness of inter-rogation itself. A suspect's discovery that a promise or statement is false might lead to subsequent resistance even to legitimate offers, thus possibly resulting in loss of a confession. On a more systemic level, knowledge that police interrogators lie may make all suspects more reluctant to talk, for fear that police importunings are based on fabrication. A general dis-trust of police interrogators might even create an unwillingness on the part of nonsuspects to cooperate with authorities.

As a general summary of these points, Maurice Punch's observations are apt:

> [Police] deviance elicits a spe-cial feeling of betrayal. In a sense, they are doubly condemned; that is, not just for the infringement itself but even more for the breach of trust involved. Something extra is involved when public officials in general and policemen in particu-lar deviate from accepted norms: "That something more is the viola-tion of a fiduciary relationship, the corruption of a public trust, of public virtue."

These effects of police deceit are espe-cially likely in communities which rou-tinely interact with the police.

Perhaps less obvious than its effects on the duped and on society is the insidious impact of investigative lying on the police themselves. For the reasons discussed in Part I, police may genuinely believe that this type of lying is morally justified. However, as Klockars has pointed out, "as the police officer becomes comfortable with lies

and their moral justification, he or she is apt to become casual with both." Thus, as Bok would predict, police lying feeds on itself. It can also lead to other effects. Barker and Carter assert that "police lying contributes to police mis-conduct and corruption and under-mines the organizatio[n's] discipline system." In the undercover context, Marx has documented even more dra-matic impacts, including accounts of officers whose undercover role is so all-consuming that they become criminals themselves. Police clearly are not immune from the corrupting influence of deceit that Bok describes.

In short, investigative lying can produce significant negative conse-quences of the type hypothesized by Bok and should therefore, under Bok's scheme, presumptively be avoided even if truthful alternatives are not available. However, this conclusion does not mean that such lying is impermissible in all instances. Recall that the two scenarios in which Bok is most likely to countenance lying involve lies in "crisis" and lying to publicly declared "enemies." Both might occur during police investigation, the first occasion-ally, the second with some regularity.

The crisis exception might apply, for instance, when police believe they need information to avert harm to themselves or someone else (e.g., a kid-napping situation). Indeed, given the general maxim about the relationship of force and deception subscribed to by Bok, lying would be permissible in any situation in which the police are autho-rized to use physical coercion (e.g., lying to get a suspect to "come in quietly"). At the same time, the crisis exception should not be stretched to cover every effort to apprehend criminals who might harm another. Bok, at least, would require some showing of imminent danger to another person's interests before recognizing a crisis. In many cases in which lying to catch a criminal is practiced, police are not even sure their prey is a criminal, much less that harm is imminent.

Of considerably more significance to investigative lying is Bok's "open declaration of hostilities" scenario, the primary exception to the notion that lying to liars and to enemies in noncrisis situations is unjustifiable. As indicated above, Bok herself uses criminals as an example of an "enemy," who if openly pinpointed as such, can be foiled through lying, at least if truthful alternatives do not exist. However, unless applied with caution, this exception too could easily swallow the rule against lying. Recall that, according to Bok, identification of the person as a criminal must be a public enterprise, so as to minimize the possibility that he will be the target of personal spite or prejudice. Simply asserting that there is a "war on crime" and handing over to the police discretion to decide who is the enemy in that war (and who is lying about not being one) obviously does not meet Bok's demands in this regard; as she notes, discrimination can only be combatted by removing that discretion through public evaluation. The issue thus becomes how to effectuate this public identification of the criminal.

Implementing the Public Identification Predicate

Based on Bok's work, the principle most relevant to analyzing investigative lying seems to be the moral need to identify publicly the "enemy"—the criminal—before engaging in deception. If this public identification occurs, investigative deception that has no good, truthful alternative can be used against the person so identified. If it does not, deception is much less likely to be morally justifiable under Bok's scheme.

The difficulty arises in operationalizing the public identification idea in the investigative context. Of course, the legislature, presumably through public debate, has already identified the conduct that is criminal (and is therefore "enemy") conduct. However, as suggested in Part II, a public vote authorizing police to use deception to "apprehend criminals" is insufficient because it begs the all-important questions of who (as opposed to what) is criminal. At the same time, public debate about the criminality of particular individuals would not only be cumbersome but counterproductive; it would alert the targets to the fact they are under suspicion. The best compromise between these two positions is a requirement of ex ante review by a judge, analogous to what occurs in the warrant process. After explaining this conclusion, the rest of this Article applies it to deception used in undercover operations, searches and seizures, and interrogation.

The Case for Judicial Review as a Proxy

One way to avoid the inefficiency and counterproductiveness of a public debate about particular suspects is to focus the discussion on particular police "practices." This is, in fact, the approach Bok suggests with respect to use of unmarked police cars. She asserts that the propriety of this investigative technique should be publicly debated and that it should be permitted only if a consensus develops in its favor. If the technique is eventually adopted, not only does the public debate enhance its acceptability, but it ensures that "those who still choose to break the speed laws will be aware of the deceptive practice and can decide whether to take their chances or not."

However, in contrast to use of unmarked police cars, many deceptive police practices cannot be discussed without reference to what the police know about the target of the practice. The public's response to decoy stings, pretextual stops, or trickery during interrogation is likely to vary greatly depending upon whether these practices are used randomly or aimed at people thought to be guilty. Should the police be able to pose as door-to-door encyclopedia salespeople? The answer might be yes if they use the ruse to gain entry into the house of a person suspected of kidnapping children but no if they simply go door-to-door to see what they can find. Should the police be able to stop a car for violation of a minor traffic law that is usually not enforced to get a peak into the backseat or consent to a full search? The answer might be yes if the police suspect the car driver of being a drug courier but no if the police stop any violators they "feel like" stopping. Should police be able to lie to someone about finding his fingerprints at the scene of the crime to scare him into confessing? The answer might be yes if he's arrested but no if investigators with few or no leads come to the person's house and make the statement simply to see how he'll respond.

To the extent the public cares about all its members (including, as Bok requires, those who will be duped), it will want to take steps that limit investigative lying to those likely to be criminals. If a "practice" can be defined to meet that goal, then no further guidance is necessary. If, on the other hand, the practice as defined could be used against anyone, then some further effort at ensuring that it will be employed only against authentic suspects should be attempted.

One method of doing so would be to say to the police: "Make sure you use this technique only against suspects." However, leaving identification of the criminal up to the police—those who will do the lying—violates Bok's notion of public debate among reasonable persons. This would be so even if we added a requirement that the individual officer seek a second opinion from another officer. As she notes, "more than [mere] consultation with chosen peers is needed whenever crucial interests are . . . at stake." People of all allegiances should be consulted so as to avoid the impact of prejudice and personal spite on the decision to deceive.

We are thus again back to the original dilemma: how to obtain public input about who is to be considered a criminal-enemy, when public input would be cumbersome and might alert the enemy. Another answer is to appoint a proxy for the public, who would act as a check on police discretion on the public's behalf. Although not an entirely satisfactory solution, the proposition defended here is that the magistrate—the person who, in our current system, makes probable cause decisions and issues search and arrest warrants—can fulfill this role. . . .

Furthermore, the involvement of a judge should assure the public that deceit by the executive branch is cabined. The fact that a judge, presumptively divorced from law enforcement, has signed off on a particular use of investigative lying should extinguish or at least significantly diminish any feelings of betrayal. Indeed, its effect might be analogous to the way in which a warrant guarantees the propriety of overt police actions. . . .

The assumption I will make, then, is that the judicial or "official" identification of a person as a criminal is both necessary and sufficient to meet Bok's demand for public debate as to whether a person is an "enemy." If this official identification occurs (the cause showing), then the police are morally justified in using deceit to gather evidence from the identified individual, at least when good truthful alternatives are not available (the necessity showing). If, on the other hand, the judge is not willing to label the person a suspect, or finds that deceit isn't necessary to investigate him further, then deception would not be permissible. The concrete implications of this official-identification predicate are several.

Distinguishing Passive and Active Undercover Work

Consider first the implications of the official identification idea for undercover work. To understand these implications, it is useful to divide covert investigative techniques into two types: passive and active. Passive covert investigation would not require judicial authorization, whereas active undercover work would.

Passive undercover operations are those which merely provide people with the opportunity to commit the crime, without importuning any particular person. Posing on a street corner as a prostitute waiting for a john is an example of a passive operation, as is putting out the word that cocaine can be bought in a particular alley or that stolen property can be sold at a specified location. These types of passive-undercover operations can be meaningfully debated in the abstract: should citizens be tempted by police posing as prostitutes, drug dealers, or fences? If it were determined, after such debate, that a certain kind of baiting operation is or may be efficacious, any particular operation of that kind need not be preceded by judicial authorization, since people who take the bait are likely to be criminals. Like the use of an unmarked police car to catch speeders, the only people against whom the police intervene are those they know to be committing crime. Abuse of discretion and the potential for betraying innocent people and damaging citizen trust in government are minimized.

These potential harms are much greater, however, when the undercover operation takes on an active mode by going after a specific target or targets thought to be criminal rather than seeking to lure criminals out of the general population. The propriety of infiltrating a particular organization or establishing an intimate relationship with a particular individual cannot be the subject of an abstract public debate. Moreover, there is no guarantee that the direct impact of such covert deception will be visited only on those who are clearly criminals, making the potential for the discrimination that Bok fears much greater. Thus, where active undercover operations are contemplated, judicial authorization should be obtained. The police should not be able to use such techniques unless the public, in the form of the judge, decides that good reason to do so exists and that more straightforward methods are not likely to work. . . .

Curtailing Pretextual Actions

Ex ante judicial authorization would also be required for deceptive searches and seizures. As with active undercover operations, a search or seizure requires the police to target a particular individual. Thus, police should not be able to use deception to effectuate such an action unless the target has been identified as a potential criminal by the public's proxy, the judge.

This second proposal is in some ways more radical than the previous one, since in effect it would eliminate almost all deception in connection with overt searches and seizures. In situations in which the police misrepresent their authority (e.g., by saying they do not need a warrant when in fact they do), they usually lack sufficient suspicion to authorize their action. Assuming so, a judge is unlikely to find the target is a criminal-enemy to whom police can lie. Pretextual actions misrepresenting the motivations of the police would also be significantly curtailed. Because the latter are also usually based on hunches rather than articulable suspicion approval of a pretextual action would seldom be sought and, if sought, would seldom be granted. . . .

Trickery during Interrogation: Pre- and Post-Arrest

. . . In contrast to the typical undercover operation or search and seizure, most interrogation in which deceit is practiced takes place after a person has been taken into custody. It thus follows either an indictment, a judicially issued arrest warrant, or a formal assertion by the police that they believe the interrogated person is a criminal, an assertion they know will be tested in front of a judge within a short timespan. As a result, the public declaration that is the cornerstone of Bok's enemy exception either precedes or hangs over the typical interrogation process, at least if one accepts the notion of the judge acting as the public's proxy. Furthermore, the official identification here is overt. Thus, as Bok would prefer, the person subjected to interrogation is on notice that the police view him or her as an enemy. . . .

In short, under Bok's framework as interpreted in this Article, a good case can be made for the proposition that postarrest trickery is permissible. Because the arrest threshold both limits police deception to openly identified "enemies" and alerts the potential dupe to the adversarial relationship, such trickery is not inherently immoral, at least when, as will often be the case, a colorable claim can be made that direct questions will not obtain the desired information. . . .

Recall, however, that Bok would permit deceit only when a truthful alternative is not available. By the time of formal charging (in contrast to the time between arrest and charging) the state presumably has developed a prima facie case against the defendant.

At this point, then, interrogation of any type, with or without trickery, should not be necessary to fulfill the state's objective. If this is so, similar to the outcome under Sixth Amendment law, formal charging should mark a cut-off beyond which investigative lies of any sort are not allowed.

Two caveats to this discussion of interrogation trickery must be made. First, Bok's admonition that deceptive practices should be publicly debated is especially pertinent here. Although the official identification of particular individuals as enemies probably must, by default, fall on judges, various interrogation practices can also be the subject of scrutiny in the abstract. Indeed, the public could decide, contrary to what has been argued to this point, that all deception during interrogation is improper. Certainly, plausible arguments have been advanced in this regard. More specifically, public debate might focus on certain types of practices. For instance, one deceptive technique that has occasioned much comment involves a police officer posing as another type of professional, say the defendant's court-appointed lawyer, a clergyperson, or a psychiatrist. As Joseph Grano has argued, the virtually universal legislative recognition of lawyer–client and psychiatrist–patient privileges could be construed to stand for a decision by the public that statements made to these individuals are confidential and that therefore police cannot learn of them through deception. Public debate might also address whether prosecutors, as distinct from the police, can ever lie to suspects. Perhaps, as officers of the court and members of the bar, they should be prohibited from doing so. Obviously, a number of other general issues of this sort can and should be debated.

A final consideration in determining what types of deception, if any, might be permitted during interrogation is the degree of coercion created by the deceptive practice. The Supreme Court itself has recognized that certain types of deceit can render a confession involuntary. Bok also notes that deception can create coercive circumstances, particularly when it limits knowledge of one's alternatives.

Conclusion

A central lesson of Sissela Bok's analysis is that, once lying becomes a practice, it is rarely justifiable. Routine deceit coarsens the liar, increases the likelihood of exposure, and when exposed, maximizes the loss of trust. When the deceptive practice is carried out by an agent of the government, it is even more reprehensible, both because the liar wields tremendous power and because government requires trust to be effective. Thus, limitations on police lying are justifiable and perhaps necessary. . . .

The extrapolation of Bok's analysis developed in this Article suggests that once an individual has been identified as a suspect through the public proxy of a judge, noncoercive deception in the investigative setting is often permissible. On the other hand, in the absence of such an identification, or when deception leads the dupe to believe he has no choice but to provide the sought-after evidence, investigative lying is wrong and should be prohibited. On this premise, warrantless "active" undercover operations and pretextual police actions are improper, unless necessary to save a life or useful as a substitute for legitimate use of force. On the other hand, deception associated with passive, bait-type stings is proper, so long as the general propriety of the sting has been subject to public debate. Trickery in connection with postarrest, precharge interrogation is also proper, so long as it does not coerce the dupe. . . . ■

Lying to Ourselves

Margaret L. Paris

Christopher Slobogin's article contributes to the emerging dialogue regarding police lying in two important ways. First, the article challenges us to categorize and morally evaluate the lies in which police engage during investigations. The article's focus on moral questions is a welcome change from the "ends-justifies-the-means" approach of some current criminal procedure scholarship that advocates the lifting of restrictions on police conduct on the basis of a questionable belief that fewer restrictions mean more convictions. Second, the article appears to invite legislatures and rulemaking bodies to debate the morality of police lying. Historically, legislatures and rulemaking bodies have left it to the courts to regulate police lying and other forms of police misconduct. Slobogin points out, however, that courts applying constitutional law have "acquiesced in, if not affirmatively sanctioned," police lying. Because constitutional law permits courts little room to impose meaningful restrictions on police lying, those of us desiring to address that social ill must not only oppose any further erosion of current doctrine in the courts, but also must affirmatively address the problem of police lying in legislative and administrative forums. I hope that Slobogin's article and the accompanying responses are read broadly by police, legislators, administrators, and other rulemakers, to whom the responsibility of tackling the issue falls.

I am also enthusiastic about Slobogin's project because I agree with his tentative conclusion that police lies are often unjustifiable. I would, however, go farther than Slobogin . . . and prohibit all police lying except when necessary to save lives. Slobogin employs Bok's evaluative method to suggest that police may justifiably lie to suspects who have been publicly identified as criminals even in noncrisis situations—that is, even in situations in which lives are

Margaret L. Paris. "Lying to Ourselves," *Oregon Law Review*, Volume 76 (Winter 1997).

not at stake. According to Slobogin, Bok acknowledges that an otherwise unjustified lie might be justifiable if it is told to an enemy to avert a crisis, and criminal suspects can be considered "enemies," as that term is used by Bok. Slobogin advances this rationale to justify police lies to suspects undergoing custodial interrogation as well as deceptive undercover techniques used against people "likely to be criminals" or those about whom judicial authorization to lie has been obtained. I will focus specifically on Slobogin's discussion of lies during interrogation because I tend to think lying during interrogation is more damaging than other types of deception.

Working within Bok's framework, I disagree with Slobogin's proposal to permit lies during interrogation on two grounds. Bok disapproves of all lies except those that can be publicly justified. According to Bok, lies can be publicly justified when: (1) there are no alternatives to lying (the necessity principle); and (2) lying would produce a surfeit of benefits versus harms (the utility principle). While Bok suggests that lies to enemies sometimes pass these tests, Slobogin's equation of arrested suspects with "enemies" does not meet these tests. Slobogin's proposal to permit lies during interrogation condones unnecessary lying because truthful alternatives exist. Slobogin's proposal also creates negative consequences that will likely outweigh the benefits, although costs and benefits are difficult to quantify in this context.

Before I address these issues, however, I will explore whether Slobogin's proposal to permit lying during interrogation is capable of public justification,

an important predicate to Bok's "lying to enemies" exception.

Public Justification

Bok generally finds lies justifiable only if they are told to avert a crisis. However, Bok does seem to acknowledge, in principle, a "narrow justification" for deception in noncrisis situations involving self-defense against enemies, and Bok indicates several times that "criminals" are among those to whom the label "enemy" would apply. Bok stresses that one of the more critical features of this justification is public identification of the enemy.

Slobogin uses Bok's passages referring to criminals as enemies to construct a rule permitting police to lie to persons who have been identified as criminals. He proposes several limitations on this license. First, Slobogin would not permit police to lie to suspects who are interrogated before arrest because the police at that stage might not have probable cause to believe those suspects are guilty of criminal behavior. Slobogin would not consider those suspects to be "enemies" until police have developed probable cause to support an arrest. For the same reason, Slobogin would not permit lying to nonsuspects and witnesses. Second, Slobogin proposes that we permit police to lie only before formal charges have been lodged against suspects. Slobogin imposes this limit because criminal charges usually are initiated only when the prosecution has sufficient evidence to proceed. After that point, it would be unnecessary to extract a confession by lying or, presumably, any other means. Third, Slobogin would prohibit "coercive" lying, which he considers immoral because it limits suspects' knowledge of alternatives.

Despite these limitations, Slobogin's proposal would permit lying in the vast majority of custodial interrogations. I believe that Bok would reject Slobogin's proposal because the generous permission to lie would soon overwhelm the limits that Slobogin advocates. Bok's language is susceptible to more than one interpretation, but nowhere does Bok state that lying to enemies is justifiable on a broad scale. To the contrary, she argues that deception is analogous to violence and that, while both are justifiable in principle when used in preemptive strikes against enemies, they are, in practice, unrestrainable in such a context. Because the practical application of justificatory schemes is of great importance to Bok, she ultimately suggests that we should resort to deception and violence only in crisis situations.

It is worthwhile to explore why Bok predicts that, as a practical matter, if deception (and violence) against enemies are condoned they are likely to proliferate. Those reasons are especially pertinent in the context of Slobogin's proposal to permit lying during interrogation. Bok believes that all significant lies (including lies told by those, like police, who occupy positions of trust) must stand up to the scrutiny of unbiased, reasonable people. Bok argues that public justification avoids the malleability of the liar's own conscience, which would all too easily assess the balance in favor of the lie. Public justification brings objectivity and wisdom, eliminates bias, challenges assumptions, and exposes fallacious reasoning. Bok asserts that a necessary part of public justification is the ability of the public to "adopt the perspective not only of liars but of those lied to; and not only of particular persons but of all those affected by lies—the collective perspective of reasonable persons seen as potentially deceived." The importance of the public's objectivity cannot be overstated: Bok rejects lies in situations in which the public justification test cannot function in an unbiased manner.

According to Bok, in situations involving enemies, the public justification test will inevitably break down as the public's reasonableness and objectivity disappears. When the public perceives an enemy, it will react with hostility, precluding the kind of balanced, perspective-shifting analysis that the public justification test requires. Bok states that if the public has been "whipped into a frenzy of hostility, one cannot speak of 'publicity' in the sense in which it has been used up to now in this book." Because the public cannot put itself in the enemy's shoes, Bok ultimately concludes that deceptive schemes based on the "lying to enemies" justification should not be sanctioned. Even deceptive practices that are carefully circumscribed at the outset will eventually expand beyond reasonable limits because the public's hostility will prevent it from objectively maintaining limits on lying. Bok explains that, in practice, neither deception nor violence can "be contained within . . . narrow boundaries; they end up growing, perpetuating themselves, multiplying, and feeding on one another, to produce the very opposite of increased safety."

If Bok were asked to comment on Slobogin's use of the "lying to enemies" justification to support police lying during interrogations, I believe she would point out that her public-justification test cannot function well in the atmosphere of public hostility that surrounds crime, and that public sympathies will inevitably allow deceptive police practices to expand beyond the limits proposed by Slobogin. For this practical reason, I believe Bok would not agree that lying during interrogation can be justified by reference to her narrow "lying to enemies" exception.

The problem of maintaining public objectivity in the "enemies" context might be alleviated if the parameters on police lying that Slobogin proposes were defined in legislation or administrative rules. It is not clear, however, that legislative or administrative bodies are capable of maintaining greater objectivity than the general public when it comes to crime and police lying or that those politically accountable bodies can avoid endless tinkering with Slobogin's parameters if the public demands change. There have been few intelligent public discussions of issues related to crime or law enforcement since the presidential election of 1968, when national politicians began inciting a public panic about crime. The political dangers inherent in advocating limits on police lying may mean that the issues cannot be fully aired. On the other hand, a few productive national conversations about law enforcement have occurred recently in connection with situations such as Waco and Ruby Ridge, in which relatively large numbers of the public were able to empathize with the suspects. These dialogues provide at least a glimmer of hope that the public may be capable of critically examining law enforcement practices and maintaining reasonable limits on deception. The malleability of public opinion of law enforcement suggests to me (as I believe it would to Bok) that the wisest course would be to enact a nearly absolute prohibition on police lying. An absolute rule would have a better chance of long-term survival than a nuanced one.

I would like to see Slobogin address in more detail Bok's reservations about the practical problems of implementing a limited "lying to enemies" exception to the general presumption against lying. The present article does not explain adequately how those problems could be overcome. Even if Slobogin were able to convince me that the limitations of his proposed "license to lie" would not be lifted quickly, however, I would still oppose his approach because he does not demonstrate that police lying during interrogations is either necessary or beneficial, both of which are required before a lie can be justified under Bok's method. The next section addresses those points in turn.

The Necessity and Utility of Lying

Bok acknowledges that lies to avoid a crisis with an enemy may sometimes be necessary, but she nevertheless requires an exacting search for truthful alternatives, even when an enemy is involved. Despite Bok's exhortation that alternatives must be sought before lying can be justified, Slobogin does not explore the alternatives to lying during interrogation. If Slobogin had examined the alternatives, he would have perceived an obvious one: police can interrogate truthfully. Of course, to be considered a viable alternative, truthfulness would have to advance the goals sought during interrogation. Slobogin does not clearly articulate the goals of interrogation, but he appears to assume that gathering information from suspects is the chief objective. I would add another objective: interrogations provide important opportunities for police to distribute information to suspects (and more indirectly, the public) about such things as integrity, honest dialogue, and trustworthiness. The dissemination of this kind of information is essential to a successfully functioning criminal justice system. Because this information is transmitted in large part by exemplification, it cannot be conveyed through deceit.

Even if we focus exclusively on the information-gathering objective of interrogations, we must recognize the possibility that truthful interrogations can produce confessions or useful information. It is far from clear that the amount of information derived from interrogations would be significantly reduced if police were required to tell the truth. Certainly, interrogators, who place great stock in the tools of manipulation and deception, would argue that their effectiveness would be jeopardized. However, the fact that professional interrogators believe deceit to be essential is not persuasive. There is no evidence that those in the law enforcement business have seriously considered, much less tried, the alternative.

Even if lying increases confession rates, it is not certain whether confession rates affect conviction rates. Professor Paul Cassell has attempted to establish a relationship between confessions and convictions in his efforts to compute the cost of Miranda, estimating that Miranda has resulted in lost convictions in 3.8% of all serious criminal cases and concluding that such a loss amounts to a significant social cost. Other scholars disagree with both his estimate and his conclusion, however. For example, Professor Stephen Schulhofer argues that Miranda affected fewer than one percent of all cases in the period shortly after the Court issued that decision, its "net damage to law enforcement is zero," and even if Cassell's 3.8% figure is accurate, that figure represents a small cost.

In addition, both Slobogin and Cassell overestimate the utility of confessions. Both assume that deception is successful if it produces confessions. Confessions are of limited use, however, if they are ruled inadmissible. Slobogin admits that lies can sometimes cause a court to rule a confession inadmissible on voluntariness grounds. Lies might also produce statements that run afoul of the corpus delicti rule, which excludes confessions unless they are supported by independent evidence of guilt. The corpus delicti rule represents a judicial determination that confessions are of questionable reliability—a determination that casts doubt on the utility of obtaining a confession through any means. In fact, wrongful convictions based on erroneous deception-induced confessions must be considered a cost of, not a benefit from, those confessions. It is not mere speculation that lies might induce untruthful statements. Psychological and sociological studies indicate that suspects are susceptible to police pressure and sometimes confess even when they are innocent. The vulnerability of suspects and the possibility that they might confess even when innocent are magnified in the hands of an interrogator well-versed in deceit and other interrogation techniques. Even "experienced" suspects are vulnerable to sophisticated interrogation techniques. Thus, although a broad rule permitting lies during postarrest, precharge interrogations might facilitate confessions, some of those confessions would be inadmissible and some would undermine the accuracy of the criminal justice system.

Slobogin acknowledges that there is conflicting research on whether confession rates affect conviction rates, and he acknowledges that a relationship between the two is necessary to his analysis. He nevertheless assumes that postarrest, precharge deceit is necessary to obtain convictions. Slobogin's failure to seriously consider the alternative of being truthful in interrogations and to demonstrate any conclusive link between confessions and convictions undercuts his conclusion that lying in interrogations is necessary and useful.

If we take Bok's test seriously, then, we would have to reject Slobogin's conclusion that lying in postarrest, precharge settings is justifiable. There are alternatives to lying, and the benefits of lying are not clear. Slobogin might fine tune his proposal by limiting lying to situations in which a judicial officer has found no viable alternative to lying and has concluded that lying is likely to produce useful information

or admissible evidence. Moreover, the judicial officer would have to determine that the benefits from lying outweigh the harms caused by lying. The time and effort involved in that kind of judicial oversight, however, would make lying too expensive in all but the most pressing circumstances.

In my discussion of the benefits and costs of lying, I have saved for last the special harm that police lying causes. As I explain in the next section, those harms, while difficult to quantify, are substantial.

Special Harms

Bok's evaluative method for determining when lying may be justified requires a careful assessment of the harms that lying causes and a rejection of lies whose harms outweigh the benefits to be gained. Bok stresses that lying damages the liar, the dupe, and society in general. Slobogin acknowledges the nature of some of those damages in the criminal investigation context. He and I differ, though, in the weight we assign to those harms. This kind of disagreement may be intractable because the relative weights of benefits and harms is a very subjective matter. Nevertheless, a few brief points might help to highlight the nature of our disagreement.

First, lies harm the liars. Slobogin acknowledges that lying has an "insidious impact" on police themselves, and he is particularly aware of the danger that lying in the interrogation context may lead to police perjury under oath. This, of course, is a widespread harm that also damages the dupe and society in general. Given Slobogin's concern for "testilying," I would have thought that he would seek to reduce the sheer number of lies that police tell. Yet his rule permitting lies during interrogation would mean that police would continue to lie extensively and presumably would continue to incur the kinds of damages that he describes so well. Slobogin explains his acceptance of lying during postarrest, precharge interrogations in part by the fact that arrested suspects are likely to be guilty. He may reason from this that police would have difficulty complying with a rule forbidding them from lying to guilty people and would therefore lie twice as much as they do now to cover up what happened during interrogations. I agree that this could be a problem, but presumably sufficiently strict sanctions for lying would correct the problem. I also would expect cover-ups to diminish if lying becomes generally unacceptable among police.

Slobogin also underestimates the damage that lying does to subjects of interrogation, although he acknowledges that some damage occurs. Slobogin's willingness to characterize arrested suspects as "enemies" helps mask the damage caused by lying because the word enemies implies hostile outsiders—persons outside our social or national connections, whose loyalty and trust we do not seek. I might (but only might) agree that we need not worry as much about the damage caused by lying when we deal with true outsiders because we are not so concerned about maintaining social bonds with them. But when it comes to persons in this country who are suspected (or even convicted) of criminal behavior, we ignore at our own peril the damage caused by lying. As the

commentators to whom Slobogin refers have argued, the loyalty and trust of "suspects" are of great concern to us because they will continue to live among us or will return to us after a period of incarceration, unless they are locked up for life without the possibility of parole. As a result, it is important that we behave honorably and truthfully with them to initiate, maintain, or renew their loyalty and trust and to exemplify appropriate behavior.

Slobogin suggests that those who are probably innocent should fare better in our calculations than those who are probably guilty, but this distinction conceals many troubling subtleties that make it unworkable in practice. For example, I am not certain how Slobogin would view the suspect whose behavior might ultimately be determined to have been lawful based on self-defense or some other excuse or justification and who might therefore be legally innocent although appearing guilty to police at the outset. In the same way, it would be useful to know how Slobogin would deal with the suspect whose crime was minor and nonviolent, the first-time offender, the suspect whose behavior might be decriminalized, or the offender whose behavior was previously acceptable but has been recently criminalized. Suspects in each of these categories would enjoy more sympathy than the violent criminal, and they probably make up a larger portion of criminal suspects than violent offenders. Add to these complexities the pervasive nature of racial, ethnic, and class bias in the criminal justice system, and an outright prohibition on all interrogation lying seems far preferable to a rule with a rationale that depends on a simplistic distinction between innocence and guilt.

Finally, there are the social costs of Slobogin's proposal. It harms a society when the officers who enforce its laws behave like the worst used car salesmen. That harm is compounded because deceptive tactics employed by police to obtain evidence reflect poorly on courts that supervise the admission of that evidence. The U.S. Supreme Court used these harms to justify the Fourth Amendment exclusionary rule, although more recently it has abandoned the "judicial integrity" rationale in favor of deterrence of police misconduct alone. These unquantifiable but very real harms deserve renewed attention and increased weight in the emerging dialogue about police lying. Unfortunately, Slobogin gives them short shrift when he evaluates the morality of lying during interrogations.

Conclusion

Professor Slobogin's article initiates an important discussion about the morality of police lying. Nevertheless, Slobogin's approach falls short when it evaluates police lying during interrogations. Police lying is unjustifiable in that context because it is unnecessary and harmful as well as impossible to restrain within reasonable limits. A thorough moral evaluation of police lying suggests that all police lying should be prohibited, except that which is necessary to save lives. ∎

▥ The Continuing Debate

What Is New

Recent cases of false confessions to major crimes have raised hard questions concerning the potentially coercive power of deceptive police interrogation techniques. In 1989, five young men confessed to a brutal attack on a Central Park jogger—an attack that left the victim near death and very severely injured, and made newspaper headlines for weeks. In 2002, the convicted men were exonerated by DNA testing, and the obvious question was, Why had they confessed to a brutal crime they had not committed? And rather than being an isolated case, false confessions are a common feature of wrongful conviction cases. When deceptive interrogation techniques are used to convict the guilty, some will still have qualms about their use, though for others the importance of correctly solving crimes may mitigate concern about methods; but when deceptive interrogation techniques convince innocent people to plead guilty to crimes they did not commit, almost everyone would agree the techniques require closer scrutiny.

Where to Find More

Sissela Bok, *Lying: Moral Choice in Public and Private Life* (1978), is an important examination of lying and its effects; Christopher Slobogin refers to Bok's book at several points in his article. For further insight on when deception may be used in the interrogation process, see Christopher Slobogin, "Lying and Confessing," *39 Texas Tech Law Review* 1275 (2007).

Wesley G. Skogan and Tracey L. Meares, "Lawful Policing," *Annals, AAPSS*, Volume 593 (May 2004): 66–83, review research on police adherence to laws and rules; they note the difficulty in determining the degree to which police are following or violating the rules, and argue that internal processes are the best means of improving compliance. Jerome H. Skolnick and Richard A. Leo, "The Ethics of Deceptive Interrogation," *Criminal Justice Ethics*, Volume 11, Number 1 (Winter/Spring 1992): 3–12, examine the legal history of deceptive interrogation, explore various types of police deception, and warn of its dangers; the quotation in the introduction to this debate is from their article. An essay by Welsh S. White, "Deceptive Police Interrogation Practices: How Far Is Too Far?: Miranda's Failure to Restrain Pernicious Interrogation Practices," *Michigan Law Review*, Volume 99 (2001): 1211–1247, examines deceptive interrogation techniques in the context of false confessions and legal protection for the rights of suspects.

A classic manual for police interrogation, which coaches interrogators in the use of deceptive techniques, is Fred E. Inbau and John E. Reid, *Criminal Investigation and Criminal Interrogation*, 3rd Edition (Baltimore: Williams and Wilkins Co., 1962), which expands their earlier *Lie Detection and Criminal Investigation*, 3rd Edition (Baltimore: Williams and Wilkins Co., 1953); its most recent edition is *Criminal Interrogation and Confessions* (Boston: Jones & Bartlett Publishers, 2004). Another standard manual advocating deceptive techniques is Charle E. O'Hara and Gregory L. O'Hara, *Fundamentals of Criminal Investigation*, 7th Edition (2003). An incisive critique of Inbau's manual can be found in Yale Kamisar, "What Is an 'Involuntary' Confession? Some Comments on Inbau and Reid's *Criminal Interrogation and Confessions*," *Rutgers Law Review*, Volume 17 (1963). Fred Inbau gives arguments in favor of deceptive interrogation techniques in "Law and Police Practice: Restrictions in the Law of Interrogation and Confessions," *Northwestern University Law Review*, Volume 52 (1957); and "Police Interrogation: A Practical Necessity," in the *Journal of Criminal Law, Criminology, and Police Science*, Volume 52 (1961). (Inbau's enthusiasm for deceptive interrogation methods may well seem excessive by contemporary standards; however, when evaluating Inbau's work, it should be remembered that when he originally developed his interrogation model in the early 1950s, Inbau was attempting to move police interrogation practices away from methods of violent coercion: the beating and threatening of suspects was not an uncommon interrogation technique, and Inbau was campaigning to abolish that method. Whatever one thinks of the deceptive techniques advocated by Inbau, they are surely an improvement over police torture of suspects.)

Paul Cassell voices doubts concerning false confessions in "The Guilty and the 'Innocent': An Examination of Alleged Cases of Wrongful Conviction from False Confessions," *Harvard Journal of Law and Public Policy*, Volume 22 (1999). Concern about false confessions and the techniques that induce them is voiced by Miriam S. Gohara, "A Lie for a Lie: False Confessions and the Case for Reconsidering the Legality of Deceptive Interrogation Techniques," *Fordham Urban Law Journal*, Volume 33 (March 2006): 791–842; she also examines the law concerning deceptive interrogation techniques. Other good examinations of psychological techniques leading to false confessions are Richard A. Leo and Richard J. Ofshe, "The Consequences of False Confessions: Deprivations of Liberty and Miscarriages of Justice in the Age of Psychological Interrogation," *Journal of Criminal Law and Criminology*, Volume 88 (1998); and Hollida Wakefield and Ralph Underwager, "Coerced or Nonvoluntary Confessions," *Behavioral Sciences and the Law*, Volume 16 (1998): 423–440. Psychological examinations of why innocent persons might confess to crimes—especially when confronted with deceptive interrogation techniques, including fake fingerprint or DNA identifications—include Richard J. Ofshe and Richard A. Leo, "The Decision to Confess Falsely: Rational Choice and Irrational Action," *Denver University Law Review*, Volume 74 (1997); and two articles by Saul M. Kassin, "The Psychology of Confession Evidence," *American Psychologist*, Volume 52 (1997), and "On the Psychology of Confessions: Does Innocence Put Innocents at Risk?" *American Psychologist*, Volume 60 (2005).

3

Should a Victims' Rights Amendment Be Added to the U.S. Constitution?

The Constitution Should Include a Victims' Rights Amendment
   Advocate: Steven J. Twist, Chief Counsel for National Victims
   Constitutional Amendment Passage; served as Chief Assistant
   Attorney General for the State of Arizona from 1978 to 1990, and
   authored the Arizona constitutional amendment for victims' rights.
   Source: "The Crime Victims' Rights Amendment and Two Good and
   Perfect Things," *Utah Law Review*, Volume 369 (1999).
There Should Be No Victims' Rights Amendment
   Advocate: Bruce Shapiro, contributing editor to *The Nation* and execu-
   tive director of the Dart Center for Journalism and Trauma.
   Source: "Victims & Vengeance: Why the Victims' Rights Amendment Is
   a Bad Idea," *The Nation* (February 10, 1997): 11–19.

"Victims' rights" hardly seems a controversial issue. Everyone sympathizes with
the innocent victim of a crime, and no one wants to deny innocent victims their
genuine rights. But the issue is not that simple. The push for "victims' rights" is
sometimes motivated by the claim that the rights of the *accused* have crowded
out the rights of crime *victims*; that is, the victims' rights movement is sometimes
part of a "get tough" movement to limit the rights of criminal defendants and
make criminal convictions easier. "Victims' rights" means different things to different people, and it requires careful scrutiny.

Several different groups with distinctively different goals have championed
"victims' rights." One group—Robert Mosteller calls it the "Victim Protection
and Aid" group—was the major U.S. victims' rights group in the 1960s and 1970s.
It promoted programs that would compensate crime victims (for example, make

payments to victims of robbery or provide medical care for victims of assault) and policies to provide special protection for those likely to be repeat victims (such as victims of spousal abuse). A second group favoring "victims' rights" is (what Mosteller calls) the "Prosecutorial Benefit" group. In their program, "victims' rights" is a way of providing stronger tools to criminal prosecutors, and thus making it more likely that criminal defendants will be convicted on severe charges and receive harsh penalties. In Europe the primary agenda of the "victims' rights" movement is helping the crime victim gain material compensation from the criminal. In other areas—notably New Zealand, Australia, and Canada—the "victims' rights" movement is often an element of the "restorative justice" model (see Debate 8), with emphasis on restoring wholeness and harmony to the community and all its members (including both victims and perpetrators of crimes).

A key demand of the contemporary U.S. victims' rights movement is the right to make a "victim impact statement" during the defendant's trial (describing in detail the suffering experienced by the victim and/or the victim's friends and family). Such statements raise special questions: A victim who is warm and appealing may influence a jury to more readily convict the defendant of a more serious offense but does the defendant deserve harsher punishment for harming a charming rather than a repulsive victim? Furthermore, the presence of a "victim" may destroy the defendant's "presumption of innocence."

Steven Twist maintains that our criminal justice system focuses on protecting the rights of the accused and on prosecuting crimes on behalf of the public good, and the result is a shift away from the crime *victim* and her loss and toward concern for the *accused* and for the good order of the *state*. Twist sees the proposed Victims' Rights Amendment restoring the individual crime victim's legitimate place in the criminal process. Bruce Shapiro argues that the Victims' Rights Amendment is a blunt instrument that is badly designed to handle a complex problem, and that the supposed "imbalance" between the rights of victims and the rights of the accused is a myth that has been exploited for political gain.

▬▬▬ Points to Ponder

- Jones commits a brutal murder: He stabs to death an affluent accountant who had just walked away from an ATM machine, and steals the $200 the man had just withdrawn. At Jones' trial, the accountant's widow speaks movingly of her terrible loss, and how much she grieves for the husband she dearly loved. The jury, deeply moved by her sorrow, sentences Jones to death. Smith also commits a brutal murder: He stabs to death a homeless and friendless old man who was sleeping in a homeless shelter after cashing his social security check, stealing $200 from this homeless drifter. At the sentencing phase of Smith's trial, no one appears to speak of the loss of this friendless drifter, and the murderer is sentenced to life imprisonment. Are the verdicts just?

- Of the 19 procedural and substantive victims' rights proposed under the amendment, are there any you regard as particularly *desirable* or *undesirable*?
- You and I were involved in a fight. I suffered significant injuries, complained to the police, and assault charges are filed against you. I claim that we were having a political debate, and you suddenly became enraged and struck me. You claim that this was a case of self-defense: *I* became enraged and took several swings at you, and your act of self-defense caused my injuries. If I am allowed to make a special statement to the court as a "victim," does that imperil your right to a fair trial?
- Should there be a special government program designed to help those who are victims of crime? For example, a government-funded program to help those who are victims of identity theft, or of injuries caused by a drunk driver, or to help the families of murder victims? The victims of the 9/11 disaster received generous support from the federal government; should a similar program be established for all crime victims?

The Crime Victims' Rights Amendment and Two Good and Perfect Things

Steven J. Twist

At the soul of America's justice system lie two "good and perfect things": (1) the principle that the procedural and substantive rights of the accused must be preserved and protected as a proper restraint on the state's power to infringe individual rights to life and liberty; and (2) the practice of public prosecution, based on the theory that when a crime occurs, while it surely involves harm to a victim, it also represents an offense against the state, which tears at the fabric of our peace and community and hence creates a harm that is greater than simply the harm to the victim involved.

These two "good and perfect things" have served America well. The first respects each individual as an end, as "created equal, [and] endowed by their Creator with certain unalienable Rights [to] Life, Liberty and the

Steven J. Twist. "The Crime Victims' Rights Amendment and Two Good and Perfect Things," *Utah Law Review*, Volume 369 (1999). Reprinted with permission from Steven J. Twist.

pursuit of Happiness." These protections of the accused include rights of habeas corpus, to a speedy and public jury trial, to know the nature and cause of the accusation, to confront adverse witnesses and have compulsory process; rights to counsel, due process and equal protection; and rights against unreasonable searches and seizures, double jeopardy, self incrimination, excessive bail or fines, cruel and unusual punishment, bills of attainder, and ex post facto laws. Overall, these rights form a zone of protection around the law-abiding, as well as the lawless, and serve to deter the abuses of government power with which the history of the world is all too familiar.

These fundamental rights formed the core of the essential fairness shown to accused and convicted criminals that became, and rightly so, a hallmark of our civilization. Through the course of history, while certainly not always faithful to them, we have seen their inexorable expansion even as we have seen repeated sacrifices at their altar. Thus, Justice Cardozo could write, in 1934:

> The law, as we have seen, is sedulous in maintaining for a defendant charged with crime whatever forms of procedure are of the essence of an opportunity to defend. Privileges so fundamental as to be inherent in every concept of a fair trial that could be acceptable to the thought of reasonable men will be kept inviolate and inviolable, however crushing may be the pressure of incriminating proof.

Indeed, there have been many times in the history of our country when the "pressure of incriminating proof" has been "crushing"; yet, the criminal has been freed so that the "fundamental privileges" of the law-abiding could be preserved.

The second "good and perfect thing" springs not from the rights of the individual so much as from the rights of the community. Private prosecutions, whereby the victim or the victim's relatives or friends brought and prosecuted criminal charges against the accused wrongdoer, were the norm in the American justice system at the time of the colonial revolution and the drafting of the Constitution. The origin of private prosecution has been traced to early English common law, but even today the civilized British retain the private right to bring criminal charges.

In America, however, while some vestiges of private prosecutions continue to this day, there was a "meteoric rise of public prosecutions" during the nineteenth century, and the office of public prosecutor grew in stature. The origin of the office remains an "historical enigma," but it certainly is consistent with the views that we often express about the nature of crime and its assault on the social compact. Former Chief Justice Weintraub, of the New Jersey Supreme Court, expressed a classic formulation of these views in 1971:

> The first right of the individual is to be protected from attack. That is why we have government, as the preamble to the Federal Constitution plainly says. In the words of Chicago v. Sturges:
>
> > Primarily, governments exist for the maintenance of social order. Hence it is that

the obligation of the government to protect life, liberty, and property against the conduct of the indifferent, the careless, and the evil-minded, may be regarded as lying at the very foundation of the social compact.

To protect the social compact, government assumed the burden of maintaining the social order and marshaled for itself the powers of state to achieve its end: a virtuous goal, a "good and perfect thing." But are there in these two good and perfect things seeds of destruction? I suspect so, and to preserve the essential goodness of them, we must seek ways to temper the excesses of their virtue.

In combination, these two ideas— the centrality of both defendants' rights and state power—have been responsible for diminishing the role of the victim to that of just another witness for the state, just another piece of the evidence. In focusing on the centrality of the rights of the accused, we have forgotten about the rights of the accuser. In stressing the centrality of the state, we have neglected the pain of the injured. Unfortunately, we do these things at our own peril, for a justice system that abandons the innocent loses moral authority and will soon lose the confidence of those it is meant to serve.

In *State v. Bisaccia*, Chief Justice Weintraub severely criticized *Mapp v. Ohio's* exclusionary rule; however, in expressing his criticism, the Chief Justice offered an insight that stretched beyond merely the Fourth Amendment to the core of the principle of state centrality. After noting the passage from the U.S. Supreme Court about the primary function of government, he wrote, "When the truth is suppressed and the criminal is set free, the pain of suppression is felt, not by the inanimate State or by some penitent policeman, but by the offender's next victims for whose protection we hold office." Here, in a few short words, is the sum of the excess virtue of the principle of state centrality. The principle goes too far when it ignores the pain of victims.

Similarly, Justice Cardozo saw the dark horizon of the principle of the centrality of defendants' rights almost sixty-five years ago when he continued after the passage just quoted above, stating, "But justice, though due to the accused, is due to the accuser also. The concept of fairness must not be strained till it is narrowed to a filament. We are to keep the balance true."

Here also, stated succinctly, is the sum of the excess virtue of the principle of the centrality of defendants' rights. A justice system that affords its only rights to accused and convicted offenders, but preserves and protects none for its crime victims, has lost its essential balance. Moreover, such a system continues to lose the public's confidence and its claim to respect.

The idea of a federal constitutional amendment for victims' rights has a pedigree born of these same considerations. In 1982, the President's Task Force on Victims of Crime identified the need for a constitutional amendment in similar terms:

In applying and interpreting the vital guarantees that protect all citizens, the criminal justice system has lost an essential balance. It should be clearly understood that this Task Force wishes in no way to vitiate the safeguards that shelter anyone accused of crime; but it must be urged with equal vigor that the system has deprived the innocent, the honest, and the helpless of its protection.

The guiding principle that provides the focus for constitutional liberties is that government must be restrained from trampling the rights of the individual citizen. The victims of crime have been transformed into a group oppressively burdened by a system designed to protect them. This oppression must be redressed. To that end it is the recommendation of this Task Force that the Sixth Amendment to the Constitution of the United States be augmented.

The Crime Victims' Rights Amendment ("the Amendment"), as passed by the Senate Judiciary Committee, is a modest proposal that embodies these goals and will preserve for victims a reasonable, but not intrusive, role in the matter of their case, and protect minimal rights to fair treatment. The rights it proposes may be grouped into two general categories: procedural and substantive.

In the procedural category, the Amendment includes the rights to:

1. reasonable notice of any public proceedings relating to the crime;
2. not be excluded from any public proceedings relating to the crime;
3. be heard, if present, at all public proceedings to determine a conditional release from custody;
4. submit a statement at all public proceedings to determine a release from custody;
5. be heard, if present, at all public proceedings to determine an acceptance of a negotiated plea;
6. submit a statement at all public proceedings to determine an acceptance of a negotiated plea;
7. be heard, if present, at all public proceedings to determine a sentence;
8. submit a statement at all public proceedings to determine a sentence;
9. reasonable notice of a parole proceedings that is not public, to the extent those rights are afforded to the convicted offender;
10. not to be excluded from a parole proceeding that is not public, to the extent those rights are afforded to the convicted offender;
11. be heard, if present, at a parole proceeding that is not public, to the extent those rights are afforded to the convicted offender;
12. submit a statement at a parole proceeding that is not public, to the extent those rights are afforded to the convicted offender;
13. reasonable notice of a release from custody relating to the crime;
14. reasonable notice of escape from custody relating to the crime;
15. reasonable notice of the rights established by this the Amendment; and
16. standing to assert the rights established by the Amendment.

In the substantive category, the Amendment includes the rights to:

17. consideration for the interest of the victim in a trial free from unreasonable delay;

18. an order of restitution from the convicted offender; and

19. consideration for the safety of the victim in determining any release from custody.

These rights are hardly radical, and are reflected in state laws around the country. Yet, it is important to underscore why these rights are vital to victims. The right to be informed of proceedings is fundamental to the notions of fairness and due process that ought to be at the center of any criminal justice process. Victims have a legitimate interest in knowing what is happening to *their* case, and such information can sometimes allay a victim's fears regarding the whereabouts of a suspect or defendant.

However, holding criminal justice hearings without notifying victims can have devastating effects. For example, the Director of Parents Against Murdered Children recently testified at a Senate Hearing that many of the concerns of the family members with whom she works "arise from not being informed about the progress of the case. . . . Victims are not informed about when a case is going to court or whether the defendant will receive a plea bargain." What is most striking about this testimony is that it comes on the heels of concerted efforts by the victims' movement to obtain notice of hearings. In 1982, the President's Task Force on Victims of Crime recommended that victims be kept appraised of criminal justice proceedings. Since then, many state provisions have been passed requiring that victims receive notification of court hearings. However, those efforts have not succeeded fully. As the Department of Justice recently reported:

> While the majority of states mandate advance notice to crime victims of criminal proceedings and pretrial release, many have not implemented mechanisms to make such notice a reality. . . . Victims also complain that prosecutors do not inform them of plea agreements, the method used for disposition in the overwhelming majority of cases in the United States criminal justice system.

The Victims' Rights Amendment will also guarantee that victims have the right to attend court proceedings. This also builds on the recommendations from the President's Task Force on Victims of Crime, which concluded that victims, "no less than the defendant, have a legitimate interest in the fair adjudication of the case, and should therefore, as an exception to the general rule providing for the exclusion of witnesses, be permitted to be present for the entire trial." Allowing victims to attend trials provides them a variety of benefits. The victim's presence may help to heal the psychological wounds from the crime. Giving victims the right to be present also helps them to reassert control over their own lives, a dignity that criminals often have impaired by the criminal act. Victims can even further the truth-finding process "by alerting prosecutors to misrepresentations in the testimony of other witnesses."

While some have argued that a victim's exclusion is needed to avoid the possibility of tailored testimony, this concern can be addressed in other ways, such as having the victim testify first or relying on pre-trial statements to police officers or the grand jury. After several hearings on the Victims' Rights Amendment, the Senate Judiciary Committee recently concluded that there is "no convincing evidence that a general policy [of] excluding victims from courtrooms is necessary to ensure a fair trial."

Victims also should be given the right to be heard at appropriate points in the criminal justice process. However, the Victims' Rights Amendment does not propose to make victims "co-equal parties in the criminal justice process," free to speak whenever they wish. Instead, the proposed Amendment extends to victims the right to be heard where they have useful information to provide. One such point is a hearing to determine whether to accept plea bargains. As Professor Beloof has explained in his excellent casebook on victims' rights:

> The victim's interests in participating in the plea bargaining process are many. The fact that they are consulted and listened to provides them with respect and an acknowledgment that they are the harmed individual. This in turn may contribute to the psychological healing of the victim. The victim may have financial interests in the form of restitution or compensatory fine which need to be discussed with the prosecutor. . . . The victim may have a particular view of what . . . sentence [is]

appropriate under the circumstances. . . . Similarly, because judges act in the public interest when they decide to accept or reject a plea bargain, the victim is an additional source of information for the court.

Victims also deserve to be heard at bail hearings. By informing courts of the risks posed by a criminal defendant, victims allow judges to reach appropriate decisions on pretrial release. This is not to say that victims should be able to dictate to judges whether and on what terms a defendant should be released. However, victims should have, while not a veto, at least a voice in the process. Indeed, the failure of the system to hear from victims of crime at this stage sometimes has led to tragic consequences from release decisions, consequences that might well have been averted if the judge had heard from the affected victims.

In addition, victims should be heard before a judge imposes sentence. This furthers fundamental due process, for "when the court hears, as it may, from the defendant, his lawyer, his family and friends, his minister, and others, simple fairness dictates that the person who has borne the brunt of the defendant's crime be allowed to speak." While all states now recognize some form of a victim's right to be heard at sentencing, shortfalls remain. A federal constitutional amendment clearly would vindicate a victim's right to be heard in all these areas.

Victims also should be given the right to receive notice whenever a defendant or a convicted offender escapes or is released. Without such notice, victims are placed at grave risk of harm. As the Department of Justice recently explained:

> Around the country, there are a large number of documented cases of women and children being killed by defendants and convicted offenders recently released from jail or prison. In many cases, the victims were unable to take precautions to save their lives because they had not been notified of the release.

The risk of attack is particularly serious in cases involving domestic violence. By providing victims with a right to "reasonable notice," the Amendment would help alert such victims to potential dangers.

Victims should also be given a right to a trial free from unreasonable delay. In today's criminal justice system, defendants often can prolong the start of trials for no good reason. Let me make plain that I am not speaking here of delays for legitimate reasons. But there can be no doubt that in a number of cases defendants have sought—and obtained—delay for delay's sake. The Senate Judiciary Committee recently concluded that "efforts by defendants to unreasonably delay proceedings are frequently granted, even in the face of State constitutional amendments and statutes requiring otherwise." Such practices should be eliminated by plainly recognizing a victim's interest in a trial brought to a conclusion without unreasonable delay. This right does not conflict with defendants' rights; defendants, of course, have long enjoyed their own right to a "speedy . . . trial."

Similar arguments could be offered in support of all of the other provisions of the Amendment, but I will not tarry any longer on the subject here. Indeed, it is interesting to observe that even the Amendment's most ardent critics usually say that they support most of the rights in principle. If there is one thing certain in the victims' rights debate, it is that these words, "I'm all for victims' rights, but . . . ," are heard repeatedly. Nonetheless, while supporting the rights "in principle," opponents in practice end up supporting, if anything, mere statutory fixes that have proven inadequate to the task of vindicating the interests of victims. As Attorney General Janet Reno testified before the House Committee on the Judiciary, "Efforts to secure victims rights through means other than a constitutional amendment have proved less than fully adequate." The best federal statutes have proven inadequate to the needs of even highly publicized victim injustices, as Professor Cassell's writing about the plight of the Oklahoma City bombing victims has ably demonstrated. In my state, the statutes were inadequate to change the justice system. And now, despite its successes, we realize that our state constitutional amendment also will prove inadequate to fully implement victims' rights. While the amendment has improved the treatment of victims, it does not provide the unequivocal command that is needed to completely change old ways. In our state, as in others, the existing rights too often "fail to provide meaningful protection whenever they come into conflict with bureaucratic habit, traditional indifference, sheer inertia or the mere mention of an accused's rights— even when those rights are not genuinely threatened." Sadly, the experience in my state is hardly unique. A recent study by the National Institute of Justice found that "even in States where victims' rights were protected strongly by law, many victims were not notified about key hearings and proceedings, many were not given the opportunity to be heard, and few received restitution." In addition, the victims most likely to be affected by the current haphazard implementation are, perhaps not surprisingly, racial minorities.

The precise reasons that victims fail to be afforded all their rights today are complex. . . . Part of the problem results from perceived conflicts between victims' rights and defendants' rights. Our courts have already stated the obvious, that "the Supremacy Clause requires that the Due Process Clause of the U.S. Constitution prevail over state constitutional provisions." Of course, victims' rights advocates do not seek to diminish the constitutional rights of those accused of offenses, and nothing in the proposed Victims' Rights Amendment would do so. Even a cursory review of the rights proposed must lead one to the conclusion, as Professor Tribe has concluded, that *"no actual constitutional rights* of the accused or of anyone else would be violated by respecting the rights of victims in the manner requested." However, without parity in the Constitution, crime victims will always be second-class citizens, and their rights never will be accorded the respect and protection that they would and should otherwise receive. They

will simply be left out of our "adversary" system. Thus, it is the consensus view of victims' advocates recently assembled by the Department of Justice that

[a] victims' rights constitutional amendment is the only legal measure strong enough to rectify the current inconsistencies in victims' rights laws that vary significantly from jurisdiction to jurisdiction on the state and federal levels. Such an amendment would ensure that rights for victims are on the same level as the fundamental rights of accused and convicted offenders. Most supporters believe that it is the only legal measure strong enough to ensure that the rights of victims are fully enforced across the country.

The criminal justice system that we have developed since our nation's founding is now simply inadequate to meet the needs of the "whole people." The system has come to respect, perhaps more than ever, the rights of those accused or convicted of crimes. Moreover, the system fairly well serves the interests of the professionals in the system—the judges and lawyers, and the police, probation, and jail officers. Unfortunately, our criminal justice system does not serve adequately the whole of the people, because it forgets the victim. . . .

Professor Tribe has observed this failure: "There appears to be a considerable body of evidence showing that, even where statutory or regulatory or judge-made rules exist to protect the participatory rights of victims, such rights often tend to be honored in the breach. . . . " As a consequence, he has concluded that crime victims' rights are "the very kinds of rights with which our Constitution is typically and properly concerned."

After years of struggle, we now know that the only way to make respect for the rights of crime victims "incorporated with the national sentiment" is to make these rights a part of the sovereign instrument of the whole people, the Constitution. The movement for constitutional rights for crime victims, properly understood, constitutes neither an attack on the rights of defendants, nor on the power of public prosecutors, but rather is a movement to save these two good and perfect things in the American justice system by tempering their excessive virtue with true balance. Indeed, this Amendment just might save the very things its critics fear it will destroy. ■

Victims & Vengeance
Why the Victims' Rights Amendment Is a Bad Idea

Bruce Shapiro

In the language of American politics today, victims of violent crime are accorded uniquely sanctified status. They are elevated to the podium at party conventions and honored at the White House. "I draw the most strength from the victims," Attorney General Janet Reno told a victims' rights conference on August 12, "for they represent America to me people who will not be put down, people who will not be defeated, people who will rise again and stand again for what is right. . . . You are my heroes and heroines. You are but little lower than the angels."

This is not just rhetoric. Over the course of a year that has brought cutbacks and setbacks to the poor, to immigrants and to African-Americans, victims of violent crime have managed to enhance dramatically both their political status and their share of the federal budget. On Election Day, voters in eight states added victims' rights language to their state constitutions, joining twenty-one others. Carolyn McCarthy, the widow and mother of shooting victims, won a seat in Congress. Thanks to a windfall in criminal fines, the Justice Department doubled its victim assistance budget to nearly $400 million.

Most significant, President Clinton, standing in the Rose Garden during the presidential campaign in the company of family members of crime victims, declared that "the only way to give victims equal and due consideration" is to amend the Constitution. Bob Dole had

Bruce Shapiro. "Victims & Vengeance: Why the Victims' Rights Amendment Is a Bad Idea," *The Nation* (February 10, 1997): 11–19. Reprinted by permission of *The Nation*.

already declared his own support for such an amendment. This far-reaching proposal—introduced into the current session by Senator Dianne Feinstein on January 21, with bipartisan promises of quick movement to the floor—must be seriously considered. The so-called Crime Victims Bill of Rights enjoys the backing of legislators ranging from Henry Hyde to Joseph Biden. Its off-stage supporters include the law-and-order right and liberal constitutional scholar Laurence Tribe. It's hard to imagine many state legislatures voting this amendment down.

The amendment's express-train momentum reflects the growing political power and savvy of crime-victim organizations. Over the past fifteen years, a handful of self-help and advocacy groups have evolved into a diffuse but effective, well-funded confederation of 8,000 organizations ranging from neighborhood rape crisis centers to Mothers Against Drunk Driving (despite its homey name, MADD last year operated on a $44 million budget). These groups have become a strikingly influential movement, appearing to confound conventional distinctions between right and left. Any organization claiming to speak for victims can now command the attention of every legislature and news outlet in the nation. But to what end? What do crime victims want?

The constitutional amendment itself is straightforward in its language, if uncertain in implication. As introduced by Feinstein, it would automatically apply only to violent crime (a limitation demanded by Reno's Justice Department, which apparently deems victims of white-collar thuggery

less in need of protection). The amendment would grant to the victims of violent crime the right to:

- a court order of financial restitution from offenders;
- trials "free of unreasonable delay";
- register objection to (but not veto) a pre-trial release, proposed sentence or plea bargain;
- attend the accused's trial and parole hearings;
- be notified about court dates and other developments in the case, including the transfer or release of prisoners.

When this amendment was first floated last year, I was in a quandary. I harbored civil libertarian suspicions, but I have also spent enough time in courtrooms to know that the interests of lawyers and judicial bureaucrats are not necessarily those of crime victims, any more than the interests of physicians are the same as those of medical consumers. Just as patients are sometimes regarded as ignorant, passive receptacles for pharmaceuticals, so, until recently, were crime victims often treated as nothing more than convenient sources of evidence. So why not spell out some minimal rights?

I was mulling this over when I was invited to participate in the first Connecticut statewide crime-victims' conference last September, a few miles up the road from my home. I had written about my own experience of a near-fatal stabbing, and the organizers asked me to take part in a panel discussion on the subject of crime victims and the media. . . .

Much of the two-day gathering (paid for by the Justice Department's

Office for Victims of Crime) was devoted to practical subjects like bereavement counseling and domestic violence. But this was not just a skills workshop; it was also a political rally.

The first day's luncheon speaker was Janice Harris Lord, MADD's national director of victim service. Lord launched into a fervent call to arms for what she called "the single most important thing you can be involved in as an advocate": the Victims' Rights Amendment.

Some people say, "Don't mess with the Constitution." But the Constitution was formed to be changed. There was a time to abolish slavery, and a time for women to get the vote. . . . Now is the time to balance the system.

I listened carefully to Lord's talk, hoping that she'd ease my concerns. But she swiftly left behind the specifics of the amendment, instead posing, with evangelical conviction, a series of what-ifs that could define the crime-victim movement's mission. As she did so I found myself growing uncomfortable, then alarmed. While some of the hypotheticals were sensible and humane policy prescriptions—"what if driving drunk with a child in the car were considered a form of child endangerment?"—many reflected a radically privatized notion of justice more likely to satisfy a longing for personal vengeance or extract a kind of moral satisfaction than to meet any substantive need:

What if restitution also included a punitive component? . . . What if every person who kills a parent were compelled to pay child support? . . .

What if every offender were required to put a photo of his victim in his prison cell? . . . This is what it will take to reestablish a balanced system for victims of crime.

Lord soon left the realm of crime victims altogether; she praised a Texas judge who requires shoplifters to parade with a sandwich board in front of the establishments they steal from, and settled on a condemnation of contemporary American society straight out of the Bill Bennett playbook: "Parents have lost the capacity to raise children with respect for values. . . . We must acknowledge that some families are rotten to the core."

It's fair to say that Lord speaks from the heart of the victims' rights movement; no organization has put more time or money into the constitutional amendment than MADD. Her comments were typical of language that appears over and over in a movement whose central perception is that criminal justice has evolved to serve everyone— lawyers, government bureaucrats and especially defendants—except victims. A nuanced version of this argument was put forth in Congressional testimony last April 23 by Steve Twist, a former Arizona deputy attorney general and a leading proponent of the amendment. When the Constitution was drafted, Twist said, there were few public prosecutors; victims brought charges themselves. But since then, with the rise of modern bureaucratized prosecution,

the criminal justice system has lost an essential balance. . . . The victims of crime have been transformed into a group oppressively burdened by a system designed to protect them. This oppression must be redressed.

Usually it is put more bluntly: "I realized that the system wasn't for the victim, it was for the murderer," says Harriet Salarno, a California law-and-order lobbyist whose daughter Catina was murdered in 1979. Not long ago my household received a direct-mail appeal from the family of Ronald Goldman, raising funds for their civil suit against O.J. Simpson:

> You see ... we continue to get a surprising number of letters from other victims of violent crime. Like us they were victimized a *second* time by a system that treats criminals better than law-abiding citizens.

"Victimized a second time." "The system wasn't for the victim, it was for the murderer." "Lost an essential balance." These are articles of faith of the victims' rights movement and of the campaign for a constitutional amendment. If those articles of faith and the amendment itself seem to blur easy distinctions, it is because today's crime-victim lobby draws water from several divergent streams of grass-roots activity going back to the sixties. A Quaker social worker in New Zealand pioneered crime-victim compensation. Feminists articulated the essential awareness that women are often re-victimized by police and the courts. In the mid-seventies, the federal Law Enforcement Assistance Administration began funding the first generation of professional victim-services providers. The late seventies saw the emergence of self-help groups for crime victims and their next of kin. All these efforts reveal victims' deep hurt at how they were depersonalized in the criminal justice system, and they led to valuable campaigns for reform.

What first gave the movement distinct political momentum, however, was not grass roots at all; it was patronage by Ronald Reagan and other conservatives, who saw crime victims as a crucial wedge against liberals.

In 1982 Reagan and Attorney General Edwin Meese convened a President's Task Force on Victims of Crime. The task force issued a report still cited as the movement's watershed event; in fact, it was that report that first proposed a constitutional amendment. It was also notable for its emotional language and absence of verifiable data—an important precedent for a movement that still largely relies on the politics of the anecdote. Its centerpiece was an undocumented nine-page "composite" describing an imaginary 50-year-old rape victim who is betrayed by hospitals, police, judges, every conceivable social institution:

> Having survived all this, you reflect on how you and your victimizer are treated by the system ... called justice ... [while the rapist] had a free lawyer; he was fed and housed; given physical and psychiatric treatment ... support for his family, counsel on appeal.

That report inspired Congress to launch an Office for Victims of Crime in the Justice Department and establish a mechanism for funding valuable victim services. Unnoted at the time, however, was its political impact. The language of the report, and subsequent Reagan patronage, were designed to draw politically diverse victim advocates securely within the compass of the right.

Today one significant slice of the victims' rights movement explicitly remains a vengeance-rights lobby, demanding faster executions and longer prison sentences and practicing a particularly vindictive brand of electoral politics. (Last June in Tennessee one victim-advocacy group, You Have the Power, orchestrated a campaign that drove from office state Supreme Court justice Penny White, solely for concurring in overturning a single death sentence. "Victims' rights advocates are the sleeping giant in this state," an exultant assistant D.A. said.)

Often presenting itself as a grass-roots victims' campaign, the vengeance-rights lobby is in fact integrally tied to right-wing funders and politicians. California's Doris Tate Crime Victims Bureau—the driving force behind the state's "three strikes" law—gets 78 percent of its funding, along with free office space and lobbying staff, from the California Correctional Peace Officers Association, the prison guards' union, which has an obvious interest in longer, meaner sentences and is a key ally of Governor Pete Wilson. The same jailers' association provides 84 percent of the funding for a "Crime Victims United" PAC headed by the aforementioned Harriet Salarno, which gave $80,000 to Wilson's 1992 campaign. Salarno, in turn, has seen her influence magnified thanks to Wilson's patronage. She was a delegate to the Republican National Convention; in 1995 he named her to California's powerful Commission on Judicial Performance; the year before that, he appointed her to a board overseeing San Francisco's juvenile justice system.

By no means is everyone in today's crime-victim movement a political conservative or in thrall to the G.O.P. There are feminists and liberal social service advocates; there are moderate Democrats like Marc Klaas, who, though supporting capital punishment, opposed "three strikes" and lent his name to a campaign called "Fight Crime, Invest in Kids." Some advocates like the idea of "restorative justice," suggesting that victims' needs are ill served by the retributive focus of current law.

Yet even compassionate voices in the movement have over the past fifteen years been subtly manipulated into a political bargain that severely limits the dialogue about crime victims and society. The vehicle for this bargain is the mechanism for funding victim services around the country: Where most strands in the frayed social safety net are paid for with hard-fought Congressional appropriations, victim programs are supported entirely from fines levied against those convicted of federal crimes.

At first glance this scheme seems sensible and fair—even inspired. Fines from crooks go to compensate those injured by crime, and victim aid gets its own self-sustaining cash stream. (Let me be clear: I value these programs deeply, indeed have benefited from them myself.) But this appealing formula locks victim advocates into a dangerous dependence on the country's law-and-order climate. If the war on drugs, for instance, were to be modified, the financial impact on victim-services funds would be catastrophic. Few victim advocates challenge even the most extreme demands of the vengeance-rights lobby; "don't bite the hand that feeds you" is the rule.

Even more important, this artificially sequestered budget isolates crime victims politically, effectively segregating their interests from all other recipients of social services, from any common struggle for safe cities or access to health care. (How many tens of millions of dollars in federal assistance now going to pay for medical care to uninsured victims would be unnecessary in a single-payer system?) Congress and the public avoid a direct tax-dollar commitment to crime victims, while the victims' rights movement may forever see itself as an island.

This isolation mirrors a vision that cloisters crime from broader social or economic forces. At the Connecticut conference, victims and their advocates heard for two days about the erosion of authority in society, about the need to make offenders more accountable to victims. Economics and race were simply not on the table—particularly notable at a conference whose participants were, like the victim movement nationally, overwhelmingly white, suburban and middle class, even though crime in Connecticut, as it is nationally, is overwhelmingly a problem faced by cities and the poor.

I felt obliged to mention this when it came my turn to speak. Afterward a half-dozen conference participants approached me to voice agreement. But my remarks were the only time such sentiments were heard from the government-sponsored podium.

Might there still be some merit in the victims' rights amendment, despite such vexing parentage? Laurence Tribe put it this way on *The Charlie Rose Show:*

There are more than just a few stories that are troubling. A woman in Florida isn't even notified when the man convicted of raping her is released and then he finds her, hunts her down and kills her. A woman in Maryland wants to attend the trial of the gang accused and ultimately convicted of murdering her husband and, in fact, there is a provision of state law that says she has a right to do it, but because there's a chance she might be called as a witness, the defense manages to keep her out of the trial. . . .

I think it is possible, with enough care, to craft a modest amendment that would be enforceable. . . . It can be done in a way that balances the rights of the accused. And it represents a fundamental principle, not just a policy preference.

Tribe's arguments are compelling. Anyone who has placed her or his own desire for justice and safety into the hands of an impersonal, slow-moving and overburdened court system knows how it can leave a victim feeling uninformed, voiceless and frustrated. There seems little reason victims should not have some right to be heard in court, and certainly no reason states can't make a good-faith effort to notify victims when their assailants are released.

Yet this amendment still seems to me a dangerous route. For one thing, it upends the historic purpose of the Bill of Rights. As President Reagan's own

Deputy Attorney General, Bruce Fein, told the Senate Judiciary Committee last April, crime victims, whatever their grievances, "have no difficulty in making their voices heard in the corridors of power; they do not need protection from the majoritarian political process—in contrast to criminal defendants whose popularity characteristically ranks with that of General William Tecumseh Sherman in Georgia." Organized victims have no difficulty persuading Congress to pass reforms.

I also fear that most of this amendment's well-meaning provisions would at best accomplish little and at worst make the lives of victims more difficult. Consider one clause that exemplifies these dangers: constitutionally mandated restitution. Under the amendment, all convicted offenders would become debtors to their victims. Most states now permit (rather than require) judges to impose restitution as part of a sentence or a condition of probation, a sensible way of recognizing the victim's individual injury.

But constitutionalizing restitution is another matter. The problem with restitution today is not the Constitution, it is collections. Most defendants are poor, and are likely to remain so. The U.S. Attorney's Office in Chicago, investigative journalist Deborah Nelson reported in the *Chicago Sun-Times* in 1995, collects just 4 cents on every fine-and-restitution dollar owed. The collections record of state courts is even worse. Not even a constitutional amendment can get blood from a stone.

Many criminal justice professionals are convinced an inflexible constitutional mandate will make the situation worse—and ultimately make the streets more dangerous. Tom Rue, a psychologist and former New York State probation officer, wrote me recently that if constitutionalized restitution becomes a condition of release or probation, "a greater number of indigent defendants will spend time behind bars than ever before.... Many of these are folks who could otherwise be considered good risks for community-based supervision." Federal Judge Maryanne Trump Barry, president of the American Judicial Conference, recently warned Congress that inflexible restitution would so raise the stakes for probationers as to cause "greater rates of recidivism and more crime."

Constitutionalized restitution, in other words, is a set-up: It's guaranteed to fail, and that failure will further amplify victims' sense of betrayal by the criminal justice system. The same is true for most of the amendment's other provisions; their emotional resonance masks some irrational and counterproductive consequences.

I have also come to oppose this amendment because of those articles of faith, those movement mantras that lie behind it: *"Victimized a second time." "The system wasn't for the victim, it was for the murderer." "Lost an essential balance."* There is a certain emotional truth to such statements. The harrowing disillusionment of the Brown and Goldman families is a reminder of the suffering perpetuated when any violent crime goes unresolved. Yet emotional and factual truth are not necessarily the same thing; and constitutional amendments based on sentiment rather than fact are dangerous business—witness the disaster of Prohibition. (The language of moral reform that permeated the Connecticut conference bears more than a passing resemblance to the temperance crusade.)

Recall, for instance, the assertion that victims' rights have "lost an essential balance" since the colonial days of private prosecution. In fact, as legal historian Lawrence Friedman notes, private prosecution meant victims paid for the case out of their own pocket; far from balanced, it "bent the administration of justice toward the interests of the rich and powerful."

It is even harder to find a factual basis for the sentiment that today's system is "for the murderer" rather than the victim. Certainly the nation's million-plus imprisoned offenders and 500,000 defendants jailed awaiting trial would have a hard time seeing it that way. Every day the overwhelming force of the state—police, prosecutors, courts, prisons, parole officers—is used to redress violence committed against people. Those accused of crime, on the other hand, get only the guarantee of an overworked public defender and an ever-shrinking handful of procedural rights.

As attorney and political philosophy professor Joy Gordon of California State University, Stanislaus, pointed out to me, victims' rights literature almost never mentions one well-established privilege, at least for those victims who can afford a lawyer: the right to sue even an unconvicted criminal—even someone who has been *acquitted*, like O.J. Simpson—in civil court for wrongful death or injury. As anyone who has heard a thirty-second update on the Goldman-Simpson civil suit knows, victims can prevail in civil court with a far lower standard of proof than in any criminal trial. "There's not an 'imbalance' if you look at the whole structure," Gordon says. Any system giving victims such a wide-open second shot—whether for money or moral vindication—is hardly "for the murderer." (How many of the politicians trumpeting their "victims' rights" records have offered to spend money on court-appointed lawyers for indigent victims in civil suits?)

These unquestioned myths allow politicians to tap into victims' extreme vulnerability. It is certainly true, and understandable, that survivors of crime often feel "victimized a second time" by reporters, police, judicial-bureaucrats and defense lawyers. Yet it is equally true and understandable that in the chaotic wake of criminal violence, anger at those we wish had done a better job of protecting us can be experienced well out of proportion to the actual scope of a betrayal.

I claim no special immunity to such emotions. When I wrote about the attack in which I was injured, I recounted shouting to a woman who saw the incident from her window, and how she refused to come to the street. "Victimized a second time" pretty accurately describes my feelings at the time. Not long ago, I met someone who by chance knew that woman. Although I didn't see it, she did come down to the street; in fact, she ran frantically in search of help. My perceptions were limited, and my sense of betrayal aggravated, by the extreme circumstances.

It's natural, maybe even inevitable, that extreme violence or loss can provoke a feeling of extreme betrayal. But those distortions are being exploited and perpetuated by politicians and victims' rights lobbyists. It is also politically relevant—I say this uneasily—that the angriest voices in the victims' rights movement, and especially in the vengeance-rights lobby, are not those who physically endure violent crime but their families. Sometimes, of course, that's because a loved one has been silenced by death, or because traumatized victims may find it difficult to speak for themselves.

But there's more to it than that. Dr. Frank Ochberg, a psychiatrist, victim advocate and nationally recognized specialist in post-traumatic stress disorder, has written, "Survivors often do less hating than one might expect. . . . The co-victims, the next of kin of the injured and dead, are more often the ones moved to rage and vengeance, if not hatred." Ochberg is profoundly concerned about where such sentiments may lead: "Obsessive hatred," he writes, "is a corrosive condition."

Corrosive, and ultimately self-defeating. In her book *Dead Man Walking*, Sister Helen Prejean recounts her unlikely but deep friendship with Vernon Harvey, whose daughter Faith was brutally murdered by a young man named Robert Willie. Harvey campaigned hard for Willie's execution, while Prejean counseled the murderer on death row. Prejean recalls her visit to Harvey in 1986, two years after Louisiana killed Willie in the electric chair:

> Vernon begins to cry. He just can't get over Faith's death. It happened six years ago but for him it's like yesterday. . . . He had walked away from the execution chamber with his rage satisfied but his heart empty. No, not even his rage satisfied, because he still wants to see Robert Willie suffer and he can't reach him anymore. He tries to make a fist and strike out but the air flows through his fingers.

Prejean's humane attempt to find common ground between the survivors of crime and those who speak for perpetrators suggests another reason I find this proposed amendment dangerous: It reinforces a constricted definition of who crime victims are, and of what our political goals might be.

An order of restitution, or the right to comment on a sentence, may sometimes prove healing or morally satisfying. But those benefits—involving a victim's individual relationship to an assailant—are for the most part speculative and intangible. On the other hand, all survivors of crime have an immediate and concrete need for medical care, or for lost wages, or for psychotherapy for themselves and their families, or for legal counsel: Why not fight to guarantee those far more substantial social rights, which join our needs to the broader community (including, sometimes, offenders and their families)? Could it be because the crime-victim movement's patrons in government, as well as the corporations that pour funding into groups like MADD by the barrowload, prefer it that way?

In fact, a substantial number of victim advocates privately question whether this constitutional amendment is, as MADD's Janice Lord put it, "the single most important thing you can be involved in as an advocate." So do many prosecutors and elected officials—though such is the moral sanctity of the victims' rights lobby, and so fearsome its political clout, that few are willing to express their unease publicly.

There are also crime survivors turned activists who reject both the movement's isolation and its self-perpetuating rage at defendants' rights. There is, for instance, Murder Victims' Families for Reconciliation, which campaigns against capital punishment. There are Freddie Hamilton and Katina Johnstone, two women who lost, respectively, a son and a husband to semiautomatic gunfire; a lawsuit they filed together in Brooklyn federal court is threatening gun manufacturers with unprecedented exposure of their corrupt marketing practices. "You are not worthy of my time or thoughts or energy," Carolyn McCarthy said to Colin Ferguson when he was sentenced for the murder of her husband and others on the Long Island Rail Road; she left the courtroom to fight the N.R.A. and run for Congress. How different from the prescriptions offered by Janice Lord, which reinforce victim status and preserve in an attenuated way the relationship between victim and assailant.

It is possible for those injured by crime to embrace a far more expansive political identity—but only if we recognize that crime victims' suffering does not trump all other social and political claims. And as emotionally appealing as the victims' rights amendment may seem, let us recognize that its principal beneficiaries will be not survivors of violent crime but politicians. It is time to exchange sainthood for solidarity across the breadth of social issues, and to refuse being drafted into the vengeance-rights battalion. ∎

⊞ The Continuing Debate

What Is New

In the decade between 1988 and 1998, 33 states passed "victims' rights" legislation or amendments to state constitutions. There has also been a national movement to amend the U.S. Constitution by adding a victims' rights amendment; the proposed "Amendment to the Constitution to Protect the Rights of Crime Victims," sponsored by Republican Senator John Kyl and Democratic Senator Dianne Feinstein, has yet to pass the Senate, though it has been put forward several times. While it has wide support, it has also generated intense opposition from the American Bar Association, the American Civil Liberties Union, and many other groups. Though the Victims' Rights Amendment has yet to pass the full Congress, in 2004 Congress did pass substantial victims' rights legislation which was signed into law by George W. Bush.

Where to Find More

A document entitled *Justice for All* (Home Office, 2002, Cm. 5563; it can be found online at http://image.guardian.co.uk./sys-files/Politics/documents/2002/07/17/Criminal_Justice.pdf) lays out the British Labour Government program for reform of the criminal justice system by placing greater emphasis on the rights of crime victims. A critique of that policy paper is offered by John D. Jackson, in "Justice for All: Putting Victims at the Heart of Criminal Justice?" *Journal of Law and Society*, Volume 30, Number 2 (June 2003): 309–326. Another critique was produced by Liberty (The National Council for Civil Liberties), and can be found online at http://www.liberty-human-rights.org.uk/pdfs/policy02/oct-2002-cj-white-paper.pdf.

One of the key cases concerning victims' rights—and especially Victims' Impact Statements—is *Booth v. Maryland*, 107 Supreme Court 2529 (1987); an interesting comment on that case is by Paul Bourdreaux, *Journal of Criminal Law and Criminology*, Volume 80 (Spring 1989): 177–197.

For a very helpful description of the various and differing groups that have been lumped together under the "victims' rights" rubric, see Robert P. Mosteller, "Victims' Rights and the Constitution: Moving from Guaranteeing Participatory Rights to Benefiting the Prosecution," *St. Mary's Law Journal*, Volume 29 (1998): 1053–1065. A major advocate of what Mosteller calls the "Participatory Rights" group is legal scholar Laurence H. Tribe. An enthusiastic supporter of the "Prosecutorial Benefit" group—which sees a victims' rights movement as a way of gaining greater advantages to criminal prosecutors (to offset what they regard as unfair current advantages for defendants)—is Paul Cassell, in "Balancing the Scales of Justice: The Case for and the Effects of Utah's Victims' Rights Amendment," *Utah Law Review* (1994): 1373–1470. Critics of Cassell's arguments (and of this version of victims' rights) include Susan Bandes, "Empathy, Narrative, and Victim Impact Statements," *University of Chicago Law Review*, Volume 63 (1996): 361–394; Robert P. Mosteller, "Victims' Rights and the Constitution: An Effort to Recast the Battle in Criminal Litigation," Volume 85 (1997); and Lynne N. Henderson, "The Wrongs of Victim's Rights," *Stanford Law Review*, Volume 37 (April 1985): 937–1021. An interesting set of articles, all appearing in the *Utah Law Review* (1999), are Susan Bandes, "Victim Standing," which critiques Cassell's position; Paul G. Cassell, "Barbarians at the Gates? A Reply to the Critics of the Victims' Rights Amendment"; and Susan Bandes, "Reply to Paul Cassell: What We Know About Victim Impact Statements."

A good collection of articles on the topic is *Integrating a Victim Perspective Within Criminal Justice*, edited by Adam Crawford and Jo Goodey (Aldershot, UK: Ashgate, 2000); many of the papers in the volume consider victims' rights from a restorative justice perspective.

DEBATE 4

Should the Use of Jailhouse Informants Be Abolished?

Jailhouse Informants Are a Legitimate Part of the Criminal Justice System
Advocate: Representative Bill McCollum, Republican Congressman from Florida's Fifth District; former Chair of the House Crime Subcommittee.
Source: Interview for *WGBH Frontline* documentary program *Snitch*.

Use of Jailhouse Informants Promotes Injustice
Advocate: Eric E. Sterling, counsel to the U.S. House Committee on the Judiciary, 1979–1989; currently President of The Criminal Justice Policy Foundation and Co-Chair of the American Bar Association Committee on Criminal Justice, Section of Individual Rights and Responsibilities.
Source: Interview for *WGBH Frontline* documentary program *Snitch*.

Those accused of crimes often testify against others. In fact, when several people are involved in a crime, it is not uncommon for a prosecutor to offer a "deal" of significantly reduced charges or a shorter sentence to one defendant if he or she agrees to testify against the others. Jailhouse informants fall into a somewhat different category. Jailhouse informants are persons who have already been convicted of a crime, and in return for a reduced sentence or early parole agree to testify against someone charged with a completely different crime (a crime in which the jailhouse informant had no involvement). Or a jailhouse informant may be someone awaiting trial on criminal charges, who works out an agreement to have the charges against him reduced or dropped in exchange for testifying against some other inmate charged with a different crime. For example, if I am in jail on charges of burglarizing a house, and you are brought to jail to await trial on charges of murder, then I might contact the District Attorney's office and offer to testify that you confessed the murder to me while we were eating lunch—that is, I'll testify that you confessed to me *if* the District Attorney reduces the charge against me from burglary to illegal trespass.

There is an obvious problem with the testimony of jailhouse informants. The testimony of jailhouse informants is given in exchange for a very important pay-off: a payoff of reduced prison time, which many would regard as a more valuable payoff than cash. As noted by the Fifth Circuit Court, "It is difficult to imagine a greater motivation to lie than the inducement of a reduced sentence." And as John Madinger, Senior Special Agent with the Criminal Investigation Division of the IRS, describes them, "Jailhouse informants are highly motivated. They want out, or at least out sooner. It is probably not surprising that quite a few will lie, cheat, and steal to get what they want; after all, this may be how they wound up in jail in the first place."

Points to Ponder

- You are sitting in jail, charged with drug possession. You have two previous possession charges on your record, and you're facing a long mandatory prison sentence if convicted a third time. You're eager to make a deal that will win you a reduced sentence, and you know the District Attorney is eager to convict someone for a drive-by shooting in which two children were killed. From your time on the streets, you heard rumors that the killer might be Albert, a ruthless big-time drug dealer who is very willing to use extreme violence to eliminate rivals. But you also know James, a small-time dealer who hates guns and violence, and is basically a rather gentle person whose drug habit led him to small-time drug dealing. In order to get a deal from the District Attorney, you have to go into the witness box and publicly accuse someone of committing a terrible murder. Whom would you consider it safer to accuse?

- Congressman McCollum argues that "Informants are the way of life in American justice, whether it's a drug issue or not. It's part of our judicial system." How would you evaluate that argument for the continued use of jailhouse informants?

- Some advocate the total elimination of jailhouse informant testimony; others suggest that the testimony should be admitted, but that the judge should warn the jury of the special problems related to jailhouse informant testimony; others would allow the testimony of jailhouse informants, but also allow the defense to call expert witnesses to cast doubt on such testimony; and still others take the position that the testimony should not be treated as special and no warning from the judge should be given (though of course the informant should be subject to cross-examination, like any other witness). Which of those positions seems best? Is there another option that is still better?

- Some people maintain that the testimony of jailhouse informants should be excluded, because it is so inherently unreliable and because the jury is unlikely to recognize how unreliable such testimony is. Others argue that excluding the testimony of jailhouse informants deprives the jury of its right to make its own judgment concerning all the evidence: whether testimony is reliable or unreliable should be a question for the jury, and only for the jury. Which side has the stronger argument?

- Bribing a witness is, of course, a crime; and if it is known that a witness accepted a bribe in return for his or her testimony, that testimony is excluded from the trial. If a jailhouse informant receives a reduced sentence for his or her testimony, should that count as bribing the witness?

Snitch

Bill McCollum

How Is the War on Drugs Doing?

Well, I don't think it's doing as well as it should be doing, because it's not seeing the leadership from the top, especially from President Clinton, that it deserves. We have a larger quantity of drugs on the streets today than we've had in the history of this nation, and they're cheaper in terms of price. We have teenage drug use in the country that's doubled since 1992, and the resources that were being used—that is, the ships and the planes and the military as well as many other resources in interdiction—have dissipated, . . . have been sent overseas to Bosnia or the Middle East or whatever. . . .

We see parents not as concerned perhaps as they should be. A whole generation who grew up with marijuana smoking, who don't realize maybe that marijuana is 10 times more potent today in many cases than it was when they heard about it in the 1960s. I think there is a general laxity in society on use. And there's no leadership, so it's in bad shape in that sense and it needs to be jumpstarted, in my judgment.

Even Though We've Spent Billions of Dollars and Have Thousands in Jail?

Well, there are a lot of people in jail today. Most of those who are in jail in our prisons in the United States

---

Bill McCollum, Interview for *WGBH Frontline* documentary program *Snitch*. From www.pbs.org/wgbh/pages/frontline/shows/snitch/procon/mccollum.html. Copyright © 1999 WGBH Educational Foundation. All rights reserved. Reprinted by permission of WGBH.

for drug involvement . . . are either violent criminals or multiple drug offenders. . . . We need to have criminals who traffic locked up and the key thrown away. But . . . you can't expect law enforcement to provide the solution to the drug problem. . . . I think what we're doing in law enforcement is the correct message and the correct way of going about it. What I think we need to be doing is more efforts to stop drugs from coming into this country in the first place. . . .

What is the Correct Message?

There are a lot of messages that need to be sent to the criminal who is out there dealing in this on the streets of the United States. We need to send the message of swiftness and certain punishment. We need to take the big cocaine dealer and lock him up and throw away the key for as long as we can, and if he deals in large enough quantities we need to give him the death penalty which federal law provides. . . .

Why Do Prosecutors Go After Small Dealers?

There are actually very few small dealers that are being prosecuted. You got people in the law enforcement community today who occasionally, and not very often, but occasionally are trying to get deals to find the big guys, and so they offer a deal to somebody to testify. It's the only way they get the case made against the big guy, and sometimes, once in a while, the small runner doesn't cooperate and they wind up

getting an extraordinarily long sentence because the law permits that. . . . But I can tell you, I'm not very sympathetic to that. I'm sympathetic to the kids on the streets who are losing their lives to these drugs, and to the effort we need to be expending to correct the problem. The minimum mandatory sentence is not nearly the problem today that the drug issue is itself and the loss of life connected with that. . . .

So You Agree with the Current Domestic Enforcement Policies?

I have no problem with the judicial system in regard [to] what we're doing. We're trying to lock up people, most of them very bad people who are causing a problem. Ninety-three percent of those who are in our state prisons for drug dealing are there because of violent offenses or they're there for multiple offenses, and almost all of the people who are there in the system for cocaine trafficking are there for large quantities; in the federal system it's an average of 183 pounds on the person, not some little pocket change amount. So I think we're doing the right thing by what we're doing in our federal law enforcement system. The problem is that we're having them inundated. They're being swamped. They're having to arrest everybody they can because we have this huge quantity pouring into the country and a president and an administration that is not doing what it's required to do and should do to stop that quantity from getting here in the first place. . . .

Are There Many Small-Time Dealers in Prison Who Were Convicted on Conspiracy Charges?

There are very few people in jails today in the United States [who] didn't deal in large quantities of the drugs. You've got people who are involved in major drug dealing who are the vast, vast majority of those who are in our prisons today. . . . Occasionally you'll run into somebody that's in there on a conspiracy charge because that's the easiest way to get them convicted, but that doesn't mean they haven't committed multiple offenses. They're violent offenders with a long track record—look at their histories. When they put out the statistics that seem to show these poor innocent people who are involved, they're not poor innocent people. They're people who have long histories and the judges have probably sentenced them to long sentences in large measure, or they're getting the minimum mandatories because they are repeat, multiple offenders. There are very few people out there who [did not have substantial] drug trafficking histories before they were ever put away, and for those that are there, they're there usually because the prosecutor has tried to get them to cooperate and they've refused to squeal on somebody who is higher up. Now I don't necessarily condone that process for those handful, but I'm going to tell you, the problem isn't with these people. These aren't the innocents. The innocents are the drug victims. The newborns that are born drug addicted because these guys are selling the stuff on the street.

Do You Respect Squealers?

I don't care whether I respect them or I don't respect them. I respect a system that says we're going to put every bit of pressure on anybody we have to put it on to get to the drug dealer who is bringing his poison into the country. I think Americans want to see that happen, they want to see people locked up who are the bad drug dealers who are dealing in these huge quantities. . . .

You Have No Problem with Informants?

I have no problem with informants whatsoever.

But Isn't There a Tremendous Incentive for Them to Lie?

I am much more concerned about the loss of life to drugs and to the crime that's going on out there and the need to stop it and protect our innocents and our citizens than I am about anybody's concern over informants. Good Lord. Informants are the way of life in American justice, whether it's a drug issue or not. It's part of our judicial system. It's a good system, if it's run properly.

Now you have to have a check on law enforcement, and that's why we can't have coerced confessions. You have lots of other constitutional protections. And everybody who gets a trial gets the right under our system to appeal if any of their constitutional rights have been abused, but let me tell you, informants are one of the [best] ways of getting information and the other way is to get it through wire taps. It's about the only way you can get at organized criminal behavior in this country today. When you get a lead, you follow that lead and the most important part of it is you're getting at somebody really bad, nine times out of 10 [someone] higher in a really major drug trafficking operation. . . .

But Most Drug Busts Aren't Major

Most busts lead to major ultimate results. . . . I know what Rudy Giuliani's done in New York is terribly impressive in reducing the rate of violent crime and heavy crime in his city, because he's gone after the lower level of crime. He's proven by what he's done that by community policing, and that means getting at misdemeanor crimes, getting at low level drug traffickers, he has gotten at the big guys more effectively than he would otherwise, because one leads directly to the other. The bottom line is that most of the efforts that go on into turning people into jail for any lengthy jail time, minimum mandatory sentences and so forth, deal with major traffickers, deal with people who are dealing with multiple offenses and violent crimes and long histories or some combination thereof.

So Most People in Jail Are Big Dealers?

You bet they are. Most of them are those kind of people and if you see a study that shows you something different, you got to look at the details of that study because you probably missed the fine print and the fine print's going to tell you that the criminal histories of these people is horrible and they're there for a reason. There are rare cases somebody can cite . . . but you're not going to find a consistent pattern of people who are there who are dealing in very small quantities that have no criminal histories and are really innocent. Most of those who are there are really the bad people that should be there.

You Have No Problems With Snitches?

I have no problems with informants because while they may not always be reliable, they give us leads and you go on and find other proof and when you go to try somebody in court, you have to prove they're guilty to a jury beyond a reasonable doubt, and if you can gain information from informants or snitches, that's fine. That's not what necessarily convicts somebody. That would be just one piece of evidence. But it does give you a lead. And you need that lead. How else are we going to find the bad guy? If you don't have informants and you can't eavesdrop, law enforcement would never be able to protect society from these major criminal enterprises. ∎

Snitch

Eric E. Sterling

Looking Back Now, How Do You Measure the Success of Your Work Enacting Mandatory Minimum Sentences for Drug Offenses?

The work that I was involved in in enacting these mandatory sentences is probably the greatest tragedy of my professional life. And I suspect that the chairman of the subcommittee feels that way too. There [have] been . . . literally thousands of instances of injustice where minor co-conspirators in cases, the lowest level participants, have been given the sentences that Congress intended for the highest kingpins. Families are wrecked, children are orphaned, the taxpayers are paying a fortune for excessive punishment. You know there's nothing conservative about punishing people too much. That's an excess. And it's just a waste. It is such a waste of human life. It's awful.

How Did These Laws Come About?

These laws came about in an incredible conjunction between politics and hysteria. It was 1986, Tip O'Neill comes back from the July 4th district recess and everybody's talking about the death of the Boston Celtics pick, Len Bias. That's all his constituents are talking to him about. And he has the insight, "Drugs, it's drugs. I can take this issue into the election." He calls the Democratic leadership together in the House of Representatives and says, "I want a drug bill, I want it in four weeks." And it set off kind of a stampede. Everybody started trying to get out front on the drug issue. . . . I mean every committee . . . not just the Judiciary Committee—Foreign Affairs, Ways and Means, Agriculture, Armed Services. Everybody's got a piece of this out there, fighting to get their face on television, talking about the drug problem. And . . . these mandatories came in the last couple days before the Congressional recess, before they were all going to race out of town and tell the voters about what they're doing to fight the war on drugs. No hearings, no consideration by the federal judges, no input from the Bureau of Prisons. Even the DEA didn't testify. The whole thing is kind of cobbled together with chewing gum and baling wire. Numbers are picked out of air. And we see what these consequences are of that kind of legislating. . . . Ten-year mandatory minimum, routine sentences are 15, 20, 30 years, without parole. . . . Then you have conspiracy, and suddenly . . . you have people facing 50 years, people facing either life in virtual terms or as a real sentence. That's what's happening. Fifteen thousand federal drug cases a year. Bulk of them mandatory minimum cases. Most of them minor offenders. Only 10% of all the federal drug cases are high level traffickers. You wonder, who's asleep at the switch at the Justice Department? . . . What you have is conviction on the basis of testimony. You have drugless drug cases. You don't need powder, all you need is the witness to say, "I saw a kilo," . . .

With No Drugs to Be Found?

There don't have to be drugs. People are amazed, "Well, aren't there drugs?" There don't have to be drugs. All there have to be are witnesses who say, "I saw the drugs," or, "He said there were drugs." That's what you need.

Couldn't You Guess This Would Happen?

I don't think any of us fully anticipated what these numbers would generate. Remember, at the time that we were doing this, the federal prison population was in the range of 30,000. It's over 100,000 today. None of us envisioned that the Justice Department would so profoundly misuse this statute. Congress said, "We're giving the Justice Department these high-level sentences so that you will go after the highest level traffickers." DEA agents and assistant U.S. attorneys are misusing this statute, with the complicity of their managers in the Department of Justice, to engage in what now has really become a pattern and practice of racial discrimination in almost overwhelmingly prosecuting people of color for tiny amounts of drugs and sending them away for king-pin sentences.

Why Are They Doing It?

They're doing it because it's easy. These cases are the easiest cases to prosecute. They're cut and dried. The lawyers are public defenders. There's not any kind of real defense. . . . These are little cases. However, it's good training for young ambitious attorneys who want to acquire jury experience. And some day they may go after the kingpins, but at this point they're able to learn their craft. For DEA agents, this is safe. I mean when DEA agents go to Columbia or Mexico, their life is in danger. Going after some poor schnook who's the corner crack dealer, that doesn't threaten their lives. The statistics look good. . . .

How Did Conspiracy Law Emerge?

If the mandatory minimums were a result of haste and excess by Congress, conspiracy as applied to these mandatories was completely by oversight and by accident. It was submitted as part of a simple technical corrections amendment. No one even thought at all about what the implications were of applying conspiracy. It was presented as though this was simply a slight little loophole that had been inadvertently created and just had to be rectified by inserting the words, "or conspiracy." No one envisioned that by applying [the statute] to anyone in a conspiracy, no matter how low they were in the conspiratorial chain, that they would get the maximum that could be imposed for the kingpin. Nobody figured that out as we were working on it in 1988. It was a total oversight. Now of course you can't change [it], because that's soft on drugs.

Isn't This All a Deadly Mix?

The current sentencing situation is a sort of witch's brew of three poisons put together making an abominable poison: mandatory minimums designed for kingpins with very long sentences; conspiracy bringing in the lowest level offenders who become eligible for those; [and "substantial assistance" policies]. The only way they can avoid those mandatories is to provide substantial assistance to a prosecutor and if it means telling a wild story to avoid spending almost life in prison without parole, there are many people who will do that.

. . . It's the prosecutor who decides whether or not your substantial assistance, your testimony, is good enough to get the prosecutor's motion to reduce your sentence. . . . So the incentive is, "I'll tell any story I can." I mean these aren't exactly saints that we're dealing with here, dope dealers. [They are] people who are often very desperate. They realize, "If I can get five years instead of 30 years, if I tell a story against that other guy, tell me what I have to say, I'll say it."

Doesn't the Prosecution Know that People Are Lying?

The entire criminal justice system knows that perjury is the coin of the realm. In New York City police officers call it "testalying." In Los Angeles they call it "the liar's club." Everybody knows that lying takes place. The prosecutors don't feel bad about it, this is simply part of the system. They just justify it by saying, "We have to get the bad guy." . . . Police officers conform their testimony to what they know the courts expect to hear in order to get the results that they want, not on the basis of what the facts are.

Prosecutors Say that Judges Tell Witnesses Not to Lie, Under Penalty of Perjury

When a judge tells a witness, "Let me remind you, you're under oath and if you lie under oath, you'll be prosecuted for perjury," this is a disclaimer. The judge in effect is washing his hands or her hands of any responsibility for the lie which is forthcoming. This is part of the ritual; it's a ritual statement, it's not a real statement. It's like when you ask a defendant who's pleading guilty if they understand what they're doing. They always say, yes. They're supposed to. They often don't have a clue what they're doing. . . .

Informing has been one of the great problems of the criminal justice system. When a codefendant testifies, almost always the defense can ask for an instruction to the jury that the testimony of a codefendant is suspect. The courts have recognized that. But this testimony becomes the cornerstone of the prosecution. And the jury understands, "Well, this is one dope dealer against another dope dealer and if the government is trying to convict this dope dealer, well probably this person is guilty, or else why else would we be here?" We believe in the presumption of innocence as a society. Once you get in the courtroom, that presumption is very, very thin. It's not a whole lot of protection. And when you have a witness who says, "Yes, I am getting a deal, but I was there and this is what the defendant did," jurors will say, "Even if I don't believe all that he's saying, I believe enough of it and that enough is proof beyond a reasonable doubt for me." . . .

Do You Feel Guilty About Your Involvement in The Development of These Laws?

The war on drugs is one of the great evils of our times. Drugs are a serious problem, but it's very hard to tease out where the problems of drugs and the problems of the war on drugs are not overlapping. Some day there probably will be war crimes trials in which those responsible for these crimes against the American people, and other peoples, may be brought to justice. . . . We have federal judges who have resigned, federal judges who have wept on the bench. Senior federal judges who say, "We refuse as a matter of conscience any longer to take these kinds of cases." Those are people at least who have the opportunity to step out. I had the opportunity to step out by leaving my job in the government and [am] now working to help expose what I think are these problems. When I meet with the family members of people serving these sentences, it is very hard. At times I am moved to tears when I sit across from someone whose loved one is serving a 30-year sentence for

something that I played a role in getting enacted. It's an awful feeling.

Is Conspiracy Law the Worst Element in Creating These Unjust Situations?

Many nations do not have conspiracy laws because they see how they can be so badly abused. Our conspiracy law is such that long after you've dropped out of the conspiracy, you're still responsible for things that you may have done way in the past. The criminal organization marches forward. You've gone straight. But when the chain gets connected all the way to the back, you can still be held liable and you can be held liable often for things that you had no responsibility for and you could not foresee. It's a terrible problem, the way in which conspiracy is being used in these cases. . . .

I had a conversation with a federal judge about the implications of the war on drugs. And the sense of how alien it is to American values, the use of informants, paying informants. . . . We have hundreds of thousands of informants. Informants can make a living professionally in their role as informants. This is simply an anathema to the way in which we think a free society ought to operate. The role of wiretapping, of monitoring telephone conversations, of taping conversations. Defense lawyers now are afraid that their clients may be trying to entrap them. The government has said, "We believe we have the power to go to a man represented by an attorney and unbeknownst to that attorney, try to get that man to incriminate the attorney." To think that we would undermine our legal system in this way is reminiscent of the Soviet Union. . . .

Are We Becoming What We Hated?

If we look at the way in which so much of our society functions today, it looks like the kind of highly regimented Soviet system that we were repulsed by in the early 1950s. Informants in the work place. Fear of having conversations with people. Fear of our children informing against us. Not knowing what the charges might be. Offenses for which bail is no longer available. . . .

Does the Public Understand What's Going On?

The ignorance about what's going on exists on a bunch of different levels. Number one, the offenders themselves are ignorant of what the penalties are that they could incur. Congress says, "We're going to pass these tough laws to send a message to the criminals to stop." But there's a complete disconnection between what Congress hopes and what criminals actually understand. They don't watch C-SPAN, they don't read "Congressional Record." They simply don't know. They're astonished when they get punished. Congressmen also don't know what the laws are. Many of them don't even know that parole was abolished. The public doesn't know what the laws are. The public still believes that people are getting slapped on the wrist. These are examples which then allow a member of Congress to say

with a straight face, "We need to get tougher." . . .

What Is the Substantial Assistance Clause?

One of the oldest prosecutorial techniques is working up the ladder. Finding someone who's not centrally involved, but who has evidence and who you in effect squeeze and say, "Testify up." This was a very common way in which an organized crime investigation would work. It's a very old theory in the law and they believed that that would [work] here. The difference in part is between being sort of a soldier in a traditional La Cosa Nostra family was you actually knew who your supervisors were. You knew what they did. They spoke to you. Drug organizations now are so large and so diverse that someone can be involved as an unloader, as a seller, as a mule, as a courier. They're insulated, they don't know who the principals are. . . . So very often low level people have nothing that they can really offer. However, the higher ups are in a position, very often, to testify down. They say, "I'll testify against six people." The prosecution of General Manuel Noriega is a prime example where a whole bunch of high level dope dealers got great sentence bargains for going after General Noriega.

Snitching Up?

That was snitching up, but these were already people who were high level people. Manny Noriega was not dealing with the guy who was unloading the boats.

Does the System Encourage Those on the Lower Levels of a Drug Organization, Who Don't Have Useful Information to Pass on to Prosecutors, to Set Up Others Who May Be Innocent?

This was one of the things that really did mystify me when our subcommittee did investigations of the way in which informants were used and misused back in the 1980s. If you are a professional informant, it's a whole lot safer to set up someone than to actually inform against somebody in the business, because that person may have you killed. And so we came across cases in which an informant would pretend to be a government agent, and enlist somebody to [whom] they say, "We want you to help catch a dope dealer. Now, in order to do that, you have to tell the dope dealers this story about all the stuff you've done." Now what happens then is actually the patsy thinks that these people he's talking to are dope dealers, [but they] are actually the DEA agents. And so the patsy is telling the DEA agents what he's been told by the informant to say, all about all this stuff that he did. So the patsy then gets prosecuted as a dope smuggling pilot, the informant gets his reward, DEA gets the case, who cares about the patsy? He's now a convicted dope dealer....

These Witnesses Are Facing Time?

... It's [often] somebody who's saying "Geez, I'm facing 30 years or 50 years in prison, I can get out? What do I have to do? What do I have to testify? Who do I have to testify against? I have to say he was a dope dealer, sure. How much do you need to say you saw? How bad do you think this guy is? He's real bad? Oh, he said he sold fifty kilos, he was the biggest dealer in town. Is it true? I swear it's true, honest." Who's going to dispute it? So you've got this guy sitting with the majesty of the federal court, presented by the United States. "Your Honor, this is the witness on behalf of the United States. You don't believe him? You don't believe the United States, your own government? Who can you trust if you can't trust us, if you can't trust our witnesses?" I don't know how judges can sleep at night, sending people to prison on what they know is perjured testimony. Well, how do they do it? "Wasn't my decision, was the jury.... If the jury believed him, who am I to say that he wasn't telling the truth?"

But the Jurors Often Don't Know What the Penalty for a Guilty Verdict Will Be

The jurors don't know the penalty. We don't let the jurors know the penalty.... If everybody thinks that dope dealers are getting off with a slap on the wrist, jurors are in the same box. After all, we know that prosecutors try to keep informed people off the jury. We don't want informed people on the jury. They're not so easily manipulated. ■

⚏ The Continuing Debate

What Is New

In a 1998 Appeals Case, a panel of the Federal Tenth Circuit Court of Appeals, in *United States v. Singleton*, ruled unanimously to overturn the conviction of Sonya Evette Singleton, on the grounds that the prosecution bribed a star witness by promising not to prosecute him for several crimes and also to inform the court (in another case against the witness) of the witness' cooperation and thus make a shorter sentence likely. Since bribery violates Title 18, Section 201 of the federal criminal code, the prosecutors acted illegally in giving the witness a substantial "bribe" of significantly reduced prison time in exchange for his testimony; and any conviction based on that testimony must be overturned. Though the full Tenth Circuit Court eventually reversed the ruling of the panel and allowed the conviction to stand, there is still the question of whether "paying" a witness with reduced prison time counts as bribery, and that issue will probably be taken up in future cases. The National Association of Criminal Defense Lawyers has long argued that there is a double standard: If a defense lawyer bribes a witness, he or she is disbarred and may be subject to criminal prosecution; but a prosecuting attorney can "bribe" a witness with the promise of a reduced sentence, and there is no penalty.

Where to Find More

A very important book that examines in detail the part played by jailhouse informants in many wrongful convictions is Jim Dwyer, Peter Neufeld, and Barry Scheck, *Actual Innocence* (New York: Doubleday, 2000). John Madinger writes extensively about the role of informants in *Confidential Informant: Law Enforcement's Most Valuable Tool* (Boca Raton, FL: CRC Press, 2000); see especially pages 29 and 193–197. For a detailed account of some of the problems with jailhouse informants and the law related to jailhouse informants, see Robert M. Bloom, *Ratting: The Use and Abuse of Informants in the American Justice System* (Westport, CT: Praeger, 2002), especially Chapter 4. Robert Bloom has also written a good article, "Jailhouse Informants," *Criminal Justice Magazine*, Volume 18, Number 1 (Spring 2003); it is available online at www.abanet.org/crimjust/spring2003/jailhouse.html. Jack Call, "Legal Notes," *The Justice System Journal*, Volume 22, Number 1 (2001), is a very clear review of the legal issues surrounding the use of jailhouse informants.

The PBS documentary series *Frontline* produced an excellent documentary on jailhouse informants entitled *Snitch*. The website associated with the documentary contains much valuable information; it can be found at www.pbs.org/wgbh/pages/frontline/shows/snitch. A superb report on jailhouse informants, "The Snitch System," was developed by the Northwestern University School of Law Center on Wrongful Convictions. The report describes in detail the contribution of false "snitch" testimony to the wrongful conviction of 15 persons who were sentenced to death, and who have since been exonerated of the crimes for which they were charged. The report concludes that false testimony by snitches is the leading cause of wrongful convictions in U.S. capital cases, and recommends important policy changes governing the testimony of jailhouse informants. Another particularly good site on jailhouse informants is the record of the Manitoba Justice Inquiry Regarding Thomas Sophonow. Thomas Sophonow was wrongfully convicted of a brutal murder, largely on the testimony of a jailhouse informant whose nickname was "Father Confession": He claimed that nine prisoners had confessed murders to him. After spending four years in prison, Sophonow was finally exonerated. An inquiry was made into the causes of his wrongful conviction and what steps could be taken to prevent such miscarriages of justice; the results are detailed in the Inquiry Report, which can be found at www.gov.mb.ca/justice/sophonow/toc.html. The report has a number of sections, and some of the most significant deal with jailhouse informants. Among the major conclusions of the Sophonow Inquiry are that "Jailhouse informants are polished and convincing liars," "All confessions of an accused will be given great weight by jurors," and that "Jurors will give the same weight to 'confessions' made to jailhouse informants as they will to a confession made to a police officer." Therefore, the recommendation of the Inquiry is that "as a general rule, the evidence of jailhouse informants should be inadmissible" (though they allowed some exceptions).

Is Plea Bargaining a Legitimate Way of Settling Criminal Cases?

Plea Bargaining Should Be Abolished

Advocate: Timothy Lynch, Director of the Cato Institute's Project on Criminal Justice.

Source: "The Case Against Plea Bargaining," *Regulation* (Fall 2003): 24–27.

Plea Bargaining Can Be Acceptable and Fair

Advocate: Timothy Sandefur, Lead Attorney of the Economic Liberties Project at the Pacific Legal Foundation.

Source: "In Defense of Plea Bargaining," *Regulation* (Fall 2003): 28–31.

Over 90% of criminal cases do not get settled in courtrooms, but instead in "backrooms": in negotiations between the defendant (or the defendant's lawyer) and the prosecutor, where the defendant agrees to plead guilty to a lesser charge to avoid the risk of conviction for a more serious crime. Under mandatory sentencing rules, the threat of conviction under certain criminal charges can be very scary indeed. If I'm charged with my third criminal offense, the prosecutor might threaten to charge me as a habitual offender under the "three strikes" law—and if convicted, I'll spend several decades locked in a prison. Even if I'm innocent of the mugging I was charged with—it's a case of mistaken identity—I may plead guilty and spend 18 months in prison, if it means I don't have to take a chance of being convicted under the three strikes law. If the prosecutor threatens to charge me with a sex crime, I may plead guilty to a lesser charge of assault in order to avoid the stigma for myself and my family and to avoid being placed on a permanent public list of sexual offenders.

There are two main forms of plea bargaining: *charge* bargaining involves bargaining for reduced charges (for example, from burglary to larceny) in return for a plea of guilty; *sentence* bargaining is bargaining for a reduced sentence recommendation (under mandatory sentencing, sentence bargaining is now more difficult).

Timothy Lynch argues that the plea bargaining process unjustly pressures defendants to give up their basic right to a trial before a jury of their peers. Lynch acknowledges that plea bargains are convenient and less expensive, but he believes that they also erode one of our most basic rights. Furthermore, Lynch believes that recent Supreme Court decisions that legitimize the plea bargaining process were wrongly decided. In contrast, Timothy Sandefur acknowledges that the current practice of plea bargaining has problems, but he believes that plea bargaining can be a legitimate part of the criminal justice system. Sandefur argues that offering reduced charges to a defendant as an incentive to forgo a jury trial does not violate any genuine right held by the defendant, but instead enlarges the defendant's options.

⚏ Points to Ponder

- If I am accused of a crime, I have a fundamental constitutional right to a trial by jury, in which I have the right to confront the witnesses against me, the right to a lawyer to defend me, and the right to a presumption of innocence (that is, the prosecution must prove my guilt beyond a reasonable doubt). However, if I exercise that right and demand a jury trial, I am likely to be charged with a more serious crime, and if convicted my sentence will be substantially longer. Thus there seems to be a substantial penalty for exercising my right to a trial by jury. Does that undercut my right to a jury trial?
- Over 90% of criminal cases are settled by plea bargains rather than by trial. Suppose that plea bargaining resulted in just verdicts, or that it resulted in verdicts at least *as* just as those produced by jury trials. In that case, would the general loss of jury trials still be a significant loss?
- If I am a suspect in a criminal case, and I accept the prosecutor's offer of a plea bargain (because I fear that I will be convicted of a more serious offense if I demand a jury trial), is my choice *free*, or is it *coerced*? Suppose that I am charged with first degree murder, but I am entirely innocent of the charges (this is a case of mistaken identity, in which a witness has wrongly identified me); the prosecutor offers a deal: If I plead guilty to second degree murder, then she will not charge me with first degree murder; I will have to serve a sentence of approximately ten years, but I will not face either the death penalty or life imprisonment. I accept the offer, and plead guilty. Was my acceptance of the plea bargain a free choice?
- "You have a right to an attorney; but if you exercise that right, and call an attorney, then I'm going to charge you with first-degree burglary, which

carries a long prison sentence; if you forgo your right to an attorney, then I'll accept your plea of larceny, and you will only spend one year in prison. It's your choice." Suppose the District Attorney makes that offer to a burglary suspect. Would such an offer (a reduced sentence if you give up your right to an attorney) be legitimate? Would that offer be analogous to the offer of a plea bargain (a reduced sentence if you give up your right to a jury trial)?

The Case Against Plea Bargaining

Timothy Lynch

Plea bargaining has come to dominate the administration of justice in America. According to one legal scholar, "Every two seconds during a typical workday, a criminal case is disposed of in an American courtroom by way of a guilty plea or nolo contendere plea."

Even though plea bargaining pervades the justice system, I argue that the practice should be abolished because it is unconstitutional.

The Rise and Fall of Adversarial Trials

Because any person who is accused of violating the criminal law can lose his liberty, and perhaps even his life depending on the offense and prescribed penalty, the Framers of the Constitution took pains to put explicit limits on the awesome powers of government. The Bill of Rights explicitly guarantees several safeguards to the accused, including the right to be informed of the charges, the right not to be compelled to incriminate oneself, the right to a speedy and public trial, the right to an impartial jury trial in the state and district where the offense allegedly took place, the right to cross-examine the state's witnesses, the right to call witnesses on one's own behalf, and the right to the assistance of counsel.

Justice Hugo Black once noted that, in America, the defendant "has an absolute, unqualified right to compel the State to investigate its own case, find its own witnesses, prove its own facts, and convince the jury through its own resources. Throughout the process, the defendant has a fundamental right to remain silent, in effect challenging the

Timothy Lynch. "The Case Against Plea Bargaining," *Regulation* (Fall 2003): 24–27. Reprinted with permission from The Cato Institute.

State at every point to 'Prove it!' " By limiting the powers of the police and prosecutors, the Bill of Rights safeguards freedom.

Given the Fifth Amendment's prohibition of compelled self-incrimination and the Sixth Amendment's guarantee of impartial juries, one would think that the administration of criminal justice in America would be marked by adversarial trials—and yet, the opposite is true. Fewer than 10 percent of the criminal cases brought by the federal government each year are actually tried before juries with all of the accompanying procedural safeguards noted above. More than 90 percent of the criminal cases in America are never tried, much less proven, to juries. The overwhelming majority of individuals who are accused of crime forgo their constitutional rights and plead guilty.

The rarity of jury trials is not the result of criminals who come into court to relieve a guilty conscience or save taxpayers the costs of a trial. The truth is that government officials have deliberately engineered the system to assure that the jury trial system established by the Constitution is seldom used. And plea bargaining is the primary technique used by the government to bypass the institutional safeguards in trials.

Plea bargaining consists of an agreement (formal or informal) between the defendant and the prosecutor. The prosecutor typically agrees to a reduced prison sentence in return for the defendant's waiver of his constitutional right against self-incrimination and his right to trial. As one critic has written, "The leniency is payment to a defendant to induce him or her not to go to trial. The guilty plea or no contest plea is the quid pro quo for the concession; there is no other reason."

Plea bargaining unquestionably alleviates the workload of judges, prosecutors, and defense lawyers. But is it proper for a government that is constitutionally required to respect the right to trial by jury to use its charging and sentencing powers to pressure an individual to waive that right? There is no doubt that government officials deliberately use their power to pressure people who have been accused of crime, and who are presumed innocent, to confess their guilt and waive their right to a formal trial. We know this to be true because prosecutors freely admit that this is what they do.

Watershed precedent Paul Lewis Hayes, for example, was indicted for attempting to pass a forged check in the amount of $88.30, an offense that was punishable by a prison term of two to 10 years. The prosecutor offered to recommend a sentence of five years if Hayes would waive his right to trial and plead guilty to the charge. The prosecutor also made it clear to Hayes that if he did not plead guilty and "save the court the inconvenience and necessity of a trial," the state would seek a new indictment from a grand jury under Kentucky's "Habitual Criminal Act." Under the provisions of that statute, Hayes would face a mandatory sentence of life imprisonment because of his prior criminal record. Despite the enormous pressure exerted upon him by the state, Hayes insisted on his right to jury trial. He was subsequently convicted and then sentenced to life imprisonment.

On appeal, Hayes argued that the prosecutor violated the Constitution by threatening to punish him for simply invoking his right to a trial. In response, the government freely admitted that the only reason a new indictment was filed against Hayes was to deter him from exercising that right. Because the indictment was supported by the evidence, the government maintained that the prosecutor had done nothing improper. The case ultimately reached the U.S. Supreme Court for a resolution. In a landmark 5–4 ruling, *Bordenkircher v. Hayes*, the Court approved the prosecutor's handling of the case and upheld the draconian sentence of life imprisonment. Because the 1978 case is considered to be the watershed precedent for plea bargaining, it deserves careful attention.

The *Hayes* ruling acknowledged that it would be "patently unconstitutional" for any agent of the government "to pursue a course of action whose objective is to penalize a person's reliance on his legal rights." The Court, however, declined to overturn Hayes's sentence because he could have completely avoided the risk of life imprisonment by admitting his guilt and accepting a prison term of five years. The constitutional rationale for plea bargaining is that there is "no element of punishment or retaliation so long as the accused is free to accept or reject the prosecution's offer."

Why the Supreme Court Was Wrong

Initially, the Court's proposition in *Hayes* seems plausible because criminal defendants have always been allowed to waive their right to a trial, and the executive and legislative branches have always had discretion with respect to their charging and sentencing policies. But a closer inspection will show that the constitutional rationale underlying plea bargaining cannot withstand scrutiny.

First, it is important to note that the existence of some element of choice has never been thought to justify otherwise wrongful conduct. As the Supreme Court itself observed in another context, "It always is for the interest of a party under duress to choose the lesser of two evils. But the fact that a choice was made according to interest does not exclude duress. It is the characteristic of duress properly so called."

The courts have employed similar reasoning in tort disputes between private parties. For example, a woman brought a false imprisonment action against a male acquaintance after he allegedly forced her to travel with him in his automobile when it was her desire to travel by train. According to the complaint, the man boarded the train, seized the woman's purse, and then disembarked and proceeded to his car. The woman then left the train to retrieve her purse. While arguing with the man in the parking lot, the train left the station. Reluctantly, the woman got into the vehicle to travel to her destination. The man maintained that the false imprisonment claim lacked merit because he exercised no physical force against the woman and because she was at liberty to remain on the train or to go her own way. The court rejected that defense and ruled that the false imprisonment theory had merit because the woman did not wish to leave the train and she did not wish to depart without her purse. The man unlawfully interfered with the woman's liberty to be where she wished to be. The fact that the man had given the woman some choices that she could "accept or reject" did not alter the fact that the man was a tortfeasor.

Second, the Supreme Court has repeatedly invalidated certain governmental actions that were purposely designed to coerce individuals and organizations into surrendering their constitutional rights. In the 1978 case *Marshall v. Barlow's Inc.,* the Court ruled that a businessman was within his rights when he refused to allow an Occupational Safety and Health Administration inspector into his establishment without a search warrant. The secretary of labor filed a legal brief arguing that when people make the decision to go into business, they essentially "consent" to governmental inspections of their property. Even though the owner of the premises could have avoided such inspections by shutting down his business, the Court recognized that the OSHA regulations penalized commercial property owners for exercising their right under the Fourth Amendment to insist that government inspectors obtain search warrants before demanding access to the premises.

In the 1978 case *Nollan v. California Coastal Commission*, the Court ruled that the state of California could not grant a development permit subject to the condition that the landowners allow the public an easement across a portion of their property. Even though the landowners had the option of "accepting or rejecting" the Coastal Commission's

deal, the Court recognized that the permit condition, in the circumstances of that case, amounted to an "out-and-out plan of extortion."

Similarly, in the 1974 case *Miami Herald Publishing Co. v. Tornillo*, the Supreme Court invalidated a so-called "right of reply" statute. The Florida legislature made it a crime for a newspaper to criticize a politician and then to deny that politician a "right to equal space" in the paper to defend himself against such criticism. Even though Florida newspapers remained free to say whatever they wished, the Court recognized that the statute exacted a "penalty" for the simple exercise of free speech about political affairs.

Finally, the ad hoc nature of the *Hayes* precedent becomes apparent when one extends its logic to other rights involving criminal procedure. The Court has never proffered a satisfactory explanation with respect to why the government should not be able to use its sentencing powers to leverage the waiver of constitutional rights pertaining to the trial itself. Can federal prosecutors enter into "negotiations" with criminal defendants with respect to the exercise of their trial rights? For example, when a person is accused of a crime, he has the option of hiring an experienced attorney to prepare a legal defense on his behalf or representing himself without the aid of counsel.

Can a prosecutor induce a defendant into waiving his right to the assistance of counsel with a recommendation for leniency in the event of a conviction? Such prosecutorial tactics are presently unheard of. And yet, under the rationale of the *Hayes* case, it is not obvious why such tactics should be constitutionally barred. After all, under *Hayes* there is no element of punishment or retaliation so long as the accused is free to accept or reject the prosecutor's offer.

Sophistry to pretend otherwise Plea bargaining rests on the constitutional fiction that our government does not retaliate against individuals who wish to exercise their right to trial by jury. Although the fictional nature of that proposition has been apparent to many for some time now, what is new is that more and more people are reaching the conclusion that it is intolerable. Chief Judge William G. Young of the Federal District Court in Massachusetts, for example, recently filed an opinion that was refreshingly candid about what is happening in the modern criminal justice system:

> Evidence of sentencing disparity visited on those who exercise their Sixth Amendment right to trial by jury is today stark, brutal, and incontrovertible. . . . Today, under the Sentencing Guidelines regime with its vast shift of power to the Executive, that disparity has widened to an incredible 500 percent. As a practical matter this means, as between two similarly situated defendants, that if the one who pleads and cooperates gets a four-year sentence, then the guideline sentence for the one who exercises his right to trial by jury and is convicted will be 20 years. Not surprisingly, such a disparity imposes an extraordinary burden on the free exercise of the right to an adjudication of guilt by one's peers. Criminal trial rates in the United States and in this District are plummeting due to the simple fact that today we punish people — punish them severely — simply for going to trial. It is the sheerest sophistry to pretend otherwise.

Sandefur's Challenge

Attorney Timothy Sandefur, whose comments follow this article, concedes that plea bargaining is "rife with unfair prosecutorial tactics" and needs "reform." But he rejects the proposition that plea bargaining is unconstitutional. Let us examine Sandefur's defense of plea bargaining.

First, everyone acknowledges that the state may not punish or penalize a person for simply invoking a right that is supposed to be guaranteed under the Constitution. And yet, this is precisely what the government does with plea bargaining. For example, every month police officers in Washington, D.C. encounter tourists who are carrying handguns. The tourists are unaware of the District's strict laws against handgun possession. They regularly surrender handguns to police officers who are supervising metal detectors at museums around the capital. When the tourists openly surrender their firearms, they mistakenly believe that they are doing nothing illegal. The gun is then confiscated and the tourist is arrested. If a tourist agrees to forgo a trial and plead guilty, prosecutors do not request jail time. However, if a tourist were to seek a jury trial, prosecutors would respond with additional charges, such as possession of illegal ammunition (conceivably, a count for each bullet in the pistol chamber). Not surprisingly, 99.9 percent of the tourists decide to plead guilty.

Sandefur argues that, in such cases criminal defendants are not being punished for a refusal to bargain; they are instead being punished for "violating the law." According to Sandefur, the tourists have no right to complain because they have no "right to leniency." That line of argument has surface appeal, but it is defective. The logical fallacy of division says that what may be true for the whole is not necessarily true for the parts. Thus, a prosecutor can indeed "throw the book" at any given tourist. However, if it came to light that the prosecutor was targeting, say, Hispanics for harsher treatment, we would know that something was very wrong. The retort that Hispanic arrestees do not have a "right to leniency" would be an unsatisfying defense of the prosecutor's handling of such cases. Plea bargaining tactics fail for similar, though perhaps more subtle, reasons. Just because the state can throw the book at someone does not mean that it can use its power to retaliate against a person who wishes to exercise his right to a trial.

Sandefur's defense of plea bargaining repeatedly returns to the idea that criminal defendants have the "right to make a contract," as in other free-trade situations. But plea bargaining is not free trade. It is a forced association. Once a person has been charged with a crime, he does not have the option of walking away from the state.

Sandefur argues that because individuals can waive many of their constitutional rights, they can also "sell" their rights. Even if that argument had merit, it is not the law. But, more importantly, one suspects that it is not the law because the argument lacks merit. Imagine four people who are charged with auto theft. One defendant pleads guilty to the offense and receives three years of jail time. The second defendant insists upon a trial, but sells his right to call his own witnesses. After conviction, he receives four years. The third defendant insists on a trial, but sells his right to be represented by his famous attorney-uncle, F. Lee Bailey. Instead, he hires a local attorney and, in addition, sells his right to a speedy trial. After conviction, he receives five years. The fourth insists upon a trial, presents a rigorous but unsuccessful defense and, after conviction, receives a prison sentence of 10 years. Are the disparate punishments for the same offense sensible? The courtroom just does not seem to be the proper place for an auction and haggling.

The constitutional defect with plea bargaining is systemic, not episodic. The rarity of jury trials is not the result of some spontaneous order spawned by contract negotiations between individuals.

Conclusion

Thomas Jefferson famously observed that "the natural progress of things is for liberty to yield and government to gain ground." The American experience with plea bargaining is yet another confirmation of that truth. The Supreme Court unleashed a runaway train when it sanctioned plea bargaining in *Bordenkircher v. Hayes*. Despite a steady media diet of titillating criminal trials in recent years, there is an increasing recognition that jury trials are now a rarity in America — and that something, somewhere, is seriously amiss. That "something" is plea bargaining.

As with so many other areas of constitutional law, the Court must stop tinkering around the edges of the issue and return to first principles. It is true that plea bargaining speeds caseload disposition, but it does so in an unconstitutional manner. The Framers of the Constitution were aware of less time-consuming trial procedures when they wrote the Bill of Rights, but chose not to adopt them. The Framers believed the Bill of Rights, and the freedom it secured, was well worth any costs that resulted. If that vision is to endure, the Supreme Court must come to its defense. ■

In Defense of Plea Bargaining

Timothy Sandefur

Plea bargaining, like all Government activities, is liable to abuse. Defendants, often too poor to afford their own attorney, unfamiliar with court proceedings, and threatened by the full force of the prosecutor's office, are likely to be very intimidated. They find themselves confronted by experienced and confident officers of the state, in suits and robes, speaking the jargon of the law and possessing wide discretion to engage in hardball tactics before trial. Prosecutors know how to exploit limits on habeas corpus rights, mandatory sentencing rules, and loopholes that allow evidence collected under questionable circumstances to be admitted. All of this would scare even the most hardened criminal, let alone an innocent defendant. And it could intimidate a defendant into accepting a plea bargain that may not be truly just.

Yet the mere fact that a process can be abused does not necessarily make that process unconstitutional or immoral. Plea bargaining is rife with unfair prosecutorial tactics, and it needs reform. But the process itself is not unconstitutional, nor does it necessarily violate a defendant's rights.

An Alienable Right to Trial?

A plea bargain is a contract with the state. The defendant agrees to plead guilty to a lesser crime and receive a lesser sentence, rather than go to trial on a more severe charge where he faces the possibility of a harsher sentence. Plea bargaining is enormously popular with prosecutors; according to researcher Douglas Guidorizzi,

Timothy Sandefur. "In Defense of Plea Bargaining," *Regulation* (Fall 2003): 28–31. Reprinted with permission form The Cato Institute.

something like 90 percent of criminal cases end in a plea bargain.

In recent decades, courts have upheld extreme and unfair prosecutorial tactics in negotiating plea bargains. Last year, in *United States v. Ruiz*, the U.S. Supreme Court held that the Constitution does not require prosecutors to inform defendants during plea bargaining negotiations of evidence that would lead to the impeachment of the prosecution's witnesses. As Timothy Lynch noted in his 2002 article "An Eerie Efficiency," this rule would allow the prosecution to not disclose during plea negotiations that its only witness was too drunk at the time of the crime to provide any reliable evidence. Such tactics are unfair. If a plea bargain is a contract, it should be subject to the same rules that apply to other contracts, including the requirement that parties disclose relevant information. If a car dealer must tell you that the car he sells you is defective, prosecutors ought to be required to disclose when their cases are defective. But the sad fact that such inappropriate bargaining tactics exist does not obviate the freedom of contract itself.

One argument against plea bargaining is that the Sixth Amendment guarantees a right to a jury trial, not to a faster, more potentially error-prone procedure like plea bargaining. As Lynch has written, "The Framers of the Constitution were aware of less time-consuming trial procedures when they wrote the Bill of Rights, but chose not to adopt them." But that does not prove plea bargaining is unconstitutional. After all, at the time the Sixth Amendment was written, there were no Federal Rules of Evidence, no Miranda

rights, no court-appointed attorneys, and no bench trials. The Framers' notion of a "fair trial" differs greatly from ours. The Constitution's limits on criminal procedure are certainly indispensable protections for individual liberty, a great advance over British rule, and a testament to the Founders' greatness—but they only go so far.

The fundamental question is, is the right to a jury trial inalienable? Although some natural rights are inalienable, most rights make sense only if they can be bought and sold. In which category does the right to a trial belong? In early American history, a defendant could waive his right to a jury in felony cases, but by the time of the American Revolution, that practice had died out. In the 1858 case *Cancemi v. People*, a New York court held that a defendant could not waive a jury trial because, while "the law does recognize the doctrine of waiver to a great extent . . . even to the deprivation of constitutional private rights," the public's interest in fair trials overrode the defendant's right to choose his own trial tactics.

But after the Civil War, the bench trial reappeared. In 1879, the Iowa Supreme Court held in *State v. Kaufman* that a defendant could waive a jury trial if he wished—after all, defendants can waive other procedural rights, including the right to a speedy trial. A guilty plea, the court noted, also "dispenses with a jury trial, and it is thereby waived." Yet the defendant still had the right to plead guilty. "This, it seems to us, effectually destroys the force of the thought" that public interest could prohibit defendants from waiving their right to a jury. According to the court:

Reasons other than the fact that he is guilty may induce a defendant to so plead ... yet the state never actively interferes in such case, and the right of the defendant to so plead has never been doubted. He must be permitted to judge for himself in this respect. ... Why should he not be permitted to do so? Why hamper him in this respect? Why restrain his liberty or right to do as he believed to be for his interests? Whatever rule is adopted affects not only the defendant, but all others similarly situated, no matter how much they desire to avail themselves of the right to do what the defendant desires to repudiate. We are unwilling to establish such a rule.

The debate over inalienability continued, however. The Iowa Supreme Court changed its mind a few years later in *State v. Carman*, then changed back in the 1980 case *State v. Henderson*. Connecticut prohibited jury waivers in the 1878 case *State v. Worden*; Louisiana allowed them in the 1881 case *State v. White*. At the California Constitutional Convention of 1878, a lengthy debate ensued over a provision allowing criminal defendants to waive their right to a jury; proponents argued that a defendant had the right to do as he pleased in his own defense, while opponents claimed the public interest was too great and defendants were often too intimidated to make reasonable decisions in their own defense. The proposal was defeated, although today California does allow defendants to waive a jury trial.

The U.S. Supreme Court held in the 1979 case *Gannett Co. Inc. v. DePasquale* that the public does not

"have an enforceable right to a public trial that can be asserted independently of the parties in the litigation." That seems reasonable; while requiring jury trials may make sense as a matter of policy, it is not an inalienable right. Life, liberty, and the pursuit of happiness are inalienable by nature. But the right to a jury is a civil right, not a natural right. If defendants can waive personal jurisdiction, and waive their right to an attorney, there seems little sense in saying that the jury right is inalienable. Today, it seems to be universally conceded that the right to a jury trial is alienable, and nothing in the Constitution says otherwise. It follows that a defendant can "sell" his right to trial if he so chooses. And at least some defendants—often guilty ones—benefit from doing so.

The Right to Leniency?

Another argument against plea bargaining is that it punishes defendants for invoking their right to a trial. Consider the landmark case *Bordenkircher v. Hayes* (1978). The defendant, Paul Lewis Hayes, was indicted for a relatively minor fraud charge, punishable by a two- to 10-year sentence. The prosecutor offered Hayes a bargain: If he pled guilty, the prosecutor would seek a five-year sentence. If not, the prosecutor would indict him under the state's Habitual Criminal Act. Because he was a repeat offender, conviction under the Act meant a lifetime sentence. Hayes refused the deal, and the prosecutor got the second indictment. Hayes was tried and convicted under the Act, and given a life sentence. On appeal to the U.S. Supreme Court, he argued that the sentence was an unconstitutional punishment for insisting on his right to a jury trial.

The Court ruled against him. In a confusing opinion, it held that so long as the procedure included no actual coercion, the plea bargain did not amount to punishment. But the Court frankly appealed to necessity: "The imposition of these difficult choices," the Court wrote, is an "inevitable attribute of any legitimate system which tolerates and encourages the negotiation of pleas." The Court thus upheld the practice of plea bargaining solely on pragmatic grounds: "A rigid constitutional rule that would prohibit a prosecutor from acting forthrightly in his dealings with the defense could only invite unhealthy subterfuge that would drive the practice of plea bargaining back into the shadows from which it has so recently emerged."

This begs the question. If a practice offends the Constitution, it ought to be driven into the shadows, just as segregation was. By basing its entire theory on pragmatism rather than the Constitution, the *Hayes* Court opened itself to the charge that it was editing the Constitution to suit current needs. If a practice is unconstitutional, efficiency cannot excuse it. "It is highly probable that inconveniences will result from following the Constitution as it is written," wrote dissenting New York Court of Appeals chief judge Greene Bronson in the 1850 case *Oakley v. Aspinwall.* "But that consideration can have no weight with me. . . . There is always some plausible reason for the latitudinarian constructions which are resorted to for the purpose of acquiring power—some evil to be avoided, or some good to be

attained by pushing the powers of the government beyond their legitimate boundary. It is by yielding to such influences that constitutions are gradually undermined, and finally overthrown."

There is a far better reason for the *Hayes* decision: The defendant was simply not being punished for his refusal to plea bargain; he was being punished for violating the Habitual Criminal Act. Had he been tried for that at the outset—which he legitimately could have been—he would have received the very same punishment: life in prison. Regardless of whether such habitual offender laws are wise, Hayes violated that law, and had, so to speak, incurred the liability of a lifetime prison term. He thus had no right, strictly speaking, to any lesser sentence, let alone to escape indictment completely. Instead, the prosecution had the right to indict him for all the crimes he committed, and Hayes had the right to a jury trial on all those charges. Once each side possessed those rights and liabilities, they had the right to exchange them; Hayes could trade his jury right for prosecutorial leniency. The prosecution's bargaining tactics may have been severe, and perhaps statutory reform of those tactics is called for. But the legitimacy of the procedure itself is not refuted by abuses. In short, because Hayes had no right to leniency, his failure to get leniency is not a deprivation, and he could not claim his rights were violated when he failed to receive it.

Other analogies   This is the response to Lynch's analogy regarding tourists arrested in Washington, D.C. for possessing firearms. He argues that the government must not permit the tourist to waive his right to a jury trial on the charge of firearm possession, because that decision is "coerced" by the fact that, if the tourist refuses to plead, the prosecutor will also bring charges for ammunition possession. But the tourist who possesses a gun and ammunition has violated both the gun law and the ammunition law; assuming those laws to be otherwise constitutional, the tourist has therefore incurred the liability of sentence for both crimes. There is nothing unjust (or, more relevantly, unconstitutional) in the prosecutor offering to drop one of the charges in exchange for a guilty plea on the other. If the tourist refuses and goes to trial on both charges, the tourist has incurred no greater punishment than he deserved at the outset.

Or consider another analogy Lynch adopts from the 1935 false imprisonment case *Griffin v. Clark*. In *Clark*, the defendant was found liable for false imprisonment when he seized the plaintiff's purse and would not return it unless she rode with him in a car. Since the plaintiff's freedom of movement could not rightly be conditioned on her giving up her purse, the court found that the defendant could not escape liability by arguing that he had not physically restrained her. Lynch argues that government bargains requiring defendants to give up the right to a trial are, in the same way, illusory choices.

But the analogy dissolves on closer inspection: The woman had a natural right to freedom of movement with her purse at anytime. A criminal defendant, by contrast, has no right not to be indicted for his crimes. As Lynch says, the criminal may not walk

away from the state; he is rightfully subject to any indictment consistent with the facts and law. The government may offer leniency and give up its right to indict him in exchange for a plea, just as it may offer to forgive other debts or confer other benefits. But the defendant has no grounds for complaint if the government chooses not to. (On the other hand, if the state indicts him without a factual or legal basis, his due process rights have been violated regardless of the legitimacy of plea bargaining.)

In the 2001 case *Berthoff v. United States*, Judge William Young decried the disparity of plea bargaining and criminal sentences:

> Between two similarly situated defendants ... if the one who pleads and cooperates gets a four-year sentence, then the guideline sentence [imposed under federal sentencing rules] for the one who exercises his right to trial by jury and is convicted will be 20 years. Not surprisingly, such a disparity imposes an extraordinary burden on the free exercise of the right to an adjudication of guilt by one's peers. Criminal trial rates in the United States and in this District are plummeting due to the simple fact that today we punish people— punish them severely—simply for going to trial.

But both of the criminals in Judge Young's example committed crimes for which they might be sent to jail for 20 years; neither has a right to demand a four-year sentence. A four-year sentence for one does not increase the punishment for the other; it simply fails to decrease the other's sentence—something to which neither defendant is entitled to begin with. The disparity of their sentences does not represent greater punishment being visited on the party that refuses the bargain; rather, it represents a benefit conferred on the party that did bargain.

Conviction of the Innocent?

Some commentators claim that plea bargaining creates an incentive system designed to discourage the exercise of constitutionally protected rights. If the defendant faces a far greater potential sentence at trial than through a plea bargain, this increases the incentive to bargain, which increases the potential that innocent parties will be sent to prison for crimes they did not commit.

Government policies that chill the exercise of constitutional rights ought to be regarded with great suspicion. But they are not per se unconstitutional or unjust. Government, like private businesses, often purchases the rights of citizens: members of the military are forbidden to criticize the president, for instance, and private contractors doing business with the government must often comply with "living wage" requirements. Unwise as those policies may be, they arc not a violation of anybody's rights, because they are based on the parties' consent. If the tactics used to induce consent are so overbearing as to obviate that consent, then the procedure should be reviewed under due process standards and, in a case in which the prosecution's tactics are fraudulent, they should be struck down. But where that is not the case, a plea bargain does not itself violate the Constitution.

Disparate punishments In short, Lynch's claim that plea bargaining is unconstitutional comes down to his complaint that "disparate punishments for the same offense [are not] sensible." But similarly situated defendants who make different choices in legal strategy often end up with different sentences. One defendant might choose to waive his right to testify, while another might exercise that right. The result might be disparate sentences, or even sentences that are insensible to outside observers. But that choice is entirely constitutional. The courtroom may not seem like a place for haggling, but that is exactly what it is, in both civil and criminal contexts. A civil defendant can settle his case for a certain sum; a criminal defendant for a certain amount of time. If the calculations made by prosecutors, or plaintiffs, and defendants are influenced by fear or intimidation rather than calm deliberation, then statutory reform is certainly warranted. But nothing in the Constitution compels it.

Lynch makes many valid points in criticizing plea bargaining. *Ruiz* was wrongly decided; courts should not give free reign to prosecutors; the criminal justice system should not be manipulated, or constitutional guarantees watered down, in order to prosecute the war on drugs more efficiently. But those criticisms surround plea bargaining without quite hitting the target. For instance, Lynch wrote in his 2002 article, "It is easy for some people to breezily proclaim that they would never plead guilty to a crime if they were truly innocent, but when one is confronted with the choice of two years in jail or quite possibly 20 years' imprisonment, the decision is not so easy." That is true, but note that Lynch assumes that the innocent defendant will be convicted and sentenced to 20 years. Without that assumption, the hypothetical defendant's risk profile changes, and surely innocent defendants have reason to believe that they are less likely to be convicted. If not, then our target should be the trial system, not plea bargaining.

Innocent defendants are convicted all too often, but if defendants are so afraid of trials that they regularly plead guilty to crimes they did not commit in order to avoid a trial, then that is an indictment of the trial system, not plea bargaining. And while it is true that plea bargains are often the product of over-bearing prosecutorial bargaining tactics, that is a criticism of the negotiating process, not of the right to make the contract. Finally, it is true that the Framers included a right to trial by jury among our vital constitutional guarantees, but that does not mean defendants lack the freedom to waive that right or trade it to the state in exchange for a lighter sentence. Mere efficiency does not justify resorting to a constitutionally flawed procedure. But there are sufficient justifications for plea bargaining. Its flaws are procedural, not constitutional, and it needs reform, not abolition. ■

⸬ The Continuing Debate

What Is New

Alaska abolished plea bargaining in 1975, the only state to do so. Many predicted that Alaska's court system would become clogged with a backlog of cases, but that has not happened; in part, because the number of offenders who chose to face trial rather than plead guilty did not greatly increase (perhaps because they suspected that judges would impose more severe sentences on defendants demanding a trial than on those who pleaded guilty). One apparent effect of the ban was that cases were screened more carefully by the District Attorney's office, and there was an increase in the number of cases that were dropped for insufficient evidence. While there is still an official Alaskan ban on plea bargaining, *charge* bargaining (the defendant bargains for a reduced charge) has become fairly common since the 1980s; sentence bargaining, however, has almost disappeared.

Where to Find More

An excellent critique of plea bargaining was developed by Kenneth Kipnis, in "Criminal Justice and the Negotiated Plea," *Ethics*, Volume 86 (1976). A strong attack on plea bargaining is by Jeff Palmer, "Abolishing Plea Bargaining: An End to the Same Old Song and Dance," *American Journal of Criminal Law*, Volume 26 (1999): 505–536. Other criticisms of plea bargaining are made by B. L. Gershman, editor, "Abuse of Power in the Prosecutor's Office," *The World and I* (Washington, DC: The Washington Times Corporation, 1991): 472–487; Stephen Schulhofer, "Is Plea Bargaining Inevitable?" *Harvard Law Review*, Volume 97 (1984); Patricia Payne, "Plea

Bargaining: A Necessary Evil?" in Albert R. Roberts, editor, *Critical Issues in Crime and Justice* (Thousand Oaks, CA: Sage Publications, 1994): 232–239; John H. Langbein, "On the Myth of Written Constitutions: The Disappearance of Criminal Jury Trials," *Harvard Journal of Law and Public Policy*, Volume 15, Number 1 (Winter 1992): 119–127; Robert Weisberg, "The Impropriety of Plea Agreements: An 'Anthropological' View," *Law and Social Inquiry*, Volume 19, Number 1 (1994): 145–148; and Albert W. Alschuler and Andrew G. Deiss, "The Repeal of the Sixth Amendment by the Courthouse Crowd," *The University of Chicago Law Review*, Volume 61, Number 3 (Summer 1994): 921–928. George B. Palermo, Maxine Aldridge White, Lew A. Wasserman, and William Hanrahan, "Plea Bargaining: Injustice for All?" *International Journal of Offender Therapy and Comparative Criminology*, Volume 42, Number 2 (1998): 111–123, raise questions about the ethics of plea bargaining, but conclude that it cannot be eliminated.

Defenders of plea bargaining include Scott Howe, "The Value of Plea Bargaining," *Oklahoma Law Review*, Volume 58 (2005); and Mike McConville, "Plea Bargaining: Ethics and Politics," *Journal of Law and Society*, Volume 25, Number 4 (December 1998): 562–587.

Stephanos Bibas recommends ways of improving plea bargaining in "Plea Bargaining Outside the Shadow of Trial," *Harvard Law Review*, Volume 117, Number 8 (June 2004): 2463–2547; recommendations for improvements are also offered by Douglas D. Guidorizzi, "Should we Really 'Ban' Plea Bargaining? The Core Concerns of Plea Bargaining Critics," *Emory Law Journal*, Volume 47 (Spring 1998): 753–783.

A good debate on plea bargaining (involving Robert E. Scott, William J. Stuntz, Frank Easterbrook, and Stephen J. Schulhofer) is in *Yale Law Journal*, Volume 101, Number 8 (June 1992). Further debate between Easterbrook and Schulhofer can be found in Frank H. Easterbrook, "Criminal Justice as a Market System," *Journal of Legal Studies*, Volume 12 (1983): 289–332; and Stephen J. Schulhofer, "Criminal Justice Discretion as a Regulatory System," *Journal of Legal Studies*, Volume 17 (1988): 43–82.

An excellent history of plea bargaining is George Fisher, *Plea Bargaining's Triumph: A History of Plea Bargaining in America* (Palo Alto, CA: Stanford University Press, 2003).

The PBS (WGBH Boston) documentary series *Frontline* produced a documentary on plea bargaining, entitled *The Plea*. To accompany the program, they developed an excellent website: www.pbs.org/wgbh/pages/frontline/shows/plea; see especially the interviews and the readings and links.

The most significant Supreme Court ruling on plea bargaining is *North Carolina v. Alford*, 400 U.S. 25 (1970), in which the Court approved of the basic process of plea bargaining.

The Alaskan ban on plea bargaining is examined by Teresa White Carns and John Kruse (1992) in "Alaska's Plea Bargaining Ban Re-Evaluated," which is available online at http://www.ajc.state.ak.us/_download/plea.pdf.

6

Must Juries Be Cross-Sectional Representations of the Community?

Fair Deliberation Rather Than Cross-Sectional Representation
Is the Goal
    Advocate: Jeffrey Abramson, Louis Stulber Distinguished Professor of
      Law and Politics, Brandeis University.
    Source: *We, the Jury: The Jury System and the Ideal of Democracy*,
      Chapter 3 (Cambridge, MA: Harvard, 2000): 61–95
Cross-Sectional Representation Is Essential for Jury Fairness
    Advocate: Deborah Ramirez, graduate of Harvard Law School and
      Professor at Northeastern University School of Law.
    Source: "Affirmative Jury Selection: A Proposal to Advance Both the
      Deliberative Ideal and Jury Diversity," *The University of Chicago
      Legal Forum* (1998): 161–177.

The jury system in the United States has undergone significant changes over the
years. Women were regularly excluded from juries well into the twentieth century; and as late as 1966 the Alabama Supreme Court ruled that women could be
excluded from criminal cases in Alabama, in order that

> they may contribute their services as mothers, wives, and homemak-
> ers, and also to protect them (in some areas, they are still upon a
> pedestal) from the filth, obscenity, and noxious atmosphere that so often
> pervades a courtroom during a criminal trial.

Juries were often selected from the voting rolls, and areas in which African
Americans were excluded from voting also excluded them from juries. Even

today, there continues to be a problem with blacks being excluded from juries. In Dallas County, prosecution lawyers were given a handbook containing these instructions for selecting jury members:

> You are not looking for a fair juror, but rather a strong, biased, and sometimes hypocritical individual who believes the Defendants are different from them in kind, rather than degree; you are not looking for any members of a minority group which may subject him to oppression— they almost always empathize with the accused.

It is obvious that an impoverished black woman tried by an all-white jury of affluent males would not be tried by a "jury of her peers," and thus there has been strong positive pressure to open up juries to a more representative cross-section of the community. The general acceptance of the importance of fair and open and representative jury membership has prompted a new and important question: What is the purpose and value of seating juries that are genuine cross-sections of the community? Suppose that you, a young African American woman, are seated on a jury in a criminal case: What is your *role* on that jury? Are you there to represent the views of a certain group? That is, are you there to represent the views of young people? Of women? Of blacks? That will be a difficult task since you obviously hold views that are quite different from those of many people in all those groups. Or rather than "representing" the views (or even biases) of some group, is your role to contribute your special range of experience and knowledge to the deliberative process? On this view, it is important to have women on juries *not* because they are there to represent the interests of women, but because women bring experience and perspective and knowledge that enlarge and strengthen the deliberative process: A jury of affluent Protestant white middle-aged males will not have the breadth and depth of experience that a more diverse jury will bring to its deliberations. Or is there some other reason for promoting jury diversity?

⠇⠇⠇ Points to Ponder

- As a college student, your age is probably around 20, and very likely under 30. If you were charged with a serious crime and were facing a jury trial, would you feel comfortable if none of the jurors were under 60?
- What specific steps could be taken to secure more diverse and representative juries?
- In some cultures, a young woman who has sexual relations before she is married is regarded as bringing shame upon her family, and her brothers may kill her in order to wipe away the family shame. Obviously most people in our culture would regard such a killing as a morally horrific act, in addition to being the criminal act of murder. Suppose that a young man, aged 28 (who has become a U.S. citizen, but who grew up in such a culture), is on trial for murder: He is accused of murdering his unmarried 22-year-old sister after discovering that she had engaged in premarital sex with her boyfriend. Assuming that you are interested in seating a *fair* jury, would you

seek out jury members who are (like the accused) immigrants from the same culture? Would you exclude such immigrants from the jury? (Obviously any potential jury member who states that he or she is not willing to follow the law in deciding a verdict could be excluded.)

- Suppose that you are a 20-year-old part-time college student who is an African American woman and a single mother of an infant daughter, and you are quite poor. You are the defendant in a criminal trial. Obviously you want fair and unprejudiced jurors on your jury; but all else being equal, what would be the three most important characteristics you would want represented on your jury? That is, would it be most important to you that there were African Americans on the jury? That there were women? That there were poor people? Young people? College students? Single parents? Would the charges against you influence your choice? That is, if you were charged with shoplifting, would you look for different characteristics than if the charge were vehicular homicide? A charge of homicide stemming from a domestic conflict? A charge of passing bad checks? Can you specify ways in which, for example, a poor person would contribute special knowledge and improve the deliberative process in your trial? A student? A woman? A young person? An African American? A single parent?
- Suppose that *you* were charged with a crime; what would be the most important characteristics you would favor for your own jury?

Jury Selection and the Cross-Sectional Ideal

Jeffrey Abramson

In the United States today, it is common to describe the ideal jury as a "body truly representative of the community." To practice this ideal, all jurisdictions rely on a computerized version of the oldest and most direct of democratic selection methods: the random drawing of names by lot. The basic principle behind the lottery is that the pool of persons from which actual juries are drawn must approximate a fair, representative cross section of the local population. Because of the luck of the draw, as well as uneven patterns of excuses and challenges, the particular jury a person gets may not itself form a cross section of the

Jeffrey Abramson, "Jury Selection and the Cross-Sectional Ideal," *We, the Jury: The Jury System and the Ideal of Democracy*, Chapter 3 (Cambridge, MA: Harvard University Press, 2000): 99–141. Copyright © 1994 by Basic books, a division of HarperCollins Publishers, Inc. Reprinted by permission of Harvard University Press.

community. But so long as jurors are summoned randomly from an initially representative list, the democratic nature of jury membership is said to be preserved.

The cross-sectional jury is so familiar to us today that we forget how modern is its triumph. As recently as 1960, federal courts still impaneled blue-ribbon juries. The theory was that justice required above average levels of intelligence, morality, and integrity. In place of random selection, therefore, jury commissioners typically solicited the names of "men of recognized intelligence and probity" from notables or "key men" of the community. A 1967 survey of federal courts showed that 60 percent still relied primarily on this so-called key man system for the names of jurors.

In 1968, with the Jury Selection and Service Act, Congress abandoned this system for federal courts, declaring it henceforth to be "the policy of the United States that all litigants in Federal courts entitled to trial by jury shall have the right to grand and petit juries selected at random from a fair cross section of the community." In 1975, the Supreme Court extended the ideal of the cross-sectional jury to state courts as well, ruling that the very meaning of the constitutional guarantee of trial by an impartial jury required that the jury pool be a mirror image or microcosm of the eligible community population.

Both Congress and the Court justified the new theory as a remedy for the discrimination practiced under the guise of searching for elite jurors. The slippery and subjective standards for jury eligibility under the elite model provided convenient cover for systematic exclusion of certain people, African-Americans in particular; they also allowed for the perpetuation of the all-white jury in the South nearly a century after the Supreme Court outlawed, in theory, such juries. The immediate task of the cross-sectional reform was to strip away such discrimination, making all persons equally eligible for jury duty who met minimum and objective standards of citizenship, age, residency, and literacy.

But the ideal of the cross-sectional jury speaks to more than the abolition of intentional discrimination in jury selection. To say, as the Supreme Court did in its landmark 1975 decision, that only "representative" juries are "impartial" juries is to suggest a new way of thinking about how to make jurors capable of impartial justice—a way that stands the classical view of impartiality on its head.

Common law defined an impartial juror as genuinely capable of bracketing his own interests and preconceptions and of deciding the case solely upon evidence presented in open court. In the words of the great common-law jurist Lord Coke, "He that is of a jury, must be *liber homo*, that is, not only a freeman and not bond, but also one that hath such freedome of mind as he stands indifferent as he stands unsworne." This is a demanding notion of impartiality, requiring jurors to be independent not only from the dictates of others but also from their own opinions and biases. It requires jurors to achieve "a mental attitude of appropriate indifference."

The ideal of the cross-sectional jury rejects this common-law view of impartial deliberation. It sees individual jurors as inevitably the bearers of the diverse perspectives and interests of their race, religion, gender, and ethnic background. Deliberations are considered impartial, therefore, when group differences are not eliminated but rather invited, embraced, and fairly represented. To eliminate potential jurors on the grounds that they will bring the biases of their group into the jury room is, we are told, to misunderstand the democratic task of the jury, which is nothing else than to represent accurately the diversity of views held in a heterogeneous society such as the United States. If the jury is balanced to accomplish this representative task, then as a whole it will be impartial, even though no one juror is. The jury will achieve the "overall" or "diffused" impartiality that comes from balancing the biases of its members against each other.

In the rise of the modern view of the jury as a representative body . . . [there occurred], an unacknowledged and unfortunate shift that courts have made over time in their arguments about what or whom jurors are supposed to represent. In the earliest cases describing the jury as a representative body—cases dating to 1940—the drive to democratize jury membership was justified in terms of the contribution persons from different walks of life would make to realizing the traditional goal of informed and impartial deliberation. The worthy vision was never one of the races and sexes voting their preconceived preferences through their juror representatives. Rather, the democratic aim of the cross-sectional jury was to enhance the quality of deliberation by

bringing diverse insights to bear on the evidence, each newly evaluating the case in light of some neglected detail or fresh perspective that a juror from another background offered the group.

The noble purpose of such a jury was also to silence expressions of group prejudice and to ratchet up the deliberations to a higher level of generality. Jurors wishing to be persuasive would now have to abandon arguments that depended on the particular prejudices or perspectives of their own kind. Their arguments would have to resonate across group lines.

More recently, courts have begun to sever the connection between the deliberative and representative features of the jury and to justify the cross-sectional jury in terms borrowed from the world of interest group politics. Cases and law reviews are full of language about the mythical nature of impartial deliberation as the common law conceived it and about the ubiquitous presence of subtle bias embedded in group identity in America. The new purpose of the cross section becomes to give voice or representation to competing group loyalties, almost as if a juror had been sent by constituents to vote their preferred verdict. Such a description of the representation we expect from jurors might explain why we call the jury a democratic institution. But it is a vision of democracy so tied to different groups voting their different interests that it cannot inspire confidence in the jury as an institution of justice. This is the predicament we find ourselves in today. . . .

The leading question is whether we have democratized jury selection by accomplishing the so called negative goal of not discriminating. Or does the principle of the cross-sectional jury go beyond traditional color-blind norms, to impose on jury commissioners the affirmative duty to achieve demographic balance on the jury rolls? The difference between these two approaches is crucial. In the first, it does not matter, for example, what race jurors are; justice is satisfied so long as selection procedures make all persons equally eligible for jury duty. In the second, "proportional representation" view, an all-white jury cannot possibly do justice to a black defendant, black victim, or black civil litigant (or vice versa) no matter how color-blind the procedures are for selecting the jury. . . .

I acknowledge the many empirical studies showing that race especially, but other demographic factors as well, influence jurors. But just because jurors start from different places does not mean that they are doomed to deadlock; in fact, only about one in twenty juries fails to reach a unanimous verdict. Nor do the empirical studies show that jurors are so captivated by narrow group loyalties that they typically vote in blocs, with conversation powerless to change views and deliberation a meaningless sideshow. Indeed, research indicates that "when jurors of different ethnic groups deliberate together, they are better able to overcome their individual biases."

From personal experience as an assistant district attorney, I can add my own testimony that jurors cross demographic boundaries to reach unanimous verdicts in cases every day. The crossing is far from perfect, and in some areas—notably, death penalty cases—a breakdown in color-blind justice continues to haunt the system.

But it would be wrong to ignore the considerable progress American juries have made from the openly bigoted deliberations reported for all-white juries of the 1950s or to sour on continued efforts to devise a jury system that defines our common values, not just our different interests. The aspiration for jury behavior may outstrip the reality, but it is still an aspiration within our reach.

The story of how American society has struggled, failed, forgotten, and struggled again to create representative juries is a long one, and I turn to it now. My purpose is to defend the rise of the cross-sectional ideal insofar as it speaks to enriched deliberation across group lines and to criticize it insofar as it recommends mere proportional representation for group differences. . . .

The Shifting Meaning of a Representative Jury

Between the time of the Court's first mention of the representative ideal in 1940 and its constitutionalization of the concept in 1975, there occurred a subtle, unacknowledged but unmistakable, shift in the arguments the Court made to justify the cross-sectional ideal. . . .

Taylor v. Louisiana

Billy J. Taylor was a man tried, convicted, and sentenced to death by a Louisiana jury for the crime of aggravated kidnapping. The death sentence was set aside, but Taylor appealed his conviction to the Supreme Court in 1975, claiming that his constitutional right to "trial by a jury of a representative segment of the community" was denied to him by the systematic underrepresentation of women on the jury list.

Taylor's appeal presented the Supreme Court with the intriguing question of how a male defendant could be claiming prejudice from the absence of a fair number of women in the jury pool. Taylor could hardly be understood as claiming that as a man he suffered prejudice at the hands of a virtually all-male jury panel. Nor was it plausible for a person charged with kidnapping to suggest that the state had an interest in excluding women from the trial of a kidnapper! Given the absence of any showing of bias or prejudice to the defendant, a minority of the Court would have upheld Taylor's conviction and dismissed the underrepresentation of women as harmless error in his case.

Interestingly enough, the Court majority never disputed the fact that Taylor was unable to show any actual bias to himself. Nonetheless, the Court held that Taylor was denied his constitutional right to an impartial jury because, by definition, no jury was impartial unless it was drawn from sources representative of all segments of the community.

But what did the *Taylor* court mean by so conflating the meaning of "impartiality" and "representativeness"? Traditionally, the first term referred to the mental state of an individual juror—the person's ability to hear the evidence with disinterested and dispassionate neutrality. But in *Taylor*, the term came to mean something quite different, almost opposite. The claim that only a representative jury was an impartial jury rested on the argument that, because we live in a community of "diversely biased people," a jury achieved impartiality only by representing the full range of the people's prejudices. In other words, impartiality was accomplished by turning the traditional search for disinterested jurors on its head: we should realistically admit that jury deliberation is but the interplay of group biases. Paradoxical as it sounds, the *Taylor* court was committed to the notion that the most impartial jury was the jury that most accurately reflected the mix of popular prejudices. The Court itself quoted with approval this passage in a House report urging passage of the 1968 Jury Selection and Service Act:

> It must be remembered that the jury is designed not only to understand the case, but also to reflect the community's sense of justice in deciding it. As long as there are significant departures from the cross-sectional goal, biased juries are the result—biased in the sense that they reflect a slanted view of the community they are supposed to represent.

The revealing aspect of this quotation is how it connected one view of an impartial jury (the jury that understands the case) to another view (the jury that understands the community). The implication was that there is not one but many ways to understand cases. In the critical words of Sen. Sam Ervin, the cross-sectional principle could easily degenerate into "suggest[ions] that the search for truth ... is ... a partisan operation, [that] justice is one thing for the hyphenated American, another for the New England Yankee." Or as Van Dyke, a sympathetic commentator, summarized the shifting sense of impartiality implicit in the cross-sectional ideal:

[A] randomly selected jury will not necessarily be "impartial" in the strict sense of that term, because the jurors bring to the jury box prejudice and perspectives gained from their lifetimes of experience. But they will be impartial in the sense that they will reflect the range of the community attitudes, which is the best we can do.

Perhaps the clearest statement of the new theory of impartiality driving the need to construct cross-sectional juries came from a California Supreme Court opinion in 1978. The Court started out with a noncontroversial statement that it would be "unrealistic to expect jurors to be devoid of opinions, preconceptions, or even deep-rooted biases derived from their life experiences in such groups." Given these deep roots of bias in prospective jurors of this race or that religion,

the only practical way to achieve an overall impartiality is to encourage the representation of a variety of such groups on the jury so that the respective biases of their members, to the extent they are antagonistic, will tend to cancel each other out.

This reference to canceling out the competing biases built into identity in America was striking. Absent was

any sense that members of different groups brought much of value to the conversation; the cross-sectional requirement lost the high ground it deserved and became a weak prophylactic attempt to "balance the biases." Philosophically, such a checks-and-balances program for the jury was reminiscent of Madisonian solutions to interest group politics elsewhere in America. But to hear juries conceived of in interest group terms, one group's juror checking another group's juror, was jarring. The cross-sectional ideal, which promised so much in the way of enriching jury deliberation, instead became wed to a cynic's view of juries, in which there was not one justice for juries to represent but multiple justices reducible to whom a juror happened to be by race, sex, national origin, religion, occupation, income, educational level, and on and on.

In *Ballard*, the chief justification for the cross-sectional requirement remained the contribution that people from different walks of life made to the deliberative process—a contribution that sometimes took the form of silencing the prejudice of others and at other times of bringing more knowledge to bear on the problem. Because the *Ballard* Court was still a believer in the classical ideal of informed and impartial deliberation, it felt compelled to show how the deliberations in the particular case before it might indeed have been enriched by the arguments (not biases) of women jurors.

In *Taylor*, the Court continued to refer to the contribution the cross-sectional requirement made to impartial deliberation. But this was no longer the chief rationale behind the ideal. Instead, the principal virtue of a representative jury was its contribution to the jury's political function.

"Political function" is the Supreme Court's exact term in *Taylor*. And the justices were, to their credit, frank about the politics of justice. The jury's political function, according to the Court, was to legitimize the verdict to the population at large and to preserve public confidence in the justice of the verdict. The jury best played this role of "selling" the verdict when all parts of the community saw the verdict as its own. But this legitimizing function of the jury, the Court warned well before the world ever heard of Rodney King, was threatened any time the jury failed to represent adequately a particular group in the community. As one federal judge explained:

> Our jury system has often fallen short of the mark. Its deficiency has inhered not in the quality of the verdicts individual juries have reached, which in the main have reflected understanding and judgment, but in the failure of the institution to include all segments of the community in its operation, thereby . . . jeopardizing that appearance of justice which . . . is as important as the actuality of justice.

This attempt to justify the cross-sectional ideal by reference to its contribution to the appearance rather than the actuality of justice is disturbing. It makes the purpose of the cross-sectional theory a nakedly political one, bent on popularizing the verdict, and divorces the concept wholly from what in the earlier cases was the contribution it indeed would make to insulating justice from popular prejudice.

When the cross-sectional ideal is justified in terms of its ability to sell the verdict, the representative jury is brought into line with the general theory of representative government. Just as Congress helps keep the peace among competing interest groups by giving each group the opportunity to participate in making the politics of the nation, so the jury keeps the peace among competing groups by giving each of them the opportunity to participate in making the justice of the community. But now there is no longer anything special about the jury as an institution of justice that exempts it from the normal barter and compromises of representative democracy. The way to justice, we are told, is not through some mythic course of impartial deliberation floating free of racial, gender, ethnic, and economic bias. Justice, alas, is reached by miring the jury in representing those subtle, imponderable but inescapable biases and preferences we all imbibe along with our group identities.

The Cross-Sectional Ideal Versus Proportional Representation: Emerging Conflicts

Has the Supreme Court proved willing to carry through with the full implications of its 1975 decision equating a jury's impartiality with its representativeness? Logically speaking, *Taylor* pushes toward the conclusion the Court most wishes to disown—namely, that groups need to be proportionately represented on the trial jury itself. After all, as numerous commentators have pointed out, if balancing group perspectives is as important to achieving impartiality as the *Taylor* decision says it is, then the place to represent groups is not just on the jury list or jury pool; the desired interaction takes place only in the jury room.

A number of practical considerations explain the Court's hesitancy to play out the full logic of the cross-sectional ideal. Americans are divided into so many different and overlapping groups that there would not be room on the jury to represent all groups in the community. Moreover, in the United States, "groups" means many things; it is a fluid term. In one case, the issue might be whether white ethnics constitute a group needing to be represented as such; in another case, any requirement to make the jury a mirror of the community might raise the question about whether African-American women are a distinct group from African-American men or Norwegian-Americans are a distinct group from Swedish-Americans. There would be no end to the calculations. Thus, for sufficient practical reasons, the *Taylor* Court drew the line where it did.

Still, the line drawn where it is lacks sense. *Taylor* and the 1968 congressional reform law suggest one theory—proportional representation—for drawing up master jury lists, yet they are not posed to maintain any balance for group views on actual juries.

That the Court balks at following through with the logic of proportional representation tells us much about the instability of the Court's starting point. At its best, the cross-sectional principle represents the common sense that "different groups have different contributions to make to the jury." But *Taylor* went awry by

adopting a skeptic's account of the "something" that diversity contributes to jury deliberations: group identity was reduced to the baggage of bias and prejudice, one group's bias necessary only to counter another group's bias. Such a description of the cross-sectional jury could quite easily suggest to those chosen that "he or she is filling some predetermined 'slot.'"

The Court's flight from such implications of cross-sectional analysis shows the need for going back and regaining our bearings. There, the purpose of the cross-sectional jury was not to recruit jurors to represent the "deep-rooted biases" of their section of town; it was to draw jurors together in a conversation that, although animated by different perspectives, still strove to practice a justice common to all perspectives. This is a noble justification for the cross-sectional ideal and one that defends the aspiration for jurors who render verdicts across all the fault lines of identity in America. . . .

Two Justifications for the Cross-Sectional Ideal

What will the future of the cross-sectional jury bring? If the only replacement for the peremptory challenge system were a jury selection system that dictated particular and proportional levels of representation for groups on juries, then the Court would be right to object, for practical and philosophical reasons. We do not want jurors to see themselves as filling reserved "slots" on the jury, nor are there enough seats on the jury to carry out any such divisive theory of representation.

But does the cross-sectional ideal have to rest cynically on the supposed incapacity of jurors to put aside their group biases? Must we concede that justice in a multiethnic society reduces in the end to balancing the biases of one group against another? The cross-sectional ideal understood as merely a method for balancing group bias on the jury is an invitation to jurors to abandon even the attempt to approach the evidence from a disinterested point of view. After all, what are jurors of diverse backgrounds to understand about their task from a description of the jury system that stresses the need to balance the inevitable prejudices built into group identity in America?

Suppose, for instance, that jurors were to begin to practice this way of representing the community. Such jurors would approach their task as the more or less mechanical job of voting or recording the preconceptions or preferences of their group. They would be less prepared to enter into the kind of independent and impartial deliberations that historically have differentiated jury behavior from voting behavior. When we vote in an election, we vote in private behind a closed curtain—the better to express freely our individual preferences. But when we serve as jurors, we talk and deliberate and argue face-to-face first and "vote" only to make official the consensus already achieved in the deliberations. The emphasis on the need to deliberate until unanimity is achieved is a sign that what we want is not the mere recording of individual opinions but the more considered and cautious judgment achieved by twelve persons acting in concert.

It takes a certain kind of moral character for a person to be able to enter into the free and independent deliberations we expect of jurors. No doubt the common law's description of the impartial juror was a naive and exaggerated view of the ability of ordinary people to achieve the kind of disinterest expected of them. The cross-sectional ideal arose to correct the common-law fiction that jurors were pure pieces of disembodied reason. But it is possible to carry the correction too far, as happens when cynics conclude that we should no longer even aspire to impartial deliberations, that the best we can do is balance the biases expressed during deliberation. Such skepticism, often expressed in cross-sectional terms, leaves us without any reason to trust the competence of ordinary persons to render justice. It allows us to forget the oldest of democratic truths, which jurors are actually constantly verifying—that twelve persons of diverse backgrounds are capable of achieving a wisdom together that no one person is capable of achieving alone.

In the end, what is at stake is whether we want jurors to understand their task primarily in terms of deliberation or representation. I have argued that the deliberative ideal is preferred for the jury. Jurors recruited randomly from different corners of the community may never be able to practice perfectly the deliberations we ask of them. But we know at least why we cherish the jury when it aspires to act as the common conscience of the community and not just as the register of our irreconcilable divisions. ■

Affirmative Jury Selection: A Proposal to Advance Both the Deliberative Ideal and Jury Diversity

Deborah Ramirez

In 1994, Professor Jeffrey Abramson observed:

> In the end, what is at stake is whether we want jurors to understand their task primarily in terms of deliberation or representation. I have argued that the deliberative ideal is preferred for the jury. Jurors recruited randomly from different corners of the community may never be able to practice perfectly the deliberations we ask of them. But we know at least why we cherish the jury when it aspires to act as the common conscience of the community and not just as the register of our irreconcilable divisions.

Implicit in Professor Abramson's critique are two conclusions about jury deliberations. First, he suggests that since jurors' racial, religious, and ethnic background are irrelevant to their deliberative task, as a matter of social and legal policy we should be indifferent to these criteria when we select them. Second, he presumes that if we permit jurors to be selected on the basis of their racial, religious, or ethnic background, jurors may come to believe that their task during jury deliberation is to represent the views or interests of their particular group rather than impartially to determine the guilt or innocence of the defendant.

This essay will explore and challenge these two conclusions. My thesis is that the racial, religious, and ethnic diversity of the jury has a positive and important influence on the jury process. Accordingly, I believe we should select jurors in a way that encourages and enhances such diversity. While I recognize the danger that jurors who are chosen in part because of their racial, religious, or ethnic affiliation may come to believe that they have a duty to represent their particular group in some fashion, I offer a procedure for enhancing juror diversity—affirmative peremptory challenges—that minimizes this danger as much as possible. In short, this article exposes the fallacy of believing that the best way to ensure

Deborah Ramirez, "Affirmative Jury Selection: A Proposal to Advance Both the Deliberative Ideal and Jury Diversity," *The University of Chicago Legal Forum* (1998): 161–177. Reprinted with permission.

a race-neutral jury verdict is through a race-neutral selection process. Its thesis is that a racially diverse jury is more likely to render a race-neutral verdict, because it is more likely to suppress racial bias in deliberations and to challenge inferences based on thoughtless racial stereotypes. Consequently, to best ensure race-neutrality in a jury's verdict, we need to acknowledge our racial differences in selecting that jury and take steps necessary to increase the likelihood of racial diversity among the twelve jurors who will render that verdict.

The Advantages of a Racially Mixed Jury

Should we care about the racial composition of the jury and aspire to create a racially mixed jury? My own answer is yes. All else being equal, a racially diverse jury enjoys significant advantages.

One important advantage lies not in the process of jury deliberation but in the legitimacy of the jury's verdict. Simply put, when a jury is racially mixed, the verdict it reaches is more likely to be seen as fair, considered, and impartial than one reached by a verdict emerging from a racially homogenous jury. This country has a sad historical legacy of all-white juries that has brought distrust and cynicism to our justice system. Even if we would like to believe that the days are gone in which a white man could murder a black man with impunity because he knew that an all-white jury would never convict him of such a crime, we still must face the fact that a verdict reached by a homogenous jury is likely to evoke at best skepticism and at worst outrage from the unrepresented

community. It is hardly surprising that statistical survey information indicates that a racially mixed jury can enhance the appearance of fairness.

The public's perception cannot be attributed solely to the historical residue of racism and intolerance. Rather, I submit that it reflects the public's quite accurate recognition that a racially diverse jury is likely to deliberate differently and more fairly than a homogenous jury. First, the presence of even one minority juror is likely to suppress the direct expression of racial bias or stereotypes and to mute any positive reinforcement of such views if they were expressed. Post-trial interviews with jurors suggest that the presence of a minority juror improves jury deliberations through what I will refer to as the "prejudice suppression effect." Since racial prejudice and stereotyping always impede accurate fact-finding, this is a truth-enhancing substantive reason in favor of a racially mixed jury. Moreover, the empirical support for this suppression effect resonates with my own life experience. Although by definition I have never been present when an all-male group discusses women, I have been in all-female settings when men are the topic of conversation, and the conversation does change when even a single, silent man joins the group. My male colleagues assure me that their experiences are similar.

In addition to enhancing the legitimacy of the verdict and suppressing the expression of prejudice, a racially diverse jury can sometimes affirmatively reduce or eliminate the racial prejudices and stereotypes that accompany jurors to the courtroom. At least one study has shown that with a racially mixed jury, jurors are more likely to respect different racial perspectives and to confront their own prejudice and stereotypes when such beliefs are recognized and addressed during deliberations. This prejudice reduction effect is yet another reason to believe that racially mixed juries enhance the truthseeking function of jury deliberations.

Finally, racially diverse juries bring to their deliberations a broader range of life experiences that allow them to use their common sense more effectively when they evaluate the facts presented at trial. I will refer to this phenomenon as the "perspective-sharing" effect. Let me give some examples. In a case where a cross-racial identification is the critical evidence, a black juror may offer an important perspective concerning how many whites may look at blacks, and vice versa. Similarly, where the propriety of police conduct is at issue, black jurors may offer a quite different perspective on the conduct of a police force in a minority area. To the extent that a racially mixed jury facilitates the sharing of diverse perspectives, information, and experiences, that sharing may lead to a more thoughtful and informed verdict. While it may be debatable whether these points of view assist or divert the jury in reaching the truth, they certainly redefine and sharpen that search.

For all these reasons, it is not surprising that the empirical evidence shows in some close cases, where small differences in perspective matter, the racial composition of the jury affects substantive outcomes and verdicts. This empirical evidence is extremely heartening. It shows that the racial composition of the jury is irrelevant where the evidence is overwhelming,

as one would hope it would be. But it also shows that, in those close cases where the verdict is properly in doubt when the deliberations begin, the different perspectives and dynamics of a racially mixed jury can generate results that are different from those reached by homogenous juries. I would take this empirical evidence one step further. I submit that the verdict of a racially mixed jury in a close case is not only sometimes substantively different from that of a homogenous jury; it is more often than not fairer and more accurate. It is fairer because the verdict is less likely to be infected by racial bias and it is more accurate because it reflects a judgment and inferential findings based upon a broader range of life experiences.

Are the Costs of Obtaining a Racially Diverse Jury Greater Than the Benefits of Obtaining It?

If we decide that racial diversity in the petit jury is desirable, the next question is whether the benefits of having a mixed jury outweigh the costs of obtaining it. Just as changes made with the best of intentions sometimes lead to unanticipated adverse effects, we may alter jury deliberations by changing the way we select jurors. A racially diverse jury may be very desirable, but we may rationally decide that we cannot afford the dangers of ensuring diversity. At the very least, we need to examine closely whether creating a racially mixed jury solves one problem at the cost of creating another more serious one.

Since the question posed here is whether the means of achieving a racially mixed jury produces dangerous side-effects, we need to define carefully what means we are contemplating. There are three ways to achieve a racially diverse jury. One way to do so would be to increase the diversity of the jury venire. A second alternative would be to implement a quota system. A third way to achieve diversity would be to implement a new program of affirmative jury selection. Certainly, the surest way to ensure racial diversity is to use quotas. While the prospect of such quotas may seem far-fetched, it is hardly implausible. Indeed, for 600 years English law used quotas to create mixed juries. Beginning in the Twelfth Century, the legal principle called de medietatae linguae or "the jury of the half tongue" guaranteed Jewish civil and criminal defendants in England that one-half of their jurors would be fellow Jews. After the Jews were expelled from England and their economic role was taken over by alien merchants, this same right was extended to them. As England developed, so did the concept of de medietatae linguae, eventually becoming a right enjoyed by all aliens to a jury divided equally between English nationals and fellow countrymen. When the English colonized the New World, they brought with them this principle of de medietatae linguae. Records of the Plymouth Colony in Massachusetts show that in 1674, when a Native American was tried for murder, he was given the privilege of a mixed jury comprised of half-colonials and half-Indians. De medietatae linguae ended in England by an act of Parliament in 1870, but it continued in certain states in this country until at least 1911.

While jury quotas are effective in producing a mixed jury and enjoy a long historical pedigree, they create more problems than they solve. Professor Abramson is correct to suggest that a quota system may make a jurors feel as if they represented the victim or the defendant, on the one hand, or the juror's own racial groups, on the other. This burden may divert jurors from focusing on the evidence and may interfere with their ability to render a fair and impartial verdict. We want jurors to be color-blind in their deliberations; we certainly do not want the jurors to focus on the race or ethnicity of the defendant or the victim when such factors have no bearing on the fair consideration of the evidence.

Similarly, although jurors may understand intuitively what it means to represent the victim or the defendant, it is not at all clear what it would mean to represent a particular racial or ethnic group. That a juror's race or ethnicity may affect her perspective and life experience does not mean that one can identify a Black or Latino style of fact-finding. In addition, asking jurors to represent a particular racial group's point of view invites racial stereotyping.

Third, and dispositively, implementing a quota system would prove too difficult and demeaning. Assuming a quota were in place, who would be entitled to choose jurors of their race or ethnicity—the defendant or the victim? Would a quota be the entitlement of only minority jurors or would it be made available to all jurors? Would we permit a juror to be removed from the jury pool simply because his race is overrepresented on the panel? Even if we could overcome those problems, how would we decide how to classify jurors in order to implement the quota? Would we permit jurors to self-identify their race, or would we try to use another criterion? What would we do with jurors of mixed race? Would a black Latino be entitled to a quota of both black and Latinos, or of only one group? Would we sort the jurors into subpanels and permit strikes for cause and peremptory challenges separately for the black panel and the white panel? In short, no matter how well intentioned, any quota system would quickly deteriorate into a morass that would carry with it all the stupidity and insensitivity of Jim Crow. In sum, I oppose a quota system for two reasons. First, such a system seems inherently unworkable. Second, even if it were workable, we should not aspire to implement a system which requires the State to sort, identify and definitively determine the racial and ethnic status of all potential jurors. A quota system places unwarranted emphasis and primacy on the State-determined racial or ethnic identity of each juror. For the State to engage in that process would be demeaning to the individual jurors and unseemly. It is simply out of the question.

Beyond Quotas: Alternative Ways to Diversify the Jury

If we exclude quotas, we are left with essentially two alternatives. The least controversial alternative would be to do all we can to diversify the juror pool. If successful, this would increase the number of minorities who sit as jurors and would statistically increase the likelihood that some minorities would find their way onto petit juries.

Enhancing Minority Representation in the Jury Pool

There are identifiable, systemic sources of minority underrepresentation in the jury pool. First, many states and almost all federal jurisdictions draw their jurors from voter registration lists. Since minorities are underrepresented on those lists, minority representation on the jury venire can be increased by selecting jurors instead from street lists or motor vehicle lists, supplemented by welfare and unemployment lists. Since minority residents are more transient than their white counterparts, it would also be important to update these lists frequently.

Second, in most of the jurisdictions that qualify jurors by mailing them a jury questionnaire to complete, the return rate for minority jurors is lower than it is for whites. Not only do fewer minorities mail back the questionnaires, but fewer receive them; because minorities are more transient than whites, a larger proportion of minority jury questionnaires are returned undeliverable. Any successful program that would either increase the minority response rate or reduce the incorrect address rate would result in more minority jurors.

Third, the disproportionate racial impact of the criminal justice system affects both voter registration and juror service. In this country, one out of three black males between the ages of 20 and 29 is currently in prison, on parole, or on probation. A felony conviction permanently restricts the right to serve as juror in 31 jurisdictions, while the remaining 20 states permit juror service but impose varying restrictions. Changing the connection between criminal conviction and jury service, or easing the burden on a convict seeking restoration of rights, would help increase the number of minority jurors.

Fourth, many states still permit jury selectors to disqualify jurors for purely subjective reasons. In many states, juror selectors are asked to make subjective determinations about prospective jurors such as whether each potential juror has "natural faculties," "ordinary intelligence," "sound judgment," or "fair character." These purely subjective evaluations play an important role in determining the racial compositions of the jury pool.

Fifth, most, perhaps all, states compensate jurors inadequately for their jury service. In New York, for example, jurors are only paid $40 a day. The failure of the system to compensate jurors adequately means that fewer minorities are in the venire, for minorities are disproportionately represented in low paying jobs and are thus disproportionately excused because of economic hardship.

While it would be worthwhile to make a concerted effort to increase the number of minority jurors in the venire, such an effort, no matter how successful, will be of only limited value when there are few minorities in the venire pool. The smaller the percentage of the population the minority comprises, the more often minorities will not be fairly represented, even if a truly random selection system were employed throughout all of the jury selection stages. Consequently, for those jurisdictions, merely increasing minority representation in the venire will not ameliorate the problem of racial representation in the petit jury because even fully proportional representation will still leave few minorities in the venire. Therefore, if we are truly committed to increasing the racial diversity of our juries but are unwilling to accomplish this goal through racial quotas, we must do more than simply tinker with the existing system.

Affirmative Jury Selection

Having explored the first non-quota alternative, I now turn to the second. One way to obtain the benefits of a racially mixed jury without triggering the costs of racial quotas would be to create an affirmative mechanism allowing each litigant a limited opportunity to create a jury of his or her peers. My particular proposal would be to provide each litigant with a fixed number of affirmative peremptory choices. Each litigant would be allowed to use these peremptory choices to include his or her "peers" within the petit jury. This next section will describe how this basic procedure would operate within the context of jury selection.

In many ways, my affirmative selection process would mirror the current jury selection process. Like ordinary jury selection, the process would begin by calling a venire to the courtroom. This large pool of potential jurors would then be subject to a limited voir dire conducted by a judge. Each party would then be allowed to make challenges for cause. After challenges for cause are exercised, the remaining potential jurors would be considered the "qualified venire."

The next step would be to create a second smaller group of jurors from the "qualified venire," which I will call the "relevant qualified venire." From that group a jury of twelve with two alternates will be left after both sides have exercised their peremptory challenges. Since, in my proposed system of jury selection, each party would be entitled to two negative peremptory challenges, a judge seeking to impanel a jury of twelve jurors and two alternates in a one-defendant case would need to select a "relevant qualified venire" of eighteen potential jurors. Up to this point, apart from the number of peremptory challenges, my system of jury selection does not differ significantly from the conventional process.

The difference lies in the selection of the "relevant qualified venire." Rather than having the court select potential jurors randomly, as is done now, each party would be allowed to select three potential jurors from the qualified venire to become part of the relevant qualified venire. The parties would do this by writing down the juror numbers of their affirmative peremptory choices and then handing them to the courtroom clerk, who would mix their names with the twelve that are randomly chosen. Thus, neither party would know which members of the relevant qualified venire were chosen by their opponent rather than randomly.

This proposal allows a party to exercise affirmative peremptory choices for any reason, including race. Parties would not need to explain their choices; indeed, if done well, the parties would be unable to discern which jurors were affirmatively selected and which were chosen randomly. At this point, the parties and the court will have created an eighteen member relevant qualified venire that is two-thirds randomly selected and one-third affirmatively selected.

At the next stage, both sides would be allowed to exercise two negative peremptory challenges. Of course, the Batson doctrine would cover this stage of the proceeding in order to ensure that neither side exercised its negative peremptory challenges in a racially discriminatory manner. This type of procedure provides minority parties with a fighting chance of securing racial representation on the jury, if the parties deem that important. It also allows each party to create its own vision of a "jury of . . . its peers" by selecting people it believes can fairly judge its case.

In Order to Reap The Benefits of a Racially Mixed Jury, We Must Require a Unanimous Jury Verdict

There is widespread consensus that a racially mixed jury offers many benefits. It enhances legitimacy, improves deliberation, reduces pre-trial prejudices, and promotes the exchange of different perspectives and ideas. These benefits only occur, however, when jurors can deliberate. When non-unanimous verdicts are allowed, the quality of deliberations diminishes and the voices and perspectives of those jurors with minority positions are muted. Non-unanimous verdicts would defeat the whole point of struggling for jury diversity because they would fail to ensure that all voices and perspectives were fully explored and fairly considered during the jury deliberation process. For these reasons, I believe that a unanimous verdict is essential to reaping the benefits of a racially mixed jury.

The United States Constitution does not require unanimous verdicts in criminal cases; as a matter of constitutional law, nine out of twelve jurors are enough to convict a defendant of a felony. Currently, however, only Louisiana and Oregon allow non-unanimous verdicts for felony criminal trials. Some jurists and scholars have called for statutory changes that would permit non-unanimous convictions in other jurisdictions, arguing that such a reform would shorten jury deliberations and would reduce the likelihood of a hung jury.

While I acknowledge that allowing non-unanimous verdicts is constitutional and has the virtue of reaching closure in a greater share of criminal cases, I nonetheless believe that such reform would harm our justice system. Empirical studies have established that non-unanimous juries pose certain dangers to the interests of justice. First, non-unanimous juries tend to conclude deliberations more quickly. Doubts of the dissenting jurors, even reasonable doubts, can be ignored when their votes are not needed to convict.

Second, non-unanimous jury verdicts change the deliberation process. Where unanimity is required, "minority faction members participate with greater frequency and are perceived as more influential." In addition, the quality of deliberation is more thoughtful and considered. Jurors charged with unanimity are more likely to believe that all arguments and facts relevant to the case "have been fully explored and that the deliberation has been thorough."

Third, jurors in courts requiring unanimity tend to view the jury decision-making process more favorably, perhaps because they believed the process was thorough. Their overall satisfaction with the process is higher than is the satisfaction of their counterparts on non-unanimous juries.

The fundamental problem with allowing a non-unanimous verdict is that it permits the members of the jury who are in the majority to ignore the voices and experiences of minority jurors by outvoting them. Such a result is anathema to the very nature and function of a jury. I support requiring a unanimous verdict because I believe that such a system encourages jurors to respect, confront, discuss, and resolve different points of view and positions during the deliberation process.

Conclusion

The goal of our jury system should be to ensure that jurors deliberate fairly and impartially in reaching a final verdict. That deliberative ideal is furthered when jurors engage in a fact-finding process that produces accurate results. As part of that ideal, the system should discourage decision-making based on race or thoughtless racial stereotypes.

The fundamental question is: How do we best achieve this deliberative ideal? Professor Abramson believes that the best way to obtain an impartial, race-neutral verdict is to adopt a race-neutral jury selection process. This article exposes the fallacy of this proposal's thesis by demonstrating how and why a multi-racial jury is more likely to embody the deliberative ideal and render an impartial, fair, and race-neutral verdict than its all-white counterpart.

A multi-racial jury functions differently than an all-white jury. First, the presence of even one racial minority on the jury suppresses prejudice. Second, when different racial groups deliberate together, there is some evidence that they are better able to overcome their individual biases. Third, the presence of diverse groups adds different voices, perspectives, and experiences to deliberations. Finally, a verdict rendered by a multi-racial jury is fairer, more accurate, and less likely to be infected by racial bias, thoughtless racial stereotypes, or racial misconceptions. Indeed, it is perhaps for these very reasons that the public correctly perceives a multi-racial verdict to be fairer and more legitimate.

This article argues that the best way to reap the benefits of a multi-racial jury is by encouraging jury diversity through an affirmative jury selection process. The virtue of the affirmative peremptory system limned in this article is that it is transracial in its design. It allows all parties, regardless of race or ethnicity, to affirmatively select a jury of their peers. Because it allows each individual to determine the extent to which race matters, it is color-conscious. It allows inclusion, based upon race, but prohibits race-based juror exclusion. In contrast, however, to a quota system, it does not require the State to sort and identify all potential jurors by race.

Finally, this article argues that in order to preserve the benefits of a racially mixed jury, the criminal deliberative process must be unanimous. Having struggled long and hard to create diversity on the petit jury, allowing a non-unanimous verdict would undermine the benefits of a multi-racial jury by permitting majority jurors to ignore the perspectives, voices, and views of minority jurors simply by outvoting them. This result is contrary to the very nature and function of a deliberative process designed to ensure fairness and accuracy. In order to advance the deliberative ideal and equal justice, the system should require a unanimous verdict because such a verdict encourages jurors to respect, confront, discuss, and resolve differences during the deliberative process. Only then can we realize the promise of the deliberative ideal: impartial justice for all. ■

⠿ The Continuing Debate

What Is New

The continuing underrepresentation of some groups—including African Americans, Latinos, young adults, and particularly the poor—remains a concern, and policies for achieving greater diversity on juries have been widely discussed. One obvious reason why the poor are underrepresented on juries is that they simply cannot afford jury service. Those who have higher earnings are more often salaried workers, who continue to be paid during their jury service. But the poor are typically hourly employees, working at or near minimum wage levels. When they serve on juries, their income from their jobs—low as it is—disappears; and instead the juror receives a small stipend (which may be as little as $6 a day).

Another major concern in trying to seat a fair or a representative jury is the frequent exclusion of African Americans from juries. This may occur when an attorney uses *peremptory* challenges to exclude blacks. When seating a jury, both sides can challenge potential jurors for *cause*; that is, an attorney can argue that a potential juror should be excluded because the juror would not be a fair judge of the case (for example, if a potential juror is a friend or enemy of someone involved in the case). In addition to excluding jurors for cause, both sides have a set number of *peremptory* challenges they can use as they wish, without justification; for example, you might choose to exercise a peremptory challenge because you sense that one of the jurors dislikes you, though you can't give any *reason* for your feeling. But suppose that there are only three blacks in the jury pool, and the District Attorney uses her three peremptory challenges to exclude all the blacks from the jury. Since blacks are typically underrepresented in jury pools, it is often possible for one side or the other to seat an all-white jury by using peremptory challenges to exclude all potential black jurors. In 1986, in *Batson v. Kentucky*, the U.S. Supreme Court ruled that prosecutors cannot systematically use peremptory challenges to exclude blacks from juries: that such systematic exclusion violates the rights of black jurors to serve and of black defendants not to have members of their own race systematically excluded. The *Batson* rule is difficult to enforce, but it is a start at preventing some of the most blatantly prejudicial practices in jury selection.

Where to Find More

For an excellent history and extended discussion of the issue of jury diversity, see Jeffrey Abramson, *We, the Jury: The Jury System and the Ideal of Democracy* (New York: BasicBooks, 1994), especially Chapter 3. See also Abramson's, "Two Ideals of Jury Deliberation," *The University of Chicago Legal Forum* (1998): 125–160, and his "Abolishing the Peremptory but Enlarging the Challenge for Cause," *APA Newsletters*, Volume 96, Number 2 (Spring 1997). A particularly good study of the importance of diversity in jury make-up—that carefully documents both its advantages, as well as its general absence—is Hiroshi Fukurai and Richard Krooth, *Race in the Jury Box: Affirmative Action in Jury Selection* (Albany, NY: State University of New York Press, 2003).

There have been a variety of proposals aimed at securing more diverse and representative juries. The possibility of selecting jury members on the basis of distinct districts similar to small electoral districts is proposed by Kim Forde-Mazrui in "Jural Districting: Selecting Impartial Juries Through Community Representation," *Vanderbilt Law Review*, Volume 52 (March 1999): 353–404. An excellent review of some efforts at achieving more representative juries is Nancy J. King, "Racial Jurymandering: Cancer or Cure? A Contemporary Review of Affirmative Action in Jury Selection," *New York University Law Review*, Volume 68 (October 1993): 707–776.

How does the racial composition of juries affect jury deliberation? Samuel R. Sommers and Phoebe C. Ellsworth review current research on that question in

"How Much do We Really Know about Race and Juries? A Review of Social Theory and Research," *Chicago-Kent Law Review*, Volume 78 (2003): 997–1031.

While there is broad concern with the underrepresentation (or even exclusion) of blacks on juries, the problem of the severe underrepresentation of the poor has been less obvious. The problem is made clear in Mitchell S. Zuklie, "Rethinking the Fair Cross-Section Requirement," *California Law Review*, Volume 84 (January 1996): 101–150; and the extent and causes of the problem are examined in Robert C. Walters, Michael D. Marin, and Mark Curriden, "Jury of Our Peers: An Unfulfilled Constitutional Promise," *SMU Law Review*, Volume 58 (Spring 2005): 319–355.

The question of how jury diversity affects the public's *perception* of the fairness of the judicial system is examined by Leslie Ellis and Shari Seidman Diamond in "Race, Diversity, and Jury Composition: Battering and Bolstering Legitimacy," *Chicago-Kent Law Review*, Volume 78 (2003): 1033–1057.

7

■ ■ ■ ■ ■ ■ ■ ■ ■ D E B A T E ■ ■ ■ ■ ■ ■ ■ ■

Jury Nullification: Should Jurors Ever Refuse to Follow the Law?

Jurors Should Be Permitted to Follow Their Consciences
Advocate: Jeffrey Abramson, Louis Stulber Distinguished Professor of
Law and Politics, Brandeis University.
Source: *We, the Jury: The Jury System and the Ideal of Democracy*,
Chapter 2 (Cambridge, MA: Harvard, 2000): 99–141.
Jurors Should Always Follow the Law
Advocate: Mark Dwyer, Assistant District Attorney and Chief of the
Appeals Bureau, New York County.
Source: From "Law, Justice, and Jury Nullification: A Debate,"
Criminal Law Bulletin, Volume 29, Number 1 (1993): 40–69.

When you serve on a jury in the United States, the judge may give you the following instruction:

> Members of the jury, it will be your duty to find from the evidence
> what the facts are. You and you alone will be the judges of the facts. You
> will then have to apply to those facts the law as the court will give it to
> you. You must follow that law whether you agree with it or not.

Through most of U.S. history, the courts followed the British tradition: Juries
could decide that a law (or its particular application) was unjust, and thus legitimately return a verdict of not guilty even if the jury thought the defendant had
violated the law. Of course, juries in the United States still sometimes refuse to
convict when they believe that a law is unjust, and juries clearly have the *power* to
do that; but for the past several decades (with the exception of Indiana and

Maryland) juries have officially not been *supposed* to do so. It's easy to find cases where we might like the result of jury nullification (juries that refused to convict those who violated the Fugitive Slave Act by helping escaped slaves); but equally easy to find results that are profoundly disturbing (the notorious refusal of Southern all-white juries to convict for civil rights violations and even murders). Sometimes jury nullification occurs when jurors reject a specific law: jury nullification of laws requiring the return of fugitive slaves is a clear example. But jury nullification can also occur when jurors believe that the law is legitimate but special circumstances make conviction unjust; for example, if a defendant broke the law without knowledge or intent (such as, a young man who carries a pocket knife to school without being aware that it is a banned item).

📷 Points to Ponder

- A standard argument *against* jury nullification is that in a democracy, laws should be decided by *all* the people, through our elected representatives, and not by some small group of jurors. What do you think of that argument?
- If a law in our democracy was passed by an unjust or unfair process—for example, a law was passed because a group of lobbyists bribed members of Congress to pass the law, not because it was the will of the people—would that justify jury nullification of that law?
- Another argument against jury nullification is that every defendant has the right to be tried under the same law. If jurors in Miami do not like a law and decide to nullify it, while jurors in Jacksonville favor and uphold the law, then defendants in Jacksonville and Miami are not being treated equally. Is that a strong argument against jury nullification?
- David C. Brody (in "*Sparf* and *Dougherty* Revisited: Why the Court Should Instruct the Jury of its Nullification Right," *American Criminal Law Review*, Volume 33 (1995)) proposed that judges give this instruction to juries:

  While it is proper and advisable for you to follow the law as I give it, you are not required to do so. You must, however, keep in mind that we are a nation governed by laws. Refusal to follow the court's instructions as to the elements of the crime(s) charged should occur only in an extraordinary case. Unless finding the defendant guilty is repugnant to your sense of justice, you should follow the instruction on the law as given to you by the court.

  Do you approve of that jury instruction? Is it too lenient, too strict, or just right?

- Those who favor jury nullification believe it should be used only to prevent the unjust conviction of a defendant; but jury nullification should *never* be used to convict someone who is actually innocent under the law. For example, suppose that in our state there is no "good Samaritan" law; that is, no law requiring that one give assistance to those who are in danger or warn others of danger. While driving at dusk, Joe notices that a bridge has been washed out; he stops his car and turns around, but makes no effort to warn a car that he meets of the severe danger, and in the gathering darkness the driver of that car plunges into the river and drowns. The jury concludes that Joe is not guilty under the law; but they think he is morally repugnant, and that there *ought* to be a law against Joe's act, so they decide he should be convicted anyway. Advocates of jury nullification would insist that the jury acted *wrongly* in not following the law in this case, but that it may be right for the jury to *refuse* to convict someone who has violated the law. Is that a consistent view?

Jurors Should Be Permitted to Follow Their Consciences

Jeffrey Abramson

. . . Philosophically, jury nullification is a close cousin to the theory of civil disobedience. In our own time, Martin Luther King, Jr., was a leading advocate for the view that individuals have a "moral responsibility to disobey unjust laws." But King accepted the state's authority to punish his acts of lawbreaking. In fact, willingness to accept punishment was a sign that the disobedience was a challenge to a particular unjust law and not to the state as a whole.

Jury nullification takes the classic theory of civil disobedience one step further by inviting the jury not to punish justified acts of lawbreaking. If the jury agrees that the broken law is unjust, then, say proponents of nullification, it should acquit rather than convict the defendant. The jury should

also acquit when it finds the broken law just but agrees that enforcing it against the particular defendant on trial would be unjust.

Jury nullification is an appealing doctrine, promising to give meaning to the sometimes empty phrase "verdicts rendered according to conscience." Authorized to nullify, a jury might move from merely finding that the defendant violated the law to further deliberation about the ethical claims raised by acts of civil disobedience; instead of mechanically convicting because the law has been broken, the nullifying jury would have to consider the justice of the cause for which the law was violated. Sometimes the causes are grand, as was the case when juries deliberated whether to enforce the Fugitive Slave Law against those

Jeffrey Abramson, "Juries and Higher Justice," *We, the Jury: The Jury System and the Ideal of Democracy*, Chapter 2 (Cambridge, MA: Harvard University Press, 2000): 61–95. Copyright © 1994 by Basic books, a division of HarperCollins Publishers, Inc. Reprinted by permission of Harvard University Press.

who helped runaway slaves attain freedom. At other times, the tension between law and conscience concerns lesser matters, such as enforcing liquor laws during Prohibition. But, for anyone who takes seriously the jury as a bridge between community values and the law, jury nullification is a strong plank. In essence, nullification empowers jurors to appeal to fundamental principles of justice over and above the written law.

There is, however, a vicious side to jury nullification that Americans know all too well. The moral case for this right foundered and sank over the issue of race. In the South especially, all-white juries repeatedly refused to convict whites charged with murdering blacks or civil rights workers of any race. Few bothered to use the word "nullification" to describe the horror of the not guilty verdicts for Emmett Till's or Viola Liuzzo's murderers, but it was also no secret that the verdicts flew in the face of both the evidence and the law. As the sociologist Gunnar Myrdal noted in his classic study of American racism, the Southern all-white jury became a shield for local racism and a prime obstacle to enforcement of national civil rights legislation. The obstacle was all the more solid because, in our trial system, a not guilty verdict is final and unreviewable.

This is not just a story about the distant past. In Mississippi in the late 1960s, a former Ku Klux Klan leader accused of plotting to murder a black leader reportedly told an associate, "Don't worry.... No jury in Mississippi would convict someone over killing a nigger." The KKK leader was tried twice, the jury deadlocking each time. In 1979, Ku Klux Klan gunmen opened fire on marchers in an anti-Klan rally in Greensboro, North Carolina, organized by the Communist Workers' Party. Five marchers died. An all-white jury (including one juror who said, "It's less of a crime to kill communists") found the gunmen not guilty on all charges. The not guilty verdict barred any state retrial of the Klansmen on the same charges. (The Klansmen were subsequently tried in federal court on separate federal civil rights charges, but an all-white jury acquitted the defendants again in 1984.)

Episodes such as the Greensboro and Mississippi trials undercut any innocent faith in nullification to pardon defendants. Once we grant jurors the right to set conscience above law, we have to live with consciences we admire as well as those we despise. As one critic put it, an "invitation to jurors to vote their consciences is inevitably an invitation to greater parochialism.... Local biases ... are legitimated and activated ..., immuniz[ing] criminal acts visited upon members of society's 'discrete and insular minorities.'"

Stripped of moral stature by its service to racism, the doctrine of nullification is in virtual eclipse today. Only two states, Indiana and Maryland, recognize the doctrine and require judges, upon the request of a defendant, to apprise the jury of its right to disregard the law in favor of an acquittal.

In every other state and in the federal system, the doctrine has passed into history. In California, Operation Rescue jurors heard, as all California jurors hear, that they had "a duty to apply the law as I give it to you to the facts as you determine them." The Massachusetts *Trial Juror's Handbook* states that the jury "decides the facts ... [but] does *not* decide the rules of law to be applied to the facts in the case. . . . The judge tells the jury the proper rules of law required to resolve the case." Pennsylvania's *Handbook for Jurors* is similar: "It is the jury's function to determine what facts are established by competent evidence [but it] is the judge's responsibility to tell . . . the jury the proper rules of law required to resolve the case. . . . [The] judge instructs the jury on the law which must guide and govern." During deliberations, "the jury is free to determine the procedures it will follow . . . as long as the judge's instructions are followed."

In some federal courts, the jury is greeted with an even more explicit statement of its duty to follow the law:

> Ladies and gentlemen: You now are the jury in this case and I want to take a few minutes to tell you something about your duties as jurors. . . . It will be your duty to decide from the evidence what the facts are. You, and you alone, are the judges of the facts. You will hear the evidence, decide what the facts are, and then apply those facts to the law which I will give to you. That is how you will reach your verdict. *In doing so you must follow that law whether you agree with it or not* [emphasis added].

These instructions illustrate the strict division of labor between judges deciding questions of law and juries deciding questions of fact. But, for all its familiarity, the idea that jurors must have nothing to do with the law marked a fundamental shift, a deep decline, in the democratic functions the jury once exercised in England and America. Well into the nineteenth century, criminal juries frequently (and civil juries occasionally) were instructed that the judge's statement of the law was not binding on them, that they could determine for themselves what the law was. Juries in England used this authority to become the first to extend legal protection to Quakers assembled in peaceable worship. Juries in the American colonies found that newspapers had a lawful right to print "true" criticisms of government long before legislatures recognized truth as a defense in seditious libel cases. And up until the Civil War, defendants charged with violating the Fugitive Slave Law appealed to juries to judge the law invalid. Well-known examples such as these illustrate the substantial contributions that juries, equipped with the right to decide questions of law, once made to upholding civil liberties.

The fact/law distinction, so starkly posed in judges' instructions to juries today, is, however, a fiction that seldom corrals the behavior of actual jurors. Even critics of jury nullification concede that criminal juries have the raw power to pardon law-breaking because there is no device for reversing a jury that insists on acquitting a defendant against the law. Opponents of jury nullification therefore fall back on a technical distinction between the conceded power to nullify and the denied right to nullify. They insist on this distinction because it has one major practical implication: judges should not instruct juries about nullification because it is not a power jurors have any lawful right to exercise.

Much of the debate over jury nullification is about this formal issue of whether to instruct or not. Defenders of jury nullification argue in favor of open instruction; anything less mis-leads the jury about the full extent of its powers and may produce convic-tions a jury knowing about nullifica-tion would have rejected as unjust. Jurors who grudgingly convict because they mistakenly believe that they have no choice may feel deceived if they learn after trial that they had the power to acquit.

Critics retort that nullification instructions conflict with instructions to jurors that they are duty-bound to apply the law whether they accept it or not. Officially informing jurors that they have the power to nullify would confuse them; it would also threaten the unpartiality of justice with the anarchy of conscience, as jurors pick and choose against whom to enforce the law. Open instruction might even encourage jurors to nul-lify, by portraying nullification as a right rather than a power. The present arrangement of keeping mum about nullification may be hypocritical, but it ensures that jurors will nullify only in extreme cases of conflict between law and conscience.

The debate over nullification instructions is important, but it some-times obscures the overriding fact that jurors continue to nullify, whether offi-cially instructed about their options or not. Ultimately, I think all sides must admit that verdicts according to con-science are so deeply entwined with popular images of the jury that jurors follow their conscience rather than the law in a good many cases, and the more visible cases at that. . . .

[J]ury nullification lives on, even when officially banished from the approved list of jury rights. But its life is secret because jurors are discouraged from openly deliberating about the justice of enforcing the law and are no doubt forced frequently into smug-gling their views on the justice of law into "approved debate" about the evi-dence or facts. But, if jurors continue to nullify on the sly, would we not do better to recognize in theory what jurors do in practice? Would not the quality of the debate about law versus justice be better if jurors were told that such debate was part of their function, that we cherish trial by jury precisely because we expect ordinary citizens to repudiate laws, or instances of law enforcement, that are repugnant to their consciences? These are the questions I wish to pursue, by revisiting the history of jury nullification.

Nullification's Rise and Fall

Jury nullification grew out of a general claim that jurors have the right to decide all questions of law necessary to reach a verdict. According to this broad claim, jurors have the right to disregard judicial instructions and arrive at their own resolution of all contested matters of law at trial.

Jurors' right to decide questions of law gives them considerably greater authority than jury nullification itself requires. The right to nullify is narrow, permitting jurors only the right not to apply the law. The crucial significance of this restriction is that juries can nullify only to acquit, never to convict. By con-trast, the right to decide questions of law entitles jurors to apply their own interpretation of the law to either the detriment or the benefit of a defendant.

Logically speaking, it is possible to defend jury nullification while rejecting the notion that juries have any general right to decide questions of law. After all, it is one thing for a judge to tell the jury what the applicable law is; it is quite another for the judge to require the jury to apply the law. But historically, jury nullification was debated as one example of the broader claim that jurors decided questions of law. The classic arguments came into English law in the middle of the seventeenth century, made by dissenting groups such as Levellers or Quakers on trial for treason, seditious libel, unlawful assembly, or disturbance of the peace. Defendants appealed to the jury to be "judges of the law," never quite specifying whether they were calling upon the jury to reject English law as unjust (to nullify it) or simply to find them innocent under existing laws (despite judicial instructions to the contrary). At any rate, the right of juries to decide questions of law became a rallying cry for political and religious minorities throughout the seventeenth century; in the colonies it turned local juries in times of crisis into centers of resistance to parliamentary law. . . .

In virtually every jurisdiction's handbook for jurors, the same mechanical description appears: find the facts, and reach a verdict by applying whatever the judge says about the law to those facts.

But the search for a strict division of labor between jury and judge creates a number of practical problems for trials today. First, . . . the division of labor does not hold up well in practice. The more we emphasize the remoteness of law from the experience of the average juror, the less credible it is that jurors receive sudden enlightenment on legal matters simply by listening to the judge's furious, quick-paced, jargon-laced set of instructions.

For instance, if I do not understand what differentiates murder from manslaughter in Massachusetts, I am unlikely to suddenly understand it because a judge instructs that murder requires malice and that malice does not require any ill-will toward the victim but includes a deliberate purpose to injure without legal excuse or palliation. Nor were jurors in the Bernhard Goetz trial likely to understand from the judge's instructions whether Goetz acted lawfully in self-defense, if he *mistakenly* thought he was facing deadly attack. In a Philadelphia racketeering trial in 1993, several jurors said that they did not believe the defendant guilty but voted to convict because they mistakenly thought a hung jury was unacceptable.

Legal realist critics have pointed out since the beginning of the century that modern jury procedures mask a charade: we have judges go through the motions of instructing jurors on the law and tell them they must abide by the instructions, but we suspect that jurors do not fathom the instructions and fall back on their own gut reactions or common sense in deciding how the case should come out. To anyone who has ever witnessed a judge instructing a jury, it is clear that our system does not even pretend that the instructions are meaningful. Rarely are jurors even provided with written copies of the instructions; little attempt is made to translate jargon into common language. Most annoying of all, juror questions about the instructions are usually rebuffed with verbatim rereadings of the same instructions.

The second difficulty, as our predecessors appreciated, is that the world outside the courtroom does not neatly divide questions of fact from questions of law. When we ask jurors to decide, as a matter of fact, whether the defendant acted with malice, we are asking them to make a complicated assessment of the nature of the defendant's mental state—an inquiry far different from finding facts in the who did what, when, and where sense. To label the defendant's behavior malicious is partly to find the historical facts, but it is also to render a judgment about its blameworthiness. Juries are constantly presented with these mixed questions that jump the artificial law/fact boundary. This is true in negligence cases, where juries decide the fact of whether a defendant's behavior fell below the behavior expected of a reasonable person. It is true in obscenity cases, where juries apply "contemporary community standards" to decide the fact of whether the work in question is pornographic. So here too, against official theory, we have to admit that juries do what we say they are not equipped to do: they decide what the law means by "negligence" or "obscenity" or even "murder."

The practical impossibility of abiding by the fact/law distinction casts a new light on the earnest attempts of American law to stamp out the tradition of jury nullification. History teaches us that jurors escape from all kinds of legal straitjackets designed to restrain conscientious acquittals in criminal trials.

And this is the way it ought to be. Many of the arguments that the Supreme Court laid down in *Sparf* stripping juries of any right to decide legal questions, have no relevance to what jury nullification is about—the right to set aside the law only to acquit, never to convict. As a doctrine, jury nullification poses no threat to the accused; it is in fact the time-honored way of permitting juries to leaven the law with leniency.

To permit juries to show mercy by not enforcing the law in a given case is hardly to destroy the fabric of a society under law. Indeed, putting pressure on jurors to convict against their conscience would seem to threaten the integrity of the law far more seriously. Our current system, in which we tell jurors they must apply the law in every case no matter how unjust the results seem to them, opens the chasm between law and popular beliefs that the jury system exists to prevent.

This is not to deny that jury nullification sometimes goes badly … There is no denying, as the Supreme Court said in another context, that "the power to be lenient is the power to discriminate." It is for this reason that the Massachusetts affiliate of the American Civil Liberties Union (ACLU) took a firm stance against a bill, introduced in the state legislature in 1991, that would have amended the jury trial handbook to inform jurors that they could acquit "according to their conscience" if they felt "the law as charged by the judge is unjust or wrongly applied to the defendant(s)." The ACLU chapter believed that "jurors often manage to control their own strong prejudices because the judge tells them they must." Its fear was that jury nullification would be an open invitation for jurors to unleash their prejudices in the name of conscience.

The ACLU affiliate's stance against jury nullification is a succinct expression of the collapsed faith in the virtue of jurors that drives the declining role of jurors at trial. In that group's judgment, jury nullification encourages jurors not to rise above law to consult fundamental justice but to fall below law into brute bias. One is left to wonder whether the rejection of jury nullification is not a rejection of the idea of the jury altogether.

Suppose we were to inform jurors that nullification is an option. Is the Massachusetts chapter of the ACLU right to fear dire consequences—a sudden bursting of prejudice through legal dikes? In the two states that do instruct about nullification—Indiana and Maryland—judges have not detected any dramatic rise in the frequency of nullification. Alan Scheflin and Jon Van Dyke, the leading scholars of jury nullification, reported recently on an empirical study where the effect of jury nullification instructions on mock jurors depended on the issue involved. Juries given nullification instructions were not more likely to acquit a college student charged with driving drunk and killing a pedestrian; in fact, they were less likely to acquit than juries given standard instructions. On the other hand, receiving a nullification instruction did increase the number of mock juries that acquitted a nurse charged with the mercy killing of a terminally ill cancer patient. It is encouraging that nullification instructions left the mock jurors able to distinguish the merits of pardoning the nurse and not acquitting the drunk driver.

In 1983, a California murder trial demonstrated the dwarfing of deliberation that comes from denying juries the right to nullify. A seventeen-year-old shot and killed a marijuana-growing farmer during a botched attempt to rob crops from the farm. In accordance with the felony murder rule, the judge instructed the jury that a killing committed during armed robbery was to be considered first-degree murder. After deliberating some time, the jury returned to ask the judge whether it was compelled to find the defendant guilty of first-degree murder if it found that the killing occurred during an armed robbery. At this point, there was only one forthright answer; the jury should have been apprised of its power to nullify.

Clearly, the jury was struggling with the issue of the harsh consequences of the felony murder rule and was searching for a way to convict the defendant of less than first-degree murder. In reacting this way to the felony murder rule, the jury was not behaving strangely but rather in tune with sentiments that had caused many other states to abandon the rule by 1983. But the judge remained silent about nullification and simply repeated the instruction that felony murder is first-degree murder. Even if the judge was not originally obliged to volunteer information about nullification, surely he answered incorrectly when the jury broached the issue on its own. An entire line of deliberation was cut off, or at least it appears to have been cut off, because the jury returned a first-degree murder conviction.

Whether such a verdict represented the jury's considered and independent judgement of justice in the case, we will never know. We do know that the California Supreme Court upheld the conviction but reduced the punishment to that for second-degree murder, finding the punishment of first-degree murder to be so "grossly disproportionate to the offense" in the case as to constitute cruel and unusual punishment. Thus, the Court ended up reaching exactly the judgment the jury was not permitted to make. . . .

Either openly displayed or hidden, nullification remains a timeless strategy for jurors seeking to bring law into line with their conscience.

This reconciliation is what the jury system is about, for better or worse. Official disapproval of jury nullification may drive it underground, . . . But, as long as we have juries, we will have nullification and verdicts according to conscience. Some of those verdicts will outrage us, others will inspire us. But always nullification will give us the full drama of democracy, as citizen-jurors assume on our behalf the task of deliberating about law in relation to justice. ■

Jurors Should Always Follow the Law

Mark Dwyer

I'm not in favor of letting juries nullify the meaning of the law. Obviously, it is simply a fact that they can do it when they want to. But I don't think that it is a good principle to instruct the jurors and remind them they can do that. There are some philosophical reasons and some very practical reasons for my views. Let me share a few of those with you.

You and I elect the legislators that make our laws; you and I elect the judges and prosecutors to enforce our laws. When someone, even a juror, nullifies existing law, he is nullifying *our* laws, which we are free to change, if we oppose them. But we are entitled to ask others to respect the laws as long as

they remain in force. We don't live in the days of John Peter Zenger, where a royal governor was enforcing the rule of the King of England. We live in a society where we may change the law if we think it unjust. If we think that those who abet suicide do not deserve to be punished then we can change the laws. If we think battered wives should be free to shoot their husbands, then we can say that is a defense under the law. If people believe that certain principles should be enacted into the law, then they can vote for representatives who will enact those principles into the law.

The question for us is whether any group of twelve people, chosen

Mark Dwyer, "Law, Justice, and Jury Nullification: A Debate," *Criminal Law Bulletin*, Volume 29, Number 1 (1993): 40–69. Reprinted by permission of the publisher and author.

through an imperfect system of jury selection to judge a particular case, should be free to ignore our law and impose their own view of how society should be run. I think it is democratic to impose the law rather than their individual views. . . .

I don't think there is a need to encourage this minority of twelve to upset the rule of law. The practical consequences will be far more deleterious than advantageous. You can, of course, conjure up some difficult issues such as abetting suicide, but frankly I have not seen a suicide abettor prosecuted in New York State, certainly not in New York County, since I've been around. We don't have that many wives who kill their husbands either, whether battered or otherwise. Frankly, I think those who do it should be punished. But for every one of those cases, if you disagree with me, I can give other situations where you are likely to feel differently about the ability of juries to nullify what is our law.

Suppose, for example, someone in Suffolk County should burn down an abortion clinic. I take it under this proposal that those jurors in Suffolk County who consider the case would be asked to consider whether they believe abortion is murder, even though that is not the law of the land, and it is therefore justifiable to burn down abortion clinics. . . . I don't think that's a good idea.

If you look at Alabama in the 1960s and posit federal civil rights violations, you wouldn't want those jurors told that they may reflect community sentiments and override the law that would otherwise govern a criminal case. If it is necessary that a principle like the ability to kill one's spouse be recognized, then let's recognize it in legislation. Let's not have juries randomly decide that they are going to recognize it in a particular case.

The last thing I want to talk about is an individual trial where this kind of instruction might be given to a jury. The proposed instruction is not designed to cover only those cases where one might have a philosophical disagreement with a statute. This is to be an instruction that any defendant can get. It would tell the jury that they can feel sympathy for the defendant, which is exactly the opposite of what we now tell jurors, since every judge now charges the jury that sympathy has no place in their deliberations, they are only to consider the facts.

But how would this change affect the trial in the jury room? Does the jury ask: "Which laws do we agree with and which do we not agree with? Do we like the burden of proof in this case or should we impose a different burden of proof? Do we agree that an affirmative defense should be an affirmative defense or should it be something the government ought to disprove beyond a reasonable doubt? Which defendant here do we like and which defendant do we dislike? Does one defendant seem like a nice guy for whom we want to let sympathy into our verdict, but not his codefendant who did the same thing?" Only after these considerations does the jury try to figure out whether someone committed a crime. I don't think that is what jurors are supposed to do.

What implications would the instruction have for earlier portions of the trial? I assume that any principle that can determine a criminal case must be one that the parties can sum up on. So the defendant could argue for sympathy and the prosecutors could argue that safe streets require a conviction.

If we are going to determine matters this way, how are we going to get the facts before jurors so that they can make this type of judgment? If, for example, the defendant appears to be a first offender to the jurors, do we let them know, when an appeal for their sympathy is charged, that he actually has a long record? What does that have to do with the jury's fairly considering whether he committed a particular crime?

Judges considering motions and legislators determining what laws to pass have access to a wide variety of information that doesn't belong before a jury in a criminal trial. This proposal would allow jurors to be informed of and judge irrelevancies, and this is not what jurors do best. The end result is that the rule of law would be sacrificed to the whims of a few citizens. I think the results would wreak harm, since the rule of law protects minorities against the majority. Arbitrariness and injustice would be introduced into the criminal justice system. This is a bad idea.... ■

⠿ The Continuing Debate

What Is New

In San Francisco in early 2003, Ed Rosenthal was convicted in a federal court on federal charges of marijuana cultivation and conspiracy to grow and distribute marijuana. Jurors did not know that Rosenthal was growing marijuana for the relief of patients suffering from cancer, cerebral palsy, and other severe illnesses, and that his activities (though in violation of federal law) were legal under California's Compassionate Use Statute (which California voters had passed as proposition 215), and that Rosenthal had been deputized by the City of Oakland to provide medical marijuana for patients unable to grow their own. Jurors were told by the judge that they must follow the law, and under the provisions of the federal Controlled Substances Act, Rosenthal was clearly guilty. After they learned more details of the case (that had been kept from them during the trial), six of the jurors—who had returned a unanimous verdict of guilty—called a press conference to denounce the verdict. The foreman of the jury, Charles Sackett, concluded that the jury reached the wrong verdict, and said he believes that if the jurors had known about jury nullification the verdict would have been not guilty.

In 2003, a bill was introduced in the New Hampshire Legislature that would have required judges to instruct juries that jurors have a right to find a defendant not guilty even when there is sufficient evidence to establish that the defendant is guilty under the law. The bill passed the New Hampshire House by vote of 220–149, but failed in the Senate.

Where to Find More

Sparf and Hansen v. U.S., 156 U.S. 51, October Term, 1894, is the U.S. Supreme Court case in which the Court ruled that judges need not tell jurors of their power to nullify law by judging both fact and law. Justices Gray and Shiras wrote a strong dissent. (This case can be found at www.Oyez.org.)

Alan W. Scheflin, "Jury Nullification: The Right to Say No," *Southern California Law Review*, Volume 45 (1972): 168–226, is an excellent source for the legal history of jury nullification; see also Alan Scheflin and Jon Van Dyke, "Jury Nullification: Contours of the Controversy," *Law and Contemporary Problems*, Volume 43, Number 4 (Autumn 1980): 51–115; Irwin A. Horowitz and Thomas Willging, "Changing Views of Jury Power: The Nullification Debate, 1787–1988," in *Law and Human Behavior*, Volume 15, Number 2 (1991); Paula Di Perna, *Juries on Trial: Faces of American Justice* (New York: Dembner Books, 1984); and William L. Dwyer, *In the Hands of the People: The Trial Jury's Origins, Triumphs, Troubles and Future in American Democracy* (New York: St. Martin's Press, 2002), Chapter 5. David A. Pepper, "Nullifying History: Modern-Day Misuse of the Right to Decide the Law," *Case Western Law Review*, Volume 50, Number 3 (Spring 2000): 599–644, argues that advocates of jury nullification have misinterpreted the history of jury nullification in the United States.

Richard St. John argues against jury nullification in "License to Nullify: The Democratic and Constitutional Deficiencies of Authorized Jury Lawmaking," *Yale Law Journal*, Volume 106 (June 1997): 2563–2597. Other opponents of jury nullification are Erick J. Haynie, "Populism, Free Speech, and the Rule of Law: The 'Fully Informed' Jury Movement and Its Implications," *The Journal of Criminal Law & Criminology*, Volume 88, Number 1 (1998); and Gary J. Simpson, "Jury Nullification in the American System: A Skeptical View," *Texas Law Review*, Volume 54 (1976).

Among supporters of jury nullification are Jack B. Weinstein, "Considering Jury 'Nullification': When May and Should a Jury Reject the Law to do Justice?" *American Criminal Law Review*, Volume 30, Number 2 (1993): 239–254; Alan W. Scheflin and Jon M. Van Dyke, "Merciful Juries: The Resilience of Jury Nullification," *Washington & Lee Law Review*, Volume 48 (1991); and Clay S. Conrad, *Jury Nullification: The Evolution of a Doctrine* (Durham, NC: Carolina Academic Press, 1998).

Arie M. Rubenstein, "Verdicts of Conscience: Nullification and the Modern Jury Trial," *Columbia Law Review*, Volume 106 (2006): 959–993, proposes an interesting compromise solution to the controversy over jury nullification. Nancy J. King, "Silencing Nullification Advocacy Inside the Jury Room and Outside the Courtroom," *University of Chicago Law Review*, Volume 65: 433–501, provides an excellent study of the current law as well as current controversies related to jury nullification.

Jury Ethics: Juror Conduct and Jury Dynamics, edited by John Kleinig and James P. Levine (Boulder, CO: Paradigm Publishers, 2006), contains excellent papers on jury nullification; see especially Chapter 3, which contains Norman J. Finkel, "Jurors' Duties, Obligations, and Rights: The Ethical/Moral Roots of Discretion," with a response by Adina Schwartz; Chapter 4, "The Constitutional and Ethical Implications of 'Must-Find-the-Defendant-Guilty' Jury Instructions," by B. Michael Dann, and the response by Shari Seidman Diamond; and "Jury

Deliberation: Fair and Foul," by Jeffrey Abramson, with a response by James P. Levine. *The Jury Trial in Criminal Justice*, edited by Douglas D. Koski and Michael J. Saks (Durham, NC: Carolina Academic Press, 2003), contains several interesting articles on jury nullification.

The "Fully Informed Jury Association," or FIJA, is a nonprofit organization that promotes the principle of jury nullification; it can be found at www.fija.org.

Is the Restorative Justice Model the Best Model for Criminal Justice?

Restorative Justice Promises Much More Than It Can Deliver
  Advocate: Richard Delgado, University Distinguished Professor of
  Law and Derrick Bell Fellow, University of Pittsburgh.
  Source: "Prosecuting Violence: A Colloquy on Race, Community, and
  Justice," *Stanford Law Review*, Volume 52 (April 2000).
Restorative Justice Is a Major Advance Over Conventional Criminal Justice
  Advocate: Allison Morris, formerly Professor in Criminology and
  Director of the Institute of Criminology at Victoria University of
  Wellington, Wellington, New Zealand.
  Source: "Critiquing the Critics: A Brief Response to Critics of
  Restorative Justice," *British Journal of Criminology*, Volume 42 (2002):
  596–615.

The Restorative Justice movement calls for significant changes in the traditional retributive justice system. In the restorative justice model, criminals have caused significant harm to their communities and to people within those communities, and the offender must recognize the harm done (and ideally, feel shame and remorse for the harm inflicted on the community and the individual victim). Both the crime victim and the community should be recognized as having been wronged, and must be restored to the greatest degree possible. Under the restorative justice model, the demands and penalties on the criminal may be substantial—they may include efforts to restore the victim to financial and psychological security, demonstration of genuine contrition and recognition of the wrong done, and sometimes quite significant punishment (such as a term of imprisonment). But the criminal is not branded as a criminal outcast; rather, the offender must be recognized as a member of the community who has done something wrong, and who must ultimately be restored to the community to make that community whole.

Supporters of the restorative justice model do not suppose that restoration of communities and offenders is easy or automatic. In many cases the process will be very challenging, and may involve requiring the community itself to undergo significant self-evaluation: for example, have past community practices—such as discrimination, or favoritism toward a privileged sector—made the offender feel alienated from the community? Does the community offer the offender a genuine opportunity to achieve success and acceptance? Has the offender been treated with respect as a community member? "Restoring" the community may involve more than merely re-establishing the status quo; it may involve restoring principles of respect and justice that the community had neglected. Restorative justice requires that people have a genuine interest in, a stake in, their community, and if that community discriminates against a group and deprives it of opportunities, then no process of genuine restoration can succeed.

Richard Delgado focuses on Victim–Offender Mediation (VOM) as a representative of the restorative justice model, and argues that this process of restorative justice is fundamentally flawed: It imposes inconsistent sentences, places defendants in a position of weakness with fewer constitutional protections, and fails to satisfy the demands of victims and society for adequate punishment. Furthermore, Delgado claims, restorative justice may make heavy psychological demands on crime victims, is unlikely to have genuine restorative effects on offenders, and makes little or no contribution to changing the social and institutional structures that shape criminal behavior. Delgado agrees that the current criminal justice system is in need of reform, but thinks that a better system should involve elements of both restorative and traditional retributive justice. In her defense of restorative justice, Allison Morris acknowledges that restorative justice does not meet all the demands of retributive justice; but in her view, many of the demands of retributive justice are not worth meeting. Morris maintains that if we compare the two systems, we will find that restorative justice is the better system for protecting the rights and interests of offenders, victims, and communities.

⠇⠇⠇ Points to Ponder

- Both Delgado and Morris emphasize the importance of discovering and changing the *causes* of crime, with Delgado claiming that restorative justice fails to address that problem and Morris insisting that restorative justice can contribute to solving such problems. What about the traditional retributive justice model? Does it make any contribution to discovering and changing the causes of crime? *Could* the retributive system do so? Does the restorative justice system have the potential for doing better at those tasks? Are those tasks part of the proper role of a justice system?

- Jim, 19, is a first-year student at your university. While walking home one evening, he is robbed at knifepoint by John, an unemployed 19-year-old who lives in the neighborhood. John is apprehended, and under questioning admits committing the robbery. Compare how the current retributive system and a restorative justice system would deal with this case.
- Victims' rights, as discussed in Debate 3, is a prominent issue in contemporary criminal justice. Considered from the perspective of crime victims, would a restorative justice approach be more likely, or less likely, to protect their legitimate interests and improve their ultimate outcome?
- Your college or university probably has a campus "judicial system" that deals with cases of academic dishonesty, and perhaps with other alleged offenses. Does it operate more on a retributive or a restorative model, or on some other model altogether?
- Could a restorative system of justice ever accept capital punishment? That is, are there any circumstances in which you can imagine someone who favors restorative justice also regarding the death penalty as legitimate?

Prosecuting Violence: A Colloquy on Race, Community, and Justice

Richard Delgado

The Restorative Justice Movement and Victim-Offender Mediation

Restorative Justice

Many proponents of restorative justice believe that our current approach to criminal justice should be reexamined. Specifically, restorative justice advocates argue that incarceration offers little in the way of rehabilitative opportunities for offenders. Many emerge from prison more hardened and angry than when they entered, setting up a cycle of recidivism that serves neither them nor society. Moreover, although the victims' rights movement has begun to clamor for restitution as a part of court-ordered sentencing, relatively few victims receive compensation for their injuries, and fewer still receive anything resembling an apology from the perpetrator.

The movement's proponents argue that the traditional criminal justice system does a second disservice to victims, by forcing them to relive their ordeal at trial. Because the American criminal justice system conceptualizes crime as a wrong against the state, it uses the victim for her testimony, while offering little, if anything, in the way of counseling services or support. For the same reason, district attorneys rarely consult with the victim at key times during the course of the trial, so that he experiences a lack of control as key events take place without his input.

In response to these perceived shortcomings, proponents of the Restorative Justice Movement believe that those affected most by crime should play an active role in its resolution. The movement intends to redefine crime as an offense against an individual, providing a forum for the victim to participate in the resolution and restitution of that crime. This is achieved through programs in which the victim, offender, and community play an active role.

Victim–Offender Mediation: Restorative Justice in Action

Of the numerous programs bearing restorative justice roots, Victim–Offender Mediation (VOM) is the most well established. Although VOM takes slightly varying forms, all share the same basic structure. Most receive referrals from the traditional justice system, are predicated on an admission of guilt, and, if successful, are conducted in lieu of a conventional trial. The VOM process generally consists

of four phases: Intake, Preparation for Mediation, Mediation, and Follow-up. During intake, a pre-screening occurs. Here, the mediator, who is either a trained community volunteer or a staff person, accepts the victim and offender into the VOM process if both parties express a readiness to negotiate and show no overt hostility toward each other. In the Preparation for Mediation stage, the mediator talks with the victim and the offender individually and schedules the first meeting. If the mediator does not feel she has effectively established trust and rapport with each of the parties, the case is remanded to court. In the Mediation stage itself, the parties are expected to tell their versions of the story, talk things over, come to understand each other's position, and agree upon an appropriate solution, usually a restitution agreement or work order. If they cannot do so, the case is remanded to court. A final Follow-up stage monitors the offender's performance and cooperation with the work or restitution agreement, with the goal of assuring compliance.

VOM success: far-reaching and still growing. While the majority of VOM programs concentrate on first- and second-time juvenile offenders, some include adult felons, including alleged killers, armed robbers, and rapists. In a recent year, VOM dealt with 16,500 cases in the United States alone, while the number of programs in the United States and Canada approached 125. Endorsed by the ABA, the movement shows no sign of slowing.

VOM's departure from today's criminal justice system. Like other programs born of the Restorative Justice Movement, VOM seeks to cure perceived problems with the traditional criminal justice process. While an adversarial dynamic may create the appearance of greater justice, it also provides minimal emotional closure for the victim and little direct accountability by the offender to the victim. On the other hand, VOM deals more openly with the direct human consequences of crime. Through a face-to-face meeting and discussion, the victim is able to receive information about the crime, express to the offender the impact his actions have had on her, and, it is hoped, gain a sense of material and emotional restoration. Similarly, the offender is forced to face the consequences of his actions and accept responsibility for them, while also playing a role in fashioning the remedies. The offender's restitution should also lead to increased public confidence in the fairness of the system. A further advantage for the offender is that VOM offers an alternative to the ravages of incarceration: Because successful mediation serves in lieu of a trial, a defendant who cooperates and performs the agreed service will escape confinement entirely.

In summary, proponents of VOM maintain that the program will empower the victim while reducing recidivism among offenders. It offers the hope that victims and offenders may come to recognize each other's common humanity and that offenders will be able to take their place in the wider community as valued citizens. Through restitution, the victim will gain back what was lost. Accordingly, VOM proponents advocate the program as "a challenging new vision of how communities can respond to crime and victimization . . . deeply rooted in . . . the collective western

heritage . . . of remorse, forgiveness, and reconciliation."

Can Restorative Justice Deliver on Its Promises? An Internal Critique

Critics of the Restorative Justice Movement and VOM voice two concerns: (1) they charge that restorative justice does not deliver what we expect from a system of criminal justice, and (2) they contend that the movement may render a disservice to victims, offenders, or society at large. The following two sections discuss these two sets of criticisms in turn.

Can Restorative Justice Deliver What We Expect from a System of Criminal Justice?

Among the elements that society may reasonably expect from a criminal justice system are consistency, equality of bargaining power, due process, punishment, state control, and widespread applicability.

Consistency. Consider first the problem of inconsistent results. The traditional criminal justice system aims at uniformity, employing a system of graded offenses and sentencing guidelines designed to assure that like cases are treated alike. Although far from perfect in realizing this goal, the system at least holds consistency up as an ideal and includes measures designed to bring it about. Moreover, judges, prosecutors, and defense attorneys are repeat players who tend to see cases in categorical terms (e.g., a car accident: pedestrian versus driver) rather than in terms of ascribed qualities of the participants (e.g., black driver, white pedestrian). However, VOM lacks both an obvious "metric" (e.g., what is the appropriate number of hours of community service for a shoplifting offense?) and the repeat-player quality of formal adjudication. The mediator may have seen many cases similar to the one at hand, but the victim and the offender will most likely be in their situation for the first time. Without any prior experience, different victims and offenders may decide similar cases differently, leading to inconsistency in punishment.

Inequality of bargaining power. VOM gives great power to the victim, and mediators and judges reinforce that power, placing defendants in an almost powerless position. For example, the mediator frequently advises the offender that he will be referred back to the court system for trial if he and the victim cannot reach a restitution agreement. The mediator may also tell the offender that the judge will take his lack of cooperation into account at the time of sentencing. This leaves the victim with the power to price the crime based on her subjective reaction, while at the same time confronting the offender with a harsh choice: cooperate or go to jail.

Waiver of constitutional rights. Related to the above-mentioned coercive quality of mediation is the issue of waiver of constitutional rights. Enacted during a period when the "king's peace" view of crime and criminal justice prevailed, rather than during the earlier period when private restitution served as chief remedy, our Constitution and Bill of Rights guarantee the criminally accused certain rights, including the right to confront witnesses, to be represented by counsel, and to avoid self-incrimination. Fearing abuse by the powerful state, the Framers incorporated these protections against overzealous prosecution and police practices. However, because VOM pressures offenders to accept informal resolution of the charges against them and to waive representation by a lawyer, trial by jury, and the right to appeal, it would seem to stand on constitutionally questionable ground. Moreover, mediation takes place early in the criminal process, at a time when the offender may be unaware of the evidence against him, or the range of defenses available. Furthermore, social science evidence compiled by VOM's defenders is one-sided, adulatory, and lacking basic elements of scholarly rigor—such as blind studies, controls for variables, and randomization—that one would wish in connection with a widespread social experiment. In the current state of research, neither offenders nor their advisors can predict what mediation will really be like. Thus, a defendant may be unable to waive his rights "knowingly and intelligently" as required by the Constitution.

Punishment. Our society has further expectations of any system of criminal adjudication. These include the traditional goals of criminal punishment—deterrence, rehabilitation, increased societal safety, and retribution. Mediation may accomplish some of these objectives in individual cases, but only incidentally and as a byproduct of its principal objectives of compensating the victim and avoiding incarceration for the offender. During mediation, if an offender is willing to apologize and make restitution, he is released immediately into society with little check on whether he is fully rehabilitated. Accordingly, society's need for retribution or vengeance remains unsatisfied. This is not surprising: Most restorative justice theorists consider retribution an illegitimate relic of a more barbaric age.

State control. Another troubling aspect of VOM is that it may upset social expectations by casting a wider net of state control than we expect. One way this may happen is that minor cases that ordinarily would have been dismissed or treated summarily in the traditional system receive full-blown treatment under VOM. Indeed, one study showed that VOM increased incarceration because many offenders who would not have received jail time entered into a restitution agreement, but then failed to carry it out. These offenders were then referred back to court, where they were sentenced for failure to complete their restitution bargain.

VOM's limited applicability. Finally, mediation cannot be applied, without radical modification, to victimless crimes, such as drug offenses or crimes of attempt, or to offenses against the state or a corporation. In these cases, no ordinary victim is available to meet with the perpetrator and discuss restitution, nor has the perpetrator victimized a specific individual or community who could be made whole.

Disservice toward particular groups. Defenders of restorative justice and VOM frequently assert that this type of informal justice is beneficial to society, offenders, and victims. What they neglect to mention, however, is that informal justice may also have a number of downsides for both victims and offenders.

Victims. Mediation may disserve victims by pressuring them to forgive offenders before they are psychologically ready to do so. Mediators, who typically want both parties to put aside their anger and distrust, may intimate that victims are being obstructionist or emotionally immature if they refuse to do so. Such victims may in fact harbor perfectly understandable anger and resentment over the crime. A victim who already blames herself may magnify that self-blame; this risk is most severe if the offender is an acquaintance or intimate partner of the victim. Furthermore, VOM casts the victim in the role of sentencer, holding the power of judgment over the offender. Not only does this lead to a lack of proportionality and consistency, but it may also place an unwelcome burden on the victim who will end up determining the fate of an often young and malleable offender. Not every victim will welcome this responsibility. In pressuring the victim to "forgive and move on" and handing him the power of sentencer, VOM may end up compounding the injury received from the crime itself.

Offenders. At the same time, VOM may disserve offenders, who lose procedural guarantees of regularity and fair treatment. Offenders are urged to be forthcoming and admit what they did, yet often what they say is admissible against them in court if the case is returned. Finally, as mentioned earlier, mediation may not meet social expectations for a system of criminal justice: It dismisses retribution, a valid social impulse; abjures incapacitation, even for serious offenses; offers little in the way of deterrence (a forty-five minute session is not unpleasant enough); and reduces recidivism little, if at all, perhaps because offenders' basic attitudes are unchanged, and the compulsory nature of the mediation induces only superficial expressions of shame and regret.

External Critique: Larger, Systemic Problems with Restorative Justice and Victim–Offender Mediation

As we have seen, restorative justice, in some respects, falls short of achieving its professed goals, or, indeed, those that any system of criminal justice, even narrowly understood, should be expected to accomplish. This section examines restorative justice in light of broader political and social values, such as its ability to spark needed social change, moral reflection, or altered relationships between offender and victim communities. As will be seen, restorative justice raises troubling issues when viewed through this lens as well.

Restoration of the Status Quo Ante

One difficulty with restorative justice inheres in the concept itself. Restorative justice, like tort law, attempts to restore the parties to the status quo ante—the position they would have been in had the crime not occurred—through restitution and payment. But if that status quo is marked by radical inequality and abysmal living conditions for the offender, returning the parties to their original positions will do little to spark social change. The mediation agreement ordinarily requires payment from the offender to the victim, when in many cases it will be the offender who needs a better education, increased job training, and an improved living environment.

Offenders rarely are assigned work that will benefit them or lead to new job opportunities; rather, they end up performing menial services for the victim, such as cutting his grass, painting his porch, or making simple repairs. When the offender performs services for the community, they typically take the form of unskilled labor, such as clearing brush, picking up trash in city parks, or painting over graffiti.

A key component of VOM consists of shaming the offender—making him feel the full force of the wrongfulness of his action, thus causing him to experience remorse. Yet, this adjustment is all one-way: No advocate of VOM, to my knowledge, suggests that the middle-class mediator, the victim, or society at large should feel shame or remorse over the conditions that led to the offender's predicament. Of course, many offenders will be antisocial individuals who deserve little solicitude, while many victims will have well-developed social consciences and empathize with the plight of the urban poor. But nothing in restorative justice or VOM encourages this kind of analysis or understanding. In most cases, a vengeful victim and a middle-class mediator will gang up on a young, minority offender, exact the expected apology, and negotiate an agreement to pay back what she has taken from the victim by deducting portions of her earnings from her minimum-wage job. Little social transformation is likely to arise from transactions of this sort.

Unlikelihood of Sparking Moral Reflection and Development

By the same token, it seems unlikely that VOM will produce the desired internal, moral changes in the offender. In theory, bringing the offender to the table to confront the victim face-to-face will enable him to realize the cost of his actions in human terms and to resolve to lead a better life. Some offenders may, indeed, have a crisis of conscience upon meeting the person she has victimized. But a forty-five minute meeting is unlikely to have a lasting effect if the offender is released to her neighborhood and teenage peer group immediately afterwards. If the offender–victim encounter is brief and perfunctory, and the ensuing punishment demeaning or menial, young offenders will learn to factor the cost of restitution into their practical calculus the next time they are tempted to commit a crime and to parrot what is expected of them when caught. Most offenders are at an early stage of Kohlberg's moral development, seeing right and wrong in pragmatic terms—the action is right if you can get away with it, wrong if you are caught and punished. A short encounter with a victim is unlikely to advance them to a higher stage. Reports of young offenders show that most have little self-esteem, yet both the mediation and the ensuing work an offender performs for the victim or his community come perilously close to degradation rituals. Rarely, if ever, is the offender ordered to do something that will benefit him. For all these reasons, VOM is apt to do little to make an offender a better person; indeed, in a few studies, recidivism increased, compared to a similar group subject to the ordinary criminal justice system.

Inequality of Treatment of Offenders and Victims

Mediation treats the victim respectfully, according to him the status of an end-in-himself, while the offender is treated as a thing to be managed, shamed, and conditioned. Most surveys of VOM programs ask the victim if he felt better afterwards. By contrast, offenders are merely asked whether they completed their work order and whether they recidivated. Offenders sense this and play along with what is desired, while the victim and middle-class mediator participate in a paroxysm of righteousness. In such a setting, the offender is apt to grow even more cynical than before and learn what to say the next time to please the mediator, pacify the victim, and receive the lightest restitution agreement possible.

The offender's cynicism may not just be an intuition; it may be grounded in reality: Informal dispute resolution is even more likely to place him at a disadvantage than formal adjudication. In court, a panoply of procedural devices serve as a brake against state power and overzealous prosecution. Each defendant is assigned a lawyer, who has a prescribed time and place for speaking. The state bears a heavy burden of proof. Moreover, visible features of the American Creed, such as the flag, the robes, and the judge sitting on high, remind all present that principles, such as fairness, equal treatment, and every person receiving his day in court, are to govern, rather than the much less noble values we often act upon during moments of informality. In less formal settings, the same individuals who will behave with fairness during occasions of state will feel much freer to tell an ethnic joke or deny a person of color or a woman a job opportunity. This "fairness and formality" thesis, solidly grounded in social science understandings of the dynamics of prejudice, counsels against using VOM for offenders who are young, black, Latino, or otherwise different from the white, middle-class norm many Americans implicitly embrace.

Racial and Social Inequality

The prime architects of the VOM movement seem to believe that mediators can balance, or counter, inequalities among the parties. However, their own writing about race is replete with stereotypes. Rather than breaking down the barriers and preconceptions that parties bring to the table, mediation is apt to compound preexisting power and status differentials even more systematically and seriously than formal, in-court resolution. VOM sets up a relatively coercive encounter in many cases between an inarticulate, uneducated, socially alienated youth with few social skills and a hurt, vengeful victim. This encounter is mediated by a middle-class, moralistic mediator who shares little background or sympathy with the offender, but has everything in common with the victim. To label this encounter a negotiation seems a misnomer, for it is replete with overt social coercion.

Prompting Recognition of Common Humanity

Nothing is wrong with requiring persons who have harmed others without justification to make restitution. But forcing a needy person who has stolen a loaf of bread to do so is regressive, unless accompanied by measures aimed at easing his poverty. In VOM, all the onus is placed on the offender to change; the victim is required only to come to the bargaining table, discuss how the crime has affected him, negotiate a restitution agreement, and accept an apology. Why not require victims to take a bus tour of the offender's neighborhood and learn something about the circumstances in which he lives? In traditional adjudication, judges, prosecutors, defense attorneys, and jurors will all be privy to this information and be able to consider it when charging and sentencing, but with mediation, the mediator and the victim often will not. Mediation aims at emotional closure, but without a reciprocal exchange of information, any closure is apt to occur only on the most superficial level. If the objective of VOM is to have both sides recognize their common humanity, measures of this sort ought to be considered. Why not even encourage the victim, in appropriate cases, to perform service to the offender or his or her community as a condition of receiving restitution (for example, by serving as a mentor or big brother/sister to a youth like the offender)? Countless studies of mediated crime adopt the feelings of the victim as the principal measure of success or failure—the better the victim feels afterwards, the more successful the mediation. Yet, sometimes in a successful mediation, the victim should feel worse, or at least realize that matters are not as simple as she might have thought.

Which Community is to be Restored?

In a similar vein, VOM will frequently lead to a restitution agreement that includes service to "the community." Indeed, one of the principal advantages of VOM is said to be its ability to repair the breach that the offender's crime has opened between himself and that same community. Yet proponents of restorative justice rarely focus on the precise nature of that community. In a diverse, multicultural society, many collectivities may vie for that status. To which does the offender owe restitution? If, for example, the offender is to rake leaves, should he be required to do it in a park near where the victim lives? In a large municipal park serving the entire city? In one in his own neighborhood? Descriptions of successful mediation abound with stories of offenders made to perform services to victims' churches, for example. Apart from obvious issues of separation of church and state, such privatized, particularized service is troublingly reminiscent of peonage and prison labor gangs.

Erasing the Public Dimension of Criminal Prosecution

Moreover, such particularized mediation atomizes disputes, so that patterns, such as police abuse or the overcharging of black men, do not stand out readily. It forfeits what Owen Fiss and others call the public dimension of adjudication. Mediation pays scant attention to the public interests in criminal punishment, particularly retribution. It also lacks the symbolic element of a public trial, trying instead to compensate by formalized talking among private participants. The criminal justice system, of course, is a principal means by which society reiterates its deepest values; loss of that opportunity is cause for concern.

Treating Conflict as Pathology

Perhaps the above concerns can be captured in the notion of conflict as pathology. Like many forms of mediation,

VOM treats conflict as aberrational, and the absence of it as the desired state. Yet, in a society like ours, tension among groups may be normal, and not a sign of social pathology. With a history of slavery, conquest, and racist immigration laws, the United States today exhibits the largest gap between the wealthy and the poor of any Western industrialized society. Until recently, Southern states segregated school children by race and criminalized marriage between whites and blacks. Surely, in such a society, one would expect the have-nots to attempt to change their social position (by legal or illegal means), and the haves to resist these attempts. Conflict is a logical and expected result. One also would expect the majority group to use the criminal law, at least in part, as a control device—a means of keeping tabs on any behavior of subordinate groups that threatens or irritates, such as loud music, congregating on sidewalks, writing graffiti on freeway overpasses, and shoplifting. Insofar as restorative justice aims at smoothing over the rough edges of social competition and adjusting subaltern people to their roles, it is profoundly conservative. While restoration and healing are emotionally powerful objectives, it is hard to deny that they can have a repressive dimension as well.

"But Consider the Alternative": The Criminal Justice System

Before rejecting restorative justice and VOM for the reasons mentioned in Parts II and III of this essay, it behooves us, as its advocates urge, to consider the alternative—the conventional criminal justice system. For if informal adjudication of offenders is imperfect, the traditional system may be even worse. And when one does examine the traditional system, one discovers that it is far from the safe haven that formal settings generally provide for the disempowered. Instead, as a result of a slow evolution, our criminal justice system has emerged as perhaps the most inegalitarian and racist structure in society. Our prisons are largely black and brown. Indigent defendants are assigned a lawyer from the underfinanced public defender's office and encouraged to plead guilty to a lesser offense in return for a shorter sentence, even if they are innocent or have valid defenses to the charges against them. Minority defendants receive harsher sentences than middle-class whites charged with the same offense, while black men convicted of murdering whites receive the death penalty ten times more often than do whites who kill blacks. Police focus on minority youth congregating on street corners; they stop black motorists and Latino-looking men at airports so regularly that the black community refers to the traffic stops as "DWBs" ("Driving While Black"). Meanwhile, the war on drugs causes police to target minority communities, where drug transactions tend to be conspicuous, rather than in middle-class areas where use is more covert. Black judges face recusal motions more often than their white counterparts often from white litigants concerned that the judge may rule against them because of their race. Studies of the behavior of mock jurors show that baby-faced defendants are acquitted more often than less attractive ones against whom the evidence is exactly the same.

The criminal justice system, then, may be the lone institution in American society where formal values and practices are worse—more racist, more inegalitarian—than the informal ones that most citizens share. As previously mentioned, the situation in this society is generally the opposite: Our formal values, the ones that constitute the American Creed, are exemplary every person is equal, everyone deserves full respect as a moral agent, one person one vote—while informality harbors risks for women, blacks, and members of other outgroups. In our criminal justice system, however, the opposite situation prevails. There alone, as in South Africa under the old regime, the formal values are implicitly or explicitly racist. Just as in South Africa, in former times, a black, such as a stranded motorist, might receive kind treatment from the occasional white traveler while the official police would pass him by, members of stigmatized groups today are apt to receive harsher treatment from U.S. police, judges, and juries than they might get, with luck, at a mediation table. As with Jews in Holland during the Third Reich, private kindness is at least possible; the official kind, unlikely. Despite the main drawbacks of privatized, decentralized, informal mediation, offenders will often be better off taking their chances within VOM than within the formal system.

What, Then, to Do? A Dialogic Approach Based on Competition Between the Two Systems

Assuming they have a choice, blacks, Latinos, and others subject to prejudice should examine both systems carefully before opting for one or the other. In white-dominated regions, as Rodney Hero has recently pointed out, blacks are apt to receive poor formal treatment; they may be better off taking their chances with VOM. Where, by contrast, the jury pool is racially mixed and the judge sympathetic, formal adjudication may be the better choice. While these pragmatic calculations are taking place, conscientious legislators and reform-minded lawyers should work to improve both systems.

Within the Formal Criminal Justice System

Within the formal system of courtroom justice, defense lawyers should serve as guides and native informants, helping defendants find and exploit any known niches of sympathy and fair treatment. Examples include regions where the jury pool is racially and economically mixed, where judges are trained to look behind police testimony and a record of prior convictions for possible bias and overcharging. Because the formal values have become corrupted by an overlay of discriminatory practices, participants must constantly remind everyone to follow the American Creed. Legislators and community groups should urge "superformality"—new layers of formality aimed at keeping the police, prosecutors, and other agents of official power honest. Examples include police and prosecutor review boards, laws requiring the police to keep statistics on traffic stops, and instructions aimed at encouraging members of the jury to consider whether race is affecting their judgment. In short, progressive lawyers and community activists should bolster the in-court version of criminal justice by expanding any informal links to justice, while seeking to impose new levels of formal oversight on the rest of the system.

Within Alternative, Informal Justice

Reformers and critics need to call attention to the way mediation's informality can easily conceal race and class bias underneath an overlay of humanitarian concern. Minority communities need to understand how this happens, so they can avoid its seductive appeal. Minorities should also lobby for structural improvements to VOM, such as more mediators of color, participation by defense attorneys, and studies that test some of VOM's overenthusiastic claims. Where VOM seems fairer than the formal justice system, defendants should "take the bait" and opt for it, while keeping alert for possible abuse and unfairness. The defense bar should attempt to counteract the powerfully conservative, status-quo-enforcing thrust of restorative justice by insisting that community and religious groups (its main sponsors) reform it. For example, minority groups could demand that work assignments benefit the offender and her community, rather than merely enhancing the middle-class or suburban communities where most victims live. Just as mediation now provides for a full airing of the victim's story, mediation should allow the offender's history be heard as well. If the offender is inarticulate, someone should be appointed to speak for him, so that those present become better informed of the social conditions that give rise to crime in a substantial sector of the population. Optimistically, this knowledge will inspire further social reform.

Short- and Long-Term Strategies

In short, persons dissatisfied with both approaches to criminal justice should adopt a short-term and a long-term strategy. The short-term would consist of steering defendants to the system where they are likely to experience the fairest treatment. The long-term strategy would focus on forcing dialog and competition between the two systems, drawing comparisons between them, making criticism overt, and attempting to engraft the best features of each onto the other. This frank merging and borrowing should promote dialog between practitioners of conventional, courtroom justice and informal mediation—something that, except in a few locations, is not taking place now. Both systems should be made to compete with each other for resources, participants, and approval in the eyes of the various constituencies that make up the criminal law's public.

This process, if carried out persistently and intelligently, can harness two principal theories for controlling prejudice—confrontation and social contact—by challenging the conventional system and the emerging one, reminding each of its myths and values, and demanding that each equal or exceed the other in pursuit of the common goal of racial and social justice. Ultimately, no form of criminal justice, either of the traditional or the restorative variety, will work if the target community lacks a hand in designing and operating it. Blacks, Latinos, whites, middle-class, and blue-collar people must be permitted, indeed encouraged, to work together to counter exploitative arrangements that oppress them and render our society one of the most fearful and crime-ridden in the Western developed world. ■

Critiquing the Critics
A Brief Response to Critics of Restorative Justice

Allison Morris

It is not unusual in the criminological literature to come across claims that 'reforms' have had unanticipated and negative consequences and this claim has been made with respect to restorative justice. Levrant, for example, recently described restorative justice as perhaps doing 'more harm than good'. Similarly, Johnstone cautions that we 'need to be alert to the ways in which it [restorative justice] could make things worse' and details a

Allison Morris, "Critiquing the Critics: A Brief Response to Critics of Restorative Justice," *British Journal of Criminology*, Volume 42 (2002): 596–615. Reprinted by permission of Oxford University Press.

'whole range of deleterious consequences' which might result from a shift to restorative justice. . . . And Delgado asserts that restorative justice renders 'a disservice to victims, offenders and society at large'.

In a related vein, some writers have also questioned whether or not the values of restorative justice can be translated into practical reality. Levrant, for example, described restorative justice as 'an unproved movement that risks failure' and claimed that its appeal 'lies more in its humanistic sentiments than in any empirical evidence of its effectiveness'. Kurki argued that 'there is not yet evidence that the experience yields better results'. . . . This paper takes issue with these various claims.

I acknowledge that the restorative justice literature is plagued with imprecision and confusion and I do not seek to defend all practices that claim to be restorative justice. These are as diverse as conferencing, victim-offender mediation, sentencing circles, community reparation boards, restitution programmes and much more. I acknowledge also that there is a risk that restorative justice advocates may claim too much. Thus I also try in this paper to make clear what, in my view, restorative justice represents. It seems to me that much of the critique that has emerged is based on fundamental misunderstandings of what restorative justice seeks to achieve, on diluted or distorted applications of the principles of restorative justice or on the misinterpretation of empirical research on restorative justice.

In addition, this paper considers more briefly a very different type of critique: philosophical rather than empirical. Just deserts theorists have argued that the sanctions agreed to within a restorative justice framework may not be proportionate to the severity of the offence and are unlikely to be consistent: offenders involved in similar offending may end up with different sanctions. . . . This paper takes issue with these claims and argues that restorative justice has to be evaluated against the values it represents and not against those it attacks and seeks to replace. . . .

Restorative Justice Values, Processes and Practices

Although restorative justice values, processes and practices have been around for a long time, there was a resurgence of interest in them internationally in the 1990s, in part as a response to the perceived ineffectiveness and high cost (in both human and financial terms) of conventional justice processes and in part as a response to the failure of conventional systems to hold offenders accountable in meaningful ways or to respond adequately to victims' needs and interests. Conventional justice systems see offending primarily (and often even exclusively) as a violation of the interests of the state and decisions about how it should be responded to are made by professionals representing the state. In contrast, restorative justice returns decisions about how best to deal with the offence to those most affected — victims, offenders and their 'communities of care' — and gives primacy to their interests. Thus the state no longer has a monopoly over decision making; the principal decision makers are the parties themselves. In a sense, the state's role — or the role of its representatives—is redefined: for example, they give information, they deliver services and they provide resources. Restorative justice also emphasizes addressing the offending and its consequences (for victims, offenders and communities) in meaningful ways; attempting to reconcile victims, offenders and their communities through trying to reach agreements about how best to deal with the offending; and attempting to reintegrate or reconnect both victims and offenders at the local community level through trying to heal the harm and hurt caused by the offending and through trying to take steps to prevent its recurrence.

Restorative justice also emphasizes human rights and the need to recognize the impact of social or substantive injustice and in small ways address these rather than simply provide offenders with legal or formal justice and victims with no justice at all. Thus it seeks to restore the victim's security, self-respect, dignity and, most importantly, sense of control. And it seeks to restore responsibility to offenders for their offending and its consequences, to restore a sense of control to them to make amends for what they have done and to restore a belief in them that the process and outcomes were fair and just. And, finally, restorative justice encourages cultural relativity and sensitivity rather than cultural dominance.

Thus victims, offenders and communities of care come together and, with the aid of a facilitator, try to resolve how to deal with the offence, its consequences and its implications for the future. Generally, restorative

justice offers a more informal and private process over which the parties most directly affected by the offence have more control. This does not mean that there are no rules which must be adhered to or that there are no rights which must be protected, but rather that, within a particular framework, there is the potential for greater flexibility, including cultural flexibility. Thus the procedures followed, those present and the venue are often chosen by the parties themselves. Overall, the intention—or the hope—is to create a respectful and non-shaming environment in which participants can feel comfortable and able to speak for themselves.

The aims of restorative justice meetings are primarily to hold offenders accountable for their offending in meaningful ways and to make amends to victims certainly in a symbolic sense and, where possible, in a real sense too. Restorative outcomes are sometimes viewed as focusing on apologies, reparation or community work, as ways of restoring the property stolen or of compensating the victim for the injuries endured. But, in fact, *any* outcome—including a prison sentence—can be restorative if it is an outcome agreed to and considered appropriate by the key parties. For example, it might be agreed that a prison sentence is required in a particular situation to protect society, to signify the gravity of the offending or to make amends to victims. Neither protecting society nor signifying the gravity of the offending are excluded within a restorative justice system. The difference is that the offender, victim and their communities of care have had some input in to the sentence, some increased understanding of the circumstances and consequences of the offence and, perhaps, some increased satisfaction in their dealings with the criminal justice system. Moreover, discussion of the consequences of the offences is seen as a more powerful way of communicating their gravity to offenders than simply imprisoning them.

One of the other hopes of restorative justice is that reconciliation between the offender and victim will occur. This is not always possible—victims may remain angry or bitter; offenders may remain unmoved and untouched. However, there is no doubt that reconciliation can on occasions take place between victims and offenders. Examples observed at family group conferences in New Zealand include invitations by a victim to the offender and his family to join the victim's family for a meal, hugs and handshakes all round at the end of the meeting, and victims deciding to attend the court hearing to speak on the offender's behalf.

There is no 'right way' to deliver restorative justice and this paper does not seek to argue that, for example, the New Zealand youth justice system is the 'ideal' form of restorative justice. The essence of restorative justice is not the adoption of one form rather than another; it is the adoption of *any* form which reflects restorative values and which aims to achieve restorative processes, outcomes and objectives. Restorative processes and practices, therefore, should empower offenders and victims by giving them a sense of inclusion in and satisfaction with these processes and practices; they should enable victims to feel better as a result

of participating in them; and they should hold offenders accountable in meaningful ways by encouraging them to make amends to their victims. If all these occur, we might then expect the restorative processes and practices to impact on reoffending and reintegration and to heal victims' hurt. . . .

Claim: Restorative Justice Erodes Legal Rights

A common criticism made of restorative justice is that it fails to provide procedural safeguards or to protect offenders' rights. The picture painted is that this failure is promoted by restorative justice advocates in order to obtain more readily offenders' acceptance of their responsibility for their offending and agreements among participants about how to deal with that offending. But, as the previous section made clear, restorative justice practitioners have to follow certain guidelines or practice manuals and, in some examples of restorative justice, there are statutory guidelines or regulations to follow too.

Overall, there is nothing in the values of restorative justice which would lead to a denial or erosion of offenders' legal rights (through their broad emphasis on human rights). However, different examples of restorative justice have translated the protection of offenders' rights into practice in different ways. For example, in South Australia, young people participating in conferences can consult with lawyers prior to admitting the offence and prior to agreeing with the proposed outcome though lawyers tend not to be present at the conference itself. In Real Justice conferences in the United States, lawyers at conferences have a watching brief and they can interrupt proceedings if they feel that the young person's legal rights are being breached. And, in New Zealand, if facilitators at a family group conference have any concerns about young offenders' legal rights, they may request the appointment of a lawyer (paid for by the state). In addition, young people referred to a conference by the Youth Court can have their court appointed lawyers (youth advocates) with them during the family group conference, as can adult offenders involved in the court referred restorative justice pilots.

And so it is difficult to accept, either with respect to the values of restorative justice or empirically with respect to these examples at least, the claim that restorative justice erodes offenders' rights. What restorative justice does is place a different priority on the protection of offenders' rights by not adopting a procedure whereby offenders' lawyers are the main protagonists or spokespersons and their primary purpose is to minimize the offender's responsibility or to get the most lenient sanction possible.

And, of course, it is quite farcical for critics of restorative justice to imply that, in contrast, conventional criminal justice systems adequately protect offenders' legal rights. It is uncommon for young offenders in the United States to be legally represented in the juvenile court (they tend to waive this right) and most cases in the adult criminal courts are dealt with through plea-bargaining. This is not the place to discuss plea-bargaining in any detail. Suffice to say that its principal objective is not to protect offenders' rights. . . .

Claim: Restorative Justice Results in Net-Widening

It is commonly claimed that restorative justice processes widen the net of social control because they tend to focus on minor offenders at low risk of reoffending (presumably offenders who would otherwise be warned by the police or otherwise diverted) and because they tend to result in these minor offenders being given more incursive penalties than they would otherwise receive. This is not a claim made exclusively of restorative justice, of course: it has been made about the introduction of a whole raft of diversionary practices (including with respect to the expansion of police warnings in England and Wales in the 1970s and the introduction of various alternatives to custody). The key issue in testing the validity of this claim, therefore, is the type of offenders a particular restorative justice practice is aimed at.

In New Zealand, restorative justice processes are used not for relatively minor offenders but rather for the most serious and persistent offenders in the youth justice system and for relatively serious offenders in the adult criminal justice system. Family group conferences are held for about 15–20 per cent of youth offenders; the rest are simply warned or diverted by the police. Some examples of the kinds of offenders dealt with in family group conferences there include a boy who broke into a house and raped a young woman; a group of school children who set fire to and destroyed an entire school block; a boy whose victim was beaten over the head during the process of a robbery; and a boy whose victim barely survived the assault and was left with permanent brain damage. As for the restorative justice pilots for adults, the two schemes in that evaluation dealt with aggravated robbery, threats to kill, driving causing death, driving with excess alcohol as well as the more 'routine' offences of wilful damage, theft and burglary. In the first year of the operation of the court-referred restorative justice pilots, all property offences with maximum penalties of two years' imprisonment or more and other offences with maximum penalties of one to seven years are eligible for referral to a restorative conference by the judge. Some other jurisdictions (for example, South Australia and New South Wales) also aim their restorative justice processes at medium serious juvenile offenders.

However, some examples of conferencing—particularly those which operate as part of police diversion—do focus on more minor offences and it is possible that netwidening occurs here. . . .

To repeat the point made earlier: the validity of this claim depends on the focus of particular examples of restorative justice and it certainly does not apply to all. Also, many advocates of restorative justice believe that restorative justice processes should be aimed at the more serious and persistent offenders given the practicality of limited resources and the potential in such cases for victims, offenders and communities to receive considerable benefits (in terms of having a better understanding of the offences and their consequences and of providing more opportunities for healing and reintegration).

Claim: Restorative Justice Trivializes Crime

This claim is most frequently mentioned with respect to violence against women. Critics tend to see restorative justice processes as decriminalizing men's violence against their partners and as returning it to the status of a 'private' matter. Morris and Gelsthorpe have already fully discussed this and I repeat here only the gist of their response to this criticism. Their main point is that the use of restorative justice processes does not signify the trivialization of any crime: the criminal law remains as a signifier and denouncer. In addition, however, restorative justice advocates believe that the offender's family and friends are by far the most potent agents to achieve this objective of denunciation. In the context of men's violence against their partners, denouncing the violence in the presence of the abuser's family and friends means that the message is loud and clear for those who matter most to him.

More broadly, restorative justice arguably takes crime more seriously than conventional criminal justice systems because it focuses on the consequences of the offence for victims and attempts to address these and to find meaningful ways of holding offenders accountable. Crime, on the other hand, is trivialized by processes in which victims have no role (apart, in some situations, as witnesses) and in which offenders are not much more than passive observers.

A slightly different but important point for questioning the legitimacy of this claim that restorative justice processes decriminalizes men's violence against their partners is that, for a range of reasons, only a few of the women who experience violence at the hands of their male partners rely on the law, police or courts to deal with it, at least in the first instance. The introduction of restorative justice processes in such cases, on the other hand, at the very least would increase women's choices and, through this involvement of friends and families, might well result in increasing women's safety. In this way, arguably, restorative justice could empower women.

Claim: Restorative Justice Fails to 'Restore' Victims and Offenders

By definition, we would expect restorative justice to 'restore' and it has to be accepted that there is some haziness in the restorative justice literature about what precisely this means. But, as noted earlier, for victims, I take it to mean restoring the victim's security, self-respect, dignity and sense of control. There is no doubt that research shows that victims who have taken part in restorative justice processes have high levels of satisfaction with reparative agreements, have reduced levels of fear and seem to have an improved understanding of why the offence occurred and its likelihood of recurrence. It is true, as some critics allege, that full monetary restoration is not always achieved as many offenders have limited resources. However, if we as a community take restorative justice seriously, this type of restoration could, and perhaps should, be a community (state) responsibility. But, more importantly, research consistently suggests that monetary restoration is not what victims want: they are much more interested in emotional reparation than material. Now, of course, emotional reparation also does

not always happen. But it seems to happen more often in restorative justice processes than it does not. And it certainly happens more often there than in conventional criminal justice processes. Overall, Latimer *et al.* concluded, on the basis of their recent meta-analysis of 22 studies, which examined the effectiveness of 35 restorative justice programmes, that victims who participated in restorative processes were significantly more satisfied than those who participated in the traditional justice system.

For offenders, again as noted earlier, I take restoration to mean restoring responsibility to them for their offending and its consequences, restoring a sense of control to them to make amends for what they have done and restoring a belief in them that the process and outcomes were fair and just. The evidence seems clear that this can occur. Maxwell and Morris, for example, showed that young offenders felt reasonably involved in the decisions being made in family group conferences in New Zealand. More recent data on just over 300 young people who were involved in family group conferences in New Zealand in 1998 shows, after preliminary analysis, that over half said they felt involved in making decisions; that more than two thirds said they had had the opportunity to say what they wanted to; that over 80 per cent said that they understood the decision; and that two thirds said that they agreed with the decision. Recent Australian research refers to young offenders seeing conferencing as fair and being satisfied with both conference processes and outcomes.

However, I also take 'restoring' to mean redressing the harms caused both by and to the offender. This means that action needs to be taken to address both the factors underlying their offending in the first place and the consequences of that offending. A process, no matter how inclusionary, and an outcome, no matter how reparative, is not likely to magically undo the years of social marginalization and exclusion experienced by so many offenders or remove the need for victims to receive long-term support or counselling. Restoration requires an acceptance by the community more generally that the offender has tried to make amends and the provision of programmes that address drug and alcohol abuse, the lack of job skills and so on. It also requires effective help and support for victims. And so here the critics of restorative justice may have a valid point to make—restorative justice is not 'restoring' offenders if they cannot access such programmes and is not 'restoring' victims if they cannot access what they need. However, the critics are aiming at the wrong target. Good programmes addressing the reasons underlying offending and effective support for victims need to accompany good restorative justice processes and practices, but providing (or at least funding) them is a state responsibility.

Claim: Restorative Justice Fails to Effect Real Change

Most critics of restorative justice are sceptical about what it has achieved. Of course, most examples of restorative justice have not been in existence for long enough to track the extent to which the kinds of transformations envisaged by advocates have actually occurred. The New Zealand youth justice system—implemented in 1989—is an exception. The implementation of restorative justice there has resulted in significant and real changes: fewer young offenders now appear in courts, fewer young offenders are now placed in residences and fewer young offenders are now sentenced to custody. This all, of course, had to result in considerable cost savings. The two restorative justice pilot schemes evaluated by Maxwell *et al.* also showed significant savings over those matched offenders dealt with entirely by the criminal courts: fewer offenders in one pilot were returned to court for sentence and fewer offenders in the other pilot received custodial penalties when compared with their matched controls.

The major claim made by critics here, however, is that restorative justice has failed to reduce reoffending. It could reasonably be argued that reducing reoffending is not really an objective of restorative justice; its focus is holding offenders accountable and making amends to victims. However, it can also be reasonably argued, at least in principle, that if a particular process reflects restorative values and achieves restorative outcomes then we might expect reoffending to be reduced. Thus, if the offender accepts responsibility for the offending, feels involved in the decision about how to deal with that offending, feels treated fairly and with respect, apologizes and makes amends to the victim and takes part in a programme designed to deal with the reasons underlying his or her offending, then we could at least predict that s/he will be less likely to offend again in the future.

Critics of restorative justice feel otherwise, principally, it seems, because the assumed features of restorative justice do not coincide with the principles of effective treatment. I need to make three points in response.

First, it is quite possible for the parties to reach an agreement, after a restorative process, which would involve a rehabilitative outcome based on the principles of effective treatment (as well as or instead of a reparative or, for that matter, a punitive outcome). I referred to this earlier in the discussion about 'restoring' offenders.

Second, critics seem to have confused here restorative justice processes and restorative outcomes and to have ignored the possibility that both may impact on reoffending. There is now some evidence of the importance of process in shaping attitudes and behaviour. Maxwell and Morris, for example, found that a number of restorative justice related factors were predictive of young people who had been involved in family group conferences in New Zealand not being reconvicted some six years later. These were: feeling remorse; not being made to feel a bad person; feeling involved in the decision making; agreeing with the outcome; and meeting the victim and apologising to him/her.

Third, and more importantly, there is now a considerable amount of research which suggests that restorative justice processes and outcomes can reduce reconviction. Indeed, Latimer *et al.*'s meta-analysis concluded that, on average, restorative justice programmes had lower reconviction rates than conventional criminal justice approaches. Compared to comparison or control groups, offenders who participated in restorative justice programmes were significantly more successful at

remaining crime free during the follow up periods. And, importantly, there are no studies that I am aware of that found that restorative justice processes actually increased recidivism rates.

Claim: Restorative Justice Results in Discriminatory Outcomes

Critics here claim that affluent communities are more likely to have the resources to develop restorative justice alternatives and that restorative justice reinforces existing race and class biases in the criminal justice system by excluding certain types of offenders from restorative justice processes. The validity of this claim again depends on how (and where) the restorative justice process is implemented. It is certainly *possible* for restorative justice programmes to be set up on an ad hoc and selective basis. But this is not the result of endorsing restorative justice principles or values and so this criticism cannot be made with respect to restorative justice generally.

To again take New Zealand as an example: conferencing for young offenders there operates on a statutory basis, nationwide and, in certain circumstances, referral to a family group conference is mandatory. In many Australian states, restorative justice processes are also based in statute and operate state-wide. Referral to a conference, however, tends to be discretionary and there are suggestions that certain categories of offenders (Aboriginals) are under-represented in conferencing in some Australian states and are more likely to be referred directly to courts.

In contrast, Maori (the indigenous people of New Zealand) are over-rather than under—represented in New Zealand restorative processes (because they are over-represented in the youth justice and criminal justice systems). However, on the basis of a recent analysis of young people referred to family group conferences in 1998, there is no evidence that Maori young offenders are dealt with differently from non-Maori offenders. Apparent differences are satisfactorily explained by differences in the extent, nature and seriousness of offending by Maori. And, of course, restorative justice processes were specifically introduced in New Zealand to make the youth justice system more culturally appropriate and more culturally sensitive, something which conventional criminal justice systems have found virtually impossible to achieve.

Claim: Restorative Justice Extends Police Powers

This criticism seems aimed primarily at the experiments in Australia, England and Wales and the Unites States with restorative conferencing located as part of police diversion. There, to the extent that the police dominate outcomes, it could be argued that police powers have been extended because they virtually become 'sentencers' as well as prosecutors. However, because of this, not all commentators see these examples of conferencing as meeting restorative values. The earlier comments on net-widening are relevant to these conferences too.

On the other hand, family group conferencing in New Zealand can be seen as *curtailing* police powers. The police there cannot refer young people who have not been arrested directly to the Youth Court. They must first refer the young person to a family group conference. If the conference feels it can resolve the matter without it going to court, then that is the end of it. Thus, again, this criticism is valid only to the extent that particular programmes are not based on restorative justice principles or values—the empowerment of the key participants—and is not, therefore, valid with respect to all examples of restorative justice.

Claim: Restorative Justice Leaves Power Imbalances Untouched

A common argument against the use of restorative justice is the imbalance between supposedly powerless offenders and supposedly powerful victims. However, neither the category 'offender' nor the category 'victim' is as clear cut as this: contrast, for example, the case of a middle-class conman and an elderly pensioner who is defrauded of her life savings; the case of a women abused over many years by her partner; the case of the 14-year-old immigrant boy beaten by the white racist; the female shoplifter who steals some baby-food from a large chain store to feed her hungry baby; and the drug addict who steals money from his mother. The power relationship between the victim and the offender in each of these examples is very different. But that is not the main point that I want to make here.

Within a restorative justice framework, power imbalances can be addressed by ensuring procedural fairness, by supporting the less powerful, and by challenging the more powerful. Thus restorative justice processes can provide a forum in which victims can make clear to offenders and, importantly, to their friends and families the effects of the offence on them but it can also provide a forum in which offenders can give victims some insight into the reasons for their offending. Facilitators of restorative justice processes have a responsibility to create an environment that ensures that both victims and offenders can freely participate, by whichever way is necessary. In contrast, power imbalances between defendants and professionals are entrenched in conventional criminal justice systems and the image of an adversarial struggle between two lawyers of equal might is a fiction. . . .

Claim: Restorative Justice Fails to Provide 'Justice'

As noted earlier, just deserts theorists argue that the sanctions agreed to within a restorative justice framework may not be proportionate to the severity of the offence and are unlikely to be consistent. Such criticisms can be responded to in a number of ways. First, judges in conventional criminal justice processes do not always deal with like cases alike. However, that is hardly an adequate response.

Second, and related to the above point, the different reasons for these inconsistencies are crucially important. Inconsistencies on the basis of gender, ethnicity or socioeconomic status per se—which is what research on conventional criminal justice systems points to—can never be right. Inconsistencies between outcomes which are the result of genuine and uncoerced agreement between the key parties, including victims, may be.

Third, restorative justice is premised on consensual decision making. It requires all the key parties—the victims, offenders and their communities of care—to agree on the appropriate outcome. The state continues to remain a party to decision making through its representatives—for example, the police or the judiciary—depending on the location of the particular restorative justice process in the criminal justice system. But what is different is that these representatives are not the 'primary' decision makers.

Finally, consistency and proportionality are constructs that serve abstract notions of justice. Ashworth and von Hirsch refer to desert theory providing 'principled and fair guidance'. But there are a number of criticisms that can be made of this: in particular, the oversimplification of the gradation of offences. There are some writers on restorative justice who refer in similar terms to 'uniformity', 'fairness' and 'equity' as means of ensuring that outcomes for offenders are not disproportionate to their culpability. But, in my view, uniformity or consistency of approach (as opposed to uniformity or consistency in outcomes) is what is required and this is achieved by always taking into account the needs and wishes of those most directly affected by the offence: victims, offenders and their communities of care. Specifically from a restorative perspective, desert theory does not provide outcomes that are meaningful to them. Indeed, desert theory is silent on why equal justice for offenders should be a higher value than equal justice (or, indeed, any kind of justice at all) for victims.

Conclusion

. . . Tracy writes we have experienced hundreds of years of the harmful consequences of a retributive justice system that has 'handed down a legacy of oppression against women, people of colour, and impoverished people'. And Delgado describes the (American) criminal justice system as 'perhaps the most inegalitarian and racist structure in society'. Schiff and Bazemore are surely right when they state that 'it is one thing to point out that after ten years of full implementation, restorative justice has failed to resolve pervasive justice system problems ... It is quite another to *blame* such longstanding problems on restorative and community justice'. ...

This review suggests that we have to contrast what restorative justice has achieved and may still achieve with what the alternative has achieved. At the very least, restorative justice offers us a new mode of thinking about crime and justice and a way of challenging conventional justice systems to address its failings. However, it offers much more. There is strong evidence that, at a general level, restorative justice offers more to victims than traditional criminal justice processes—they have high levels of satisfaction with reparative agreements; they have reduced levels of fear; and they seem to have an improved understanding of

why the offence occurred and its likelihood of recurrence. There is also strong evidence that, at a general level, restorative justice expects more of offenders than traditional criminal justice processes—they feel involved in the process; they have the opportunity to say what they wanted to; they understand and agree with the decisions made about how best to deal with the offending; they see restorative justice processes and outcomes as fair; and they are satisfied with both these processes and outcomes. Research has also shown that restorative justice processes and outcomes can result in fewer people appearing in the criminal courts and fewer people being sentenced to residential or custodial sentences. This consequently results in cost savings. In addition, research has shown that restorative justice processes and outcomes can impact on reoffending when compared with matched offenders dealt with solely in the criminal courts. Thus, there are many reasons to feel encouraged. Now it is time to present a challenge to the critics of restorative justice: what have conventional criminal justice systems achieved in the last ten years or so? I doubt it is as much. ∎

▨ The Continuing Debate

What Is New

Australia, New Zealand, and Canada have probably made the most extensive use of restorative justice processes. Perhaps the best known use of the model is the work of the Truth and Reconciliation Commission in South Africa, which used a restorative model to deal with the many crimes and atrocities of the earlier apartheid government. Though the Commission achieved some remarkable successes, it was severely limited by the fact that the white minority community still had great economic and military power, and the new government was not sufficiently strong to ensure that the politicians, army officers, and policemen of the brutal apartheid regime would be brought to justice; and therefore some of the worst offenders avoided the Commission altogether. (Because of the limited power and resources of the Commission, some argue that it should not count as a genuine restorative justice program, though it shared the restorative justice ideals.) As Bishop Desmond Tutu (Chair of the Commission) stated in the Foreword of the Commission Report, "by and large, the white community failed to take advantage of the Truth and Reconciliation process," though "mercifully there have been glorious exceptions." However, other restorative justice programs—Canada and New Zealand offer good examples—have had strong support and significant success (for example, in reducing recidivism of offenders).

Where to Find More

An excellent introduction to restorative justice is Gerry Johnstone, editor, *A Restorative Justice Reader: Texts, Sources, Contexts* (Cullompton, Devon UK: Willan Publishing, 2003). Johnstone also wrote his own examination of restorative justice: *Restorative Justice: Ideas, Values, Debates* (Cullompton, Devon UK: Willan Publishing, 2002). Another good anthology is Elmar G. M. Weitekamp and Hans-Jürgen Kerner, editors, *Restorative Justice: Theoretical Foundations* (Cullompton, Devon UK: Willan Publishing, 2002). An anthology that focuses on restorative justice in juvenile cases is Gordon Bazemore and Lode Walgrave, editors, *Restorative Juvenile Justice: Repairing the Harm of Youth Crime* (Monsey, NY: Criminal Justice Press, 1999); see the essay by Elmar G. M. Weitekamp, "The History of Restorative Justice," for a good survey of the program.

John Braithwaite is one of the leading advocates of restorative justice; see his *Crime, Shame, and Reintegration* (Cambridge: Cambridge University Press, 1989); "Restorative Justice: Assessing Optimistic and Pessimistic Accounts," *Crime and Justice: A Review of Research*, Volume 25 (1999): 1–110; *Restorative Justice and Response Regulation* (Oxford: Oxford University Press, 2002); and "Setting Standards for Restorative Justice," *British Journal of Criminology*, Volume 42 (2002): 563–577. See also Carter Hay, "An Exploratory Test of Braithwaite's Reintegrative Shaming Theory," *Journal of Research in Crime and Delinquency*, Volume 38 (2001): 132–153.

Critics of restorative justice include Sharon Levrant, Francis T. Cullen, Betsy Fulton, and John F. Wozniak, "Reconsidering Restorative Justice: The Corruption of Benevolence Revisited?" *Crime and Delinquency*, Volume 45, Number 1 (January 1999): 3–27; G. Pavlich, *Justice Fragmented: Mediating Community Disputes Under Postmodern Conditions* (London: Routledge, 1996); and D. Miers, "An International Review of Restorative Justice," Crime Reduction Series Paper 10 (London: Home Office, 2001).

Desmond Tutu, *No Future Without Forgiveness* (New York: Doubleday, 1999), is the classic source for the South African Truth and Reconciliation Commission; see also Alex Boraine, *A Country Unmasked: Inside South Africa's Truth and Reconciliation Commission* (Oxford: Oxford University Press, 2001).

Restorative Justice programs in Canada are examined in Robin J. Wilson, Bria Huculak, and Andrew McWhinnie, "Restorative Justice Innovations in

Canada," *Behavioral Sciences and the Law*, Volume 20 (2002): 363–380. A good overview of restorative justice in Canada is available online at http://www. justice.gc.ca/en/ps/voc/rjpap.html. Also available online from the Canadian Department of Justice is a helpful brief fact sheet on restorative justice; go to http://www.justice.gc.ca/en/ps/voc/rest_just.html. The Conflict Resolution Network has excellent detailed material on restorative justice programs in Canada; it is at http://www.crnetwork.ca/RJ/. A good essay on Canadian restorative justice programs, prepared by the Canadian Resource Centre for Victims of Crime, can be found at http://www.crcvc.ca/docs/restjust.pdf. The Correctional Service of Canada also has online information on restorative justice, at http://www.csc-scc.gc.ca/text/portals/rj/index_e.shtml. The Centre for Restorative Justice has an excellent website, with many links and papers. It is operated by the Simon Fraser University School of Criminology, and can be found at http://www.sfu.ca/crj/popular.html. Information on restorative justice in New Zealand (which has been particularly effective in dealing with youthful offenders) can be found at http://www.justice.govt.nz/restorative-justice/parta.html.

DEBATE 9

Should Shaming Be an Element of Criminal Punishment?

Legitimate Criminal Punishment Requires Shaming the Person Convicted

Advocate: Dan M. Kahan, Elizabeth K. Dollard Professor of Law, Yale Law School.

Source: "Punishment Incommensurability," *Buffalo Criminal Law Review*, Volume 1 (1998): 691–709.

There Are No Positive Grounds for Shaming Punishments

Advocate: Michael Tonry, Marvin J. Sonosky Professor of Law and Public Policy at University of Minnesota Law School.

Source: From "Formerly Unthinkable Policies," in *Thinking About Crime: Sense and Sensibility in American Penal Culture* (New York: Oxford University Press, 2004): 156–167.

Shaming punishments may seem a relic of a harsh and primitive era, but some people—including some judges—wish to revive punitive measures that are primarily designed to publicly shame the offender: punishments like standing in public with signs stating what crimes they have committed (such as shoplifting). Last year, the state of Tennessee passed legislation requiring those convicted of DUI violations to spend three supervised sessions picking up litter along public highways while wearing a bright vest stating (in bold letters) "I AM A DRUNK DRIVER."

There are two fundamentally different concepts of shaming, with very different purposes and methods: *reintegrative* shaming as distinguished from *disintegrative* shaming. In disintegrative shaming, the offender is made an object of ridicule and contempt: someone who is used as a punitive object lesson to reaffirm the importance of the community standards the offender violated. In reintegrative shaming—which some restorative justice theorists, such as Braithwaite, consider an important element of restorative justice—the offender is not so much shamed by society as by the recognition of falling short of community standards which the offender shares and embraces. While in reintegrative shaming, shame and repentance are elements of restoration of the offender to the community, disintegrative shaming labels the offender as different and despised. Moreover, in reintegrative shaming, the shame is temporary, rather than a long-term shaming that makes one a pariah to the community; and the shame is followed by forgiveness and repentance and reintegration into the society.

Disintegrative shaming is sometimes celebrated as a way of affirming the values the offender has violated, and using the offender for that purpose. Whatever its effectiveness in value affirmation, it seems unlikely to have a successful deterrent effect on the shamed offender. To the contrary, it may drive the offender into a despised subculture that rejects the values of society and bands together in defiance of those values (for example, a subculture of pedophiles).

The basic advantage of disintegrative shaming punishments is their cost. Public humiliation is less expensive than incarceration. The basic objection to shaming punishments is that they attack the dignity of the offender: they humiliate and dehumanize the offender. And they draw the larger public into this process of humiliation by making them witnesses to the spectacle. A further objection is that such sentences tend to be "quirky" and thus undermine the principle of uniform justice. As Jonathan Turley stated (in a September 18, 2005, *Washington Post* editorial): "Once you allow judges to indulge their own punitive fantasies, defendants become their personal playthings—freaks on a leash to be paraded at the judges' pleasure." And finally, shaming punishments often carry over to the family of the shamed offender.

▥ Points to Ponder

- Suppose that David has shoplifted several items from the local grocery store, and has been found guilty of that offense. The judge offers David a *choice*: spend two weekends walking around the parking lot of the store carrying a large sign saying "I am a shoplifter" or go to jail for one month. Does being offered a choice make the shaming punishment better?
- Suppose that your friend David has been sentenced to spend the weekend walking with a sign in front of the grocery store. You were not aware of David's shoplifting conviction, nor did you know that he would be carrying a sign. You stop by the grocery, and as you walk toward the grocery you encounter your friend David and his sign, and you (an innocent person) are profoundly embarrassed. Is that a reason against shaming punishments? A trivial and unimportant and irrelevant issue? A part of your duty as an upright, law-abiding citizen?
- David's shoplifting offense occurred in his hometown, one hundred miles from the university he attends; and only one other student at David's university knows about his shoplifting conviction. However, that one person happens to work as a reporter for the college newspaper, and he's home on

the weekend that David carries his sign. The reporter snaps a photo, and the newspaper runs a large picture of David and the shoplifting sign on its front page, and David's shaming experience becomes much more severe. Is that legitimate? Should shaming be restricted? *Could* it be restricted?

- Restorative justice programs (as discussed in Debate 8) often include some element of shaming. What is the difference between shaming as integrated into a restorative justice program and shaming as advocated by Dan Kahan?
- Are shaming punishments—of the sort favored by Kahan—likely to help in the rehabilitation of offenders? If research showed that such punishments do *not* play any positive role in rehabilitation, would that change Kahan's opinion of shaming punishments?

Punishment Incommensurability

Dan M. Kahan

The Alternative Sanctions Puzzle

Why do American jurisdictions insist on imprisoning so many offenders who don't need to be incapacitated and who could be effectively disciplined by alternatives such as fines and community service? I'll call this the alternative sanctions puzzle. My goal in this article is to develop the theoretical resources necessary to solve it.

The proposition that the United States relies excessively on imprisonment shouldn't be controversial. Leaving aside capital punishment, incarceration might be the only option for many violent offenders, including murderers, rapists, and armed robbers.

But they make up less than half the American prison population. The rest have engaged in nonviolent offenses—from larceny, to fraud, to drug distribution, to drunk driving. The short terms of imprisonment they typically receive deter no more effectively than fines and community service, yet are much more costly for society, not to mention harsher for offenders. Theorists of nearly every ideological stripe are thus united in their support for alternative sanctions.

Notwithstanding this expert consensus, however, the call for alternative sanctions has fallen on deaf ears, politically speaking. In the last decade, prison sentences have been dramatically

Dan M. Kahan, "Punishment Incommensurability," *Buffalo Criminal Law Review*, Volume 1, Number 2 (Jan 1998): 691–709. Copyright © 1998 by University of California Press – Journals. Reproduced with permission of University of California Press – Journals in the format Textbook via Copyright Clearance Center.

lengthened for many offenses and extended to others that have traditionally been punished only with fines and probation. Large fines have also become common—especially in federal criminal law—but almost exclusively as supplements to imprisonment, not as substitutes for it. Similarly, community service is now a common disposition, but mainly as an additional punishment for offenders who would otherwise have received straight probation.

Solving the alternative sanctions puzzle requires identifying the cause of the public's disagreement with the experts. The experts blame the public, whom they see as too uninformed or too vindictive to see the benefits of prison's rivals. I want to suggest that it's the experts who are at fault for overlooking a phenomenon that I'll call punishment incommensurability.

The conventional defense of alternative sanctions assumes that all forms of punishment are commensurable—or fungible—along the dimension of severity. The primary function of imprisonment, on this view, is to make offenders suffer. The threat of such discomfort is intended to deter criminality, and the imposition of it to afford a criminal his just deserts. But liberty deprivation, the defenders of alternative sanctions point out, is not the only way to make criminals uncomfortable. On this account, it should be possible to translate any particular term of imprisonment into alternative sanctions that impose an equal amount of suffering. The alternatives, moreover, should be preferred whenever they can feasibly be imposed and whenever they cost less than the equivalent term of imprisonment.

What this account misses is the social meaning of punishment.

Punishment is not just a way to make offenders suffer; it is a special social convention that expresses moral condemnation. Not all modes of suffering express condemnation or express it in the same way. The message of condemnation is very clear when society sentences an offender to prison. But when it merely fines him for the same act, the message is likely to be different: you may do what you have done, but must pay for the privilege. Because community service penalties involve activities that conventionally entitle someone to respect and admiration, they also fail to express condemnation in an unambiguous way. It is this gap between the suffering that a sanction imposes and the meaning that it has for society that makes imprisonment and alternative sanctions incommensurable: because imprisonment and its rivals don't say the same thing, no politically acceptable exchange rate can be constructed between them for purposes of criminal punishment.

The remainder of this essay cashes out these claims. The next part develops the related concepts of social meaning and incommensurability, and briefly spells out their significance for criminal law. The two after that use these concepts to explain the political unacceptability of fines and community service. The penultimate one shows how the constraint of punishment incommensurability can be overcome through shaming penalties. And the final sums up.

Social Meaning and Incommensurability

Actions have meanings, as well as consequences. Many of the roles we occupy (spouse, parent, teacher) and goods we value (love, dignity, status) are constructed by social norms. Against the background of these norms, actions become invested with meaning; they signify to others what a person (or community) believes and cares about. From our friends, for example, we expect shared time and experience; thus, a person's failure to share time and experiences with others—because, say, she is preoccupied with her professional life—conveys that she either doesn't value them as friends or doesn't really know how to.

Two goods can be said to be commensurable if their respective worth can be assessed according to a common unitary metric, such as monetary value; they are incommensurable if their relative worth cannot be assessed in this way. It should be obvious that commensurability of this sort is context-, purpose-, and community-specific. For a commercial dealer, two antiques may be commensurable in terms of their cash value. But for another person, the same two pieces may be incommensurable if one of them is a family heirloom; what the heirloom signifies for her may have a value that cannot be reproduced by other antiques or by any amount of money.

The phenomena of social meaning and incommensurability constrain rational choice (individual and collective). Generalizing, it is irrational to treat goods as commensurable where the use of a quantitative metric effaces some dimension of meaning essential to one's purposes or goals. It would be irrational, for example, for a person who wanted to be a good colleague within an academic community to offer another scholar cash instead of comments on her manuscript. Against the background of social norms, the comment's signification of respect cannot be reproduced by any amount of money; even to attempt the substitution conveys that the person does not value his colleague in the way appropriate to their relationship.

Punishment has a distinctive social meaning. By imposing the proper form and degree of affliction, society morally condemns the wrongdoer and reaffirms the worth of the crime victim. Moreover, this expressive function of punishment can't be flatly equated with the suffering an affliction imposes. As Henry Hart pointed out in a famous essay, military service might in some sense be equivalent to imprisonment if we consider their effect on a person's liberty. But the reason that only imprisonment and not conscription is regarded as punishment is that against the background of social norms, only imprisonment expresses society's authoritative moral condemnation.

The meanings of different forms of affliction constrain society's options for constructing punishments. Just as it would be irrational for a person who wishes to express respect and affection for a friend to offer her money rather than shared experiences, so would it be irrational for society to attempt to express condemnation of a wrongdoer through an affliction that does not have that signification within a particular cultural setting. Punishment, as a language, has a vocabulary uniquely suited for getting its meaning across.

When those who try to speak the language of punishment use the wrong vocabulary, the problem they'll encounter is punishment incommensurability. Forms of affliction that may be equivalent for some purposes—say, for inflicting suffering or for deterring future wrongdoing—might nonetheless be radically inequivalent in expressing condemnation. Since condemning is central to what society is trying to accomplish when it punishes, substituting a form of affliction that doesn't convey that meaning for one that does is expressively irrational.

That's exactly the problem, I want to argue, for fines and community service, at least in their present forms. Unlike imprisonment, these alternative sanctions just don't express condemnation. Consequently, they turn out to be incommensurable with imprisonment along the critical dimension of social meaning.

Fines vs. Imprisonment

The imposition of a prison sentence is an unambiguous sign of society's moral disapproval. This can be linked to the sacred place of individual liberty in our culture. Because liberty is such a powerful symbol of what individuals are due in a democratic society, taking it away leaves no doubt about society's condemnation of a criminal wrongdoer.

Fines, in contrast, condemn much more ambivalently. Their expressive ambiguity is captured in the distinction that Robert Cooter has drawn between "sanctions" and "prices." Sanctions are the legal detriments that society imposes on someone for doing what's morally forbidden; prices, in contrast, are the fees or taxes that society exacts for doing what's permitted. When combined with a term of imprisonment, no one doubts that fines are sanctions—

that is, that they are being imposed for doing what's morally forbidden. But when fines are used as a substitute for imprisonment, then they look and feel more like prices. That connotation, moreover, is inconsistent with moral condemnation; while we might believe that charging a high price for a good makes the purchaser suffer, we don't condemn someone for buying what we are willing to sell.

This sensibility is at the heart of the political resistance to alternative sanctions for white collar offenders. When Congress enacted the Sentencing Reform Act, for example, it directed the Sentencing Commission to use imprisonment for white collar offenders because the fines then imposed, in Congress' words, did "not accurately reflect the seriousness of [white collar] offenses." In other words, different penalties can reflect different attitudes toward crime, and fines just don't reflect how seriously society takes white collar crimes.

Private citizens often say the same thing. The use of a fine for an affluent white collar offender, for example, typically provokes the outraged retort that the offender is being permitted to "buy his way out" of the consequences of his actions. If the offense was committed in the course of commercial activities, then a fine is likely to be deribed as merely the "cost of doing business." These, too, are objections to the social meaning of fines.

Criminologists Anthony Doob and Voula Marinos provide compelling empirical confirmation of this sensibility. Doob and Marinos presented test subjects with a list of crimes and asked them to identify which ones could appropriately be punished by fines alone. For a great number of offenses, the majority of respondents indicated that no fine—of any amount—would be an appropriate substitute for a prison sentence. It might be fair to assume that the respondents demanded prison for violent offenses in order to incapacitate; but other offenses for which they also viewed fines to be inappropriate—including nonconsensual sexual touching and cocaine distribution—were relatively nonviolent. In addition, when told to assume that stipulated prison sentences were appropriate for the same offenses, the respondents were able to specify appropriate alternative fines for some but not for others.

These and like findings suggest that a politically acceptable exchange rate for fines and imprisonment cannot be constructed for at least some serious offenses. Such a translation may be possible for certain, relatively trivial offenses, but for those that exceed a certain threshold of seriousness, no fine of any amount will adequately satisfy the demand for appropriate condemnation. . . .

Punishment incommensurability has important normative as well as descriptive implications. The standard retributive critique of fines is that they don't make offenders suffer enough. A related point is that they create inequality by treating affluent white collar offenders less severely than common offenders, who are likely to be too poor to pay a large fine or too violent not to require imprisonment for purposes of incapacitation.

The standard reply to this argument asserts punishment commensurability. If potential offenders would be as deterred by a particular fine as they would by a particular term of imprisonment, it can be inferred that losing that amount of money hurts them just as much as that amount of incarceration. By thus fashioning a proper exchange rate between imprisonment and fines, and imposing the latter whenever feasible, society would get equal retribution at a smaller cost. Indeed, John Lott has argued that affluent offenders likely suffer more when imprisoned than do nonaffluent ones because they lose more income and endure greater reputational harm. Thus, the retributivist's narrow "same treatment" conception of equality not only raises the cost of punishment but in fact discriminates against wealthy offenders by making them suffer disproportionately relative to poor ones.

This argument fails, however, if we understand the retributivist argument in expressive terms. What makes fines (when viewed as mere prices) unacceptable is that they fail to impose the condemnation that the offender deserves, however much disutility they impose. Thus, even if the white collar offender who is fined suffers as much as the common offender who is imprisoned, the two clearly aren't being condemned equally given what these afflictions signify in our culture. And this matters to the public, which views expressing appropriate condemnation to be just as important as securing deterrence and inflicting deserved pain.

Imprisonment vs. Community Service

Community service is another alternative sanction that has failed the test of political acceptability. As with fines, the problem for community service is punishment incommensurability.

The substitution of community service for imprisonment creates dissonance. We don't ordinarily condemn individuals who work in "community-owned nursing homes, city parks, churches, local YMCA branches, . . . organizations restoring run-down and abandoned buildings for low-income housing, senior citizens' centers, day care centers, Salvation Army centers" and the like; we admire them. Because such activities just don't express condemnation, "it is difficult to conceive of them as 'punishments' at all." If society really took the offense seriously, it would select an affliction, like imprisonment, that unambiguously says as much. Against the background of social norms, community service—like fines— trivializes the magnitude of the offense and devalues the worth of the victim.

Even worse, community service conflicts with the positive connotations of nonpenal service. We expect society to punish individuals with a mode of affliction that signals their disgraceful status. Not surprisingly, then, for the law to say that being made to serve others is a fitting punishment for criminals insults the persons who voluntarily perform the same services and demeans those whom such services are meant to benefit:

> Many of us noncriminals perform community service not to avoid jail but because we want to. Perhaps the bench thinks the inconvenience of not being able to go after big bucks for a while is fitting punishment for corporate wrongdoers. I consider community service an honor that should not be tainted by judicial wrist slapping. Is this community service construed as some sort of penance, like having to recite

a string of Hail Marys? If so, what does that make the everyday jobs of drug counselors, educators and law enforcement officers in the antidrug effort? Or does such community service constitute punishment only when imposed on a bureaucrat fallen from the imperial heights? Doesn't the public have a choice? Suppose parents are less than thrilled with the idea of Mr. North doing his community service bit as part of their children's civics lesson. . . . And the downtrodden, homeless and needy—how do they feel about swarms of felons swooping down on them? What about their choices? It is important that people with short memories recall that not so long ago—but before Watergate, Iran-contra, junk bonds—community service was inspired only by public-spiritedness and generosity. Believe it or not, there are people who, without charisma or notoriety, work among the needy, not because they are sentenced to do so by a judge but rather because they are moved by the dictates of their own hearts. As a teacher, I find it insulting to my profession that this person, after pleading guilty to a felony, is going to perform in the capacity of an educator as punishment for his offense. The only risk is that [community service] will give honest labor a bad name: cleaning ladies shouldn't be tainted by their association with celebrities. Zsa Zsa Gabor should only be so lucky.

These are the dominant public criticisms of community service dispositions, and they lead again to punishment incommensurability. There isn't a politically acceptable exchange rate between imprisonment and hours of community service. For in no matter what amount it is imposed, community service (in its present form) always says the wrong thing.

Shame

So far I have argued that the social meaning of punishment creates the objective constraint of punishment incommensurability. But there is nothing intrinsically negative about my thesis. The lesson of punishment incommensurability is that substitutes for imprisonment must express comparable condemnation in order to be politically acceptable. So what we should be looking for are alternatives that meaningfully condemn.

The leading candidate is shaming penalties. Jurisdictions throughout the United States are rediscovering public humiliation as a criminal punishment. Some courts, for example, now require offenders convicted of drunk driving and other offenses to use special license plates or bumper stickers. Judges in other states make offenders buy newspaper adds, post signs on their property, or even wear distinctive items of clothing announcing their crimes. Many cities broadcast the names and pictures of offenders on public access television or display them on billboards. Others have experimented with even more innovative afflictions, including self-debasement and apology rituals.

Such penalties are being used, moreover, not just for petty misdemeanors, but for more serious offenses that would otherwise be punished by imprisonment. Examples include drunk driving, larceny, embezzlement, assault, burglary, perjury, toxic-waste dumping, and drung distribution. These are the same kinds of crimes, in essence, for which conventional alternative sanctions are typically advocated.

If we want to know why shaming penalties are succeeding where conventional alternatives have not, social meaning again supplies an answer. These punishments gratify rather than disappoint the public demand for condemnation. Like imprisonment but unlike fines and community service, shaming penalties supply an unambiguous and dramatic sign of the wrongdoer's disgrace. As a result, substituting shame for imprisonment doesn't offend the public's expressive sensibilities.

Of course, it's one thing to show that shaming penalties are politically acceptable, and another to show that they will work. There's good reason to think that mere status deprivation would furnish a powerful incentive for individuals to obey the law; but in fact, the utility of shaming penalties doesn't depend on that. For the simplest and most effective way to use shaming penalties is simply to add them to the conventional alternatives such as fines and community service. This strategy would combine the known deterrent effects of the conventional alternatives with the demonstrated political acceptability of shaming penalties.

Shame can buy political acceptability for the conventional alternatives by transforming their social meaning. Consider fines. American jurisdictions are reluctant to use fines as a substitute for imprisonment because they don't unambiguously express moral condemnation. The reluctance to fine, however, disappears when fines are used in conjunction with imprisonment. Even short terms of imprisonment unambiguously condemn, and against that background fines no longer carry a permissive connotation. The same effect can be achieved with shaming penalties. Where the law imposes shame in addition to a fine, the inference that the law is merely pricing rather than sanctioning an offender's conduct is impossible to sustain.

The meaning of community service is subject to similar reform. One way to infuse this sanction with shame is to order offenders to perform services that unambiguously denote humiliation. Some tasks, such as trash collection or manure shoveling, fit this description because they are believed intrinsically repulsive. But even services that are not inherently distasteful can acquire degrading connotations if strictly confined to criminal offenders. One municipality, for example, uses only offenders to maintain its community garden. Because it is known that only criminal offenders work there, being seen at work in the garden effectively stigmatizes offenders. And because offenders work nowhere else, the degrading connotations of such service don't demean the work performed by law-abiding members of the community.

Finally, simply changing the name of community service would likely ease some of the tension between this mode of discipline and public expressive sensibilities. A label like "shameful service" would underscore the law's commitment to distinguishing the types of affliction used to mark the disgrace of criminals from the forms of public service that ought to entitle citizens to admiration and respect.

Solving the Puzzle

The dominant position of imprisonment is usually attributed either to the public's ignorance or to its appetite for human suffering. My analysis suggests a more complicated but ultimately less disturbing explanation: punishment incommensurability. The public expects punishment not only to deter crime but to express appropriate moral condemnation. Because of the value of liberty in our culture, imprisonment unequivocally conveys society's denunciation of wrongdoers. The conventional alternatives, however, express condemnation much more ambivalently. Fines, when used in lieu of imprisonment, often imply that society is merely pricing, not sanctioning, offenders' behavior. Community service seems to suggest that society doesn't sincerely believe the offender to be vicious, or, even worse, that it doesn't genuinely respect the virtue of those who voluntarily serve the public. Whatever equivalence there might be between these sanctions and imprisonment along the dimensions of regulatory effect and pain, they will frequently remain incommensurable with imprisonment along the dimension of meaning. When this is so, they will be inadequate substitutes for imprisonment in whatever amount they are imposed.

The lesson of punishment incommensurability, in short, is that theorists must become much more sophisticated about the social meaning of punishment. To recognize that punishment is a convention for signifying condemnation is to understand punishment as a special kind of language. Just as the speaker of a real language can't hope to be understood if she uses words in an idiosyncratic way, so those who wish to reform a punishment regime can't hope to make their proposals acceptable if they advocate forms of affliction that don't express condemnation. The question confronting the proponents of alternative sanctions, then, is whether the alternatives to imprisonment can be translated into a punitive vocabulary that makes them a meaningful substitute for imprisonment.

I have tried to show that they can—through shaming penalties. These sanctions, used alone, are already proving to be a politically acceptable alternative to imprisonment for many offenses. If combined with fines and community service, moreover, these sanctions would likely resolve the expressive ambiguity that makes these sanctions incommensurable with imprisonment. At that point, we will not only have solved the alternative sanctions puzzle, but dispelled it as well. ■

Formerly Unthinkable Policies

Michael Tonry

Disintegrative Shaming

Twenty years ago, Kahan's arguments on disintegrative shaming would have been widely considered bizarre. In our time, they won him appointments at two of America's pre-eminent law schools, the University of Chicago and Yale. Though he has written about shaming repeatedly and at great length, the basic argument can be briefly summarized. Punishment is not, as most people who write about punishment theory suppose, primarily about attributions of culpability and imposition of deserved punishments,

or primarily about crime prevention, but about shaming. Most writers about punishment do not understand this, he says, and if they hope ever to influence policy must accept that punishments should "unambiguously express disgust" of the offender. Explaining, for example, that community penalties will not win public favor until they are made more debasing, he compares them unfavorably with imprisonment:

> Prison, in contrast, does unequivocally evince disgust.... By stripping individuals of liberty—a venerated symbol of individual

Michael Tonry, "Formerly Unthinkable Policies," *Thinking About Crime: Sense and Sensibility in American Penal Culture* (New York: Oxford University Press, 2004): 156–167. Reprinted by permission of Oxford University Press, Inc.

worth in our culture—and by inflicting countless other indignities—from exposure to the view of others when urinating and defecating to rape at the hand of other inmates—prison unambiguously marks the lowness of those we consign to it.

Elsewhere, he writes that offenders should be subjected to "intrinsically repulsive," "degrading," or at least "effectively stigmatizing" punishments and that, for example, community service should be renamed "shameful service."

So far as I can tell, these ideas derive from two intellectual developments of recent decades, both of which Kahan misunderstands or misinterprets. The first is increased attention to the norm-reinforcing, moral-educative, and expressive effects of punishment. Until the last ten years, most scholarly writing on punishment was by lawyers and philosophers, and they tended to concentrate on procedures and policies as they affected the convicted offender standing before the judge, or on the possible crime-reductive effects of particular sentences or policies. Since then, precipitated by sociologist David Garland's writing on the sociology of punishment and psychologist Tom Tyler's work on procedural justice, much more attention has been given to the broader normative and social-psychological effects of punishment.

The second development Kahan apparently misconceives is the growing and increasingly subtle literature on public understanding and opinion about punishment. This shows broadly that the general public believes sentences are too lenient, but it also

shows that public opinion is based on misconceptions of crime and punishment attributable to media concentration on exceptional cases, that judges' sentences are harsher than the public realizes, that the sentences citizens say they would prefer are less severe than are actually imposed, and that there is widespread support for rehabilitative programs and community penalties.

Kahan is an appropriate figure on whom to focus because, more than any other contemporary American writer, he offers views about criminal justice policy that seem best understood in terms of prevailing penal sensibilities. It is hard to imagine how else they could be explained. . . .

I discuss the intellectual backdrop to Kahan's disintegrative shaming analysis in some detail to make a general point and a specific point. The specific point is that, looked at with any care, existing systematic knowledge and research findings provide no credible evidentiary base for Kahan's proposals. The general point, however, is that proposals such as Kahan's make perfect sense, of a sort, in the context of the penal sensibilities of the last ten years.

Expressive Punishments

Three major literatures—in philosophy, criminal law theory, and sociology—have revived interest in expressive punishments. Philosophers have developed communicative theories in which a central aim of punishment is to express to the offender the wrongfulness of his or her behavior. Criminal law theorists have emphasized the role of criminal punishments in reinforcing or undermining social norms. Sociologists have investigated ways in which official responses to crime shape the ways offenders perceive the integrity of the system and have argued that more respectful, nurturing, and holistic approaches may increase offenders' prospects for achieving law-abiding lives.

Communicative Theories of Punishment The first is the development in the philosophical literature, exemplified by the writings of Antony Duff, Joel Feinberg, Jean Hampton, and Jeffrie Murphy, of "communicative" theories of punishment. All of these are moral theories, premised on respect for the moral autonomy of the offender, in Dworkin's terms showing "equal respect and concern" for each offender, and call in various ways for punishment to express to the offender the wrongfulness of his acts.

The prevailing image is of a judge, looking deeply into an offender's eyes, more in sorrow than in anger, and wanting to help her understand why what she has done is wrong. If it works, the offender will come to understand that she was temporarily distracted from right values by egoism, emotion, or impulse, and be ready to reclaim her place among right-thinking people. This will not happen because she was bullied, threatened, or brainwashed, but because as a morally autonomous person she now understands that, and why, her actions were wrong.

There are differences in view among philosophers working within the communicative punishment tradition as to whether the aim is solely to express norms to the offender, so that she as a morally responsible actor can come to understand the wrongfulness of her acts, or whether in addition there is a collateral aim through punishment to express norms to the general community as bystander. There are differences in view as to whether her regret, repentance, contrition, or remorse is a sufficient outcome or whether, for her sake or the larger society's, some material punishment should also be imposed or borne. There is also a question of how offenders who are insensitive, defiant, or impervious to moral reasoning should be handled. However, nowhere in this literature are there indications that the aim of punishment should be to express disgust of the offender or to debase her in order to placate public opinion. That, in the conventional Kantian language, would be to use the offender merely as a means, and that is something no mainstream moral theory would allow.

Moral-Educative Theories of Punishment A second relevant punishment literature derives from the Durkheimian functionalist notion that the criminal law serves to identify and reinforce basic social ideas about right and wrong, that "crime brings together upright consciences and concentrates them." The Norwegian writer Johannes Andenaes, who wrote about the "moral-educative functions" of the criminal law, was influential in reviving interest in such views. The criminal law is seen as performing a dramaturgical function, with punishment directed primarily at the community and not at the offender. Crime is a part of every human society, possibly a necessary part, a functional mechanism that helps set and then illuminate and reinforce the boundaries of acceptable behavior. The primary aim of punishment is to restate and reinforce prevailing norms: "[Punishment] does not serve, or else serves only secondarily, in correcting the culpable, or in intimidating possible followers. From this point of view, its efficacy is justly doubtful and, in any case, mediocre. Its true function is to maintain social cohesion intact."

There has been a revival of interest in Durkheimian ideas about punishment in Germany and Scandinavia, as an alternative to retributive and utilitarian ideas. Influential elaborations of such views have been offered by Finnish writers under the name "general prevention," and in Germany under the name "positive general prevention." Both traditions distinguish their neo-Durkheimian ideas from Anglo-American "(negative) general prevention," which operates through the utilitarian processes of deterrence, incapacitation, and rehabilitation.

The German and Scandinavian ideas emphasize that punishment has an important role to play in setting and reinforcing norms, but it is a secondary role. For the most part, extraordinary circumstances aside, people do or do not commit crimes because of the socialization they do or do not receive from primary institutions such as the home, the family, the church, the school, and the community. The primary work of crime prevention must be done in those places. It is important that the criminal law confirm basic behavioral norms, and be seen to do so, but the primary work must be done elsewhere. This has important, perhaps to most Americans surprising, implications.

First, because the law should perform its back-up role, it is important that criminal acts have penal consequences. As a result, although the Finns, Swedes, and other Scandinavians have among the lowest imprisonment rates in the world, expressed in terms of people in prison on an average day per 100,000 residents, they have among the highest prison admission rates in the developed world, expressed in terms of the number of people per 100,000 admitted to prison in a year.

Second, because the law should perform its back-up role, it is important that punishments be commensurate with the gravity of the offenses for which they are imposed. Put differently, proportionality is a first principle; unless more serious crimes receive harsher penalties and less serious crimes lesser ones, the law's normative messages will be morally incoherent and contradict the primary norm-setting processes.

Third, there is no reason to expect changes in the severity of penalties to be effective or desirable. If primary institutions play the major socialization roles, and punishment can only marginally reinforce or undermine prevailing norms, it would be unrealistic to imagine that changes in the severity of sanctions can have much effect. Patrik Törnudd thus observed, "A strong belief in general prevention as the guiding rationale of the criminal justice system thus does not imply that changes in policy, such as increases in the severity of punishment, would widely be seen as an appropriate or cost-effective means of controlling crime."

Once again, there is nothing here, express or implied, about debasement, disgust, or stigmatization. Indeed, since Northern European countries take seriously the European Torture Convention's prohibition of inhumane and degrading punishments, it would be surprising if there were.

Reintegrative Shaming "Reintegrative shaming" is a reconceptualization of punishment proposed by Australian criminologist John Braithwaite. The proposal is simultaneously a hypothesis that restorative responses to criminal offenders might have greater crime-reducing effects than criminal justice responses and a normative argument that reintegrative processes are more humane and respectful of human dignity.

Braithwaite's notion is that reactions to crime should simultaneously express disapprobation and support, in much the same way as parents communicate to children that they have misbehaved but that they are still loved. The "shaming" communicates through disapproval the importance of the norms or expectations that were violated but in a way that also communicates respect for the individual and concern for her well-being, and is therefore "reintegrative." This is contrasted with the destructive shaming of the traditional criminal justice system that ostracizes, alienates, and often breeds defiance or leads to rejection of pro-social norms and attachment to antisocial ones. Braithwaite has proposed a number of reasons why traditional criminal justice approaches are likely to be less effective at socializing offenders and preventing crime than are reintegrative approaches.

Even this brief summary should make it clear that Braithwaite's affirmative theories of shaming have nothing in common with Kahan's proposals which, to the contrary, embody,

even celebrate, the kind of destructive processes that Braithwaite decries.

Public Knowledge and Opinion

The second growing literature that might support Kahan's ideas, but does not, concerns public knowledge and opinion about punishment. In particular, Kahan cites a study by Canadian psychologists Anthony Doob and Voula Marinos of Canadians' support for the use of fines as punishments for various crimes. A majority of respondents indicated that, for many crimes, a fine would not be a normatively appropriate substitute for imprisonment. Tom Tyler and Robert Boeckmann's study of reasons (primarily "expressive") why ordinary people support three-strikes laws even though there are sound reasons to doubt their instrumental effectiveness offers comparable findings: imposing a lengthy prison sentence for a third violent crime sends a message people believe should be sent. Hans Boutellier and Joseph Kennedy more recently argue that punishment and crime control policy should be understood in our time as having primarily expressive functions. Kahan, drawing on a hodgepodge of newspaper clippings and letters to the editor as authority, makes similar arguments about community service.

There are serious problems with Kahan's claim that public support for punishment practices requires disintegrative shaming. It is poorly informed. A large literature shows that public attitudes are much more complex and less single-mindedly vengeful than he suggests. It is overbroad. Even if nonincarcerative punishments for some very serious crimes would, in Model Penal Code language, "unduly depreciate the seriousness of the offense," most crimes are not that serious. It is parochial. In many Western countries, fines and community service are commonly used as sanctions for quite serious, including violent and sexual, crimes.

Under-Informed The large multinational public opinion literature offers much more complicated findings than Kahan suggests. Surveys consistently show that the general public believes that the average crime is more serious than it is, substantially underestimates the severity of punishments imposed, and generally supports punishments less severe than are now imposed. The public has ambivalent views about punishment, wanting offenders to be punished for their crimes but, believing that social disadvantage and drug dependence are primary causes of offending, also wanting (and being willing to pay for) offenders to be rehabilitated. Finally, for all but the most serious crimes and the most incorrigible criminals, the public is willing to have criminals sentenced to community penalties in place of prison, so long as the community penalty is burdensome or restitutive (community service or work release coupled with restitution are okay, house arrest without more is not). Thus, while there is something to be said for Kahan's claim that the public wants symbolically appropriate punishments, that by itself is a partial and misleading summary of the evidence. None of the major scholars of public opinions and attitudes about crime interprets the preference for symbolically appropriate sentences as a demand for shaming punishments.

There is substantial evidence of public support for wider use of community services in place of incarceration for many kinds of offenders because it satisfies symbolic demands for punishments that are burdensome and express right values, and is in an important sense restitutive. To the contrary, community service is a sanction that Kahan argues must be made "degrading," "stigmatizing," "shameful," and "intrinsically repulsive" if it is to win public support.

Overbreadth Even if Kahan were right that the public insists on only prison sentences for violent crimes, most people now admitted to prisons have not been convicted of violence. In 1996, for example, of people committed to state prisons, 29.3 percent had been convicted of violent crimes, 29 percent of property crimes, 30.2 percent of drug crimes, and 11.3 percent of something else. In federal prisons the percentages, for the same categories in 1997 were 11.9 percent, 5.6 percent, 60.1 percent, and 22.4 percent. Among convicted jail inmates in 1996, the corresponding percentages were 21.8 percent, 28.6 percent, 23.7 percent, and 25.9 percent. The public opinion evidence summarized in the preceding paragraph shows that for the nearly 80 percent of people sentenced to prison for nonviolent crimes, there is broad support for increased use of nonincarcerative sanctions that do not debase.

Parochialism Experience in other countries suggests that the public would be willing to accept fines and community service as prison substitutes for all but the most serious crimes. Throughout Scandinavia and Germany, for example, day fines are the modal sanction. Day fines are penalties that take into account some measure of the offender's earnings or wealth, usually a day's net pay, and the seriousness of his crime. A moderately severe crime might generate a fine of thirty days' net pay. Day fines are used in these countries as punishments for most crimes, including many violent and sexual crimes and especially property crimes. In England, Scotland, and Holland, community service was established to serve as an alternative to prison sentences for moderately severe crimes and is used in that way.

Kahan's arguments for disintegrative shaming are not deducible from any of the important recent developments concerning expressive punishments or research on public opinion about crime and punishment. What is left is an idiosyncratic argument that offenders should be subjected to debasing, degrading punishments because, Kahan apparently believes, offenders have "failed to internalize society's moral norms" and populist appetites, however well- or ill-informed, would thereby be appeased or gratified.

All the consequences of penal sensibilities such as characterized the 1980s and 1990s need not be bad. Heightened willingness to adopt moralistic postures, harnessed properly, can be used to achieve positive social goals. The feminist movement has greatly sensitized Americans to issues of sexual exploitation and urged greater use of the law to address gender-related abuses of power and violence. Before the 1970s, people who were social policy liberals, and hence likely to be concerned with gender equity issues, were also likely to be due process liberals, and hence uncomfortable with criminal justice solutions to

social policy problems that treated offenders harshly. By the 1980s, criminalization of domestic violence became a central plank in the feminist platform and led to calls for mandatory arrest policies for alleged domestic assault misdemeanors. Reasonable people can differ, of course, as to when the criminal law should be invoked and for what kinds of cases. Since contemporary penal sensibilities make overreliance on the criminal law a recurring risk, it is possible that criminal law is being overused in our time as a response to domestic violence and that other, more nuanced, approaches in many cases would do more good and less harm.

Likewise, the modern victims' movement may owe much of its success to prevailing penal sensibilities. No informed person doubts that the victims' movement has enhanced attention to victims' interests and mobilized new resources to address victims' needs. There is no good reason why concern for fair handling of offenders implies lack of concern for victims, but it is clear that the contemporary victims' movement dates only from the 1970s. Before that, little programmatic or policy attention was given to victims issues. The overreactions associated with contemporary penal sensibilities predisposed advocates to the nonsensical view that they must be both "for" victims and "against" criminals. That dualism is not inexorable and may be moderating. As with the domestic violence movement, contemporary sensibilities appear to have mobilized and energized the victims' movement.

On balance, though, the most dramatic products of contemporary sensibilities have been negative. None of the three policies and proposals principally discussed in this chapter could have been seriously put forward in the 1950s or the 1960s. The penal sensibilities of those decades were radically different. These three policy ideas, however, stand as a stark warning about what can happen when, during a cyclical period of heightened intolerance of offenders and drug users, policy makers lose their senses of humility and proportion and lose sight of timeless values. ■

⠇⠇⠇ The Continuing Debate

What Is New

In 2005 the Ninth Circuit Court of Appeals approved shaming punishments as constitutional. In the case before the court, U.S. District Judge Vaughn Walker (in addition to imposing a prison sentence) required Shawn Gementera, who had been convicted of stealing mail, to stand outside a post office wearing a sign proclaiming, "I stole mail. This is my punishment." Gementera appealed the order to wear a sign, claiming that such humiliation constituted cruel punishment, in violation of the Eighth Amendment. Later that year, the U.S. Supreme Court rejected Gementera's appeal without comment, allowing the ruling of the Ninth Circuit Court to stand.

Where to Find More

In "What's Really Wrong with Shaming Sanctions," *Texas Law Review*, Volume 84 (2006), Kahan expresses doubts concerning his endorsement of shaming sanctions. Dan Markel, a resolute opponent of shaming punishment, maintains that Kahan's doubts about shaming do not go far enough; see "Still Wrong? Professor Kahan on the Fall of Shaming and the Rise of Restorative Justice," *Texas Law Review*, Volume 85 (May 2007). For Dan Kahan's earlier arguments in favor of shaming, see his "The Anatomy of Disgust in Criminal Law," *Michigan Law Review*, Volume 96 (1998); "What Do Alternative Sanctions Mean?" *University of Chicago Law Review*, Volume 63 (1996); and (with Eric Posner) "Shaming White Collar Criminals: A Proposal for Reform of the Federal Sentencing Guidelines," *Journal of Law and Economics*, Volume 42 (1999).

Relevant works by Michael Tonry include *Thinking About Crime: Sense and Sensibility in American Penal Culture* (Oxford: Oxford University Press, 2004); "Symbol, Substance, and Severity in Western Penal Policies," *Punishment and Society*, Volume 3, Number 4 (2001): 517–536; and "Rethinking Unthinkable Punishment Policies in America," *UCLA Law Review*, Volume 46 (1999).

Supporters of severe (disintegrative) shaming punishments include Aaron S. Book, "Shame on You: An Analysis of Modern Shame Punishment as an Alternative to Incarceration," *William and Mary Law Review*, Volume 40 (1999). Other advocates of shaming punishments include Amitai Etzioni, "Shaming

Criminals," *Current* (November 1999): 7–12; see also his book *The Monochrome Society* (Princeon, NJ: Princeton University Press, 2003).

James Q. Whitman, *Harsh Justice: Criminal Justice and the Widening Divide Between America and Europe* (Oxford: Oxford University Press, 2005), concludes that the goal of the American corrections system is to "degrade and demean" prisoners, and he traces the history that led to this result. See also his "What Is Wrong with Inflicting Shame Sanctions?" *Yale Law Review*, Volume 107 (1998).

Dan Markel is a leader of the opposition to shaming punishments; see "Are Shaming Punishments Beautifully Retributive? Retributivism and the Implications for the Alternative Sanctions Debate," *Vanderbilt Law Review*, Volume 54 (November 2001). Toni M. Massaro raises important objections to shaming sanctions in "Shame, Culture, and American Criminal Law," *Michigan Law Review*, Volume 89 (1991); and in "The Meanings of Shame: Implications for Legal Reform," *Psychology, Public Policy, and Law*, Volume 3 (1997). Paul Ziel critiques the Ninth Circuit Court of Appeals decision in *U.S. v. Gementera* and critiques shaming punishments generally in "Eighteenth Century Public Humiliation Penalties in Twenty-First Century America: The 'Shameful' Return of 'Scarlet Letter' Punishments in *U.S. v. Gementera*," *BYU Journal of Public Law*, Volume 19, Number 2 (Winter 2005): 499–522; Ziel notes that public shaming punishments tend to be most popular among authoritarian governments such as Afghanistan under the Taliban. Demi Smith Garcia, "Three Worlds Collide: A Novel Approach to the Law, Literature, and Psychology of Shame," *Texas Wesleyan Law Review*, Volume 6 (1999), makes interesting criticisms of shaming punishments based on their larger adverse effects. Philosopher Martha Nussbaum criticizes shaming punishments in *Hiding From Humanity: Disgust, Shame, and the Law* (Princeton, NJ: Princeton University Press, 2004).

John Braithwaite is a leading advocate of restorative justice, and of reintegrative shaming as an element of restorative justice; see his *Crime, Shame, and Reintegration* (Cambridge: Cambridge University Press, 1989); "Restorative Justice: Assessing Optimistic and Pessimistic Accounts," *Crime and Justice: A Review of Research*, Volume 25 (1999): 1–110; and *Restorative Justice and Response Regulation* (Oxford: Oxford University Press, 2002).

See also the references for Debate 8, "Restorative Justice."

10

Should There Be Mandatory Minimum Sentences for Criminal Offenses?

Mandatory Minimums Are Good Policy
  Advocate: David Risley, Assistant U. S. Attorney, Illinois; Lead
    Organized Crime Drug Enforcement Task Force Attorney.
  Source: "Mandatory Minimum Sentences: An Overview," *Drug Watch International* (May 2000); at www.drugwatch.org.

Mandatory Minimum Sentences Are a Disaster
  Advocate: The Honorable Patricia M. Wald, Chief Judge, U.S. Court of
    Appeals for the District of Columbia Circuit (retired); former Judge,
    International Criminal Tribunal for the Former Yugoslavia.
  Source: Testimony given on behalf of the American Bar Association,
    Before the Inter-American Commission on Human Rights
    (Washington, DC, March 3, 2006).

Mandatory minimum sentences are prison terms that legislative bodies require judges to impose when a defendant is convicted of a specific crime with specific features. The most common mandatory sentences are for drug crimes and crimes involving weapons, and the mandatory minimum is imposed based upon specific features of the crime or the criminal: the type or quantity of drug, proximity of a firearm to the offense, and past convictions of the offender. With mandatory sentencing, judges are barred from considering other factors (such as youth, prior exemplary record, unusual circumstances, undue influences) which might be considered relevant to appropriate sentencing.

Mandatory minimum sentencing was pushed by judicial critics who complained about the wide disparity in sentences imposed by various judges: similar offenses might draw a severe sentence from one judge and a milder sentence from another. The differences in sentencing practices drew substantial criticism, and the response to this criticism was passage of the Sentencing Reform Act of 1984, followed by passage of a number of mandatory minimum sentences for crimes involving drugs and violence. In addition to the federal mandatory sentences, every state has passed at least one mandatory sentencing law (such as the "three strikes" laws that mandate life imprisonment for a third criminal conviction).

Mandatory minimum sentences remain in effect, but opposition to them is strong. In 1993 a survey of over 400 state and federal judges found 90% opposed to mandatory minimums; Supreme Court Justice John Paul Stevens, in 1992, condemned mandatory minimum sentences as mandating prison terms "that are manifestly and grossly disproportionate to the moral guilt of the offender," and in a speech at the 2003 ABA Annual meeting, conservative Supreme Court Justice Anthony M. Kennedy stated that "In too many cases, mandatory minimum sentences are unwise and unjust."

While the overall effects of mandatory sentencing are still debated, one effect is obvious: mandatory sentencing has resulted in an enormous increase in the number of people imprisoned.

⠿ Points to Ponder

- Ben, an 18-year-old high school senior, is an occasional user of marijuana; he has no police record, has grades that place him in the top 10% of his graduating class, and has been accepted at Penn State for next fall. Occasionally Ben gives a joint to his friend Matt, also an occasional user; sometimes Matt pays Ben a few dollars. One day in the school parking lot an undercover police officer spots Ben handing a joint to Matt, and receiving a folded bill in return. The undercover officer calls in a uniformed patrol, and both Ben and Matt are quickly arrested. Ben's car is searched, and Ben's shot-gun is found in the back seat of his car: Ben had forgotten to remove it after going duck hunting with some friends over the weekend. Ben is convicted for selling drugs on school property while in possession of a firearm, a very serious offense carrying a mandatory minimum sentence; very likely the judge cannot impose a sentence of less than five years' imprisonment without parole, and may well be required to impose a more severe sentence. Obviously the law was aimed at violent drug dealers who prey on high school students, and Ben is not in that category. Should the judge have discretion to impose a shorter sentence, or is the mandatory minimum a good policy?
- Mandatory minimum sentencing was supposed to eliminate discretion, and impose uniform sentences on everyone committing the same sort of crime. But the discretion is not eliminated; instead, it is transferred from the sentencing judge to the District Attorney's office. In the case of someone like Ben (in the case above) the District Attorney can charge Ben with simple possession, or with possession and sale; and the District Attorney could include or drop the specifications of school grounds and firearm involvement, both of which make

the offense much more serious. If discretion is inevitable, is it better that the discretion be exercised by the District Attorney (in deciding what charges to bring) or by the judge at the time of sentencing?

- One of Patricia Wald's main concerns about mandatory minimum sentences is that they are too severe, imposing very long criminal sentences on offenders (especially on those involved with crack cocaine). If the mandatory minimum sentences were significantly *reduced*, would that meet most of her objections to mandatory minimum sentencing?

- David Risley notes that the mandatory minimum sentence for growing 100 marijuana plants is five years, and suggests that such a sentence is not excessive. But of course if a gun is present in the grower's house, the minimum sentence is greatly increased. Suppose that the grower, Frank, has a gun in the house, and is living with Laura, who actually owns the house but has no involvement with the marijuana. Then under the mandatory minimum provisions, Laura is subject to the same severe mandatory minimum sentence as Frank. Perhaps Laura should have kicked Frank out of the house; but does she deserve the same severe sentence as Frank? Or would it be better for the judge to have some discretion in sentencing her?

Mandatory Minimum Sentences
An Overview

David Risley

The purpose of mandatory minimum sentences is to prevent the judicial trivialization of serious drug crimes. They do that well, to which some protest. Because the federal sentencing system is the model most often cited, it will be used for illustration throughout the following discussion.

Before the advent of mandatory minimum sentences in serious drug cases, federal judges had unbridled discretion to impose whatever sentences they deemed appropriate, in their personal view, up to the statutory maximum. Because individual judges differ widely in their personal views about crime and sentencing, the sentences they imposed for similar offenses by similar defendants varied widely. What some judges treated as serious offenses, and punished accordingly, others

David Risley, "Mandatory Minimum Sentences: An Overview," *Drug Watch International* (May 2000); at www.drugwatch.org. Reprinted with permission from Drug Watch International.

minimized with much more lenient sentences.

Ironically, more lenient sentences became particularly prevalent in areas with high volumes of major drug crime, such as large metropolitan and drug importation centers. Perhaps the sheer volume of cases in such areas led to a certain degree of desensitization. When serious crime becomes routine, there is human tendency to treat it routinely, and sentences often drop accordingly. In some areas across the country, that phenomenon can even be seen with crimes such as murder.

While the ideal is that sentences be perfectly personalized by wise, prudent, and consistent judges to fit every individual defendant and crime, the reality is that judges are human, and their wide human differences and perspectives lead to widely different sentences, if given completely unbridled discretion.

Such wide disparity in sentencing is inherently unfair, at least to those who receive stiff sentences for crimes for which others are punished only lightly. But such inconsistency was welcomed by drug dealers, since it meant they could hope for a light sentence for serious drug crimes. That, of course, created a much bigger problem.

Drug dealers are risk takers by nature. Lack of certainty of serious sentences for serious crimes encourages, rather than deters, such risk takers to elevate their level of criminal activity in the hope that, if caught, they will be lucky enough to draw a lenient judge and receive a lenient sentence. The only possible deterrence for people who are willing to take extreme risks is to take away their cause for such hope.

Some counter that drug dealers are undeterrable by criminal sanctions because they sell drugs to support their own addictions, and so should be treated for their addictions rather than imprisoned. While there may be some merit to that argument for many low-level street dealers, it is generally untrue of their suppliers, and even many other street dealers. Most dealers and distributors at any substantial level do not use drugs themselves, or do so only infrequently. They are exploiters and predators, and users are their captive prey. Drug dealing is a business. As in any other business, drug addicts are unreliable and untrustworthy, especially around drugs, and so make poor business partners. Because drug dealers usually run their operations as high-risk businesses, they necessarily weigh those risks carefully, and so are deterrable when the risks become too high. Many dealers who used to carry firearms, for example, now avoid doing so when they are selling drugs due to the high mandatory federal penalties when guns and drugs are mixed.

However, drug dealers seldom view the risks as too high when they see reason to hope for a light sentence. Congress, however, can, and did, step in to take away that hope. By establishing mandatory minimum sentences for serious drug offenses, Congress sent a clear message to drug dealers: no matter who the judge is, serious crime will get you serious time.

To those who do not view crimes subject to mandatory minimum sentences as serious, including drug dealers and their support systems, that message is objectionable. To most, it is welcome. Mandatory minimum sentences put steel in the spine of our criminal justice system.

The natural question which follows is, what level of dealing must defendants reach before being subject to mandatory minimum sentences, and what are those sentences? The answer varies with the type of drug and whether the defendant is a repeat offender.

In the federal system, there are two levels of mandatory minimums, with each level doubling for defendants with prior convictions. The first tier requires a minimum sentence of imprisonment for five years (10 with a prior felony drug conviction), and the second tier requires a minimum of 10 years (20 with one prior felony drug conviction, and mandatory life with two such prior convictions). Of that, defendants can receive a reduction in the time they serve in prison of only 54 days per year as a reward for "good behavior," which means they must actually serve about 85% of their sentences.

For a prior drug offense to be considered a felony, it must be punishable by more than one year. In the federal system and most states, a drug offense is rarely classified as a felony unless it involves distribution of the drugs involved, or an intent to do so. For most practical purposes, therefore, a prior felony conviction for a drug such as marijuana can be read to mean a prior conviction for distribution. And, since most small distribution cases are reduced to misdemeanor simple possession (personal use) charges as part of plea bargains, especially for first-time offenders, a prior felony drug conviction for a drug such as marijuana usually means the prior conviction

either involved a substantial amount of the drug or a repeat offender undeserving of another such break.

In the case of marijuana, those who oppose mandatory minimum sentencing on so-called "humanitarian" grounds seldom mention that, to be eligible for even a five-year minimum sentence, a defendant must be convicted of an offense involving at least 100 kilograms (220 pounds) of marijuana, or, in the case of a marijuana growing operation, at least 100 plants. Such defendants are not low-level offenders.

With marijuana available at the Mexican border in Texas for wholesale prices between $600 and $1100 per pound, and selling in most areas at a retail price of between $1200 and $2000 per pound, and with any reasonably healthy cultivated marijuana plant producing at least one and sometimes two pounds of finished product, eligibility for even the lowest mandatory minimum sentence requires conviction of an offense involving between $132,000 and $440,000 worth of marijuana, or plants capable of producing marijuana worth a bulk retail price of between $120,000 and $450,000.

To be eligible for the next, 10-year tier of minimum sentence, a defendant must be convicted of an offense involving 1000 kilograms (1.1 tons) of marijuana or 1000 marijuana plants. Even at a low wholesale price of $600 per pound, such offenses involve marijuana worth at least $1.3 million. One kilogram equals 2.2 pounds. Conversely, one pound equals 453.6 grams, and one ounce equals 28.35 grams.

It would be difficult to describe any offense involving between $120,000 and $450,000 worth of drugs as undeserving of even a five year prison sentence. Yet, those who oppose mandatory minimum sentences for marijuana and other drug offenses do just that, usually by attempting to convey the false impression the criminals they are attempting to protect are only low-level offenders.

In examining the deterrent potential of such mandatory minimum sentences, one must consider that the profit potential for marijuana offenses is relatively high, and the penalties relatively low, which makes marijuana an attractive drug in which to deal, as evidenced by its widespread availability. To illustrate, if a dealer bought 200 pounds of marijuana in Texas for $900 per pound for a total of $180,000, transported it to the Midwest and sold it for as low as $1400 per pound, for a total of $280,000 with minimal overhead, the profit for just one such trip would be $100,000. When the street-level price of between $125 and $300 per ounce is considered, or the lower acquisition costs if the marijuana is grown by the dealer himself, the profit potential for such a venture can be huge, and yet still not involve enough drugs to trigger even the lowest mandatory minimum penalty. Since the chance of getting caught for any single trip of that sort is relatively low, the prospect of a quick $100,000 profit lures plenty of eager dealers, even with the risk of spending close to five years in prison.

Of course, if drug dealers are undeterrable, as the actions of many demonstrate they are, the only realistic options left are to either give up and allow them to ply their predatory trade unhindered (the legalization "solution"), or incapacitate them with even longer sentences.

The debate, it would seem, should be about whether the mandatory minimum penalties for marijuana offenses are currently too lenient, not too harsh.

Mandatory Minimums as a Check on Sentencing Guidelines

The next question is whether the more recent advent of the federal sentencing guidelines, which also limit judicial sentencing discretion, made mandatory minimum penalties obsolete. The answer is definitely no. As a practical matter, only through mandatory minimum sentences can Congress maintain sentencing benchmarks for serious drug crimes which cannot be completely circumvented by the commission which establishes, and sometimes quietly alters, those guidelines. One of the best illustrations is that of the sentencing guidelines for marijuana growers, who have achieved favorable treatment under the sentencing guidelines, but fortunately not under Congress' statutory mandatory minimum sentences.

To appreciate the significance of that illustration, one must understand a little about the sentencing guideline system, and its relationship to mandatory minimum sentences. As part of the Sentencing Reform Act of 1984, Congress mandated the formation of the United States Sentencing Commission as an independent agency in the judicial branch composed of seven voting members, appointed by the President with the advice and consent of the Senate, at least three of whom must be federal judges, not more than four of whom may be from the same political party, serving staggered six-year terms. That Commission was charged with the formidable task of establishing binding sentencing guidelines to dramatically narrow judges' sentencing discretion, in order to provide reasonable uniformity in sentencing throughout the country, while at the same time taking into reasonable account the myriad of differences between the hundreds of federal crimes and limitless array of individual defendants.

The result of that enormous undertaking was the adoption, effective November 1987, of the United States Sentencing Guidelines. Using its provisions, contained in a book one inch thick, courts determine the seriousness of the offense and the extent of the defendant's past criminal history, and use that information to determine on a chart the relatively narrow sentencing range within which they have sentencing discretion. In drug cases, the seriousness of the offense (offense level) is determined mostly on the basis of the amount of drugs for which a defendant is accountable, with adjustments for factors such as role in the offense, whether a firearm was involved, and whether the defendant accepted responsibility for his or her actions through a candid guilty plea.

As part of its broad delegation of authority, Congress provided that changes promulgated by the Commission to the Sentencing Guidelines automatically become law unless Congress, within a 180-day waiting period, affirmatively acts to reject them. By that means Congress avoided a great deal of detailed work, but also created the possibility that changes to the Sentencing Guidelines to which they

would object if carefully considered would become law if no one raises a sufficient alarm.

Because the Commission has only seven voting members, a change of only one member can result in the reversal of a previous 4–3 vote, sometimes with great consequences. Congress is ill-equipped to deal with the intricacies of the impact of many amendments to the Sentencing Guidelines, and is sometimes preoccupied with other, more pressing or "hot button" issues. Therefore, the only realistic check on the delegation of authority to the Commission to make changes in drug sentences is the trump card of mandatory minimums.

That is true because defendants receive the higher of whatever sentence is called for by the statutory mandatory minimums or the Sentencing Guidelines. If the Commission promulgates a change to the Sentencing Guidelines which calls for lower sentences than required by the statutory mandatory minimums, the mandatory minimums trump the Sentencing Guidelines. In other words, the mandatory minimums are mandatory, and are beyond the control of the Commission.

With that background, the vital importance of mandatory minimum sentences as at least a partial check over the Commission in drug sentences is dramatically illustrated by the changes the Commission made regarding sentences for marijuana growers. The mandatory minimum sentences for marijuana growers imposed by Congress, which kick in at 100 plants, equate one marijuana plant with one kilogram (2.2 pounds) of marijuana. Until November 1995, the Sentencing Guidelines used that same equivalency in calculating the offense level in cases involving 50 or more plants, but for cases involving less than 50 plants considered one plant as the equivalent of only 100 grams (3.5 ounces). That 10:1 ratio between the amount of marijuana to which plants were considered to represent was a major logical inconsistency, since marijuana plants do not produce significantly more or less marijuana just because they happen to be in the company of more or less than 49 other marijuana plants.

The Commission solved that inconsistency in early 1995 by promulgating an amendment to the sentencing Guidelines which, instead of eliminating the unrealistically low 100 gram equivalency for smaller cases, eliminated the one kilogram equivalency for larger cases. Congress did nothing, so, as of November 1995, the Sentencing Guidelines treat all marijuana plants as if they were only capable of producing 3.5 ounces of marijuana.

In explanation, the Commission stated:

> In actuality, a marihuana plant does not produce a yield of one kilogram of marihuana. The one plant = 100 grams of marihuana equivalency used by the Commission for offenses involving fewer than 50 marihuana plants was selected as a reasonable approximation of the actual average yield of marihuana plants taking into account (1) studies reporting the actual yield of marihuana plants (375 to 412 grams depending on growing conditions); (2) that all plants regardless of size are counted for guideline purposes while, in actuality, not all plants will produce useable marihuana (e.g., some plants may die of disease before maturity, and when plants are grown outdoors some plants may be consumed by animals); and (3) that male plants, which are counted for guideline purposes, are frequently culled because they do not produce the same quality marihuana as do female plants. To enhance fairness and consistency, this amendment adopts the equivalency of 100 grams per marihuana plant for all guideline determinations.

Contrary to those claims, no self-respecting commercial marijuana grower would ever admit his plants produce no more than 412 grams (14.5 ounces) of marijuana, much less that they average only 100 grams. Based upon long experience with actual marijuana growing operations, it is widely accepted in law enforcement circles that cultivated marijuana plants typically produce about one pound of marijuana (453 grams), and sometimes two pounds (907 grams). While it is true that some growers cull out the male plants in order to produce the potent form of marijuana known as sinsemilla, derived from the unpollinated female plant, not all growers do so. And, the observations of the Commission completely ignore the fact that a marijuana plant is a renewable resource—the seeds from one plant can be used to grow several more plants. It is unrealistic, therefore, to treat one plant as representing only that amount of marijuana it can produce itself, and to require courts to assume all marijuana growers standing before them are incapable of producing more than 100 grams of marijuana per plant.

Fortunately, Congress was more realistic in establishing its mandatory minimum sentences. And, for cases involving 100 or more plants, those mandatory minimums trump the Sentencing Guidelines. The result, however, is still a boon to commercial marijuana growers who are informed enough to keep the number of plants in their operations under 100, or under 1000. That is because the interaction between the lenient Sentencing Guidelines and the stricter mandatory minimums produces a stair step effect on sentences at the 100 and 1000 plant marks.

If a marijuana grower is caught raising 99 marijuana plants, no mandatory minimum sentence is triggered. Under the Sentencing Guidelines, those plants would be treated as the equivalent of 9.9 kilograms of marijuana ($26,135 worth, using a conservative price of $1200 per pound), which, for an offender caught for the first time, would result in an unadjusted sentencing guideline range of only 15–21 months. With the normal adjustment to reward a candid guilty plea, that guideline range would drop to 10–16 months.

In contrast, if that same grower raised just one more plant, for a total of 100, the first tier of mandatory minimum sentences would be triggered, and the court would be required to impose a sentence of five years. The jump from a maximum sentence of 20 months for 99 plants up to five years for 100 plants is due solely to the overriding effect of the mandatory minimum sentence.

Not until that same grower was caught with 800 to 999 plants, treated as the equivalent of 80 to 99.9 kilograms of marijuana (at least $211,200 worth), would his unadjusted sentencing guideline range reach the 51 to 63 month mark, and even then a candid guilty plea would drop it to 37 to 46 months. Consequently, the five year mandatory minimum would probably still control the sentence. But, if the grower was caught with just one more plant, raising the total to 1000, the second tier of mandatory minimum sentences would be triggered, requiring a sentence of 10 years. Again, the jump from a maximum sentence of 63 months for 999 plants up to 10 years for 1000 plants is due solely to Congress' mandatory minimum sentence scheme.

Without those mandatory minimum sentence, the commission's view that marijuana plants should only be treated as the equivalent of 100 grams of marijuana would be controlling, which marijuana growers would doubtless applaud. Only because of the mandatory minimums does the more sensible view of Congress that each marijuana plant should be treated as the equivalent of one kilogram of marijuana impact growing operations involving 100 or more plants.

Ultimately, whether the effect of those mandatory minimum sentences is good or bad depends upon how seriously one views marijuana use. If a person believes a sentence of five years is too harsh for growing 100 marijuana plants conservatively capable of producing between $26,400 and $120,000 worth of marijuana, or distributing 220 pounds of marijuana worth at least $264,000, the mandatory minimum sentences for marijuana should be abolished. If, however, a five year sentence for such crimes seems reasonable, or even lenient, the mandatory minimums should be retained, and perhaps toughened.

There is no doubt about on which side of that question the marijuana growers, dealers, users, and their supporters stand. There is also little room to doubt on which side those who take marijuana crimes seriously should stand. ■

Testimony given on Behalf of the American Bar Association Before the Inter-American Commission on Human Rights

The Honorable Patricia M. Wald
Chief Judge, United States Court of Appeals for the District of Columbia Circuit
(Retired), Former Judge, International Criminal Tribunal for the Former Yugoslavia

Good morning, your Excellencies. My name is Patricia Wald of Washington, D.C., and I am a former judge of the International Criminal Tribunal for the Former Yugoslavia and former Chief Judge of the United States Court of Appeals for the District of Columbia. I welcome the opportunity to testify before you on behalf of the American Bar Association concerning the impact of mandatory minimum sentencing in the criminal justice system of the United States of America. . . .

In 2003, U.S. Supreme Court Justice Anthony Kennedy, in a speech at the ABA Annual Meeting, challenged the legal profession to begin a new public dialogue about American sentencing and corrections policies and practices. He raised fundamental questions about the fairness and efficacy of a justice system that disproportionately imprisons minorities, and then returns them to their communities in worse shape than they left it. In regard to mandatory minimum sentences, Justice Kennedy said, "I can neither accept the necessity nor the wisdom of federal mandatory minimum sentences." "In too many cases," he asserted, "mandatory minimum sentences are unwise or unjust."

In response to Justice Kennedy's concerns, the ABA established a commission to investigate the state of sentencing and corrections in the United States, and to make recommendations on how to correct the problems Justice Kennedy had identified. The Justice Kennedy Commission after studying these issues reported to the 2004 Annual Meeting a series of policy recommendations that have been hailed as providing a blueprint for sentencing and corrections reform. In particular, the Justice Kennedy Commission called upon states, territories and the federal government to repeal mandatory minimum sentence statutes. The recommendations were overwhelmingly approved by the ABA House of Delegates.

The ABA's opposition to mandatory minimum sentencing is longstanding. Its 1994 Standards for Criminal Justice on Sentencing, in whose formulation I participated, state unequivocally that "A legislature should not prescribe a minimum term of total confinement for any offense." In addition, Standard 18–6.1 (a) directs that "[t]he sentence imposed should be no more severe than necessary to achieve the societal purpose or purposes for which it is authorized." This standard goes on to say that "[t]he sentence imposed in each case should be the minimum sanction that is consistent with the gravity of the offense, the culpability of the offender, the offender's criminal history, and the personal characteristics of an individual offender that may be taken into account." These standards

balance respect for the role of the judge in calibrating the severity of the punishment due in each case, with a need to avoid disparity and reduce levels of severity overall.

The ABA has also expressed concern about the racially discriminatory impact of mandatory minimum sentencing, particularly in connection with the differential penalties for trafficking in crack and powder cocaine. As early as 1995, the ABA called for the elimination of "current differences in sentencing based upon drug quantity for offenses involving crack versus powder cocaine." The report accompanying this resolution noted that African Americans were disproportionately prosecuted and sentenced under the harsh federal crack cocaine laws, and thus were likely to serve substantially more time in prison for cocaine offenses than whites.

Following receipt of the Justice Kennedy Commission report in 2004, the ABA again urged the repeal of mandatory minimum sentence statutes as well as other steps to eliminate unjustified racial and ethnic disparities. The ABA reasserted its opposition to mandatory minimum sentences in the policy it adopted in response to the Supreme Court's decision in *United States v. Booker*, 543 U.S. 220 (2005). It urged Congress to take several steps to assure fair, effective and just federal sentencing practices, including expanded sentencing ranges and increased judicial discretion in departing from those ranges.

As a matter of policy, mandatory minimum sentences raise a myriad of troubling concerns. To satisfy the basic dictates of fairness, due process and the rule of law, criminal sentencing should be both uniform between similarly situated offenders and proportional to the crime that is the basis of conviction. Mandatory minimum sentences are inconsistent with these twin commands of justice.

First, mandatory minimum sentencing laws have resulted in excessively severe sentences. Mandatory minimum sentences set a mandatory floor for sentencing. As a result, all sentences for that crime, regardless of the circumstances of the crime or the offender, tend to be arrayed above the mandatory floor. They are a one-way ratchet upwards. The Justice Kennedy Commission found that, since the advent of mandatory minimum sentencing policies, the average length of incarceration in the United States has increased threefold. I recently participated in a case where a first offender who had been charged with two sales of a modest amount of marijuana while carrying a gun on his person was sentenced to 55 years in prison. The sentencing judge expressed intense frustration but said he could do nothing as the mandatory minimums required the sentence. The Justice Kennedy Commission found that mandatory minimum sentencing was one of an "array of policy changes which, in the aggregate, produced a steady, dramatic, and unprecedented increase in the population of the nation's prisons and jails," despite a decrease in the number of serious crimes committed in the past several years.

Second, mandatory minimum statutes lead to arbitrary sentences. When the relevant considerations in sentencing shifted from the traditional wide focus on both the crime itself and "offender characteristics," to an exclusive focus on "offense characteristics," a host of mitigating circumstances could no longer be considered in determining the sentence. As a result, a person with sympathetic mitigating factors based on background, family status, or community ties would receive the same punishment as a hardened criminal. Women offenders—typically minor players in drug dealing and disproportionately the caretaker parents of minor children—bear the brunt of mandatory minimums. Their numbers and the duration of their confinements have increased dramatically.

Third, mandatory minimum sentence statutes have produced the very sentencing disparities that determinate sentencing was intended to eliminate. Because punishment as a practical matter is now determined by charging decisions made by prosecutors, judges no longer have the ability to individualize sentences or impose the minimum sanction that is consistent with the gravity of the actual offense conduct. Disparity in sentencing also arises when laws provide radically different penalties for what are more reasonably regarded as substantially similar behaviors: a person who possesses crack with intent to distribute will receive a substantially higher sentence than someone convicted of possessing the same amount of cocaine powder. In the case of the crack/powder differential, the sentencing disparities break down along racial lines, in part because black urban populations tend to use crack while white suburbanites tend to use the powdered version, and in part because of law enforcement policies that target urban areas. A person who possesses five grams of crack cocaine receives a sentence that is equivalent to that imposed for the possession of five hundred grams of powder cocaine. As the Kennedy Commission concluded, the "differential treatment of crack and powder cocaine has resulted in greatly increased sentences for African-Americans drug offenders."

Fourth, mandatory minimums undermine judicial discretion. The ABA believes that a fair and just sentencing system must allow for the sentencing judge to exercise discretion in appropriate cases. In our adversarial criminal justice system, judges are expected to take an impartial role in the resolution of cases, siding neither with the prosecution nor the defense. Thus it is the judge who is the appropriate person to decide on a particular sentence within designated ranges, and not the legislature or Sentencing Commission. Mandatory minimum sentencing regimes shift discretion from judges to prosecutors, who do not have the training, incentive, or even the appropriate information to properly consider a defendant's mitigating circumstances at the initial charging stage of a case. To give prosecutors that kind of unchecked power dangerously disturbs the balance between the parties in an adversarial system, and deprives defendants of access to an impartial decision-maker in the all-important area of sentencing.

In addition to the organized bar's objections to mandatory minimum sentencing regimes, I note that the weight of opinion within the ranks of American judges is also opposed to mandatory minimum sentencing. Both the Judicial Conference and the judges of the 12 federal circuit courts of appeals, on one of which I sat for 20 years, five as chief judge, have adopted resolutions that oppose mandatory minimum sentencing statutes. In a formal resolution, the Judicial Conference urged Congress to "reconsider the wisdom of mandatory minimum sentence statutes and to restructure such statutes so that the U.S. Sentencing Commission may uniformly establish guidelines for all criminal statutes to avoid unwarranted disparities from the scheme of the Sentencing Reform Act."

I conclude by briefly mentioning a few of the most disastrous social consequences of our overreliance on punitive sentencing policies, particularly mandatory minimum prison sentences. Society incurs a variety of collateral costs when a person is sent to prison or jail, including increased expenditures for the maintenance and health care of dependents of inmates, lost tax revenues from income that would have been earned or expenditures that would have been made by the person left free in the community. Not least of all, the families and communities from which prisoners come suffer a wide variety of tangible and intangible harms from the absence of the prisoner. These include as I have mentioned the emotional, economic, and developmental damage to the children of incarcerated offenders, and the disenfranchisement and consequent political alienation of a significant portion of the young men in minority communities.

There is no question that crimes must be punished and that prison serves a legitimate retributive and incapacitative purpose, but only if it is proportionate to the circumstances of the crime and the offender as well as the gravity of the underlying offense. Unduly long and punitive sentences are counter-productive, and candidly many of our mandatory minimums approach the cruel and unusual level as compared to other countries as well as to our own past practices. On a personal note, let me say that on the Yugoslav War Crimes Tribunal I was saddened to see that the sentences imposed on war crimes perpetrators responsible for the deaths and suffering of hundreds of innocent civilians often did not come near those imposed in my own country for dealing in a few bags of illegal drugs. These are genuine human rights concerns that I believe merit your interest and attention. ■

⠿ The Continuing Debate

What Is New

Recently there have been proposals before Congress to impose mandatory minimum sentences for street gangs and gang-related crime; in 2006 such a bill was passed by the U.S. House of Representatives, but not by the Senate (the bill would have imposed a ten-year mandatory minimum sentence for any "gang crime," and a 20-year mandatory minimum sentence for any crime resulting in serious bodily injury; and would have increased the likelihood of 16- and 17-year-old youths being tried as adults). Also *United States v. Booker*, 2005, and *United States v. Fanfan*, 2005, are key Supreme Court rulings, making sentencing rules guidelines rather than mandatory. But obviously the Congress is trying to pass more mandatory sentencing laws, and that trend appears likely to continue.

Where to Find More

An organization opposed to mandatory minimums is Families Against Mandatory Minimums; their website, which contains extensive information on mandatory minimum sentencing laws, is at http://www.famm.org.

The effectiveness of mandatory minimum sentences in reducing crime has been challenged by Jonathan P. Caulkins, C. Peter Rydell, William L. Schwabe, and James Chiesa, *MR-827-DPRC* (Santa Monica, CA: RAND, 1997), whose research indicates that drug treatment programs and conventional enforcement (without mandatory minimum sentencing) is more cost-effective in reducing drug use and drug-related crime than are mandatory minimum incarceration policies. A more extensive challenge to the effectiveness of mandatory sentences in preventing crime is offered by Michael Tonry, *Sentencing Matters* (New York: Oxford University Press, 1996); see also Michael Tonry, *Thinking About Crime: Sense and Sensibility in American Penal Culture* (New York: Oxford University Press, 2004).

Franklin E. Zimring, Gordon Hawkins, and Sam Kamin, *Punishment and Democracy: Three Strikes and You're Out in California* (New York: Oxford University Press, 2001), and Franklin E. Zimring, Sam Kamin, and Gordon Hawkins, *Crime and Punishment in California: The Impact of Three Strikes and*

You're Out (Berkeley, CA: Institute of Governmental Studies, University of California, Berkeley, 1999) extensively critique the three strikes version of mandatory sentencing, and conclude that such laws are ineffective in reducing crime. See also Franklin E. Zimring and Gordon Hawkins, *Incapacitation: Penal Confinement and the Restraint of Crime* (Oxford: Oxford University Press, 1995). Zimring can be heard disscussing the issue (in an interview with NPR's Renee Montagne) at http://www.npr.org/templates/story/story.php?storyId=4126631.

U.S. District Judge Gerard E. Lynch, "Criminal Law: Sentencing Eddie," *Journal of Criminal Law & Criminology*, Volume 91 (Spring 2001): 547–567, examines in detail the "routine and modest injustices produced by mandatory minimums." A very good anthology on the effects of prison policy on society is edited by Mary Pattillo, David F. Weiman, and Bruce Western, *Imprisoning America: The Social Effects of Mass Incarceration* (New York: Russell Sage Foundation, 2004).

David W. Garland is the editor of an excellent anthology, *Mass Imprisonment: Social Causes and Consequences* (London: SAGE, 2001). David Garland is also the author of *The Culture of Control: Crime and Social Order in Contemporary Society* (Chicago: University of Chicago Press, 2001), and *Punishment and Modern Society: A Study in Social Theory* (Chicago: University of Chicago Press, 1990). A very readable book on the contemporary U.S. use of imprisonment is Joseph T. Hallinan, *Going Up the River: Travels in a Prison Nation* (New York: Random House, 2001). Eric Schlosser, "The Prison-Industrial Complex," *Atlantic Monthly* (December 1998), details the relation between the security industry (including private prisons) and the U.S. approach to crime control and imprisonment.

A good collection of articles on issues surrounding incarceration as a social institution is Timothy J. Flanagan, James W. Marquart, and Kenneth G. Adams, editors, *Incarcerating Criminals: Prisons and Jails in Social and Organizational Context* (New York: Oxford University Press, 1998).

Judge Stanley Sporkin and Congressman Asa Hutchinson debate mandatory minimum sentencing policy in "Debate: Mandatory Minimums in Drug Sentencing: A Valuable Weapon in the War on Drugs or a Handcuff on Judicial Discretion?" *American Criminal Law Review*, Volume 36 (Fall 1999): 1279–1301. Jerome H. Skolnick, in "Wild Pitch: 'Three Strikes, You're Out' and Other Bad Calls on Crime," *The American Prospect*, Volume 5, Number 17 (March 1994), criticizes mandatory sentencing, particularly the three strikes legislation; John J. DiIulio responds and Skolnick responds to DiIulio in "Instant Replay," *The American Prospect*, Volume 5, Number 18 (June 23, 1994).

See also the readings for Debate 11 on selective incapacitation.

Is Selective Incapacitation an Effective Policy for Reducing Crime?

Selective Incapacitation Is the Best Model for Stopping Criminal behavior
   Advocate: James Q. Wilson, Ronald Reagan Professor of Public Policy,
   Pepperdine University School of Public Policy.
   Source: "Selective Incapacitation," in Andrew von Hirsch and Andrew
   Ashworth, editors, *Principled Sentencing: Readings on Theory and
   Policy*, 2nd Edition (Oxford: Hart Publishing, 1998); a revision of
   "Dealing with the High-Rate Offender," *The Public Interest*,
   Volume 72 (1983).

Selective Incapacitation Is an Ineffective Criminal Policy
   Advocate: Andrew von Hirsch, Director of the Centre for Penal
   Theory and Penal Ethics at the University of Cambridge Institute of
   Criminology; Honorary Professor of Penal Theory and Penal Law,
   Cambridge University; Honorary Fellow, Wolfson College.
   Source: "Selective Incapacitation: Some Doubts," in Andrew von
   Hirsch and Andrew Ashworth, editors, *Principled Sentencing:
   Readings on Theory and Policy*, 2nd Edition (Oxford: Hart
   Publishing, 1998); originally published in the 1st Edition, edited for
   the 2nd Edition.

The policy of selective incapacitation is the policy of singling out or *selecting* the
major criminal offenders and then locking them away or *incapacitating* them for
a long time. It incorporates several major assumptions: first, that specific
individuals are the source of a very substantial proportion of crime; second, that
removing those individuals from society for an extended period is an efficient

199

way of reducing the crime rate; and third, that such individuals can be accurately *identified*. All of those assumptions have been challenged. First, while individuals certainly commit crimes, there is a serious question of whether social structures and institutions are the major causal factors influencing the commission of crimes by individuals. The second assumption—that removal of repeat offenders from society for an extended period is an efficient way of reducing the crime rate—has come in for extensive critique. First, long-term incarceration results in keeping prisoners incarcerated long past the age when their crime activities are most likely to stop; and keeping people in prison who are unlikely to commit crimes is not very efficient. And second, incarcerating large numbers of people for long periods may break down the community social structure in such a way that more crime results. The third assumption—that we can accurately identify those likely to commit multiple crimes—has proved the most problematic. The problems with identifying which individuals are likely to commit more crimes have proved to be insurmountable: every means of identifying the target individuals turns out to also identify so many "false positives" (people who would *not* commit more crimes) that any incarceration policy using such identification procedures would be grossly inefficient (as well as profoundly unjust).

Selective incapacitation policies are deeply contrary to a basic principle of justice: that punishment should be commensurate to the crime committed; that is, the worst crimes should receive the most severe punishment. Under selective incapacitation, the focus is not on the crime committed but on the potential for committing *future* crimes. The criminal behavior of someone who commits three acts of shoplifting is not as severe as that of someone who commits an unpremeditated murder; but under such "habitual offender" statutes as the three strikes law, the shoplifter might be sentenced to life without parole, while the murderer serves only a few years' imprisonment. The justification for the incapacitating sentence is that it will prevent *future* criminal acts, not that it is reasonable punishment for past criminal behavior.

Three strikes laws are the most evident effect of selective incapacitation theory. The state of Washington passed a three strikes law in 1993: upon conviction of a third felony, the offender received a sentence of life without parole. California passed a similar law in 1994, and by 2004 most states (as well as the federal government) had passed some form of three strikes law mandating very long (often life) sentences for three-time offenders.

⠿ Points to Ponder

- James Q. Wilson claims that "one great advantage to incapacitation as a crime control strategy" is that "it does not require us to make any assumptions about human nature." Is it true that selective incapacitation makes no assumptions about human nature?
- Suppose that we lock up Paul for 20 years, and we can determine—by some extraordinary calculation—that Paul would have committed 10 crimes during that period of incarceration. Does that imply that locking up Paul for 20 years actually prevented 10 crimes from occurring?

- Suppose that we discovered that people who grew up in poverty were much more likely to commit multiple crimes in the future than were people who grew up wealthy. Rhonda and Wendy are both convicted of shoplifting the same value of goods on the same day; for both it is their first offense; Rhonda grew up in poverty, while Wendy is from a wealthy family. If our studies show that impoverished Rhonda is more likely to commit future crimes than is wealthy Wendy, would we be justified in sentencing Rhonda to a much longer prison term in order to "selectively incapacitate" her?

Selective Incapacitation

James Q. Wilson

When criminals are deprived of their liberty, as by imprisonment (or banishment, or very tight control in the community), their ability to commit offences against citizens is ended. We say these persons have been "incapacitated", and we try to estimate the amount by which crime is reduced by this incapacitation.

Incapacitation cannot be the sole purpose of the criminal justice system; if it were, we would put everybody who has committed one or two offences in prison until they were too old to commit another. And if we thought prison too costly, we would simply cut off their hands or their heads. Justice, humanity, and proportionality, among other goals, must also be served by the courts.

But there is one great advantage to incapacitation as a crime control strategy — namely, it does not require us to make any assumptions about human nature. By contrast, deterrence works only if people take into account the costs and benefits of alternative courses of action and choose that which confers the largest net benefit (or the smallest net cost). Though people almost surely do take such matters into account, it is difficult to be certain by how much such considerations affect their behaviour and what change, if any, in crime rates will result from a given, feasible change in either the costs of crime or the benefits of not committing a crime. Rehabilitation works only if the values, preferences, or time-horizon of criminals can be altered by plan. There is not much evidence that we can make these alterations for large numbers of persons, though there is some evidence that it

James Q. Wilson, "Selective Incapacitation," from *Principled Sentencing: Readings on Theory and Policy, Second Edition*, edited by Andrew von Hirsch and Andrew Ashworth (Oxford: Hart Publishing, 1998): 113–120. Reprinted with permission from James Q. Wilson.

can be done for a few under certain circumstances.

Incapacitation, on the other hand, works by definition: its effects result from the physical restraint placed upon the offender and not from his subjective state. More accurately, it works provided at least three conditions are met: some offenders must be repeaters, offenders taken off the streets must not be immediately and completely replaced by new recruits, and prison must not increase the post-release criminal activity of those who have been incarcerated sufficiently to offset the crimes prevented by their stay in prison.

The first condition is surely true. Every study of prison inmates shows that a large fraction (recently, about two-thirds) of them had prior criminal records before their current incarceration; every study of ex-convicts shows that a significant fraction (estimates vary from a quarter to a half) are rearrested for new offences within a relatively brief period. In short, the great majority of persons in prison are repeat offenders, and thus prison, whatever else it may do, protects society from the offences these persons would commit if they were free.

The second condition—that incarcerating one robber does not lead automatically to the recruitment of a new robber to replace him—seems plausible. Although some persons, such as Ernest van den Haag, have argued that new offenders will step forward to take the place vacated by the imprisoned offenders, they have presented no evidence that this is the case, except, perhaps, for certain crimes (such as narcotics trafficking or prostitution) which are organized along

business lines. For the kinds of predatory street crimes with which we are concerned—robbery, burglary, auto theft, larceny—there are no barriers to entry and no scarcity of criminal opportunities. No one need wait for a "vacancy" to appear before he can find an opportunity to become a criminal. The supply of robbers is not affected by the number of robbers practicing, because existing robbers have no way of excluding new robbers and because the opportunity for robbing (if you wish, the "demand" for robbery) is much larger than the existing number of robberies. In general, the earnings of street criminals are not affected by how many "competitors" they have.

The third condition that must be met if incapacitation is to work is that prisons must not be such successful "schools for crime" that the crimes prevented by incarceration are outnumbered by the increased crimes committed after release attributable to what was learned in prison. It is doubtless the case that for some offenders prison is a school; it is also doubtless that for other offenders prison is a deterrent. The former group will commit more, or more skillful, crimes after release; the latter will commit fewer crimes after release. The question, therefore, is whether the net effect of these two offsetting tendencies is positive or negative. In general, there is no evidence that the prison experience makes offenders as a whole more criminal, and there is some evidence that certain kinds of offenders (especially certain younger ones) may be deterred by a prison experience. Moreover, interviews with prisoners reveal no relationship between the number of crimes committed and whether the offenders had served a prior prison term. Though there are many qualifications that should be made to this bald summary, there is no evidence that the net effect of prison is to increase the crime rates of ex-convicts sufficiently to cancel out the gains to society resulting from incapacitation.

To determine the amount of crime that is prevented by incarcerating a given number of offenders for a given length of time, the key estimate we must make is the number of offences a criminal commits per year free on the street. If a community experiences one thousand robberies a year, it obviously makes a great deal of difference whether these robberies are the work of ten robbers, each of whom commits one hundred robberies per year, or the work of one thousand robbers, each of whom commits only one robbery per year. In the first case, locking up only five robbers will cut the number of robberies in half; in the second case, locking up one hundred robbers will only reduce the number of robberies by 10 per cent.

In the late 1970s, researchers at the Rand Corporation had been interviewing prisoners (first in California, then in other states) to find out directly from known offenders how much crime they were committing while free. No one can be certain, of course, that the reports of the convicts constitute an accurate record of their crimes, undetected as well as detected, but the Rand researchers cross-checked the information against arrest records and looked for evidence of internal consistency in the self-reports. Moreover, the inmates volunteered

information about crimes they had committed but for which they had not been arrested. Still, it is quite possible that the self-reports were somewhat inaccurate. However, it is reasonable to assume that inmates would be more likely to conceal crimes they did commit rather than admit to crimes they did not commit. Thus, any errors in these self-reports probably lead to an underestimate of the true rate of criminality of these persons.

The Rand Group learned that the "average" individual offence rate was virtually a meaningless term because the inmates they interviewed differed so sharply in how many crimes they committed. A large number of offenders committed a small number of offences while free and a small number of offenders committed a very large number of offences. In statistical language, the distribution of offences was highly skewed. For example, the median number of burglaries committed by the inmates in the three states was about 5 a year, but the 10 per cent of the inmates who were the highest-rate offenders committed an average of 232 burglaries a year. The median number of robberies was also about 5 a year, but the top 10 per cent of offenders committed an average of 87 a year. As Peter W. Greenwood, one of the members of the Rand group, put it, incarcerating one robber who was among the top 10 per cent in offence rates would prevent more robberies than incarcerating eighteen offenders who were at or below the median.

All the evidence we have implies that, for crime-reduction purposes, the most rational way to use the incapacitative powers of our prisons would be to do so selectively. Instead of longer sentences for everyone, or for persons who have prior records, or for persons whose present crime is especially grave, longer sentences would be given primarily to those who, when free, commit the most crimes.

But how do we know who these high-rate, repeat criminals are? Knowing the nature of the present offence is not a good clue. The reason for this is quite simple—most street criminals do not specialize. Today's robber can be tomorrow's burglar and the next day's car thief. When the police happen to arrest him, the crime for which he is arrested is determined by a kind of lottery—he happened to be caught red-handed, or as the result of a tip, committing a particular crime that may or may not be the same as either his previous crime or his next one. If judges give sentences based entirely on he gravity of the present offence, then a high-rate offender may get off lightly because on this occasion he happened to be caught snatching a purse. The low-rate offender may get a long sentence because he was unlucky enough to be caught robbing a liquor store with a gun.

Prosecutors have an understandable tendency to throw the book at persons caught committing a serious crime, especially if they have been caught before. To a certain extent, we want to encourage that tendency. After all, we not only want to reduce crime, we want to see criminals get their just deserts. Society would not, and should not, tolerate a system in which a prosecutor throws the book at purse snatchers and lets armed robbers off with a suspended sentence. But while society's legitimate desire for retribution must set the outer bounds of any sentencing policy, there is still room for flexibility within those bounds. We can, for example, act so that all robbers are punished with prison terms, but give, within certain relatively narrow ranges, longer sentences to those robbers who commit the most crimes.

If knowing the nature of the present offence and even knowing the prior record of the offender are not accurate guides to identifying high-rate offenders, what is? Obviously, we cannot ask the offenders. They may co-operate with researchers once in jail, but they have little incentive to co-operate with prosecutors before they go to jail, especially if the price of co-operation is to get a tougher sentence. But we can see what legally admissible, objective attributes of the offenders best predict who is and who is not a high-rate offender. In the Rand study, Greenwood and his colleagues discovered, by trial and error, that the following seven factors, taken together, were highly predictive of a convicted person being a high-rate offender: he (1) was convicted of a crime while a juvenile (that is, before age 16), (2) used illegal drugs as a juvenile, (3) used illegal drugs during the previous two years, (4) was employed less than 50 per cent of the time during the previous two years, (5) served time in a juvenile facility, (6) was incarcerated in prison more than 50 per cent of the previous two years, and (7) was previously convicted for the present offence.

Using this scale, Greenwood found that 82 per cent of those predicted to be low-rate offenders in fact were, and 82 per cent of those predicted to be medium- or high-rate offenders also were. To understand how big these differences are, the median California prison inmate who is predicted to be a low-rate offender will in fact commit slightly more than one burglary and slightly less than one robbery per year free. By contrast, the median California inmate who is predicted to be a high-rate offender will commit ninety-three burglaries and thirteen robberies per year free. In other states, this prediction scale may be more or less accurate.

Opinions differ as to the effect on the crime rate and prison population of making sentences for high-rate offenders longer than those for low-rate ones. Greenwood applied his scale to California and found that if all low-rate robbers received two-year prison terms (most now receive longer ones) and all high-rate robbers received seven-year terms (most now receive shorter ones), the number of robberies committed in the state would drop by an estimated 20 per cent with no increase in the prison population.

Obviously, a policy of reducing crime by selective incapacitation (that is, by adjusting prison terms to reflect predicted individual offence rates) raises a number of issues. Though these issues are important, one must bear in mind that they cannot be resolved by comparing selective incapacitation to some ideal system of criminal justice in which everyone receives exactly his just deserts. No such system exists or ever will. One must compare instead the proposed policy with what exists now, with all its imperfections, and ask whether the gains in crime reduction are worth the risks entailed when we try to make predictions about human behaviour.

The first issue is whether it is permissible to allow crime-control to be an objective of sentencing policy. Some persons, such as Andrew von Hirsch, claim that only retribution—what he calls "just deserts"—can be a legitimate basis for sentencing. To some extent, he is undoubtedly correct. Even if we were absolutely certain that a convicted murderer would never murder again, we would still feel obliged to impose a relatively severe sentence in order to vindicate the principle that life is dear and may not be unlawfully taken without paying a price. Moreover, the sentences given low-rate offenders must reflect society's judgment as to the moral blame such behaviour deserves, and the sentences given high-rate offenders ought not exceed what society feels is the highest sentence appropriate to the crime for which the offenders were convicted. And low-rate offenders should get a sufficiently severe sentence to help persuade them, and others like them, not to become high-rate offenders. Still, after allowing for all of these considerations, there will inevitably remain a range of possible sentences within which the goal of incapacitation can be served. The range will exist in part because there is no objective way to convert a desire for retribution into a precise sentence for a given offence and in part because legislatures will almost invariably act so as to preserve some judicial discretion so that the circumstances of a case which cannot be anticipated in advance may affect the sentence. Among those circumstances is a concern for protecting society from the threat that a given offender represents.

The second issue is whether our prediction methods are good enough to allow them to influence sentence length. The answer to that question depends on what one will accept as "good enough". Absolute certainty will never be attainable. Moreover, criminal justice *now*, at almost every stage, operates by trying to predict future behaviour. When a prosecutor decides how much plea bargaining he will allow, he is trying to predict how a judge or jury will react to his evidence, and he is often trying to guess how dangerous an offender he has in his grasp. When a judge sets bail, he is always making a prediction about the likelihood of a person out on bail showing up for his trial and is frequently trying to predict whether the person, if out on bail, will commit another crime while free. When a defence attorney argues in favour of his client being released on his own recognizance, without bail, he is trying to persuade the judge to accept his prediction that the accused will not skip town. When the judge passes a sentence, he is trying, at least in part, to predict whether the convicted person represents a future threat to society. When a parole board considers a convict's application for early release, it tries to predict—often on the basis of a quantitative system, called a "base expectancy table"—whether the person will become a recidivist if released. Virtually every member of the criminal justice system is routinely engaged in predicting behaviour, often on the basis of very scant knowledge and quite dubious rules of thumb. The question, therefore, is this: are the kinds of predictions that scholars such as Greenwood make about future

criminality better (more accurate) and thus fairer than the predictions prosecutors and judges now make?

A third issue is tougher. Is it fair for a low-rate offender who is caught committing a serious crime to serve a shorter sentence (because he is not much of a threat to society) than a high-rate offender who gets caught committing a relatively minor offence? Probably not. Sentences would have to have legal boundaries set so that the use of selective incapacitation could not lead to perverse sentences—armed robbers getting one year, purse-snatchers getting five.

Finally, there is bound to be a debate about the legal and even ethical propriety of using certain facts as the basis for making predictions. Everyone would agree that race should not be a factor; everyone would probably agree that prior record should be a factor. I certainly believe that it is proper to take into account an offender's juvenile as well as his adult record, but I am aware that some people disagree. But can one take into account alcohol or drug use? Suppose the person claims to be cured of his drinking or his drug problem; do we believe him? And if we do, do we wipe the slate clean of information about these matters? And should we penalize more heavily persons who are chronically unemployed, even if unemployment is a good predictor of recidivism? Some people will argue that this is tantamount to making unemployment a crime, though I think that overstates the matter. After all, advocates of pretrial release of arrested persons, lenient bail policies, and diverting offenders away from jail do not hesitate to claim that having a good employment record should be counted in the accused's favour. If employment counts in favour of some, then obviously unemployment may be counted against others. Since advocates of "bail reform" are also frequent opponents of incapacitation, selective or collective, it is incumbent on them to straighten out their own thinking on how we make use of employment records. Nonetheless, this important issue deserves thoughtful attention.

On one matter, critics of prison may take heart. If Greenwood and the others are correct, then an advantage of selective incapacitation is that it can be accomplished without great increases (or perhaps any increases) in the use of prisons. It is a way of allocating more rationally the existing stock of prison cells to produce, within the constraints of just deserts, greater crime-control benefits. Many offenders—indeed most offenders—would probably have their sentences shortened, and the space thereby freed would be allocated to the small number of high-rate offenders whom even the most determined opponents of prison would probably concede should be behind bars. ∎

Selective Incapacitation: Some Doubts

Andrew von Hirsch

Prediction research in criminology has, by and large, focused on characteristics of offenders. Various facts about criminals are recorded: age, previous arrests and convictions, social history, and so forth. It is then statistically determined which of these factors are most strongly associated with subsequent offending. The result is a "selective" prediction strategy: among those convicted of a given type of offence, some will be identified as bad risks and others not.

Traditional Prediction Methods

Traditional statistical prediction techniques pursued this selective approach. Generally, they found that certain facts about an offender—principally, previous criminal history, drug habits, and

Andrew von Hirsch, "Selective Incapacitation: Some Doubts," from *Principled Sentencing: Readings on Theory and Policy, Second Edition*, edited by Andrew von Hirsch and Andrew Ashworth (Oxford: Hart Publishing, 1998): 121–127. Reprinted by permission of Hart Publishing, Ltd.

history of unemployment—were to a modest extent indicative of increased likelihood of recidivism.

These techniques did not, however, distinguish between serious and trivial recidivism. Both the offender who subsequently committed a single minor offence and the individual who committed many serious new crimes were lumped together as recidivists. Moreover, the techniques offered no promise of reduced crime rates, as they did not attempt to estimate aggregate crime-prevention effects. Locking up the potential recidivist thus assured only that he or she would be restrained; since other criminals remained at large, it did not necessarily diminish the overall risk of victimization. By the 1970s, these limitations reduced penologists' interest in traditional prediction techniques.

"Selective Incapacitation"

Surveys of imprisoned offenders, conducted in the United States in the early 1980s, found that a small number of such persons admitted responsibility for a disproportionate number of serious offences. If that minority of dangerous offenders could be identified and segregated, perhaps this could reduce crime rates after all. These surveys thus generated a renewed interest in prediction research.

The most notable product was a Rand corporation study published in 1982 by Peter W. Greenwood. Greenwood named his prediction strategy "selective incapacitation". His idea was to target *high-rate, serious* offenders—those likely to commit frequent acts of robbery or other violent crimes in future. For that purpose he took a group of incarcerated robbers,

asked them how frequently they had committed such crimes, and then identified the characteristics of those reporting the highest robbery rates. From this, he fashioned a seven-factor predictive index, which identified the high-rate offenders on the basis of their early criminal records and histories of drug use and unemployment.

Greenwood also devised a method of projecting the crime reduction impact of this technique. On the basis of offender self-reports, he estimated the annual rate of offending of those robbers who were identified as high risks by his prediction index. He then calculated the number of robberies that, supposedly, would be prevented by incarcerating such individuals for given periods. By increasing prison terms for the high-risk robbers while reducing terms for the others, he concluded, one could reduce the robbery rate by as much as 15 to 20 per cent—without causing prison populations to rise.

Questions of Effectiveness

While the study initially attracted much interest, problems later became apparent. One difficulty is making the predictions hold up when official data of the kind a sentencing court has available are relied upon. The objective of selective incapacitation is to target the potential high-rate serious offenders, and distinguish them from recidivists who reoffend less frequently or gravely. To make this distinction, the Rand studies, including Greenwood's, relied upon offender self-reports. A sentencing court, however, is seldom in the position to rely upon the defendant facing sentence to supply the necessary information about his criminal past. The court would have to rely on officially recorded information about offenders' adult and juvenile records, and such records make the distinction poorly. When Greenwood's data were reanalyzed to see how well the potential high-risk serious offenders could be identified from information available in court records, the results were disappointing. The officially recorded facts — arrests, convictions, and meagre information about offenders' personal histories — did not permit the potential high-rate robbers to be distinguished from (say) the potential car thieves. The factors in the self-report study that had proved the most useful — such as early and extensive youthful violence and multiple drug use, were not reflected in court records. To make the predictions work, the courts would have to obtain and rely on information in school and social-service files — with all the problems of practicability and due process that would involve.

Flaws were found, also, in the projections of preventive impact. Greenwood based his crime reduction estimates on the self-reported activities of *incarcerated* robbers, and then extrapolated those estimates to robbers generally. Incarcerated robbers, however, are scarcely a representative group; they may well rob more frequently than robbers generally in the community. (It is like trying to learn about the smoking habits of smokers generally by studying the self-reported smoking activity of admittees to a lung cancer ward.) When this extrapolation is eliminated, the projected crime reduction impact is reduced by about one-half. Other

defects in the projections exist. Greenwood assumed, for example, that his high-rate robbers would continue offending for a long time. When shorter and more realistic residual criminal careers are assumed instead, the estimated preventive effect shrinks.

These doubts are confirmed by the 1986 report of the National Academy of Sciences' panel on criminal careers. The panel included several noted advocates of predictively-based sentencing, and the report endorses the idea of predictive strategies (within certain limits) *if* these could be shown to be effective. Nevertheless, the panel's conclusions on the crime-preventive effects of selective incapacitation are sceptical. After recalculating Greenwood's results and scaling his initial preventive estimates down considerably, the panel notes that even those revised estimates (1) do not hold up in two of the three jurisdictions studied; (2) would shrink further were the scale drawn from a broader and potentially more heterogeneous population than persons in confinement and were it to utilize officially recorded rather than self-reported information; and (3) could nearly disappear if the estimated length of the residual criminal career were scaled down. While the report urges further research, it does not claim that selective incapacitation methods now exist that yield more satisfactory results.

Prospects for Improvement

Can these difficulties be overcome? Greenwood's research was only the beginning, and future selective incapacitation studies might conceivably do better. The obstacles are considerable, however. If the aim is to distinguish potential high-rate, serious offenders from lesser potential criminals, this remains difficult to achieve using the scant official records courts have at their disposal. Records of early offending might become somewhat more accessible, with a change in the law concerning the confidentiality of juvenile records—but such records, notoriously, suffer from incompleteness and inaccuracy. Social histories, such as drug use and employment, will be even more difficult to ascertain accurately.

Estimation of the impact of selective incapacitation on crime rates involves difficult problems of sampling. Analyses of convicted or incarcerated offenders' criminal activities suffer from the difficulty mentioned already: it is not clear to what extent these persons' activities are representative of the activity of offenders in the community. Samples drawn from the general population are free from such bias, but may contain too small a number of active offenders.

Another obstacle concerns estimating the length of criminal careers. The serious offenders with whom selective incapacitation is concerned generally would be imprisoned in any event; the main policy issue is the length of their confinement. The strategy is to impose longer terms on the supposed high-risk offenders, but that assumes they will continue their criminal activities. Little prevention is achieved if the bad risks who are confined are those whose careers will end fairly soon. This means that selective incapacitation, to succeed, needs not merely to pick out high-risk offenders but *those who are likely to continue offending for an appreciable time*. But how much do

we know about forecasting the residual career? The National Academy panel suggests that career termination may depend on new variables—not so much prior criminal history but later events, including steady employment and marriage. Those are scarcely matters concerning which a court can readily obtain information at time of sentencing.

A valuable review of recent incapacitation research has been provided by Franklin Zimring and Gordon Hawkins writing a decade after the National Academy Report. They note that the research problems mentioned above have yet to be resolved—and notes a variety of other problems for example, failure to deal adequately with the phenomenon of group offending (where confining one member of the group does not necessarily reduce the group's level of offending) and of substitution (where incarcerated offenders' criminal activities are taken up by other potential offenders). He notes also the tendency of incapacitative strategies to yield diminishing returns, if it is indeed true that only a limited number of offenders commit large numbers of crimes. He concludes that present projection methods "tend to invite overestimation of the amount of incapacitation to be expected from marginal increments of imprisonment". Real improvements in ways of estimating incapacitative effects seem not yet to have occurred.

Proportionality Problems

Selective prediction strategies—whether the traditional sort or newer methods such as Greenwood's—suffer also from a serious ethical problem: their conflict with the requirements of proportionality. The conflict stems from the character of the factors relied upon to predict. Those predictive factors have little bearing on the degree of reprehensibleness of the offender's criminal choices.

Proportionality requires that penalties be based chiefly on the gravity of the crime for which the offender currently stands convicted. The offender's previous criminal record, if considered at all, should have only a secondary role and the offender's social status is largely immaterial to the penalty he or she deserves.

With selective risk prediction, the emphasis necessarily shifts *away* from the seriousness of the current offence. Since the aim is to select the higher risk individuals from among those convicted of a specified type of crime, the character of the current crime cannot have much weight. Traditional prediction indices largely ignored the gravity of the current offence and concentrated on the offender's earlier criminal and social histories. The newer "selective incapacitation" techniques have a similar emphasis. Of Greenwood's seven predictive factors, three do not measure criminal activity of a significant nature at all, but the offender's personal drug consumption and lack of stable employment, instead. Of the four other factors, only two measure the offender's recent criminal record; and *none* measure the heinousness (e.g., the degree of violence) of the offender's current offence.

When one tries to take aggregate preventive impact into account, matters become worse. Selective incapacitation techniques, by their own proponents'

reckoning, could promise significant crime reduction effects only by infringing proportionality requirements to a *very* great degree.

Greenwood's projection of a significant reduction in the robbery rate is made on the assumption that robbers who score badly on his prediction index would receive about *eight* years' imprisonment, whereas better-scoring robbers would receive only *one* year in jail. This means a great difference in severity—one of over 800 per cent—in the punishment of offenders convicted of the same offence of robbery; and one that can scarcely begin to be accounted for by distinctions in the seriousness of the offender's criminal conduct. When this punishment differential is narrowed—when high-risk robbers receive only modestly longer terms than robbers deemed lower risks—the crime reduction payoff shrinks to slender proportions, even by Greenwood's estimation methods.

Conclusions

Where does this leave us? A limited capacity to forecast risk has long existed: persons with criminal records, drug habits, and no jobs tend to recidivate at a higher rate than other offenders, as researchers have known for years. However, the limitations in that forecasting capacity must be recognized—for selective incapacitation as well as more traditional forecasting techniques. Identifying high-risk, serious offenders will be impeded by the quality of information available (or likely to become available) to sentencing courts. The potential impact of selective incapacitation on crime rates is far below proponents' initial estimates, and is likely to be modest. Considerations of proportionality limit the inequalities in sentence that may fairly be visited for the sake of restraining high-risk offenders; and limiting these permissible inequalities will, in turn, further restrict the technique's impact on crime. Selective incapacitation—far from being the near panacea some of its advocates have asserted it is—is both on empirical and ethical grounds a device of limited potential, at best. ■

⠿ The Continuing Debate

What Is New

"Three strikes" laws are the most obvious and most controversial manifestation of the selective incapacitation approach: in 2004, 26 states as well as the U.S. federal government had three strikes laws: in most of those cases, conviction for the third offense brings a mandatory life sentence with no possibility of parole. Though sentences under the California Three Strikes Law can be very severe—Leandro Andrade, a heroin addict, was sentenced to 50 years with no parole for shoplifting children's videotapes (valued at $154), which he wanted to give as Christmas presents to his nieces—the U.S. Supreme Court has upheld such sentences, ruling in 2003 that life imprisonment for shoplifting does not count as "cruel and unusual punishment," and so does not violate the Eighth Amendment. In the Andrade case, the Ninth Circuit Court of Appeals had ruled that Andrade's sentence was so cruel and severe as to be unconstitutional; in its 2003 decision (*Lockyer v. Andrade*), the Supreme Court split 5 to 4; it reversed the Ninth Circuit Court, and reinstated Andrade's 50-year sentence. Writing for the minority, Justice Souter stated that "The application of the Eighth amendment prohibition against cruel and unusual punishment to terms of years is articulated in the 'clearly established' principle acknowledged by the court: a sentence grossly disproportionate to the offense for which it is imposed is unconstitutional . . . If Andrade's sentence is not grossly disproportionate, the principle has no meaning."

Where to Find More

David Greenberg proposed selective incapacitation in "The Incapacitative Effect of Imprisonment, Some Estimates," *Law and Society Review*, Volume 9 (1975): 541–580. The first detailed selective incapacitation plan was Peter Greenwood, *Selective Incapacitation* (Santa Monica, CA: RAND, 1982); see also Peter W. Greenwood and Susan Turner, *Selective Incapacitation Revisited: Why the High-Rate Offenders Are Hard to Predict* (Santa Monica, CA: RAND, 1987). A detailed statistical analysis of incapacitation policies is presented in William Spelman, *Criminal Incapacitation* (New York: Plenum Press, 1994). Dean J. Champion examines the challenges of classification in *Measuring Offender Risk: A Criminal Justice Sourcebook* (Westport, CN: Greenwood Press, 1994). See also L. Sherman,

D. Gottfredson, D. MacKenzie, J. Eck, P. Reuter, and S. Bushway, "Preventing Crime: What Works, What Doesn't, What's Promising: A Report to the United States Congress" (1998); go to www.ncjrs.org/works/index.htm.

Andrew von Hirsch raises concerns about the justice of selective incapacitation in "The Ethics of Selective Incapacitation: Observations on the Contemporary Debate," *Crime & Delinquency*, Volume 30, Number 2 (1984): 175–194.

An excellent detailed critique of selective incapacitation policies is Kathleen Auerhahn, *Selective Incapacitation and Public Policy: Evaluating California's Imprisonment Crisis* (Albany, NY: SUNY Press, 2003). Auerhahn is also the author of several very insightful studies of key elements of selective incapacitation: "Selective Incapacitation and the Problem of Prediction," *Criminology*, Volume 37, Number 4 (November 1999): 703–734; "Selective Incapacitation, Three Strikes, and the Problem of Aging Prison Populations: Using Simulation Modeling to See the Future," *Criminology & Public Policy*, Volume 1, Number 3 (2002): 353–388; and "Conceptual and Methodological Issues in the Prediction of Behavior," *Criminology & Public Policy*, Volume 5, Number 4 (2006): 771–778.

A powerful statistical critique of the effectiveness of selective incapacitation policies (especially three strikes laws) is Daniel Macallair, "Striking Out: The Failure of California's 'Three Strikes and You're Out' Law," *Stanford Law and Policy Review*, Volume 11, Number 1 (Fall 1999): 65–74. A very interesting article by Scott Ehlers, Vincent Schiraldi, and Jason Ziedenberg, "Still Striking Out: Ten Years of California's Three Strikes Law," is available at the Justice Policy Institute website: http://www.justicepolicy.org/images/upload/04–03_REP_CAStillStrikingOut_AC.pdf.

A superb history and examination of California's three strikes law is Joe Domanick, *Cruel Justice: Three Strikes and the Politics of Crime in America's Golden State* (Berkeley, CA: University of California Press, 2004).

The problems associated with accurately "selecting" those who are likely to commit violent crimes is addressed by Thomas Mathiesen in "Selective Incapacitation Revisited," *Law and Human Behavior*, Volume 22, Number 4 (August 1998): 455–469; in the same issue, immediately following that article, is C. D. Webster, "Comment on Thomas Mathiesen's Selective Incapacitation Revisited," on pages 471–476.

See also the readings for Debate 10 on mandatory minimum sentences.

Supermax Prisons: Valuable or Vile?

Supermax Prisons Are a Valuable Element of the Correctional System
  Advocate: Gregory L. Hershberger, regional director for the North
    Central Region of the Federal Bureau of Prisons and former warden
    of ADX Florence.
  Source: "To the Max," *Corrections Today*, Volume 60, Number 1
    (February 1998): 54–57.
Supermax Prisons Are Part of the Problem Rather Than the Solution
  Advocates: Jesenia M. Pizarro, Michigan State University;
    Vanja M. K. Stenius, Rutgers University; and Travis C. Pratt,
    Washington State University.
  Source: "Supermax Prisons: Myths, Realities, and the Politics of
    Punishment in American Society," *Criminal Justice Policy Review*,
    Volume 17, Number 1 (March 2006): 6–21.

Over the last 25 years the United States has vastly increased its prison population and number of prisons. In 1980, the number of prisoners in state and federal prisons (not counting those in local jails, including persons jailed while awaiting trial) was 320,000; in 2005, it was 1.5 million. When prisoners in jails (including those who are being held in jail while awaiting trial) are added, the total number held in U.S. jails and prisons (according to U.S. Justice Department statistics for mid-year 2005) is 2,186,230 prisoners. In 1980, the United States was already a world leader in the number of its citizens behind bars, and the prison boom of the last quarter century has propelled the United States to the top: counting the prisoners held in local jails, the U.S. currently imprisons 738 persons for every 100,000 residents (only Rwanda has a higher rate, as a result of many convictions following the genocide). By comparison, Canada imprisons 102 persons per 100,000; Germany, 98; Sweden, 64; Japan, 37. That is, the United States imprisons at a rate more than 7 times that of Canada and Germany, 12 times Sweden's rate, and 20 times the Japanese imprisonment rate. A significant part of this prison building boom has been the construction of supermax (or "ultra-max") prisons: from 1 in 1984 to currently more than 60.

214

Supermax prisons are motivated by a desire for control of inmates, but also by the strong retributive orientation of many U.S. politicians and U.S. voters. Thus for many, there is little interest in whether the conditions of supermax prisons are inhumane, or whether they damage the psychological health of inmates, or whether they reduce violence in prisons or reduce recidivism. The harsh conditions of supermax incarceration are often regarded as an end-in-itself: prisons are *supposed* to be harsh environments where prisoners suffer retribution. Though such a justification may appeal to some politicians, criminal justice professionals make much deeper inquiries into the supermax system, exploring whether it has any legitimate purpose, whether that purpose is effectively met, whether it could be met more economically and humanely, and whether there are unacceptable secondary effects from the use of supermax prisons. All of these questions are taken up by the readings for this chapter.

Gregory Hershberger argues that supermax prisons, with their extreme resources for isolating and controlling prisoners, result in "safe, secure, and humane" incarceration for the most violent and dangerous prisoners. In particular, supermax facilities can still offer isolated inmates the opportunity to participate in educational, religious, and recreational programs—though almost always by way of closed-circuit television— while the prisoner remains in strict isolation. Furthermore, Hershberger maintains that such severe settings are essential for safely supervising large groups of violent prisoners. Pizarro, Stenius, and Pratt question whether supermax facilities are actually effective in reducing violence, and they emphasize their potential to inflict lasting psychological damage on prisoners, as well as their high monetary costs. Given the lack of empirical support for the benefits of supermax prisons, Pizarro, Stenius, and Pratt examine other possible explanations for their current popularity: in particular, development of a political orientation toward inmates as merely products to be safely contained and managed, rather than as persons who might be rehabilitated; and the rise of several accompanying political "myths."

▦ Points to Ponder

- There appears to be near consensus among criminologists that there is currently little or no empirical research showing the effectiveness of supermax prisons in reducing prison violence (though some believe that future research might show such facilities to be effective). Given the current lack of empirical support for such facilities, what should be our stance toward the building of new facilities? Of continuing to operate existing supermax facilities?
- Though it is often claimed that supermax prisons house only "the worst of the worst," in fact many in supermax prisons are placed there not because they are dangerous or violent, but because they are regarded as "troublemakers": for example, they lead prisoner protests against conditions in prison. Should there be restrictions on which prisoners can be sent to a supermax?

- If a substantial percentage of inmates in supermax prisons suffer psychological problems from their imprisonment, would that count as evidence that being confined in supermax isolation is "cruel and unusual punishment"?

To the Max

Gregory L. Hershberger

Supermax Facilities Provide Prison Administrators With More Security Options

Over the past decade, correctional systems around the nation have activated several high security prisons, which are popularly known as "supermax" institutions. These facilities are designed to hold the most violent, disruptive or escape-prone offenders. By isolating the "worst of the worst," these facilities increase the safety of staff, other inmates and the general public. They also allow inmates in other institutions to live in a more normalized prison environment, with greater freedom of movement and access to educational, vocational and other correctional programs.

In some correctional systems, offenders may be sent to supermax facilities as direct commitments from the courts, but most inmates are sent to them because of their behavior in prison. Among the roughly 400 inmates in the Federal Bureau of Prisons' (BOP) most secure facility, the U.S. Penitentiary Administrative Maximum (ADX) in Florence, Colo.,

approximately 20 percent are there for the murder or attempted murder of a fellow inmate, 18 percent for assaulting another inmate with a weapon, 16 percent for serious assault on a staff member, 10 percent for a serious escape attempt and 5 percent for rioting. Other reasons for placement in this facility include attempted murder of a staff member, taking a staff member hostage, leading a work or food strike, introducing narcotics into an institution and having a leadership role in a prison gang. Only about 3 percent of the inmates were sent there directly from court. About 6 percent are state boarders, inmates who were involved in the murder of state correctional staff, or inmates who are too disruptive or dangerous for state officials to house safely.

Dispersion vs. Consolidation

For years, correctional administrators have used various strategies for handling especially dangerous inmates and minimizing the disruption they cause to the rest of the system. Historically, they have used two basic models—dispersion and consolidation.

Gregory L. Hershberger, "To the Max," *Corrections Today*, Volume 60, Number 1 (February 1998): 54–57. Reprinted with permission of American Correctional Association, Alexandria, VA.

The dispersion model scatters offenders with unusually dangerous histories or disruptive behavioral patterns throughout the correctional system, thus avoiding a concentration of such offenders in any one location. Staff in each institution share the burden and dangers of supervising and controlling these inmates. In smaller prison systems, the aggressive conduct of these inmates often results in their placement in long-term segregation or detention status. In larger systems, administrators transfer inmates from one institution to another, if only to disrupt their alliances and give staff relief from the stress of dealing with them. In the past, entire institutions often were managed in a more rigid, highly controlled manner in order to reduce the threat posed by this relatively small number of inmates.

Among the benefits of the dispersion model is the fact that no single institution is required to deal with a large number of problem inmates. In addition, some prison administrators believe that it is easier to manage small groups of inmates of this caliber. Finally, it was once thought that a number of institutions holding a few such individuals each would require the allocation of fewer security-related resources overall.

In contrast, the consolidation model involves placing all highly dangerous inmates at one location and controlling them through reliance on heightened security procedures. The potential drawback of adopting a consolidation model is that the institution holding this group is necessarily subjected to a dramatically different routine and will, in all likelihood, require additional staff and expensive security modifications.

Alcatraz was the prototypical consolidation-model institution at the federal level. From 1934 to 1963, it operated as the prime federal prison resource, housing many of the more notorious or dangerous offenders in the federal system. Alcatraz was closed in 1963—not because of flaws in the consolidation model, but because the island prison was very expensive to operate and maintain, and because there was a shift in correctional philosophy during the so-called "medical model" or rehabilitation era.

When the BOP closed Alcatraz, it decided to disperse its hard-core offenders throughout the various federal prisons, rather than move them as a group to another single location. During most of the 1960s and the early 1970s, the BOP managed its most dangerous offenders by using the dispersion model. However, in the late '70s, the BOP began moving toward the consolidation model once again, concentrating its most troublesome inmates at the U.S. Penitentiary in Marion, Ill.

Consolidation Pros and Cons

Focusing extra security resources on a single location is thought by many corrections practitioners to be far more efficient and effective. Under the consolidation model, staff training for managing this more homogeneous group is simplified, and operational procedures are much more refined. But more important, staff and inmates in other institutions throughout the prison system see their safety enhanced, and rigid controls lessened, once the most dangerous individuals are removed to a single, more highly controlled location.

The BOP recognized that the consolidation strategy for reducing violence in its mainline institutions had its risks. While the benefits in terms of overall system safety and order clearly were worthwhile, the dimensions of those risks soon became evident. In 1979, a series of serious assaults, inmate murders and the attempted murders of two staff in Marion's dining room demonstrated the volatility and potential danger of the new population mixture. A special task force, convened to deal with the increasing violence at Marion, recommended that the institution be converted to a tightly controlled, unitized operation that would permit the continued consolidation of the most violent, assaultive and disruptive inmates at one institution and would better protect staff and inmates from violence. However, implementation of that recommendation was deferred, and Marion's daily routines continued to resemble those of a traditional institution.

By 1980, Marion's operation began to show clear signs of the underlying stresses of using this quasi-normal system to deal with such aggressive offenders. Assaults on inmates and staff continued; there were major incidents in the administrative detention unit; and inmates staged three major work stoppages, the last of which lasted for four months. The BOP decided to remove industrial operations from Marion altogether, and convert the institution into the more highly structured operation envisioned several years earlier. This was done by expanding the restricted movement and program procedures which were initiated during the strike.

Management Challenges

Prison administrators recognize better than most the difficulty of operating a minimum privilege, maximum control facility. As a result, even though numerous serious incidents underscored the difficult and dangerous nature of the inmate group at Marion, various attempts were made to return the institution to some semblance of normalcy throughout 1982 and most of 1983. Unfortunately, each step toward normalization was met by additional assaults and other serious incidents, generating increased concern for the safety of staff and inmates. In October 1983, two staff members who were working in the most secure area of Marion were murdered in separate incidents on the same day, and two other staff were seriously injured. Just days later, an inmate was murdered and several staff were assaulted during a group disturbance. These events culminated in the final realization that the type of inmates confined at Marion could not be managed in the same manner as typical penitentiary inmates. Thus, the decision was made to convert the institution into a long-term, highly controlled operation—a "supermax" facility.

While this management program seemed to control the inmate population, the BOP found that Marion's design and layout was not particularly well-suited for its mission. For example, because education, recreation, health services and other vital program areas were centrally located, inmates often had to be moved from one location to another. For security reasons, each move had to be escorted. Consequently, the high volume of inmate movement consumed an enormous number of staff hours and significantly threatened staff safety. Accordingly, in the mid-'80s, BOP administrators began thinking about a new high-security facility, one that was designed specifically for high-security operations and that took advantage of the many advances in inmate management and correctional technology that occurred between 1960 and 1980.

After years of careful planning, the BOP opened ADX Florence—one of the most sophisticated supermax prisons in the nation. Since its activation in 1994, ADX Florence has been extremely effective in housing the federal prison system's most dangerous offenders in a safe, secure and humane manner.

ADX Operations

Supermax facilities have been incorrectly characterized as "lockdown" institutions. This is misleading. Lockdowns are relatively short periods of time when all inmates in an institution are confined to their cells because of an institutional emergency, or for some other overriding reason such as a facilitywide shakedown. During a lockdown, all but the most basic services are suspended. True supermax facilities operate quite differently. A supermax facility is not simply a segregation unit in a maximum security penitentiary. It is a full institution, with unique security elements and programmatic features.

The main purpose of a supermax facility is to control the inmates' behavior until they demonstrate that they can be moved back to a traditional, open-population penitentiary. As they demonstrate increasingly responsible behavior, ADX inmates move incrementally from more to less restrictive housing units. Each successive unit allows more privileges and more interaction with staff and other inmates.

Administrative maximum security operations differ from typical penitentiary operations in several ways. Inmates are handcuffed whenever they come in contact with staff; this prevents violent offenders from assaulting staff and other inmates, and eliminates the possibility that escape-prone inmates will attempt to take a hostage or access an area of the institution that will facilitate an escape. Inmates eat and recreate individually, or in small, carefully screened and supervised groups; this differs from procedures in a typical prison, where inmates have largely unrestrained contact with each other and staff throughout the day. Inmates are confined in their cells for larger portions of the day; in a typical prison, an inmate would have 12 to 16 hours of out-of-cell time, while an inmate in an administrative maximum security institution would be much more restricted.

Programs in an administrative maximum security setting rely primarily upon individual inmate-based delivery systems (self-study courses, closed circuit television, staff visits to the housing unit) as opposed to having inmates go in groups to a central program area. Visiting in such an institution is generally noncontact, in contrast to the contact visiting that is permitted in most institutions. Staff/inmate ratios are higher, to provide increased supervision and capability for searching inmates, cells and other areas of the institution in order to prevent assaults and disruptive incidents.

Unique Confinement Conditions

While conditions of confinement for inmates in an administrative maximum security setting are highly restrictive relative to the general population of most typical penitentiaries, these facilities are an improvement on conditions in a typical detention or segregation unit at a regular penitentiary, because they provide increased movement, more contact with staff and more opportunities to participate in programs. Institutions such as ADX Florence are intended to control disruptive and dangerous behavior, yet also permit a reasonable amount of access to necessary programs and offer inmates the means to progress to a more typical penitentiary setting.

Rather than being housed in traditional lockdown conditions, inmates at ADX Florence, for example are offered a range of programs and services. Most are delivered at the inmate's cell or in the individual unit, eliminating the danger and expense associated with frequent escorted moves. Inmates do start their time at Florence under relatively close controls; they spend the majority of their time in their cells or in the cellhouse. On- and off-unit recreation, visiting, medical care, in-cell television, religious activities, education and other self-improvement programs are available from the day of arrival at Florence. The federal courts have consistently found that the BOP's administrative maximum operations are consistent with constitutional requirements related to conditions of confinement.

ADX inmates are offered an opportunity to demonstrate nondangerous behavior through compliance with institutional rules. As they do, they progress through a graduated system of housing units, with each unit providing increased freedom and work opportunities, all contingent on the inmate avoiding misconduct. Proper conduct in this program results in eventual transfer to other, less controlled institutions.

The ADX program is based on the assumption that every inmate will be given the opportunity to demonstrate that he or she doesn't need to be at the ADX. Most progress through the program in a little more than three years (42 months, on average) and then are returned to open population prisons. Once in regular penitentiaries, more than 80 percent of former administrative maximum inmates behave well enough that a return to the program is unnecessary.

Conclusion

The essential challenge of operating a supermax facility is to properly balance staff and inmate safety needs against important constitutional and correctional management principles that govern prison life. It is critical to remember that with this type of offender, good treatment starts with vital safety considerations—for both staff and inmates.

The challenges posed by these inmates are very real, as are the dangers they present to staff, other inmates and the public. If a prison system confines all of its dangerous offenders in one institution, it can increase the safety of staff and inmates at other locations in the system and operate these facilities in a more open, normalized fashion. Highly refined security procedures and appropriate programming within the supermax facility allow for safe and secure operations while providing even the most dangerous offenders with reasonable opportunities to demonstrate pro-social behavior and earn their way back into an open population institution. ∎

Supermax Prisons
Myths, Realities, and the Politics of Punishment in American Society

Jesenia M. Pizarro, Vanja M. K. Stenius, and Travis C. Pratt

Since the 1970s, the United State's correctional system has undergone dramatic changes. Prison populations have skyrocketed in response to changing sentencing policies, such as the mandatory sentences implemented during the War on Drugs, and increasing crime rates. These changes contributed to numerous problems within correctional facilities such as overcrowding and violence. In the face of inmate violence, lawsuits, federal oversight, and other problems, prison administrators sought new means for addressing these issues, one of which was the placement of violence-prone and disruptive inmates in supermax facilities or units. The growing popularity of these facilities made them "one of the most dramatic features of the great American experiment with mass incarceration during the last quarter of the 20th century".

The National Institute of Corrections defined supermax prisons as follows: "free-standing facilities, or a distinct unit within a facility, that provides for the management and secure control of inmates who have been officially designated as exhibiting violent or seriously disruptive behavior while incarcerated". The general purpose of these facilities is to increase control over inmates known to be violent, assaultive, major escape risks, or likely to promote disturbances in the general prison population. Prison administrators achieve this goal by confining inmates to their cell for 22 or 23 hours a day and by limiting human contact to instances when medical staff, clergy, or a counselor stops in front of the inmate's cell during routine rounds. The rationale behind these practices is to segregate the most dangerous inmates to protect prison staff and the inmates in the general prison population. Furthermore, proponents of supermax prisons assert that the harshness of

Jesenia M. Pizarro, Vanja M. K. Stenius, and Travis C. Pratt, "Supermax Prisons: Myths, Realities, and the Politics of Punishment in American Society," *Criminal Justice Policy Review*, Volume 17, Number 1 (March 2006): 6–21. Copyright © 2006 by SAGE Publications, Inc. Reprinted by permission of SAGE Publications, Inc.

these institutions deters other inmates from committing criminal acts inside prisons.

The number of supermax institutions in the United States has grown from 1 facility in 1984, the Federal Penitentiary at Marion, Illinois, to approximately 60 facilities in 1999 throughout more than 30 states in the country. At the end of 1998, about 20,000 inmates, or 1.8% of those serving sentences of 1 year of more in state and federal prisons, were housed in such facilities.

Despite the spread of supermax institutions over the past 20 years, little research has addressed the effect that placement of inmates in supermax prisons has on their behavior, the administration of correctional institutions, and the community. Most of what is known, or can be inferred, about supermax facilities comes from research on the effects of isolation on inmates' behavior, which suggests that supermax facilities may damage inmates' mental health while failing to meet their purported goal of reducing violence and other problematic behavior within the general prison population. Rather than serving as a panacea for dealing with problematic inmates, supermax institutions may contribute to problems for correctional administrators and increase economic cost to the community without apparent benefits, especially once inmates are released back into their communities or into the general prison population.

Given the potential for increasing costs, both fiscal and human, it is important to consider why supermax prisons have become so popular in the United States during the last 2 decades. This article explores changes in penal policy,

the politics of punishment, and the economics of crime control in the United States that help to explain why supermax prisons gained widespread support in recent years. A review of the penology literature suggests that supermax prisons gained support during recent years because of changes in the ideologies that drive corrections. Supermax prisons represent an ideology of toughness and efficacy that concurs with recent changes in penal policy and thought. This ideology is based on certain myths—in particular, the myths of novelty, public safety, and managerial efficacy—and not realities. We propose that these myths have contributed to the adoption of supermax prisons by many jurisdictions because they create a false, yet persuasive, perception that these institutions offer a tough new form of punishment that acts as an efficient tool for managing inmates while at the same time protecting society.

Changes in American Penal Culture and Policy

During the last 30 years, there have been numerous changes in penal policy. The changes that took place do not just reflect an increase in the prison population, which has been substantial, but reflect shifts in how the public, policy makers, and correctional administrators think about and respond to crime and offenders. Garland and other penologists attribute the shifts in penal policy to factors such as the decline of rehabilitation as a guiding philosophy for corrections, changes in the goals of the penal institution, the politicization of crime control, and the commercialization of prisons. Together, these changes prompted the shift in penal discourse and the politics of punishment we see today. These new politics of punishment created an environment in which supermax prisons are seen as both necessary and acceptable.

Decline of Rehabilitation

Although numerous factors contributed to the loss of faith in rehabilitation in the 1970s, Martinson's infamous review, which has been misread by most to indicate that nothing works in rehabilitation, provided an argument against rehabilitation not only for policy makers and practitioners but also for scholars who began reevaluating the goals of punishment. The reevaluation of rehabilitation created opportunities for other penal philosophies, culminating in the emergence of just deserts as the leading penal goal in the United States as well as a greater emphasis on deterrence and incapacitation. Although just deserts sought to ensure proportionality with a minimal level of punishment, the focus on desert and blameworthiness reestablished the legitimacy of a retributive discourse and increasingly punitive responses to crime. This occurred as penal policy became less concerned with achieving crime reduction through individualized sentencing and focused increasingly on fitting the punishment to the crime as prescribed in just-deserts theory. Within this structure, offenders' social situations (e.g., poverty, lack of opportunity) were of minimal significance. People who broke the law were no longer seen as victims of the system (or society) that, with treatment, would change for the better. Instead, offenders were seen as blameworthy and deserving of punishment because they broke the law....

In the absence of rehabilitation as a primary aim in corrections, prisons have acquired a different reason for being. The prisons of today are intended to punish offenders, prevent them from committing new offenses, and deter others from engaging in criminal behavior. Within this context, supermax institutions are a natural extension of a correctional environment that has lost faith in rehabilitation and seeks the most expeditious means of dealing with problematic behavior. Just as the public seeks to remove and punish those deemed dangerous for the sake of public safety, prison officials seek to remove dangerous inmates to enhance prison safety. Placement in these facilities purportedly depends on desert (as measured by dangerousness within the general prison population) and the desire to control the disruptive behavior of inmates for whom rehabilitation or less restrictive means of control are not seen as being viable options. In essence, administrators engage in selective incapacitation and deterrence of troublesome or potentially troublesome inmates by placing them in supermax facilities.

Changes in the Goals of Incarceration of Penal Institutions

New managerial styles and policies accompanied the changing criminological thought regarding the treatment of offenders. Feeley and Simon coined the term *new penology*, which refers to a new management style in corrections that focuses on managing risk. The new penology is not concerned with responsibility, fault, moral sensibility, diagnosis, or intervention and treatment of offenders but with techniques to identify, classify, and manage groups sorted by levels of perceived dangerousness. The increased emphasis on the effective management of prisons influenced sentencing policies and practices through the development of sentencing guidelines and selective incapacitation as well as the operation of prisons through increases in the bureaucracy of the institutions and risk management.

Supermax institutions fit directly under the purview of the new penology, notably in regard to the actuarial aspect of prison management, which focuses on "identifying and managing unruly groups". Supermax prisons were created specifically to manage risk. In fact, the NIC defined supermax prisons as "institutions that provide for the management and secure control of inmates". Furthermore, the inmates in supermax prisons are not those who committed the worst crimes in society. Instead, the inmates placed in supermax facilities are those whom correctional staff believes are a threat to the safety, security, or orderly operation of the facility in which they are housed. The threat that correctional staff believes an inmate presents to the institution can be based on real, tangible facts or simply their perceptions. Correctional administrators assert that placement in a supermax institution is not a penalty but an administrative decision based on a pattern of dangerousness or unconfirmed but reliable evidence of pending disruption (e.g., the prisoner is a leader or member of a gang or other radical movement). The placement of inmates in these institutions is deemed acceptable as part of the new conventional management style in corrections.

The Politicization of Crime Control

Beginning in the 1970s, sentencing (and time served), which was once under the purview of judges, correctional administrators, and parole boards, became an increasingly political issue as legislators gained more control over sentence lengths and other sentencing policies. What began as a bipartisan effort to reduce disparity and increase proportionality in sentencing established a system in which politics and public fear of crime could alter sentencing policies. The War on Crime and War on Drugs politics created a punitive climate in most states in which being tough on crime became essential for political success.

Public fear of crime, which became a major issue in contemporary society, was central to the increasing politicization of crime. Although fear and perceptions of crime do not necessarily coincide with the crime rate, perceptions are what matter to the public and frequently to policy makers. The perception that violence increased, regardless of actual violence, resulted in demands for more punitive actions from the government and the passage of harsher sentencing laws, many of them requiring mandatory sentences for specific offenses. The rise in fear of crime and media attention to crime issues along with some very well-known incidents contributed to an increased emphasis on protecting society, which made it more acceptable, if not mandatory, for policy makers to embrace punitive policies.

Policy makers used public opinion to justify the development of increasingly punitive policies. They argued that the public wants offenders to serve longer sentences under harsher conditions. Putting aside the question of whether public opinion should drive public policy, it nevertheless played an increasing role in justifying get-tough crime policy since the mid-1970s. Law-and-order proponents cited public opinion polls to support their positions and legislation, usually interpreting public opinion as more punitive than it actually is.

With the prioritization of public protection, responses to crime necessarily changed. As Garland wrote, "Today, there is a new and urgent emphasis upon the need for security, the containment of danger, the identification and management of any kind of risk." This holds true both inside and outside the prison walls. Outside of prison, the typical response to getting tough on crime and securing society has been longer sentences for those convicted. Toughness, however, is not limited to the duration of punishment but surfaces in the desire to make the conditions of confinement harsher thus providing inmates with fewer rewards and amenities. In recent years, support dropped for prison amenities ranging from weight-lifting equipment to federal Pell Grants for college courses. Supermax prisons represent the extreme case: total deprivation. Inmates housed in these facilities enjoy none of the amenities that inmates in other prisons have available to them and seem to correspond well with the apparent public mood....

Myths and Realities of Supermax Prisons

The image of supermax prisons as innovative, tough, and efficient concurs with current penal policy not only because the United States has adopted a retributive philosophy but also because these institutions fall under the paradigm of the new penology and they bring money to economically depressed communities. This image of supermax prisons, however, is founded on three myths: the myth of novelty, the myth of public safety, and the myth of managerial efficacy, all of which have promoted the spread of these institutions. These facilities seemingly present a new approach to punishment by emphasizing isolation. Furthermore, they appear to house the worst of the worst thus providing the public and prison administrators with an additional sense of safety and retribution. The reality of supermax institutions is, however, a different story.

Myth of Novelty

One of the premises that contributed to the increase in popularity of supermax facilities is that these institutions present a new form of punishment—total isolation—to deal with problematic and violent inmates. Proponents of supermax prisons assert that the new type of punishment that is carried out in these institutions is effective in deterring future deviant behavior in the general prison population. The reality of supermax prisons is that these prisons do not present a novel form of punishment. The use of solitary confinement, the primary feature of supermax institutions, has been used since the development of prisons and was considered the only desirable method of penal reform in 1787 by the Philadelphia Society for Alleviating the Miseries of Public Prisoners. Segregation was central to the operation of the first penitentiaries where solitude was seen as the means for inmates to reflect on their crimes and repent.

Isolation continued as a primary means of reforming prisoners until the late 1800s when it was abandoned in part because of the harmful effects it had on inmates' psychological health. In 1890, the U.S. Supreme Court ruled that the main features of solitary confinement were too severe, because solitary confinement caused inmates to become violently insane. As a result, solitary confinement was adopted solely as a tool to temporarily discipline disruptive inmates. As such, it became, and continues to be, the most common disciplinary action taken against inmates exhibiting disruptive behavior. This method differed from the original solitary confinement practices, because inmates would only serve, based on the seriousness of their violation, a determinate amount of time. Despite the lessons learned in the 1800s, corrections administrators once again embraced indeterminate solitary confinement policies with the advent of the supermax institution in the 1980s (although under a different rationale).

Myth of Public Safety

The claims by prison administrators that supermax prisons house the worst of the worst inmates is one of the biggest selling points of these institutions, because it provides the public and prison administrators with an additional sense of safety. The reality of supermax prisons, however, is that these assertions have not been demonstrated empirically and that they are based on speculations. Although it is true that supermax prisons can temporarily alleviate prison violence through the inca-

pacitation of problematic inmates, the long-term effects of supermax institutions on inmates potentially contribute to future violence by contributing to mental illness and decreasing inmates' level of social functioning.

Supermax prisons also fail to enhance public safety, because the inmates housed in these facilities are not necessarily the most dangerous for the general public. Contrary to popular belief, inmates placed in these institutions are not those who committed the worst crimes in society but those whom correctional staff deem as a threat to the safety, security, or orderly operation of the facility in which they are housed. Placement in a supermax institution is not a penalty but an administrative decision based on a pattern of dangerousness. Their primary function is to provide institutional (e.g., prison) safety, not public safety.

Additionally, the ideology of public and institutional safety surrounding supermax prisons is a myth, because research demonstrates that not all inmates housed in these institutions have committed violent acts *within* prisons. Wells and his colleagues found that supermax facilities also house inmates who violate institution rules, are in protective custody, or are alleged to belong to a gang. Some jurisdictions house mentally ill inmates in supermax facilities because of a lack of mental health resources in regular maximum-, medium-, and minimum-security prisons. Furthermore, some of the jurisdictions that operate supermax facilities indicate that they use these institutions to house inmates on routine segregation (e.g., discipline, protective custody, and program segregation) during shortages of segregation beds in regular facilities.

Regardless of the reason for placement in a supermax institution, most inmates placed there will one day return to society or to the general prison population. In 22 jurisdictions, inmates can complete their court-ordered sentence while in a supermax institution. Only six jurisdictions surveyed by the NIC indicated that inmates placed in supermax prison go through a transitional program (e.g., move inmates from supermax prison into a maximum-security prison, let inmates participate in group activities, place inmates in institutional jobs) before they are released into society or the general prison population. With few exceptions, inmates coming from supermax institutions find themselves returned to their communities after spending several years with minimal human contact.

Releasing inmates from supermax prisons straight into society or the general prison population poses a threat to public safety, because supermax institutions have the potential to damage inmates' mental health. Research on inmates placed in solitary confinement and highly restricted environments (such as supermax prisons) suggests that isolation contributes to psychological and emotional problems. Kupers argued that inmates placed in an environment as stressful as that of a supermax prison begin to lose touch with reality and exhibit symptoms of psychiatric decomposition including difficulty concentrating, heightened anxiety, intermittent disorientation, and a tendency to strike out at people. Similarly, Korn noted that conditions in control units, such as supermax units or facilities, produce feelings of resentment, rage, and mental deterioration. Consequently, supermax prisons potentially endanger society, beyond any criminogenic effects of regular imprisonment, if inmates housed in such facilities deteriorate mentally or become more hostile, violent, or prone to commit offenses than if they had served their sentence in the general population. The deprivation of human contact undermines the ability of inmates released from supermax facilities "to cope with social situations again".

Myth of Managerial Efficacy

The final myth surrounding supermax prisons is that they contribute to the effective management of the prison population. In accordance with the new penology, prison administrators assert that supermax prisons are effective management tools because they serve as a general deterrent within the correctional population—that their presence leads to effective prison management because they curb violence and disturbances within penal institutions. Some jurisdictions even assert that supermax facilities helped significantly reduce the number of assaults on correctional officers, and their existence provides a deterrent to gang members and inmates who endanger prisoners and correctional staff. There is, however, no empirical evidence to support this. Like the assertion that supermax prisons provide safety to the public and the general prison population, the assertions of the managerial efficacy of supermax prisons are based on speculation. One recent study of supermax facilities in Illinois, Arizona, and Minnesota found that the opening of a supermax facility in these jurisdictions did not reduce the levels of inmate-on-inmate violence. Out of the three jurisdictions that were studied, they found that only in Illinois did the opening of a new supermax facility coincide with reductions in assaults against staff. The authors, however, are reluctant to attribute this decrease to the supermax facility because of numerous confounding factors. For example, the Illinois Department of Corrections changed its policies regarding the control of inmates as well as organizational management and staffing after opening the supermax facility.

In the absence of more empirical studies, criminological research on deterrence theory offers some insight into the likely consequences of the operation of supermax facilities on violence in other prisons. Contrary to the assertions of proponents of supermax institutions, deterrence theory suggests that instead of curbing violence and disturbances, supermax prisons may exacerbate these problems. Deterrence may occur at the general or individual level. Given that inmates placed in supermax facilities rarely return to the general population, individual deterrence is not an issue. The purported deterrent mechanism for supermax prisons operates through general deterrence. In theory, general deterrence occurs as individuals observe the imposition of the threatened punishment on others or solely by the knowledge that a given behavior carries a given punishment. This theory asserts that if punishment is distributed with certainty, adequate (and appropriate) severity, and celerity, rates of offending should be low. For deterrence

strategies to be effective, offenders must not only be aware of the sanctions, but they must also believe that they will get caught and punished with the threatened sanction. What is important in the efficacy of sanctions as deterrents is not their actual certainty or severity but individuals' perceptions of certainty and severity.

It is unlikely that the certainty of punishment through placement in supermax facilities serves as a deterrent, because placement in these facilities is relatively rare. Furthermore, placement in these facilities is often based on administrative decisions using risk factors over which the inmate has little control. Twenty-two jurisdictions have specific criteria for placement in a supermax prison, yet the criteria are not always followed. As a result, the perceived certainty of placement in supermax facilities is likely to be low among the general inmate population and become increasingly so as inmates engage in, and observe, disruptive or violent behavior that does not result in placement in a supermax institution.

Experiential effects suggest that threatening inmates with placement in supermax institutions for specified behavior and then failing to do so may actually increase problematic behavior. Additionally, increasing the severity of the punishment has generally been found to be a less effective means of achieving deterrence than increasing the certainty. The argument that the severity of supermax confinement acts as a deterrent does not find support in the deterrence literature, especially if inmates question the certainty of such confinement for violent or disruptive behavior.

Appearing Tough on Crime—Selling the Myths

In 1968, Herbert Packer identified the now classical distinction between the crime control model and the due process model in criminal justice. The due process model reflects the focus on individual rights that was so evident in the 1960s as the U.S. Supreme Court increasingly focused on the rights of the accused. The politicization of crime, beginning with Nixon's adoption of the law-and-order stance, marked a switch to the crime control model. The politicization of crime increased until it was a major focal point for many election campaigns and political agendas. . . .

A popular means of appearing tough on crime was to demand harsh mandatory sentences for certain types of offenders while avoiding policies seen as being soft on crime or coddling inmates within the prison. Although supermax facilities represent a very small part of the correctional population, they have characteristics that have appealed to voters in recent years. Supporting these facilities allows policy makers to appear tough on crime while selling the myths to which the general population can readily relate. Embracing supermax prisons represents the ultimate rejection of prisons that coddle offenders while purportedly (a) offering a novel approach to enhancing public and institutional safety, (b) punishing the most dangerous offenders more severely and keeping them securely locked up, and (c) increasing managerial efficacy by deterring violence within other facilities. Safety is likely to provide the most salient argument for the public. As noted earlier, these selling points are more myth than reality, although within the political landscape, myths may serve equally well as political capital if people take them for fact. If people believe that supermax facilities house the worst of the worst, punishing and providing safety simultaneously, then support for these facilities is likely to continue. . . .

Supermax prisons emerged within a social, political, and correctional culture focused on punitive responses to crime and the need to manage large numbers of individuals. The lack of knowledge about the purpose and operation of these facilities provided politicians with myths that work well in a political environment intent on being tough on crime. Within this context, developing policies portrayed as improving public safety was one means of gaining votes. On the surface, supermax facilities represent the ideal prison for a public that desires a harsh and punitive environment. It was politically safe for politicians to support and promote supermax prisons because of the image that they portray. . . . ■

⚎ The Continuing Debate

What Is New

There have been a number of recent court challenges to supermax prisons and the treatment of prisoners in such facilities. In 2002, the Seventh U.S. Circuit Court of Appeals unanimously ruled that a Wisconsin supermax prisoner, Nathan Gillis, had the right to sue on grounds that his treatment was "cruel and unusual punishment," forbidden under the Eighth Amendment to the Constitution. Writing for the court, Judge Terence Evans prefaced his ruling with this statement:

> Stripped naked in a small prison cell with nothing except a toilet; forced to sleep on a concrete floor or slab; denied any human contact; fed nothing but "nutri-loaf"; and given just a modicum of toilet paper—four squares—only a few times. Although this might sound like a stay at a Soviet gulag in the 1930s, it is, according to the claims in this case, Wisconsin in 2002. Whether these conditions are, as a matter of law, only "uncomfortable, but not unconstitutional," as the State contends, is the issue we consider in this case.

In 2005, in *Wilkinson v. Austin*, the U.S. Supreme Court ruled that due to the special hardships imposed on prisoners at supermax facilities, "inmates have a constitutionally protected liberty interest in avoiding assignment" to such facilities, and therefore the state must satisfy due process requirements (for example, by holding hearings) before assigning inmates to such special facilities. It is well established that the supermax conditions of extreme isolation often lead to and certainly exacerbate mental illness; nonetheless, the courts have not ruled that supermax isolation constitutes cruel and unusual punishment, though they have recognized (in the words of Judge Thelton E. Henderson) that supermax conditions "press the outer bounds of what most humans can psychologically tolerate". Federal courts have, however, consistently ruled that confining the mentally ill in supermax conditions is unconstitutional.

Where to Find More

Descriptions of conditions of incarceration within a supermax prison can be found in Leena Kurki and Norval Morris, "The Purposes, Practices and Problems of Supermax Prisons," in Michael Tonry, editor, *Crime and Justice: A Review of Research*, Volume 28 (Chicago: University of Chicago Press, 2001): 385–424; and in "Cruel and Unusual Punishment," *Harper's*, Volume 303 (2001): 92. On the Web, pictures of a supermax cell, a diagram of a cell, and extensive descriptions of conditions in a supermax prison can be found at a British Broadcasting Corporation website: www.news.bbc.co.uk/2/hi/americas/4972526.stm#graphic. The National Public Radio program *All Things Considered* has an excellent website examining supermax prisons; it is at www.npr.org/templates/story/story.php?storyId-5587644. Go to www.supermaxed.com for links, articles, and newspaper accounts concerning supermax facilities.

A collection of articles in support of supermax prisons is Donice Neal, editor, *Supermax Prisons: Beyond the Rock* (Lanham, MD: American Correctional Association, 2003). Another supporter of supermax prisons is C. Riveland, *Supermax Prisons: Overview and General Considerations* (Washington, DC: U.S. Department of Justice, National Institute of Corrections, 1999). Work critical of supermax prisons includes Sasha Abramsky, "Return of the Madhouse," *The*

American Prospect Magazine (February 11, 2002); M. T. Clarke, "Ohio ACLU Challenges Supermax," *Prison Legal News*, Volume 12 (October 2001); N. D. Miller, "International Protection of the Rights of Prisoners: Is Solitary Confinement in the United States a Violation of International Standards?" *California Western International Law Journal*, Volume 26 (1995): 139–172; Jesenia Pizarro and Vanja M. K. Stenius, "Supermax Prisons: Their Rise, Current Practices, and Effect on Inmates," *The Prison Journal*, Volume 84, Number 2 (June 2004): 248–264; Richard L. Lippke, "Against Supermax," *Journal of Applied Philosophy*, Volume 21, Number 2 (2004): 109–124; and Human Rights Watch, *Out of Sight: Super-Maximum Security Confinement in the United States* (New York: Human Rights Watch, 2000).

A survey of the views of prison wardens concerning supermax facilities can be found in Daniel P. Mears and Jennifer L. Castro, "Wardens' Views on the Wisdom of Supermax Prisons," *Crime and Delinquency*, Volume 52, Number 3 (July 2006): 398–431. A detailed review of current research and debate can be found in Daniel P. Mears and Michael D. Reisig, "The Theory and Practice of Supermax Prisons," *Punishment and Society*, Volume 8, Number 1 (2006); and Daniel P. Mears and Jamie Watson, "Towards a Fair and Balanced Assessment of Supermax Prisons," *Justice Quarterly*, Volume 23, Number 2 (June 2006): 232–270.

An important case on supermax prisons, heard by the U.S. Supreme Court, is *Wilkinson v. Austin*, decided in 2005; for information on the case and the ruling, and for several other useful links, see the Medill Journalism website at Northwestern University: http://docket.medill.northwestern.edu/archives/002051.php. An excellent article on legal issues related to supermax prisons is David Fathi, "The Common Law of Supermax Litigation," *Pace Law Review*, Volume 24 (2004): 675–690; it can be accessed online at http://library.law.pace.edu/PLR24-2/PLR209.pdf.

13

DEBATE

What Are the Rights of Criminals and Prisoners?

The Rights of Prisoners Should Be Restricted
  Advocate: Wesley Smith, Deputy Director of the Governors' Forum at
    the Heritage Foundation.
  Source: "Jailhouse Blues," *National Review* (June 13, 1994): 40–44.
The Rights of Prisoners Must Be Protected
  Advocate: Franklin E. Zimring, William G. Simon Professor of Law
    and Wolfen Distinguished Scholar, University of California,
    Berkeley; and Gordon Hawkins (1919–2004), formerly Director of
    Sydney University Institute of Criminology.
  Source: "Democracy and the Limits of Punishment: A Preface to
    Prisoners' Rights," in *The Future of Imprisonment*, edited by Michael
    Tonry (New York: Oxford University Press, 2004).

In years past, prisoners were regarded as having suffered "civil death"; that is, they were thought to have lost almost all their civil rights as citizens while suffering imprisonment. Under the civil death model, the running of prisons was left up to prison administrators, and the courts tended not to intervene (since prisoners were regarded as having few if any rights to protect in any case). In the 1960s the civil death model was challenged and generally rejected by the courts, and in 1974 the U.S. Supreme Court—in *Pell v. Procunier*—explicitly recognized that prisoners continue to have First Amendment rights (including the freedoms of speech and religion), and those rights can be limited only for legitimate safety and security purposes. Subsequent cases supported the view that prisoners have all their rights that are consistent with maintaining safety and security in a custodial environment. While the "civil death" model has been largely abandoned, vestiges of such thinking remain: in many states, convicted felons are permanently deprived of the basic right to vote, and currently some 4 million U.S. citizens are denied the right to vote due to past felony convictions.

More recently, the Court has been less concerned with the protection of the civil rights of prisoners and more concerned with prison security and ease of operation; in particular, the Court has adopted policies making it more difficult for prisoners to bring suits claiming that their rights have been violated. In addition, The Prison Litigation Reform Act of 1995 increased the challenges to prisoners filing lawsuits to protect their rights: The Act requires that prisoners exhaust all internal prison procedures of appeal prior to filing suit, requires that prisoners pay filing fees (which can often be a heavy burden for prisoners), sets a much higher standard for proof of injury, and makes it more difficult for prisoners to obtain professional legal representation. Thus, while recent Supreme Court cases and legislation have not completely denied the rights of prisoners (they have not returned to the "civil death" model), they have significantly reduced the means of protecting those rights.

Wesley Smith maintains that concern for prisoners' rights has become excessive, and that it interferes with keeping order and carrying out rehabilitation programs in the prisons. His solution is to return more control of prisons to the states, with minimal federal intervention for protecting the constitutional rights of prisoners. Franklin Zimring and Gordon Hawkins defend prisoners' rights as a first line of defense against larger violations of basic civil rights.

⠿ Points to Ponder

- The right to protest against perceived wrongs or injustices is one of our most basic and cherished rights. But in prison, protests by prisoners are typically regarded as a grave threat to prison order and security, and they are severely punished. As Margaret Leland Smith notes, this raises a serious problem:

  > If a self-respecting subject, a prisoner, sees the suffering or abuse of another prisoner, what does her dignity require of her? A moral response will involve recognition of the wrongfulness and some expression of that recognition. But this response will bring her into immediate conflict with the coercive project of prison, may increase the suffering of others around her, and will very likely increase the pain and harms she bears. The experience of witnessing injustice and of being unable to give voice or aid without further penalty is a daily event for a person who is incarcerated.

  Is there any way to resolve this basic tension?
- With severe limits now placed on the opportunity of prisoners to sue for protection of their rights, are there any effective means that prisoners can use to promote recognition of their rights?

- Suppose you are a prison warden, and you wish to protect the right of prisoners to protest (and you also believe that allowing a peaceful means of voicing protests might prevent more violent expressions); however, you are also concerned to maintain order in the prison. Is there some program or policy that you could adopt that would accomplish your goal?
- Zimring and Hawkins maintain that we all have a stake in protecting the basic rights of prisoners, even if we have little concern for the prisoners themselves. What is the basis of that claim?
- One current controversy related to imprisonment policies is the question of whether convicted felons should lose the right to vote. In many states— such as Florida, Georgia, Louisiana, and Texas—convicted felons are permanently barred from voting. Should convicted felons who have completed their prison sentences be denied voting rights?

Jailhouse Blues

Wesley Smith

In 1989 Kenny Parker filed suit against Nevada state officials for "cruel and unusual punishment." His complaint? They had given him a jar of creamy peanut butter, whereas he had explicitly ordered chunky. One of Parker's jailmates—convicted first-degree murderer David Bean—is suing the state because the jeans he was given were too tight, "causing rashes and epileptic seizures." Another Nevada inmate, convicted child molester Chris Chapman, is suing for copies of the North American Man-Boy Love Association newsletter, as a matter of First Amendment rights. Iowa prisoner Art Hartsock, wanting to "see what I'm missing while I'm in here," has demanded greater access to pornography.

These "rights" violations seem less constitutional than comical, but they are taken seriously by the federal judiciary. In 1993, the nation's prisoners filed over 53,000 lawsuits in federal court, generally against state governments. While most cases are dismissed as frivolous, the litigation explosion has cost the states hundreds of millions of dollars in legal fees and in the costs of complying with the courts' orders. In 1993 Nevada alone spent about $700,000 in direct legal costs defending against suits like Parker's.

These legal costs, however, are dwarfed by the indirect costs on society as a whole. Most governors, state attorneys, and other criminal-justice officials say the prisoners'-rights movement is making state prisons ungovernable. And federally imposed prison population caps and other decrees aimed at alleviating "overcrowding" have forced the early release of tens of thousands of violent criminals.

Judicial Tsunami

In 1966 prisoners filed 218 suits in federal court to remedy arguably inhumane treatment in federal, state, and county prisons. Then the federal judiciary opened the floodgates. By 1980 prisoner suits had increased twentyfold. In 1993 prisoners field 53,713 lawsuits in federal courts—7,615 more suits than the Federal Government field against criminals.

By 1993, four-fifths of all state prison systems and roughly one-third of the five hundred largest local jails were under federal-court supervision. And the courts are mostly not content to set broad guidelines for the states to interpret. In Arizona, for example, federal judges tell state prison officials the types of publications and typewriters they must buy for prisoners and the number of law clerks they must hire for the state's prison law libraries. (Delaware Attorney General Charles Oberly II says such rulings mean state prisoners have better access to law materials than be does.)

In South Carolina, Federal Judge James McMillan has given the state orders to purchase specific recreational equipment for prisoners, including three sets of horseshoe equipment, three guitars, five frisbees, fifty decks of playing cards, and a piano. In Alabama a federal judge orders the state to provide inmates air conditioning and televisions. In other states federal judges are seeing state-sponsored "cruel and unusual punishment" in prisons lacking basketball courts, weight rooms, televisions, workshops, or single-occupancy cells.

Under the guise of constitutional jurisprudence, the federal judiciary has aggressively replaced the criminal-justice policies of the fifty states with its own. Groups like the ACLU's National Prison Project argue that states must treat prisoners much as they do citizens at large. Federal judges have agreed; and in their pursuit to elevate the legal status of prisoners to that of law-abiding people, they have removed the concept of prison as punishment, and with it much of the deterrent effect of imprisonment.

Of course, prisoners have been quick to adopt this distorted view of their moral and legal status. An Illinois inmate demanded the right to use his cell as his place of residence for conducting drug-related activities. A Nevada inmate sued for the right to cross-dress, and 14 death-row inmates in California sued for the right to procreate through artificial insemination. Florida's Robert Procup sued when he got just one bread roll on his dinner plate, and sued again when prison officials failed to provide him a salad at lunch. When told by ABC's John Stossel that he was, after all, being punished, Procup replied, "Nobody sentenced me to punishment. They sentenced me to be separated from society"—a recurring theme of the prisoners'-rights movement. Procup was convicted of murder for cementing his business partner into a storage shed.

While federal judges see such decisions as principled constitutionalism, most prisoners see them as a weakness that demands to be exploited. Art Hartsock, the prisoner who won for himself and other inmates at Anamosa State Prison the right to view pornographic magazines, is now preparing for another suit. His reasoning: "Every dollar they spend fighting a lawsuit is a dollar they can't spend building a place to lock me up."

At age 15 Willie Bosket killed two New York subway riders "for the experience." He has also tried to kill two prison guards, which is why prison officials chain him to his cell door for five minutes each day before moving him. Of the chaining Bosket says, "I feel several things. I feel humiliated. I feel an affront to my dignity. I feel vulnerable." A federal court afforded him a jury trial to decide whether he would continue to be chained. At his trial Bosket told jurors his only regret was that he had not killed the guard. He vowed to kill again.

Most criminals show a psychology of denial for their criminal actions. Nevada Deputy Attorney General Anne Cathcart says criminals "come into prison denying any wrongdoing, and they are constantly presented with further reasons to blame others. Unlimited access to federal courts gives them an added tool to vent their anger and rebel against the system."

This undermines rehabilitation efforts generally, as prisoners quickly learn that contempt for the system is rewarded. But the federal bench has even prohibited specific state rehabilitation plans as violative of prisoners' rights. After Governor Gerald Baliles discovered in 1986 that 85 per cent of

Virginia inmates were illiterate, he started a program that linked reading proficiency to early parole. The ACLU threatened suit, saying prisoners had a right to parole without literacy tests, so Baliles made the program voluntary and consequently much less successful. Governor Fife Symington thought pornography might not be healthy for Arizona inmates, many of whom are sex offenders, so he decided last January to prohibit all pornographic materials in the state's prisons. That sounded reasonable to Arizona citizens, but Federal Judge Muecke didn't agree; he has begun contempt hearings against the state.

Each to His Own Religion

Federal encroachment took a dramatic leap forward last November when Congress passed the Religious Freedom Restoration Act. RFRA severely limits the power of government to restrict a prisoner's religious activities.

Before RFRA, a state could restrict certain practices in prison to maintain order. For instance, Illinois forbade inmates belonging to Aryan Nation's religious arm, the Church of Jesus Christ Christian, to distribute literature calling for the extermination of Jews and blacks. In 1992 they sued the state for the right to do so. Shortly after RFRA became law, they amended their complaint with newfound RFRA rights. Under this new standard Illionis will almost certainly lose. Susan O'Leary, deputy chief legal counsel for the state, predicts that this will incite riots in Illinois prisons, which have a 66 per cent black population.

In 1987, the followers of Yahweh Ben Yahweh and his "Temple of Love" demanded the right to distribute hate literature among inmates and lost in court. They are now suing again under RFRA and have already won at the district-court level. The Temple of Love, like Aryan Nation, is seeking attorney fees and monetary damages for religious rights denied them before RFRA even became law. These remedies do not take into account the costs to the states of hiring additional guards or building new cells to separate these inmates from others for their protection.

Even before RFRA, some federal courts were reluctant to define what constitutes a genuine religion. A federal court in 1974 declared The Church of the New Song a religion; this church requires Harvey's Bristol Cream, filet mignon, and marijuana for its religious ceremonies. In Indiana inmates calling themselves the Black Gangster Disciples are claiming a "new Muslim" status, even though prison officials believe their aim is to infiltrate their gang into the older Muslim group. In Colorado, inmate Robert Howard, a practicing Satanist, is suing for the right to religious materials including the Satanic Bible, passages of which command the sacrificing of a "preferably Christian" female virgin and the using of candles made from the fat of unbaptized babies. With RFRA, states will have little discretion in restricting so-called religious activities such as these in order to maintain security.

Religion-based demands for special diets are particularly costly to the states. Nevada Attorney General Frankie Sue del Papa says providing a special religious diet winds up adding 65 per cent to the total cost of imprisoning one inmate. California Attorney General Dan Lungren estimates that if only 2 per cent of the national inmate population demands special religious diets, it will cost the states at least $177 million annually.

Even if a state ultimately wins such a case, its taxpayers still lose. Since RFRA allows a state to restrict a religious practice only in a way that is least burdensome to the prisoner, few courts will be able to dismiss frivolous claims on summary judgment. Evidentiary hearings, expert witnesses, and transportation of prisoners and state's witnesses to the hearings will be required to determine if the state is using a "least restrictive" penology. And since RFRA applies retroactively, cases already won by states will be relitigated.

According to a Senate staffer who worked to modify RFRA, "Congress imagined Baptist preachers holding Bible studies in prison. Who could be against that? They failed to realize it would be Satanists, white supremacists, and those wanting better lunches that would really take advantage of RFRA protections." Of course, the more reasonable inmate requests that RFRA was aimed at protecting, like Bible classes, were rarely denied. And now, since all "religions" will be entitled to equal treatment, states will be forced to eliminate legitimate religious programs in order to avoid suits by other "religious" groups demanding equal funding.

The Ignored Right

As the definition of prisoners' rights has mushroomed, basic constitutional rights like personal safety have actually diminished. Prisons have become more violent than ever before, and America's streets have become more dangerous, as federal judges force the early release of violent criminals to reduce "cruel and unusual" overcrowding.

Although the Supreme Court in Rhodes v. Chapman declared double bunking was not, per se, cruel and unusual, it reaffirmed the right of the federal judiciary to decide the constitutionality of state prison conditions by looking at the "totality of the circumstances." By the early 1980s the lower federal courts had begun to set prison population limits that forced the release of prisoners by the tens of thousands in the following years.

After a court in 1981 imposed a population cap in Texas prisons, the state parole board increased early releases by over 400 per cent, with inmates serving an average of 2 months for every year sentenced. This was followed by a 29 per cent surge of crime in Texas during the next decade, at a time when crime decreased nationally. The courts also mandated population reductions in county jails in Texas and across the country, forcing them to increase pre-trial releases. In Cook County, Illinois, almost 30,000 accused criminals are released before trial each year for this reason. Of that group, 67 per cent are rearrested on felony charges before their cases come to trial, over 25 per cent of them for violent crimes.

The personal tragedies this federal policy has created are reported with numbing frequency in the nation's newspapers. Last June, Loran Cole, like other "nonviolent" criminals, was released early from a Florida prison to alleviate overcrowding; he had served only 18 months of a 66-month sentence for grand theft. Eight months later Cole was charged with the murder of John Edwards, an 18-year-old student at Florida State, and the kidnapping and rape of Edwards's sister. In Texas, Michael Blair served 18 months of a 10-year sentence for burglary and indecency with an 11-year-old girl (his actual crime, sexual assault, had been plea-bargained down). While still on parole in 1993, he raped and murdered 7-year-old Ashley Nicole Estell after kidnapping her from a park in an upscale Dallas community. Had he served even half his time, Blair would have been in prison on the day Ashley and her family went to the park. Kenneth McDuff was convicted and sentenced to death in 1968 for first-degree murder, for killing three teenagers execution style. McDuff's death sentence was commuted to life imprisonment when the Supreme Court outlawed capital punishment in 1972. This made him eligible for parole, which he got in 1989. Since then, he has been linked to the rape and murder of four women.

Just the threat of court-ordered releases has been enough to push state parole boards to release prisoners early. Between 1983 and 1993 the Georgia parole board released 36,006 violent and sex offenders—including 2,772 multiple sex offenders—after they had served an average of 36 per cent of their sentences. In 1989, Governor Joe Frank Harris released 13,000 "nonviolent" prisoners under an emergency program to reduce prison populations when inmates threatened federal lawsuits. Since then the Georgia parole board has accelerated thousands of paroles. Although the parole board insists the released prisoners were "nonviolent," Clayton County Superior Court Judge Kenneth Kilpatrick says the early release of even nonviolent felons increases both nonviolent and violent crime, because short imprisonment suggests to criminals that any crime brings light punishment.

According to Department of Justice statistics, three-fourths of all violent criminals convicted in 1989 were back on the streets by December of 1993. Safe Streets Alliance President James Wootton points out that 3.2 million criminals are out on parole or probation. Even modest early releases have been devastating. A study in Illinois in the early 1980s found that 21,000 prisoners released just 3 months early committed 23 homicides, 32 rapes, 262 arsons, 681 robberies, 2,472 burglaries, and 2,572 assaults during that 3-month period. Nationally, almost one-third of all violent crimes are committed by criminals on parole or pre-trial release. The federal courts have no apparent concern for the victims, however, but focus exclusively on the injustices they perceive as being committed against prisoners.

A Return to Sanity

Although Congress is now posturing as the field marshal in the war on crime, it has done little to halt federal judicial intervention, and has actively undermined state criminal justice through legislation like RFRA. Congressmen Charles Canady (R., Fla.), Preston Geren (D., Tex.), and others are pushing for amendments to the 1994 crime bill that would prevent federal judges from using one prisoner's suit to take over administration of an entire prison, would prohibit federally imposed population caps, and would impose fees on prisoners filling suit. Many states are considering reforms of their own, such as delaying parole for prisoners who filed fraudulent or malicious suits, and are urging Congress to pass legislation requiring that all state grievance procedures be exhausted before a federal suit can be filed.

These proposals, however, will not substantially reduce existing caseloads, since inmates have little incentive not to sue as long as the federal courts waive most court fees for inmates and continue to entertain frivolous suits. These solutions will fail because they ultimately rely on the discretion of federal judges, who are not accountable to the states or their citizens for their actions and who reveal an outright contempt for self-governance.

If Congress wants to make a meaningful contribution to criminal-justice reform, it should dramatically limit federal-court jurisdiction over state prison administration. Article III of the Constitution gives Congress this power. If senators and congressmen refuse to use it, they should be held accountable by the voters for the foolish decisions of the federal judiciary in releasing criminals to rape and murder a second, third, and fourth time.

But there is no indication that Congress is willing to do so; therefore the states themselves will need to take matters into their own hands. They may be forced to confront Washington, as Governor Symington is doing in defying the federal court order that allows pornography in Arizona's prisons.

Governors like Symington, Mike Leavitt of Utah, and George Allen of Virginia, and hundreds of other state and local law-enforcement officials, see the current fight over control of state prisons as a small part of a larger problem. The federal judiciary's activism stems from an abstract theory of individual rights that disregards the rights of the community. Deliberately detached from the effects of their decisions on society, federal judges have acted as if they intended to strip communities of any power to defend themselves.

As recently elected Virginia Attorney General James Gilmore has said, it is the states' responsibility to make streets "as safe for our children as it was for us when we were growing up." The success of that agenda will be determined in large measure by the power of the states to free themselves from Washington's control.... ■

Democracy and the Limits of Punishment
A Preface to Prisoners' Rights

Franklin E. Zimring and Gordon Hawkins

... Criminals are the most feared and resented of a society's citizens. Public hatred of crime and criminals invites the use of extreme forms of governmental power to suppress and punish criminals.

The serious criminal offender—the rapist and the robber—is the least attractive case for claims to limit government power, but he is, for that reason, the most important frontier for defending the limits on that power. If the claim of human rights against government power is only as strong as its weakest link, that will almost always make the rules and limits of criminal punishment of central importance to respect for individual dignity as a limiting principle throughout government. Because punishment of criminals is the "weakest link" in the argument for limiting state power, those who try to keep the criminal system free from abuse of government power are guarding an important frontier....

Punishment and Governmental Power

To the extent that power held by government comes at the expense of

Franklin E. Zimring and Gordon Hawkins, "Democracy and the Limits of Punishment: A Preface to Prisoners' Rights," in *The Future of Imprisonment*, edited by Michael Tonry (New York: Oxford University Press, 2004): 157–178. Reprinted by permission of Oxford University Press, Inc.

restrictions on the liberties of individual citizens, there is a natural tendency for citizens to resent increases in governmental power and to desire limits on government. Where citizens have continuing power over governmental policy, new powers must be approved on the basis of the need for government to produce common benefits that citizens value more highly than the liberties they surrender. The need to justify governmental power in terms of collective gains that are more important than lost liberty is spread over the full range of governmental powers from taxation and spending to military force. Crime and punishment have a special strategic importance in this dynamic to establish the limits of governmental power because criminals are the most frightening and most unpopular citizens in a democratic state. Fear of crime means that citizens will cede authority to government for crime control that they might not be willing to surrender for other reasons. The public hostility toward criminals will support harsh punishments administered by government because criminals are to receive them. Citizens will approve conduct in the punishment and control of crime that they would hesitate to support or tolerate in other domains.

Because criminal punishments are the most extreme deprivations that government will inflict on any citizen, most enforceable limits in governmental power will be limits on criminal punishments. Further, because of hostility to criminal offenders, public opinion and democratic institutions will support punishments of high magnitude. Expanding power to punish in democracy will be easier than in other arenas of government operations, and limiting power through democratic institutions will be more difficult.

That the punishment enterprise is the boundary territory for the maximum exercise of negative government power explains the historic importance of criminal justice in the basic architecture of limited government. The Bill of Rights to the U.S. Constitution has eight amendments dealing with the relationship of government and individual citizens. Five of these eight amendments are chiefly concerned with criminal justice (4, 5, 6, 7, and 8).

Concern about excessive governmental power is external to the usual topics of effectiveness and individual desert in the determination of appropriate punishment. To worry about whether it is proper for modern governments to extinguish life as a criminal sanction is not to address either topics like deterrence or incapacitation that concern the effects of punishment on crime rates or to consider what particular punishment might be morally justified by the commission of a particular act. Restraints on government power of this sort are prior conditions to setting a scale of punishments based on individual desert or deterrence. The citizen is a potential victim in this setting both of criminals and of government; and he need not imagine himself a criminal offender to feel threatened by a government that is without restraints in pursuing its policies. . . .

All the major democracies in the world have substantial constitutional limits on their government's power to punish criminals, including prohibitions of torture, and all the major democracies except the United States and Japan prohibit the death penalty. All the developed democracies impose substantial minimal procedural conditions that must be met before punishing. The current pattern is that those nations with substantial democratic influence on government power also have more limits on punishment than nations with less citizen control on government, but this is no paradox. Authoritarian regimes do not choose to limit themselves and their citizens lack the power to force limits.

More interesting are the motives and mechanisms that limit punishment power in democracies. If a government responds to popular will, why not give it total discretion in the choice of punishment for criminal offenders? One problem with that position is that changing political circumstances is a risk that cannot be discounted. Governments may cease to be accountable, so that whatever safety came from popular control might disappear. But there is also a possibility of majority will supporting the excessive use of force. In almost all nations, discrete minority populations support restrictions on government power in part because of a fear of popular control. And while self-interested enthusiasm for limits on government power is easiest to imagine for those with conspicuous minority identities, there are few of us immune from being outvoted in a matter of important personal preference. All citizens are potential minorities on contested issues.

So the reason democratic regimes have more restrictions on government power than autocratic regimes is that democracies allow such limits to exist. We know this because the strongest support for limits on government will come from those who have recently experienced autocratic governmental excesses. Limits on government power are quickly imposed once iron curtains fall.

When we underscore the importance of limiting punishments in democratic government, it is not because we regard punishment abuses as more of a problem in democracy, but rather because abuse of punishment is a special threat to the positive values of liberal democracy.

How might a government constrained by limits on power tempt its citizens to remove such limits? Fear of crime and of criminals is one obvious technique, and this creates a strong motive for governments that desire additional power to exaggerate the danger of crime and criminals. The political task is to convince citizens that criminality is a greater threat to them than government excess. The motive is larger power to those in government. The major appeal is to fear.

Not all areas of criminal justice are of equal concern from a human rights perspective. The maximum dangers cluster at the extreme edges of the system—the most serious offenders, the most fear-inspiring crime problems, and the most extreme punishments.

The most serious and hated criminal offenders are the justification for new incursions of state power. The serial killer, the murderer of children, the terrorist bomber, the predatory sex offender, and the drug lord are the principal arguments put forward for extensions of the severity of punishments available and the length of incapacitation. Terrible crimes are always urged as the justification for terrible punishments. But more than the heinousness of individual offenders, the justification for new intensities of surveillance and punishment depends on the public's sense of insecurity in combating the particular problem that is urged as this year's necessity for the extension of state power. It is the citizen's sense of vulnerability more than his distaste for particular criminal offenders that justifies the extension of state power. A sense of public emergency thus becomes the leading enemy of moderation and of the limitation of government power. A powerful illustration of this general point is the aftermath of the September 11, 2001 events in the United States, where the extraordinary extensions of power were assembled in a piece of legislation labeled by its sponsors as the "Patriot Act."

The importance of public feelings of vulnerability about crime to support the expansion of punitive power explains not only the incentive of ambitious governments to scare their citizens but also the cyclicality of the public sense of emergency about particular crime problems. In late twentieth-century American experience, each campaign to make citizens feel acutely threatened had a relatively short effective life after the threatened Armageddon did not happen, from the war on drugs, to gang violence, to the juvenile super-predator. So that governments intent on consistent expansion of punishment powers felt the need to rotate the particular problems that were pushed to justify penal inflation. When drug wars are followed by panics about juvenile violence, the shift in topic may be the only way supporters of expansion in

governmental power can generate consistent levels of public anxiety. Whether the concern with terrorists and terrorism in the aftermath of the World Trade Center's destruction in 2001 will have a more sustained career as the central justification for expanding governmental power is one of the important contingencies of the first decade of the twenty-first century. Is mass destruction sufficiently compelling to avoid becoming "last year's panic" in short order?

While extreme forms of criminality are the focus of support for extensions of governmental power, extreme forms of punishment attract the attention of the enemies of unlimited governmental power, particularly when a punishment is distinct from more standard penal measures in kind as well as degrees. Torture, beatings, and execution have been the targets of choice for human rights reformers, practices that inspire citizen empathy with the subject of the punishment, and types of deprivation that are easy to distinguish from more common penal measures such as imprisonment and fines.

Penal practices that differ from those in common use in extremity but not in kind are more difficult targets for the human rights reformer to identify and to attack. An illustration of this phenomenon, which we will discuss at some length in the next section, concerns what has come to be called "the supermax prison" that has proliferated throughout the United States since the 1980s. Designed to impose unprecedented levels of individual isolation and psychological deprivation, the supermax prison is nonetheless a more difficult target for the human rights reformer than canings or torture because the institution can be defended by government as merely another form of prison. . . .

To date, these extraordinary institutions have not received the attention they deserve from either reformers or the wider community. This essay will show why a human rights approach to limits on prison is both more difficult than categorical prohibitions on types of punishment but necessary nonetheless.

Prisons and the Modern Politics of Punishment

Imprisonment is the most serious penal sanction that is frequently imposed in the modern state and a stunning example of the conflict and complexity involved in the protection of individual dignity during punishment. The imprisoning state administers an institution where the totality of the offender's life is under its control and restraint. For this reason, sociologists describe such facilities as "total institutions." For the modern prisoner, the same government that condemns and wishes to punish him controls every aspect of the offender's daily life: eating and drinking, social contact, excreting, communication with the world outside the prison, exercise, light and darkness are all state-administered conditions in the modern prison. . . .

The Politics of Gratuitous Deprivation

The totality of state power over individual life in prison means that the punitive impulse that inspires imprisonment could in theory influence every aspect of the conditions of confinement. Why should those who have murdered and raped get decent meals or the opportunity to communicate with family and friends? What is the argument for allowing those who are being imprisoned to be punished to enjoy movies on cable television or build their muscles in exercise rooms that have been equipped at public expense? One older version of objections to positive conditions in prison acquired the label "less eligibility," an argument that conditions in confinement should not be better than those available to the poorest members of the law-abiding community. But the broader argument we hear more recently is why not make the conditions of confinement in penal institutions punitive in all their details?

The contract between the rhetoric that supported concerns about less eligibility a century ago and the appeals associated with current efforts to reduce the privileges available in prisons is a useful introduction to the new politics of punishment in the United States. The hazard associated with "less eligibility" was as much a utilitarian as a moral concern. If prisoners were better off than the poor in the community, what was to make the poor fear prisons?

The modern political arguments do not compare prisoners with the poor, but instead favor making prison life less inviting for prisoners as a way of identifying with the concerns of crime victims. One branch of the modern politics of punishment begins with a premise that most if not all issues of criminal justice policy should be viewed as a status competition between criminal offenders and their victims.

The politician asks whether the citizen cares more about the welfare of criminals or of crime victims. The implication is that the answer to that question should decide any question of justice system policy. To imagine every issue as a competition between victims and offenders can easily lead to assuming that everything done to disadvantage offenders in some way also helps victims. This image, which we have elsewhere called "the zero sum fallacy," leads also to the assumption that providing any comforts to prisoners, who are after all criminal offenders, is also a way of ignoring the interests of crime victims.

In this rendering, every decision about conditions of prison confinement can be seen as a competition between crime victims and criminal offenders, and the citizen is invited to show solidarity with the victims of crime by withdrawing family visits, cable television, weight rooms, and other gym equipment. Even prison policies that humiliate prisoners can be restated as a way of reinforcing the positive social status of crime victims by humiliating those who offended against them (e.g., the Maracopa County, Arizona Sheriff who makes jail inmates who have been caught masturbating wear pink pants on the outside of their jail uniforms). Once the assumption of a zero-sum relationship is accepted, the crime victim support rationale for making the environment of prisoners less tolerable has no apparent limit.

The 1990s produced a bumper crop of legislative and administrative attempts to make prisons more unpleasant, and not all of these were concerned with unimportant or merely symbolic details. State legislation and Corrections Department regulations were frequently passed concerning weight rooms and television privileges.

Peter Finn of Abt Associates published a survey of the changes in prison and jail conditions imposed under the heading of "the no frills prison and jail" movement, with a range of examples:

> In 1994 the Arizona legislature eliminated weightlifting equipment in state prisons and established a $3.00 co-payment for health care services.
> In 1995, the Mississippi legislature mandated the phasing-in of striped uniforms with the word "convict" written on the back, banned private television and other equipment in cells.
> The Arizona Department of Corrections reduced the number of items for sale in the prison store, reduced the amount of property and clothing inmates may keep in their cells, and the number and types of movies and television programs they may watch.

Many jails eliminate weightlifting equipment, free coffee, hot lunches, girly magazines, and reduce recreation time, television programming, visitations, and items for sale in the commissary.

Not to be outdone, the Alabama Department of Corrections introduced what were called "no frills chain gangs" in each of the state's three prisons in 1994. The punitive roots and deprivational intention of these wide-ranging policies are the only common thread we can imagine.

The federal Congress passed its own version of a "No Frills Prison

Act" in 1996 that among other things provides that "[I]nmates serving a sentence for a crime that resulted in serious bodily injury to a victim are denied any television viewing and are limited to one hour a day of sports or exercise."

Legislation was also proposed to withdraw "good time" or "good behavior" credits to prisoners who file lawsuits that a court later classifies as frivolous, thus lengthening times of penal confinement as a sanction against the filing of lawsuits. This was also the era that produced "Megan's Laws" requiring released sex offenders location in a community to become public knowledge.

There are no obvious limits to the potential of this kind of politics to operate. However, since the actual incentives for victims and other groups to produce these negative impacts are not great, those restrictions that do receive legislative sanction will frequently have other constituencies who benefit from the restriction of privilege. The State Attorney Generals who must defend against inmate litigation are the real winners with good time restriction legislation.

Gratuitous restrictions on prisoners might not produce any real benefits to crime victims, but they have no powerful opponents either. Prison administrators might object to proposals that threaten the governability of prisoners and some administrators would also oppose the needless restriction of liberty and the denial of small comforts in prison. Thus, Finn reports that only 16 percent of prison administrators support television restrictions. The opposition of wardens to gratuitously downgrading prisons might not be a major bulwark against gratuitous restrictions, however, because prison administrators are not by themselves politically powerful in the legislative branch of state government. Once a political dynamic like the "zero sum" assumptions of victim's rights gets going, the political process can easily make for larger deprivations in the experience of imprisonment than are necessary or justifiable in a prosperous modern nation. . . .

Principles and Institutions of Limitation

The question we now confront is whether there are viable principles of limitation available to safeguard the prisons of the United States from unnecessary deprivations based on citizen hostility expressed through the legislative process. . . .

Restricting Gratuitous Deprivation

The purest forms of gratuitous restrictions are those imposed by the political process—the legislation taking television away from prisoners or abolishing family visits. The simplest institutional arrangement to guard against punitive deprivation by legislation is to keep decisions about the details of prison administrations from the legislative branch of government. The general strategy of separating practical decisions on punishment from the most politically sensitive and symbolically oriented institutions of government was called "insulation" in our earlier discussion of punishment and democracy. The idea is to keep decisions about conditions of confinement from legislators. The argument is put forward that conditions of confinement are best decided by the experts who hold administrative power over prisons.

An institutional theory of separating power over correctional details from legislative bodies does provide limited protection from some forms of gratutious punitive deprivation, but the prisoner protection that comes from a theory of administrative expertise is by no means complete. In the first place, legislative restrictions can always be framed as budgetary matters, to bring them within the traditional ambit of legislative control (i.e., "none of the funds allocated for the department of corrections shall be spent on television for prisoners"). Unless a reviewing body is willing to look behind the veil of budgetary authority, a formal prohibition on legislative setting of conditions of confinement will not provide much protection.

In the second place, the resort to administrative power might not protect the prisoner when the prison administration seeks to gain political favor by endorsing politically popular restrictions. To the extent that prison administrators need to curry favor with legislative bodies, they may endorse deprivations that have no functional role in prison administration. This certainly happened in the 1990s.

The third problem with relying on the prison administrator to represent the interests of the prisoner is the very large number of situations where their interests conflict. Any power or autonomy one gives to the inmate in a prison is that much power that the staff and administration does not possess. Even when prison administrators oppose broad bans on inmate recreation and television, what they tend to favor is systems where small comforts are available to prisoners but only at the discretion of those who run the prisons.

So there is no sense in which those who administer prisons have the neutrality that would make them ideal institutional agents to protect prison inmates from unnecessarily punitive deprivation. If neutral agencies of government would be the best hope for review of conditions of confinement, the choices are between executive branch personnel without any other responsibility for prison governance and judicial officers, either judges of general jurisdiction or judicial branch officers with special responsibility for prisons.

While constitutional courts are one necessary element of scrutiny for enforcing limits on governmental use of imprisonment, a variety of other executive branch controls are also helpful in maintaining human rights in prisons. Of particular value are executive officials with some administrative independence from the line and staff of a conventional department of corrections. An ombudsman or inspector general of the prisons has particular value when resources are devoted to the serious pursuit of oversight. When executive agencies operate effectively, they make the judicial system a last resort in the protection against abuse. And the capacity of executive offices to make scrutiny into an administrative routine assures that the combination of administrative and judicial oversight is much more effective than the judicial oversight alone.

The irony is that those prison systems most likely to have extensive administrative scrutiny for human rights abuses are also the places where the danger of abuses is the smallest. When a state like Alabama invents a "no frills chain gang," it is a safe bet that it will not also fund an aggressive inspector general to police against human rights abuses. The same insensitivity that invites abuses also inhibits the development of administrative controls.

Principles of Limit

But what should be the review standard for legislative acts that attempt to alter conditions of confinement for expressly punitive purposes. If the state legislature passes an act forbidding cable television services in maximum security prisons, what kind of claim should inmates be allowed to make against such regulations? Certainly there is little to suggest finding a positive legal or constitutional right of those in state custody to television service or free weights. Just as certainly, the absence of cable television should not be regarded as cruel and unusual punishment. Should judges or neutral ombudspersons have the power to order all reasonable services and amenities to those in prison?

But wouldn't that make the judge into the warden in fact of the prison? Any effort to impose such an open-ended set of conditions would become more of a usurpation of the normal authority of prison administrators than the legislative interference that removes the television service as an administrative option. . . .

There is a less artificial standard for review that may be available to courts that goes to the core of the problem posed by legislative ceremonies of punitive deprivation. A prohibition on gratuitously punitive legislative conditions could provide a method to curtail the all-but-transparently punitive provisions singled out in the last section without creating an open-ended invitation for second guessing administrative and legal authority on conditions of confinement. When a measure withholding a privilege, either by legislation or administrative action, appears punitive in intent, it could be subject to review on a due process standard that might put a nontrivial burden of justifying the condition on those who frame the rule. The prohibition of TV and weight rooms would be easy victims to any real judicial scrutiny, despite the creative imaginations of those who draft legislative findings of fact in modern government. The removal of good time credits for early release as a consequence of filing a frivolous lawsuit would also seem a likely candidate for invalidation.

But most traditional collateral conditions of imprisonment or felony conviction would survive challenge, unless they are plainly irrational in modern settings. The test case here is the permanent ban on a convicted felon's voting in many states that survives as a vestige of the "civil death" of a convicted felon in Anglo-American antiquity. It is punitive and irrational but also traditional, a close case for a standard that disapproves of the gratuitously punitive. Is history alone sufficient warrant for the perverse exclusion of the felon from political reintegration?

As a matter of principle, we see nothing wrong with a common law or constitutional rule that is suspicious of legislative disabilities that produce injury and indignity but serve no rational penal purpose. There is the danger that the standard might invite too much judicial interference, but judicial caution in application of such standards can help minimize that danger. . . .

Prison Reform as Transplant Surgery

We wish to return to our description of the strategic importance of criminal justice in the first part of this essay to suggest one method of obtaining standards of decency for American penal practices that has substantive credibility. Our earlier argument is that public fear and resentment make the criminal justice process one where a society's usual standards of decency and restraint might not be observed. This vulnerability is what makes appropriate restraint by government in the criminal justice field so broadly important. But the special pressures that often distort practices in criminal justice also are a signal that one natural place to find good standards of decency in practice that can be projected into criminal justice is from related areas of government operation without the distortive fear and hostility found in criminal justice. Practice in noncriminal justice fields provides some measure of what constitutes minimum standards when fear and loathing are not powerful pressures.

Our earlier analysis made the conclusion that:

> In one key respect, the punishment of criminals is not a frontier issue for consideration of the obligation of the state to its citizens. Criminal justice is not the area where governments can be expected to innovate in the extension of opportunities and entitlements to citizens. Such innovations will usually first be extended to dependant populations with much higher social reputations than criminals—the elderly, children and to those handicapped through no fault of their own. The strategic role of the criminal offender is in defining the absolute minimum obligation of state to citizen, so that adequate provisions for prisoners are a defensive necessity.

Our suggestion now is that the standards of decent treatment that exist with noncriminal dependant populations, "the elderly, children and those handicapped through no fault of their own" are a useful measure of standards of decency that can be applied to conditions of penal confinement as well.

Take the question of the treatment of mentally ill prisoners in the supermax facility. One measure of the decency of their treatment is whether the same conditions imposed on the mentally ill in supermax prisons would be approved or allowed in public and private hospitals for persons with the same mental health problems. If not, an additional question is whether the conviction status of the mentally ill inmate should make a critical difference. The reference to public standards in noncriminal justice fields is both a disciplined and appropriate way to construct measures of decent conditions that are specific to American culture and values.

A second example of such logic concerns the access of jail and prison inmates to smoking opportunities. Whenever persons are wholly confined in state institutions, a rule against smoking in public buildings becomes a total prohibition against smoking. The argument is made in jails and prisons that such a prohibition protects nonsmoking inmates and staff from the harms of "passive smoking." Perhaps, in the age of the "no frills" prison, there is more than a possibility of punishment as a motive for prohibiting smoking. We suggest that the policies and principles about opportunities to smoke found in military barracks and state mental hospitals should also apply in prisons as well, unless there are good reasons why different levels of smoking control are needed. And the way that the smoking problem is handled in other institutions of adult confinement provides insight into the actual motives for policy in prisons and jails.

This sort of transplantation of standards of decency from areas of governance that do not suffer the distortions of criminal justice suggests another perspective on the function of the criminal justice reformer. One technique of assuring that the distortive pressures that operate in criminal justice do not corrupt the government is to perform a sort of transplant surgery of healthy values and appropriate practices found in other domains of governmental activity. This form of transplant protects the most vulnerable areas of government operation from corruption and thus protects the health of the entire governmental organism. . . .

The Consolations of an Uphill Struggle

What can this general review tell us about prisoners' rights in the immediate future? The strategic role of the criminal offender is in defining the absolute minimum obligation of state to citizen, so that adequate provisions for prisoners is a defensive necessity. Assuring the human dignity of the murderer and the rapist is not a strategy for expanding the entitlements of school children and senior citizens; instead it is a strategy to prevent the erosion of citizen claims against government, to prevent regressions applied to the least popular of dependant populations, which might thereafter be applied more broadly.

The defensive significance of offenders' interests in the human rights dynamic has two implications when thinking about the future efforts to protect human dignity in prisons. The first is that the entirety of a human rights agenda can never be exclusively based on offenders' interests. The defense of prisoners' rights is always a necessary but never a sufficient condition for a human rights agenda.

A second corollary of the defensive strategic position of offenders' interests is that efforts to protect this particular flank will be much more important in bad times than in good times. In periods characterized by good will and the growth of government concern for citizens, the advocacy for offenders' rights will be somewhat easier in its own right and less necessary for the protection of other vulnerable populations.

When a social climate turns threatening, the defence of offenders' interests becomes at once tactically more difficult and strategically more important. It is during eras of bad feeling that the interests of vulnerable populations are most at risk. The path of least resistance to the erosion of individual rights will always be to target those domestic enemies assembled in the criminal justice process.

So there is some consolation in the current low esteem of prison reform in the United States early in the twenty-first century. The same features of politics and society that make the advocates of prison reforms unpopular also make those who question the government's hegemony in penal institutions an indispensable element in defence of human liberty. ■

⠿ The Continuing Debate

What Is New

The problems of the prison system—from massive overcrowding to endemic violence—are glaringly obvious. In 1999, federal judge William Wayne Justice gave this description of the daily circumstances of Texas prison inmates:

> Texas prison inmates continue to live in fear—a fear that is incomprehensible to most of the state's free world citizens. More vulnerable inmates are raped, beaten, owned, and sold by more powerful ones. Despite their pleas to prison officials, they are often refused protection. Instead, they pay for protection, in money, services, or sex. Correctional officers continue to rely on the physical control of excessive force to enforce order. Those inmates locked away in administrative segregation, especially those with mental illnesses, are subjected to extreme deprivations and daily psychological harm. *Ruiz v. Johnson*, 37 F. Supp. 2d 855, 940 (S.D. Tex. 1999).

The passage of long mandatory sentences has resulted in massive overcrowding in most U.S. prison systems, with California (due to its "three strikes" law and other lengthy mandatory prison sentences) being one of the most overcrowded. While Governor Schwarzenegger has proclaimed his goal of reforming the prison system (under threat of a federal takeover of the system), he has instead taken steps to keep the worst problems hidden: In 2004 he vetoed bills that would have allowed public reports from the clergy and media on the conditions of incarceration in California. However, in December of 2006 he proposed a review of California's sentencing guidelines (an essential first step in reducing overcrowding), and called for an $11 billion investment in new prisons and in reforming the parole system. A federal judge has threatened to release prisoners and cap the California prison population if the state does not institute reforms that decrease overcrowding, reduce high rates of prison violence and suicide, and improve the medical care of inmates.

Where to Find More

Discretion, Community, and Correctional Ethics, edited by John Kleinig and Margaret Leland Smith (Lanham, MD: Rowman & Littlefield, 2001), raises interesting issues concerning prisoners' rights: see especially the first chapter, consisting of a paper on "Professionalizing Incarceration" by John Kleinig and a response by Margaret Leland Smith. Good books on the prison environment, with special attention to its effects on guards, are Ted Conover, *Newjack: Guarding Sing Sing* (New York: Random House, 2000); and Kelsey Kauffman, *Prison Officers and Their World* (Cambridge, MA: Harvard University Press, 1988). A clear examination of the prison system is Franklin Zimring and Gordon Hawkins, *Incapacitation: Penal Confinement and the Restraint of Crime* (Oxford: Oxford University Press, 1997). Important reform recommendations are offered by Craig Haney in *Reforming Punishment: Psychological Limits to the Pains of Imprisonment* (Washington, DC: American Psychological Association, 2006).

Cindy Chen describes the threat to prisoners' rights posed by The Prison Litigation Reform Act (PLRA) of 1995 in "The Prison Litigation Reform Act of 1995: Doing Away With More Than Just Crunchy Peanut Butter," *St. John's Law Review*, Volume 78 (2004). 203–231. Other critics of the PLRA are Eugene J. Kuzinski, "The End of the Prison Law Firm? Frivolous Inmate Litigation, Judicial Oversight, and the Prison Litigation Reform Act of 1995," *Rutgers Law Review*, Volume 29 (1998): 361–399; and James B. Jacobs, in "Prison Reform Amid the Ruins of Prisoners' Rights," Chapter 7 in *The Future of Imprisonment*, edited by Michael Tonry (Oxford: Oxford University Press, 2004): 179–196.

A good book on the conditions and effects of the U.S. system of imprisonment is Joseph T. Hallinan, *Going Up the River: Travels in a Prison Nation* (New York: Random House, 2001). Mary Pattillo, David F. Weiman, and Bruce Western, *Imprisoning America: The Social Effects of Mass Incarceration* (New York: Russell Sage Foundation, 2004) is an excellent source for examining the effects of imprisonment.

Human Rights Watch maintains an informative website on the current conditions of imprisonment and of prisoners' rights around the world; go to http://hrw.org/prisons/. A website by Ken Strutin—Criminal Justice Resources: Prisoners' Rights and Resources on the Web—has an excellent collection of links to useful websites. The Legal Information Institute at Cornell Law School posts information at http://www4.law.cornell.edu/wex/index.php/Prisoners'_rights. A British website for prisoners' rights is at http://www.your-rights.org.uk/your-rights/chapters/the-rights-of-prisoners/index.shtml. The BBC maintains a site at http://www.bbc.co.uk/dna/actionnetwork/A1181882.

See also the readings for Debates 9, 10, 11, and 12.

14

■ ■ ■ ■ ■ ■ ■ DEBATE ■ ■ ■ ■ ■ ■ ■

Should There Be Laws Requiring Registration and Community Notification for Convicted Sex Offenders?

There Should Be Laws Requiring Community Notification of the Presence of Convicted Sex Offenders
  Advocate: Patty Wetterling, Children's Rights Advocate.
  Source: "The Jacob Wetterling Story," Proceedings of a BJS [Bureau of Justice Statistics]/SEARCH [National Consortium for Justice Information and Statistics] conference, National Conference on Sex Offender Registries, April 1998.
Community Notification Laws Do More Harm Than Good
  Advocate: Bonnie Steinbock, Professor of Philosophy at the State University of New York at Albany.
  Source: "A Policy Perspective," *Criminal Justice Ethics*, Volume 14, Number 2 (Summer/Fall 1995).

Of all the continuing life-long punishments for convicts who have been released from prison, few are as severe in their effects as the requirement to register as a sex offender. Not only are employers extremely reluctant to hire persons whose names appear on the list; there are also many restrictions on where such persons can live (there is currently a trend in many communities to pass laws prohibiting persons on sex offender lists from living within the community); and finally, the public listing of a person as a sex offender subjects the person to ostracism, verbal abuse, physical threats, and occasional violence: several murders and attempted murders have targeted listed persons.

No criminal act provokes greater public outrage than attacks on children; and when those attacks are of a sexual nature, the outrage is even greater. Thus it is hardly surprising that laws setting up registries for sex offenders are easily passed, often unanimously, by state legislatures and the U.S. Congress: whether such laws are good or bad, few politicians have the courage to challenge laws that are named for childhood crime victims (such as "Megan's Law") and are promoted as protecting children from predatory monsters. While many state legislatures had already passed sex offender registry laws, in 1994 Congress passed the Jacob Wetterling Crimes Against Children and Sexually Violent Offender Registration Act (42 USCS at 14071), which required all states to create sex offender registration laws.

Leaving aside questions of whether sex offender registries are just, and of whether they are constitutional, one basic question is whether they *work*: that is, are such registries an effective means of reducing sex crimes? Some argue that by focusing attention on "dangerous strangers," the registries may encourage people to neglect a more common threat: sexual abuse by close friends, family members, teachers, clergy, coaches, and so on. Others have argued that registries and the threat of attack may force sex offenders "underground," and thus keep them out of treatment programs. And finally, some have suggested that for some cases and categories of offenders the registration process may undermine effective treatment programs, and thus lead to more repeat offenses.

⚏ Points to Ponder

- The abuse and murder of a child—such as Megan Kanka, for whom "Megan's Law" is named—is a horrific act, which stirs deep feelings of outrage; and such outrage is often the major force behind swift passage of legislation (such as, obviously, "Megan's Law"). What are the advantages and/or disadvantages of passing legislation under such circumstances?
- Thirty years ago, when Joe was 19, he committed a terrible crime. He had been on a week-long drinking binge, and at the end of the week he violently raped a 14-year-old girl from his neighborhood. Joe was deeply appalled at his own act. He pleaded guilty, and he felt that his ten years of imprisonment was justly deserved for the awful crime he had committed. After his release from prison, Joe moved to a different state. He became a dedicated member of Alcoholics Anonymous, and has not had a drink in 30 years. He completed college, got married, and he now has three children whom he adores. He owns and operates a popular and successful restaurant, he coaches his youngest daughter's soccer team, and he is active in several civic organizations. Though Joe's wife knows about his criminal history, no one else in Joe's community—including his children—knows about Joe's past.

The state now passes a law requiring that all persons who have been convicted of violent sexual assaults against children be registered as sexual offenders, and that the registry be open to public inspection. When Joe's name appears on the list, he is dismissed as the coach of his daughter's soccer team, his children and his wife are socially ostracized, and his restaurant goes into bankruptcy. Is Joe being punished again, after already "paying his debt to society" 20 years ago? Does the fact that his wife and children also suffer have any relevance in determining whether this registry is just?

- Are public sexual offender registries a type of "shaming" punishment? Some claim that such registries are shaming punishments; others insist they are merely registries that are useful for crime control purposes. What *legal* difference does it make which way they are classified?

The Jacob Wetterling Story

Patty Wetterling

I am truly honored to be a part of this very exciting opportunity to make the sex offender registries law better and more workable in every State. A complete stranger sent me a verse from a song called "Hope," which we have lived on for the last 7 1/2 years. It is about beginnings. I would like to start with that.

Hope is intimately tied to beginnings, of this I'm certain. You're not going to start anything without hope of a successful conclusion. Unless you hope strongly, intensely enough, you may never start at all. In any endeavor, two-thirds of the battle is won simply by taking the first step. All too often through the years I've let myself be held back by lack of confidence, fear of failure, sometimes just plain inertia or laziness. But I've learned that if you force yourself to make the first move, mighty forces will come to aid. The act of beginning starts the flow of power, but those who never begin never feel that power. Between hope and action lies a chasm deep but also narrow. It can be bridged by an act of will, a decision that says firmly, "Yes, I will take steps to make this hope a reality, and I will take the first step now." Hope, the spark that ignites the actions that make the dream come true.

We have had a dream for Jacob for 7 1/2 years. I thought it might be helpful to share with you where sex offender registry legislation came from and why it is so critical for us.

Patty Wetterling, "The Jacob Wetterling Story," Proceedings of a Bureau of Justice Statistics/SEARCH conference, National Conference on Sex Offender Registries, April 1998. Reprinted with permission from the U.S. Department of Justice.

My husband and I went to a house-warming party on October 22, 1989. We called home to give the children the phone number where we were. My son, Trevor, answered the telephone and we gave him the number.

Our older daughter was not home that night. Jacob, his best friend, Aaron, and Trevor were babysitting their younger sister, Carmen. Trevor called back and said, "We're bored. There's nothing to do. Can we ride our bikes to the store and rent a video?" From our house to the video store is less than 10 minutes by bike. We live in a town of 3,000 people, but I said no. It was starting to get dark, and they had never done this before. Trevor said, "Well, let me talk to Dad." My husband, Jerry said, "If you wear my jogging vest (which is reflective) and take a flashlight, and put a white sweatshirt on Aaron, and if you go straight to the store and come straight back, it should be okay."

I truly believe it should have been okay. They called another time. I do not know if any of you are parents, but this was the third time we talked to our kids that night. "Carmen doesn't want to go," the kids said. "Is it okay if Rochelle comes over to babysit?" These were responsible kids who arranged a babysitter for their younger sister.

The next call came from a neighbor's dad who told us two of the kids came back from the store, but somebody had taken Jacob. They were biking home from the store when they looked up and saw a man with a gun standing in the road. He told the kids to get off of their bikes and to lie down in the ditch or he would shoot them. He asked their ages, which is still confusing to me. Travor was 10 years

old and Aaron and Jacob were 11 years old. The man with the gun told Trevor to run into the woods as fast as he could or he would shoot him, so Trevor took off. He said the exact same words to Aaron, and Aaron took off. But as Aaron was leaving, he saw the man grab Jacob's shoulder. When Aaron caught up to Trevor and they felt safe enough to turn around and look back, Jacob and the man were gone.

Nobody saw the man's face. He wore a mask. They did track Jacob's footsteps to where a car had been parked, so they know they left in a car. It was a generic tire track on a dusty, gravel road in October. The police have gathered little information since then; basically, we have no more than we had that very first night.

No matter what preparations you make, nothing prepares you for a high-profile investigation of a missing child case. One local television station assembled a film clip of activities during the first year Jacob was missing. The clip shows I was blessed with a sheriff who left no stone unturned. He had been a sheriff for years and years. He called in 20-year-old favors, asking, "Can you do this for me?" He pulled in everybody.

We had our state crime bureau, the Minnesota Bureau of Criminal Apprehension (BCA), involved. The FBI became involved the first night because Jacob's classmate was the son of an FBI agent and because there was a weapon used. They knew this was an unusual case right away.

The police used all-terrain vehicles and horses to search for Jacob. Everybody in the entire Midwest was aware of his abduction. The Minnesota Vikings wanted to wear "Jacob's hope" hats at a game. The National Football League said no, so the Vikings waited for a home game and then they all wore their hats on the sidelines as Jacob's picture was projected on to the Metrodome highlight screen. The effect was phenomenal. People joined hands for Jacob. The line stretched for 5 miles. The sheriff's department told me the line would have been longer, but this happened in Minnesota in the winter. People were huddled together, shivering with cold, in many places. This huge outpouring of support is still heartening to me.

We still have no suspect. We have no proof that Jacob is not alive.

I remember a sense of helplessness in the beginning. I remember crawling into bed, pulling the covers over my head and thinking, "I can't do this. It's too hard." I had this image of Jacob laying somewhere pulling covers over his head and thinking, "I can't do this. They're never going to find me."

At that point, we made a very conscious decision that we were going to do something about this issue. I began asking questions. I was lucky enough to be a stay-at-home mom. I knew a lot about childhood things, but I knew nothing about child abduction, so I asked a lot of questions. I still ask questions. I think one of the complicated issues is that most people are ignorant about those who violate children. We do not function in their world, which is why sex offenders continue to find victims.

When Jacob was abducted, law enforcement had no experience running a missing child investigation. Police train for all kinds of situations, but at that point, 7 years ago, there was

not much training for this type of investigation.

I learned that most abductions are short-term, lasting a few hours. Most of the time, it is not a stranger who victimizes a child. The way Jacob was taken was extremely rare. Most victims get tricked or lured by someone they know. The number one reason for kidnapping is for sexual purposes. We truly have to stop the child molester if we are going to stop kidnappings.

I want to read the profile of the person who may have abducted Jacob, because I think it is key. Consider how this profile might be relevant to community notification and sex offender registration. It reads, "The following is a profile of persons who have committed crimes similar to the abduction of Jacob Wetterling. Agents assigned to the FBI Academy's Behavioral Science Unit at the National Center for the Analysis of Violent Crime compiled the profile. Construction of a criminal personality profile is predicated upon careful and objective analysis of victimology and crime-scene data coupled with behavioral possibilities arising from study and extensive research in similar cases.

"The offender is likely to be a white male between the ages of 25 to 35 years old; very low self-image; likely to have committed a similar crime in the past; may have some physical deformity; and is likely to have had a recent stressful event in his life which would have precipitated the high-risk approach taken in this crime. The high-risk approach also indicates the offender may have attempted similar acts recently and failed. The offender is likely to be in an unskilled or semi-skilled job that does not include contact with the public. Persons who know the offender would likely notice heightened anxiety on the offender's part since the crime occurred."

"What do you need?" I asked law enforcement. "What would help you find Jacob?" The police responded, "It would have helped to know who was in the area at the time of Jacob's abduction." We found out sex offenders were being sent to our region by another county, and they were put in halfway houses. Our local law enforcement did not know these halfway houses were for sex offenders. When police went to find out who was living in the halfway houses when Jacob was taken, they were told, "We're not going to tell you. There are privacy issues to consider." You could find out who was staying at the Holiday Inn or Super 8 motels. Information on noncriminals was available, but not information on sex offenders. Well, police got the information they were looking for, and then the law was corrected because it did not make sense. A lot of the things did not make sense at the time.

There was a man arrested for burglary in St. Cloud a year and a half after Jacob's abduction. When police ran a criminal history check on him, they found he had victimized young boys in his past. He lived closer to the abduction site than we do, but police did not know about this person at the time. It would really help law enforcement to know. Just knowing who is in the area is a good tool.

This information can also be used to clear suspects right away, rather than searching for them for years, finding out they were not involved and then having to go back to the beginning. I was appointed to a governor's task force in Minnesota to look at this problem and to suggest solutions. We did not jump into legislation right away. I did not have the knowledge at the time, and I would encourage you to avoid reactionary legislation because it is not the best way to proceed. It is not well planned.

Eventually, we came up with a proposal to have sex offender registration in Minnesota. I was appointed by a governor who lost his next election. When we went to report our findings, we had to report to a new governor. We said we wanted to have sex offender registration. He looked me straight in the eye and said, "You can't do that. These people have rights."

That was the wrong thing to say to me at the time. We got our legislation. We proceeded in Minnesota very carefully. We are not trying to violate anyone's rights. We tried to give police some tools we felt that they could use. After we got sex offender registration legislation passed in Minnesota, we went for Federal legislation. In 1996, Attorney General Janet Reno signed a proclamation to develop a system to connect all 50 State sex offender registries. Whether it is working or not, I think it is a good idea.

At the signing of the crime bill after our Federal legislation passed, we met Megan Kanka's parents. Megan, as you know, was kidnapped and murdered by someone who had committed these types of crimes before. This was not the first set of parents I met whose children were victims of crime.

Jeanna North, who was kidnapped, still has not been found. A man who was living on the corner where she was last seen who had a history of victimizing little girls in South Dakota admitted to kidnapping and murdering Jeanna in North Dakota. He has not been charged with the crime even though he provided a full confession. He is serving 30 years in prison for victimizing two other little girls. I continually hear from these parents, If only we had known.

That statement implies that increased knowledge will lead to change. When you are out alerting the public that a sex offender is going to be released into the community, anticipate change. That is why you are spreading the information, so people can respond differently and protect their children. Not knowing is a greater risk.

How you release the information is critical. The media like to highlight cases where notification did not work or where somebody was harassed. They do not want to report on all the instances when notification worked. When letting people know that a sex offender is being released into their community, we must tell them how they should respond. We are giving them the information so they can take precautions. The media also like to play around with the word "stranger." We know stranger is a ridiculous word. I hear law enforcement using it all the time, but people do not know who a stranger is. What is a stranger? Kids do

not know. One time, I was talking to a group of social workers and a little 5-year-old girl said, "Mommy, Jacob was abducted by a stranger, wasn't he?" I was impressed; 5 years old. The girl's mommy said, "Yes, he was." The little girl said, "I'm so glad we don't know any strangers." Brilliant thought—once you know them, they are not strangers anymore.

Sex offenders victimize children by gaining their trust. We are not just telling kids to beware of the "stranger" who is moving into their community. We are denying that stranger the opportunity to befriend children so he cannot victimize them. It is so important to remember the intent of this bill. I feel we worked really hard in Minnesota so our intent was clear. Our intent is to have fewer victims. We want to prevent sex offenders released from prison from violating other children.

We are not going to make it easy for them to have innocent victims because people are going to know their style. They are going to know what these people have done in the past. Another question you need to ask is, "Who is good at talking to communities to calm them down?" People are going to be angry. They are going to ask a lot of questions.

There is a lot of concern because sex offender registries are unfunded mandates. The Minnesota registry is unfunded as well. The Minneapolis Police Department decided that if it was going to have to notify the people, it was going to do it right. Before police began the notification process, they held community meetings and met with people in every single precinct in the city. They educated the community. These people are living among us now, the police said. You are only going to be told about a few individuals, but here is some basic knowledge to stay safe. The police did that with no additional funding. We had smaller departments saying, "We cannot afford to do this." Minneapolis was not given extra money to do it. The police just decided they were going to do it, they were going to do it right, and they were going to do a good job, and they have.

The Atlanta Journal-Constitution just ran an in-depth series on sexual predators titled "why Megan's Law is Not Enough." We hear a lot about what is wrong with notification laws. They are a start. They are tools that are only as good as those who use them. I know many people have been arrested in Minnesota simply for not registering as sex offenders. They are back in jail. That is a good step.

We set up a model policy task force through our Police Officers Standards and Training Board, and I was really intrigued by the process. When Jacob was first kidnapped, I assumed the whole world was working together to try and find him. Boy, was I wrong. Agencies do not always cooperate. The sheriff's department was not necessarily used to working with the BCA and FBI. All of this was foreign to them, but they did a good job. They pulled together.

When I sat through this task force for model policy, I learned that turf battles happen everywhere. Law enforcement sometimes blames the Department of Corrections, and the Department of Corrections blames the probation or parole officers, and they think the treatment people are at fault, and what about social services? It is easy to throw blame around. You should think about this the next time you find yourself saying, "We are doing our job, but they are not."

You could call a victim's parents and explain to them why the investigation is not working and see what you can do to make it better. See what you can do to improve communication between agencies. Maybe another visit to the legislature is necessary to make the notification law more efficient. Education does not happen just with people in your community. I had to educate our governor as to why we were going to do this. We are constantly educating legislators so they know what we need.

Since most sex offenders are not in prison, the people in the community need to know what they are supposed to be watching out for— not just for one offender who is going to be released but for all those already living in the community. When notification meetings are held in Minnesota, the community hears about general safety for 30 minutes and then 5 minutes are devoted to the specific person being released. I think that is important, because the law does not cover areas that people need to be aware of.

A lot depends on attitude. Attitude is everything in terms of how you go after these people. Our intent is to have fewer victims. We want to prevent these people from harming other children. . . . ■

A Policy Perspective

Bonnie Steinbock

A Policy Perspective

On July 29, 1994, Jesse Timmendequas invited seven-year-old Megan Kanka into his home to see his puppy. Once inside, Timmendequas forced Megan into his room, strangled her with a belt, and sexually assaulted her. She died from asphyxiation. Only after Megan's death did authorities reveal that Timmendequas had two previous convictions for child sexual abuse. Timmendequas had been sentenced to ten years at the Adult Diagnostic and Treatment Center, known as Avenel. With time off for good behavior, Timmendequas was released after serving only six years. At the time of Megan's murder, Timmendequas lived across the street from the Kankas with two other convicted sex offenders whom he had met at Avenel.

The outrage of community members that convicted sex offenders could live anonymously in their communities led to the passage of "Megan's Law" in New Jersey. In 1990, Washington State enacted its Community Protection Act after a seven-year-old Tacoma boy was lured into a wooded area by a recently released sex offender who orally and anally raped the boy and then cut off his penis. The man had a twenty-four-year record of assaults on young people, including the kidnapping and assault of two teenage girls and involvement in the murder of a fifteen-year-old schoolmate.

Registration of sex offenders with police is relatively unproblematic. It is community notification that has sparked the greatest controversy. In arguments before New Jersey's Supreme Court, lawyers opposed to Megan's Law criticized the law as stigmatizing and humiliating for offenders. They also said it was punitive, increasing the punishment to which offenders had originally been sentenced, and was therefore unconstitutional. In addition, they said that the law was an invasive measure that infringed the privacy and liberties of convicted sex offenders who had supposedly paid their debt to society. Other commentators point out that the stigma attached to sex offenders by society, and reinforced by notification laws, interferes with their ability to find jobs and places to live and to resume a normal life.

Whatever the merit of these objections as a matter of law—an issue I leave to those with legal backgrounds—they do not have much

Bonnie Steinbock, "A Policy Perspective," as appeared in *Criminal Justice Ethics*, Volume 14, Number 2 [Summer/Fall 1995], pp. 4–8. Reprinted by permission of Bonnie Steinbock and **The Institute for Criminal Justice Ethics**, 555 West 57th Street, Suite 607, New York, NY 1019–1029.

moral force. As Megan's mother, Maureen Kanka, expressed it, "I have a dead little girl. How can they sit there and worry about if it's punishment? What about our kids? That's ultimately what it comes down to. Our kids have rights and it's time someone started addressing them." It seems to me that Mrs. Kanka has framed the issue correctly. When a little boy has been raped and had his penis cut off, or when a little girl has been raped and murdered, worry about humiliating the people who committed these crimes seems a little overly sensitive.

I start then with the assumption that the paramount issue is the protection of children, that their rights to be safe from violent sexual assault certainly outweigh the rights of sexual predators not to be stigmatized. The trouble is that notification laws will not protect children. They are at best ineffective and at worst create a false sense of security that may actually expose children to risk. In addition, there is the danger of vigilantism that risks harming innocent bystanders and is contrary to the rule of law even when directed at the guilty.

First, Megan's Law focuses on a tiny percentage of those who commit sexual crimes against children, namely, dangerous strangers. Between seventy-five and eighty-nine percent of child sexual abuse is committed by relatives and friends. Yet Megan's Law explicitly targets for community notification sexual predators whose "sexual preference is for minor children outside his or her immediate family." Thus, it fails to protect children from the most common kind of sexual abuse, that inflicted by friends and relatives. Indeed, such laws may "promote a false sense of

security, lulling parents and kids into the big-bad-man mindset when many molesters are in fact trusted authority figures or family members."

It might be objected that it is not unreasonable to focus on the dangerous stranger even though this accounts for a very small percentage of child sexual abusers, simply because the dangerous stranger is likely to inflict greater harm on the child than a relative or family friend. Although all sexual abuse of children is undesirable, there is a much greater need to protect children from violent sexual predators than from pedophiles who fondle children or expose themselves.

However, this raises the question whether it is possible to determine who are the truly dangerous sex offenders. At first glance, this might seem simple. Columnist Suzanne Fields notes that Jesse Timmendequas had served just six years after two convictions for sexually assaulting two young girls and asks rhetorically, "Was there any doubt that he would strike again?" Yet while it may seem obvious, with 20–20 hindsight, that Timmendequas would commit more crimes if released, in fact it is not easy to predict either dangerousness or the propensity to reoffend. Studies indicate that predictions of an offender's dangerousness or propensity to reoffend average only a one-third accuracy rate. Thus, it is relatively arbitrary which offenders are placed into tier three and subject to community notification. This is the second reason why Megan's Law is not a good bet for protecting children. Inevitably, some sex offenders who would not have committed future crimes will be placed erroneously in the third tier, and unfairly stigmatized, while others who will go on to harm other children will escape community notification.

Nevertheless, perhaps some offenders are so clearly sociopaths that professionals can tell with a high degree of certainty that they are dangerous, violent, and likely to repeat their crimes. Then the question has to be, why on earth do we release such people? Worse, why do we release them without supervision? Under current law, once sex offenders complete their sentences at Avenel, they do not have to attend outpatient therapy or report to any authorities. In a psychiatric evaluation in February 1988, shortly before he was released, Timmendequas himself said that he needed more therapy and expressed fears about adjusting to life outside of the center. His therapist also urged that he remain institutionalized, or at least undergo "intensive psychotherapy in the community following release," but this was not done since Timmendequas had completed his sentence. "[W]e have no legal jurisdiction over anyone who has completed a jail sentence," says Grace Rogers, acting superintendent of the Avenel prison. "There's absolutely nothing we can do." Why has there not been community outrage and a "Megan's Law" about this absurd flaw in the law?

Aside from the epistemological problem of correctly identifying recidivists, some dangerous sex offenders escape notification because they have not been convicted of a crime. Some just were never caught, but there are other ways to escape notification. For example, the suspect arrested in the Polly Klaas kidnapping case, Richard Allen Davis, had spent more than

fifteen years in prison since 1973 for sex convictions, but because he had avoided sex offense charges through plea bargains, he was exempt from registration and notification.

A third reason why Megan's Law will not protect children is that notifying community members of the presence of convicted sex offenders will not prevent offenders from reoffending. "Released sex offenders . . . who experience a compulsion to offend, will find a victim regardless of whether the victim resides in a notified or unnotified community." In some jurisdictions, neighbors within a three-block radius must be notified of the presence of a paroled sex offender. What's to stop an energetic pedophile from walking four or five blocks to find a victim? One demonstrated effect of community notification laws is that sex offenders tend to flee the notified community. Thus, even if notification provides some measure of protection to one community, it may be at the expense of another. Offenders are likely to relocate in areas that either do not have notification laws or that do not enforce them. "In particular, sex offenders find large cities and inner city areas attractive because law enforcement agencies in these areas usually lack the time and resources to enforce community notification laws." Community notification simply transfers the problem of dangerous sex offenders from middle and upper-class communities to poor inner-city neighborhoods.

Fourth, the success of Megan's Law depends on the cooperation of convicted sex offenders. Although they are required by law to register with the police, not all do. Some register under a phony address. Many move frequently. Police lack the resources to track down those who fail to comply, in part because New Jersey legislators passed Megan's Law without appropriating any funds for its enforcement. The inevitable conclusion is that the legislators were not really serious about protecting children, but did what was likely to be politically popular.

However, even if there is little reason to think that Megan's Law will protect children, is there any harm from such laws, which are, after all, wanted by many voters? Quite aside from the problem of promoting false security, the greatest harm posed by notification laws is vigilantism. In Washington, notification laws have prompted several incidents of vigilantism. The family home of Joseph Gallardo, a convicted child rapist, was burned down by angry neighbors who had heard he was about to be released from prison. Not only the convicted offenders, but their relatives have been subjected to death threats, eggs thrown at their homes, and eviction. Worse, in Warren County, New Jersey, a father and son broke into a house, looking for a convicted child molester whose address was made public, and beat an innocent man who happened to be staying there. Thus, Megan's Law is not harmless pandering to voter preference, but is itself a threat to innocent people and a law-abiding society.

Some commentators oppose notification because it does not address the root problems of child abuse. One writes:

[N]otifying community members of released sex offenders neither confronts the causes of child sexual abuse nor looks to help offenders control their deviant behavior. Thus, Megan's Law represents a short-term solution that will not deter convicted sex offenders from reoffending.

But can sex offenders be taught to control their behavior? This is extremely controversial. A 1989 article in the journal *Psychological Bulletin*, reviewing studies of treatment for sex offenders before 1985, concluded that there was no successful treatment. Andrew Vachss, a lawyer who represents children, characterizes sexual predators as crafty sociopaths who "laugh behind their masks at our attempts to understand and rehabilitate them." He calls rehabilitation for chronic sexual predators "a joke":

A 1992 study of 767 rapists and child molesters in Minnesota found those who completed psychiatric treatment were arrested more often for new sex crimes than those who had not been treated at all. A Canadian survey that tracked released child molesters for 20 years revealed a 43 percent recidivism rate regardless of the therapy.

However, a new generation of more sophisticated therapies is challenging the conventional wisdom that sex offenders cannot be rehabilitated. "The new view is that, as with alcoholism, there is no complete 'cure' for sex offenders, but that with help they can manage their sexual impulses without committing new crimes." The new treatment, called "relapse prevention," focuses on helping sex offenders control the cycle of troubling emotions, distorted thinking, and deviant sex fantasies that lead to their sex crimes, whether rape, child molesting, exhibitionism, or voyeurism. A first step is helping the men develop empathy for their victims by reading accounts and watching videotapes from the victims' perspective. Proponents claim that the recidivism rate of those who complete programs in relapse prevention is about half that of offenders who receive no treatment.

There is probably truth in the claims of both sides. Therapy is probably helpful for some sex offenders, but unlikely to rehabilitate sexual sociopaths who are incapable of empathy. Psychologists agree that sex offenders must be highly motivated for the therapy to work, and some offenders have no interest in changing their behavior. In any event, relatively few convicted sex offenders (about twenty-five percent) receive any treatment at all. Consider what has occurred at Avenel, once a model treatment center. When it opened in 1976, it provided inmates with individual and small group therapy, sometimes on a daily basis, and was headed by a superintendent with an expertise in mental health. However, its budget was reduced, staff was cut, the quality of therapy declined, and the inmate population, designed to be 594, grew to 681. By 1989, Avenel had changed from a treatment center into a maximum-security prison. "What passes for treatment is one and one-half hours of group therapy per week. There are no bilingual counselors and no one-to-one therapy."

It is beyond the scope of this essay to attempt to determine whether it is worthwhile to put resources into treatment programs for sex offenders. The evidence of success in Vermont and California suggests that further research and experimentation should be tried. Nevertheless, it seems likely that some sex offenders—the hardcore, violent sexual predators—cannot be rehabilitated. They should get longer sentences and be released, if at all, only under strict supervision.

The remaining avenues for protecting children are supervision and education. Indeed, notification is supported by some partly because they think it will motivate parents to educate their children about sex crimes. However, this is a weak argument for notification, in light of all its problems. Parents will be motivated to educate their children simply by understanding that this is the best way to protect them. But what should be the content of the education? I dissent from the view that we should be educating young children about sex crimes. It seems to me that this is more likely to frighten them than to protect them. Nor will pointing out individuals the children should avoid provide adequate protection. Mrs. Kanka said, "If I had known that three sex perverts were living across the street from me, Megan would be alive today." Perhaps so, but notification would not prevent another Megan in another neighborhood from becoming a victim. Nor would notification protect Megan from a sex pervert who was not registered or who had escaped tier-three classification. A better way to protect children is by giving them sensible safety rules, for example, that they are not to go with strangers: not into their houses, in their cars, or into the woods. Parents should role-play various situations with children, such as, "What if a stranger says that I'm hurt, and I've asked him to come get you? Would you get into a car with him then?" or "what if he says he has candy or a toy or a puppy for you to play with? Would you go into his house then?" Parents can teach these safety rules to children in a non-frightening way, without scaring them with the details of rape and sexual mutilation. Such rules can protect children not only from tier-three offenders, but from those in tiers one and two as well as those who have not yet committed or been convicted of a sexual offense.

Children also need to be protected from the vastly more common form of sexual abuse, that committed by friends and relatives. Children must feel that they can tell their parents, or other trusted adults, about anything that is bothering them, that they will not be dismissed or ridiculed. It is often shame or the fear of being disbelieved that makes children reluctant to reveal sexual abuse. They need to know that they will not be blamed or punished if they tell, but will be protected.

Education is only part of the story. As parents, we are responsible for supervising our children. How closely a child needs to be supervised depends on several factors, such as the child's age and maturity, and the kind of community in which one lives. Parents in New York City cannot safely let six-year-olds out of their sight; parents in suburbs and small towns can let children play by themselves with only periodic checks so long as they do not leave the yard or block. There are no hard and fast rules, and it is often a matter of judgment as to what is safe.

The difficulty that parents face is to strike a balance between teaching our children to be prudent and cautious while not making them excessively dependent or timid. After all, neighborliness is also an important virtue we want our children to learn. My children are in and out of the houses of their playmates on our street; their friends frequently visit in our house. We permit this even though it is possible that, unbeknownst to us, their friends' parents are sexual predators. That risk is too minute to worry about, any more than I would keep my children indoors to protect them from lightning (though I would call them inside if there was a thunder storm in the area) or refuse to let them ride bicycles (though they must wear helmets). Instead, we tell them that we need to know where they are, and so they must tell us before they go to play with their friends.

It may be that Megan thought of Jesse Timmendequas as a friend. Apparently, he was considered a gentle man, and the neighborhood children often played with his puppy. We do not know if Megan asked permission from her parents before going inside Timmendequas's house, but probably it never occurred to her to do so. It may not have occurred to her parents to teach her to do so. Unfortunately, in today's world, parents must be a little more suspicious than was necessary in the past. We need to have our antennae up. A childless adult who makes friends with children may be perfectly harmless, but it does not hurt to tell children that they are not allowed to go inside a grown-up's house without first getting permission. Had Megan been taught this rule, she would probably be alive today.

Supporters of community notification ask, "But wouldn't you want to know if there was a dangerous sex offender in your neighborhood?" This is not the right basis for making law or policy. Some people would want to know the HIV-status of their doctor or dentist even though the risk to patients from HIV-infected doctors is miniscule and the dangers of such notification very great indeed. We should not ask, then, what people are likely to want to know, but rather, what are the effects of community notification? If, as I have argued, it does not increase safety but rather promotes a false sense of security and furthermore is likely to lead to vigilantism, then we need to find more effective, less dangerous ways of achieving the paramount goal of protecting children. ■

⬛ The Continuing Debate

What Is New

In 2003 the U.S. Supreme Court—in *Smith v. Doe*, No. 01-729, and *Connecticut Department of Public Safety v. Doe*, No. 01-1231—upheld the constitutionality of sex offender registries (or "Megan's Laws") against two challenges. In dealing with a key issue in one case, the majority of justices ruled (over strong dissent from the minority) that such laws are regulatory rather than punitive. Though the Court upheld the laws in these cases, some justices noted that such laws might be open to challenge on grounds other than those argued in these two cases; and so the issue is likely to return to the Supreme Court.

Where to Find More

For a description of how sex offender registration laws work and are administered and enforced in several states, see Alan D. Scholle, "Sex Offender Registration: Community Notification Laws," *FBI Law Enforcement Bulletin* (July 2000): 17–24.

Mary Ann Farkas and Amy Stichman, "Sex Offender Laws: Can Treatment, Punishment, Incapacitation, and Public Safety be Reconciled?" *Criminal Justice Behavior*, Volume 27, Number 2 (Autumn 2002): 256–283, provide a good overview of the issues as well as an excellent history of sexual predator laws.

William Edwards and Christopher Hensley, "Contextualizing Sex offender Management Legislation and Policy: Evaluating the Problem of Latent Consequences in Community Notification Laws," *International Journal of Offender Therapy and Comparative Criminology*, Volume 45, Number 1 (2001): 83–101, argue that in some cases, required registration of sex offenders undercuts effective treatment programs (for example, by making family members of offenders and victims reluctant to report an offender for fear of public stigma), and so may result in increased risk of repeat sexual offenses. The fear of public stigma and ostracism is well-founded, as shown in a study by R. Zevitz and Mary Ann Farkas, "Sex Offender Community Notification: Managing High-Risk Criminals or Exacting Further Vengeance?" *Behavioral Science & the Law*, Volume 18, Number 2/3 (2000): 375–391; and also by Richard Tewksbury and Matthew Lees, "Perceptions of Sex Offender Registration: Collateral Consequences and Community Experiences," *Sociological Spectrum*, Volume 26, Number 3 (May/June 2006): 309–334. Other ways in which sexual offender registration and notification laws may inhibit effective treatment are noted by J. Billings and C. Bulges, "Comment: Maine's Sex Offender Registration and Notification Act: Wise or Wicked?" *Maine Law Review*, Volume 52 (2000): 175–259; and R. Prentky, "Commentary: Community Notification Laws and Constructive Risk Reduction," *Journal of Interpersonal Violence*, Volume 11, Number 2 (1996): 295–298.

Other critics of "Megan's Law" include R. Freeman-Longo, "Feel Good Legislation: Prevention or Calamity," *Child Abuse and Neglect*, Volume 20 (1996): 95–101; and Jonathan Simon, "Megan's Law: Crime and Democracy in Late Modern America," *Law and Social Inquiry*, Volume 25, Number 4 (Fall 2000): 1111–1150.

The very limited empirical research on the effectiveness of sexual offender registry laws in preventing new episodes of sexual abuse indicates that such laws are not working; see A. J. Petrosino and C. Petrosino, "The Public Safety Potential of Megan's Law in Massachusetts: An Assessment from a Sample of Criminal Sexual Psychopaths," *Crime and Delinquency*, Volume 45, Number 1 (1999): 140–158; and Sarah Welchans, "Megan's Law: Evaluations of Sexual Offender Registries," *Criminal Justice Policy Review*, Volume 16, Number 2 (June 2005): 123–140.

A. R. Kabat, "Scarlet Letter Sex Offender Databases and Community Notification: Sacrificing Personal Privacy for a Symbol's Sake," *American Criminal Law Review*, Volume 35, Number 2 (1998): 333–370, suggests ways of revising current policies to enhance both public protection and effective rehabilitation programs.

An interesting critique and review of U.S. Supreme Court decisions related to sex offender registries is offered by *Harvard Law Review*, "Making Outcasts Out of Outlaws: The Unconstitutionality of Sex Offender Registration and Criminal Alien Detection," Volume 117 (June 2004): 2731–2752.

A Canadian restorative justice program for sex offenders is described by Stacey Hannem and Michael Petrunik, in "Canada's Circles of Support and Accountability: A Community Justice Initiative for High-Risk Sex Offenders," *Corrections Today* (December 2004): 98–101. For a review of sex offender registration programs from an international perspective, see Lyn Hinds and Kathleen Daly, "The War on Sex Offenders: Community Notification in Perspective," *Australian and New Zealand Journal of Criminology*, Volume 34, Number 3 (2001): 256–276.

See also Debate 9 on shaming punishments.

15

Should the Death Penalty Be Abolished?

The Death Penalty Is Morally Justifiable
Advocate: Louis P. Pojman (1935–2005), recently retired from teaching philosophy at the U.S. Military Academy at West Point.
Source: From "Why the Death Penalty is Morally Permissible," Chapter 3, *Debating the Death Penalty: Should America Have Capital Punishment?* edited by Hugo Adam Bedau and Paul G. Cassell (New York: Oxford University Press, 2005): 51–75.

The Death Penalty Is Morally Wrong
Advocate: Stephen B. Bright, President of the Southern Center for Human Rights; teaches criminal law courses at both Yale and Harvard Law Schools.
Source: "Why the United States Will Join the Rest of the World in Abandoning Capital Punishment," Chapter 6, *Debating the Death Penalty: Should America Have Capital Punishment?* edited by Hugo Adam Bedau and Paul G. Cassell (New York: Oxford University Press, 2005): 152–182.

Though the death penalty has been abolished in most countries, it remains in effect in the United States, and it remains a topic of fierce disagreement. The classic argument for capital punishment is retributive: blood deserves blood, those who commit murder deserve to die, and justice is not done when a murderer is allowed to live. A more sophisticated argument gives capital punishment a symbolic or expressive function: Capital punishment is the strongest and most appropriate way for society to express its deep abhorrence of the most awful crimes. The argument that capital punishment is an effective deterrent of crime is perennially popular, though it can offer little empirical support for its claims. Those opposing capital punishment argue that capital punishment may have an expressive function, but that it expresses the wrong message: that killing is a solution, and that reform is impossible. They also argue that capital punishment is a cruel, unusual, and dehumanizing punishment. Among contemporary abolitionists, there are two prominent arguments: first, that capital punishment is administered in a capricious or arbitrary or racially discriminatory manner; and second, that because of many flaws in our system of justice and the honest mistakes of eyewitnesses, there is grave danger of wrongly executing the innocent.

Louis Pojman's case for capital punishment combines both the retributive and the deterrent arguments; and he insists that even if mistakes are made, we shouldn't give up capital punishment "because of a few possible miscarriages" of justice in which innocent people are executed. Stephen Bright argues that capital punishment is contrary to the best principles and positive image of the United States; that it is likely to result in executions of the wrongly convicted; and that it is administered in an arbitrary, unfair, and racist manner. On some points, Pojman and Bright almost argue past one another: Bright argues that the U.S. system of capital punishment is unfair and subject to serious mistakes, while Pojman insists that capital punishment is still justified even if the system *is* unfair and prone to error. But on some other key questions—especially on the fundamental nature of capital punishment and the message it conveys—they are on a collision course.

⠿ Points to Ponder

- Pojman notes that "abolitionists often make the complaint that only the poor get death sentences for murder." In response, Pojman suggests that the death penalty might also be appropriate for white collar criminals who steal millions of dollars from the pension plans of their employees. Is that an answer to the abolitionists' complaint?
- The classic argument for capital punishment is retributive: blood deserves blood, those who commit murder deserve to die, and justice is not done when a murderer is allowed to live. The retributive view is stated plainly by Igor Primoratz:

  Capital punishment ought to be retained where it obtains, and reintroduced in those jurisdictions that have abolished it, although we have no reason to believe that, as a matter of deterrence, it is any better than a very long prison term. It ought to be retained, or reintroduced, for one simple reason: that justice be done in cases of murder, that murderers be punished according to their just deserts.

  Many people (including, of course, Primoratz) regard that as a clear and certain truth. But what is the *basis* for the claim that murderers *justly deserve* to be executed? Is it a gut feeling? A matter of religious faith? An instinct?

- Based on the high number of mistaken convictions that have been overturned during the last decade—many for prisoners on death row— there seems little doubt that if capital punishment continues, the state will wrongly execute some innocent persons along with those who are guilty. *If that is true, is that a sufficient reason to halt capital punishment?*

- Pojman argues that abolishing capital punishment because we occasionally make a mistake and execute an innocent person would be like "abolish[ing] the use of fire engines and ambulances because occasionally they kill innocent pedestrians while carrying out their mission." Is that a good analogy?

- Walter Berns—a supporter of capital punishment—insists that "the criminal law must be made awful, by which I mean inspiring, or commanding 'profound respect or reverential fear.' It must remind us of the moral order by which alone we can live as *human* beings, and in America . . . the only punishment that can do this is capital punishment." Assuming that the death penalty does command "reverential fear," is that an appropriate goal for a democratic society to have toward its laws, or is it more appropriate to a monarchical or tyrannical society?

Why the Death Penalty Is Morally Permissible

Louis P. Pojman

A Defense of the Death Penalty

> Who so sheddeth man's blood, by man shall his blood be shed. (Genesis 9:6)

There is an ancient tradition, going back to biblical times, but endorsed by the mainstream of philosophers, from Plato to Thomas Aquinas, from Thomas Hobbes to Immanuel Kant, Thomas Jefferson, John Stuart Mill, and C. S. Lewis, that a fitting punishment for murder is the execution of the murderer. One prong of this tradition, the *backward-looking* or deontological position, epitomized in Aquinas and Kant, holds that because human beings, as rational agents, have dignity, one who with malice aforethought kills a human being forfeits his right to life and deserves to die. The other, the *forward-looking* or consequentialist, tradition, exemplified by Jeremy Bentham, Mill, and Ernest van den Haag, holds that punishment ought to serve as a deterrent, and that capital punishment is an adequate

Louis P. Pojman, "Why the Death Policy Is Morally Permissible," from *Debating the Death Penalty: Should America Have Capital Punishment?* edited by Hugo Adam Bedau and Paul G. Cassell (New York: Oxford University Press, 2005): 51–75. Reprinted with permission from Rowman & Littlefield.

deterrent to prospective murderers. Abolitionists like Bedau and Jeffrey Reiman deny both prongs of the traditional case for the death penalty. They hold that long prison sentences are a sufficient retributive response to murder and that the death penalty probably does not serve as a deterrent or is no better deterrent than other forms of punishment. I will argue that both traditional defenses are sound and together they make a strong case for retaining the death penalty. That is, I hold a combined theory of punishment. A backward-looking judgment that the criminal has committed a heinous crime plus a forward-looking judgment that a harsh punishment will deter would-be murderers is sufficient to justify the death penalty. I turn first to the retributivist theory in favor of capital punishment.

Retribution

A couple of years ago I spent a long evening with the husband, sister and parents of a fine young woman who had been forced into the trunk of a car in a hospital parking lot. The degenerate who kidnapped her kept her in the trunk, like an ant in a jar, until he got tired of the game. Then he killed her.

Human beings have dignity as self-conscious rational agents who are able to act morally. One could maintain that it is precisely their moral goodness or innocence that bestows dignity and a right to life on them. Intentionally taking the life of an innocent human being is so evil that absent mitigating circumstances, the perpetrator forfeits his own right to life. He or she deserves to die.

The retributivist holds three propositions: (1) that all the guilty deserve to be punished; (2) that only the guilty deserve to be punished; and (3) that the guilty deserve to be punished in proportion to the severity of their crime. . . .

Criminals like Steven Judy, Jeffrey Dahmer, Timothy McVeigh, Ted Bundy (who is reported to have raped and murdered over 100 women), John Mohammed and John Lee Malvo, who murdered 12 people in the killing spree of 2002, have committed capital offenses and deserve nothing less than capital punishment. No doubt malicious acts like the ones committed by these criminals deserve worse punishment than death, and I would be open to suggestions of torture (why not?), but at a minimum, the death penalty seems warranted.

People often confuse *retribution* with *revenge*. Governor George Ryan, who recently commuted the sentences of all the prisoners on death row in the State of Illinois, quotes a letter from the Reverend Desmond Tutu that "to take a life when a life has been lost is revenge, it is not justice." This is simply false. While moral people will feel outrage at acts of heinous crimes, the moral justification of punishment is not *vengeance*, but *desert*. Vengeance signifies inflicting harm on the offender out of anger because of what he has done. Retribution is the rationally supported theory that the criminal deserves a punishment fitting the gravity of his crime.

The nineteenth-century British philosopher James Fitzjames Stephens thought vengeance was a justification for punishment, arguing that punishment should be inflicted "for the sake of ratifying the feeling of hatred—call it revenge, resentment, or what you will—which the contemplation of such [offensive] conduct excites in healthily constituted minds." But retributivism is not based on hatred for the criminal (though a feeling of vengeance may accompany the punishment). Retributivism is the theory that the criminal *deserves* to be punished and deserves to be punished in proportion to the gravity of his or her crime, whether or not the victim or anyone else desires it. We may all deeply regret having to carry out the punishment, but consider it warranted.

On the other hand, people do have a sense of outrage and passion for revenge directed at criminals for their crimes. Imagine that someone in your family was on the receiving end of violent acts. Stephens was correct in asserting that "[t]he criminal law stands to the passion for revenge in much the same relation as marriage to the sexual appetite." Failure to punish would no more lessen our sense of vengeance than the elimination of marriage would lessen our sexual appetite. When a society fails to punish criminals in a way thought to be proportionate to the gravity of the crime, the danger arises that the public would take the law into its own hands, resulting in vigilante justice, lynch mobs, and private acts of retribution. The outcome is likely to be an anarchistic, insecure state of injustice. As such, legal retribution stands as a safeguard for an orderly application of punitive desert.

Our natural instinct is for *vengeance*, but civilization demands that we restrain our anger and go through a legal process, letting the outcome determine whether and to what degree to punish the accused. Civilization demands that we not take the law into our own hands, but it should also satisfy our deepest instincts when they are consonant with reason. Our instincts tell us that some crimes, like McVeigh's, Judy's, and Bundy's, should be severely punished, but we refrain from personally carrying out those punishments, committing ourselves to the legal processes. The death penalty is supported by our gut animal instincts as well as our sense of justice as desert.

The death penalty reminds us that there are consequences to our actions, that we are responsible for what we do, so that dire consequences for immoral actions are eminently appropriate. The death penalty is such a fitting response to evil.

Deterrence

The second tradition justifying the death penalty is the utilitarian theory of deterrence. This holds that by executing convicted murderers we will deter would-be murderers from killing innocent people. The evidence for deterrence is controversial. Some scholars, like Thornstein Sellin and Bedau, argue that the death penalty is not a deterrent of homicides superior to long-term imprisonment. Others, such as Isaac Ehrlich, make a case for the death penalty as a significant deterrent. Granted that the evidence is ambiguous, and honest scholars can differ on the results. However, one often hears abolitionists claiming the evidence shows that the death penalty fails to deter homicide. This is too strong a claim. The sociological evidence doesn't show either that the death penalty deters or that it fails to deter. The evidence is simply inconclusive. But a commonsense case can be made for deterrence.

Imagine that every time someone intentionally killed an innocent person he was immediately struck down by lightning. When mugger Mike slashed his knife into the neck of the elderly pensioner, lightning struck, killing Mike. His fellow muggers witnessed the sequence of events. When burglar Bob pulled his pistol out and shot the bank teller through her breast, a bolt leveled Bob, his compatriots beholding the spectacle. Soon men with their guns lying next to them were found all across the world in proximity to the corpses of their presumed victims. Do you think that the evidence of cosmic retribution would go unheeded?

We can imagine the murder rate in the United States and everywhere else plummeting. The close correlation between murder and cosmic retribution would serve as a deterrent to would-be murderers. If this thought experiment is sound, we have a prima facie argument for the deterrent effect of capital punishment. In its ideal, prompt performance, the death penalty would likely deter most rational criminally minded from committing murder. The question then becomes how do we institute the death penalty so as to have the maximal

deterrent effect without violating the rights of the accused.

We would have to bring the accused to trial more quickly and limit the appeals process of those found guilty "beyond reasonable doubt." Having DNA evidence should make this more feasible than hitherto. Furthermore, public executions of the convicted murderer would serve as a reminder that crime does not pay. Public executions of criminals seem an efficient way to communicate the message that if you shed innocent blood, you will pay a high price. . . .

Former Prosecuting Attorney for the State of Florida, Richard Gernstein, has set forth the commonsense case for deterrence. First of all, he claims, the death penalty certainly deters the murderer from any further murders, including those he or she might commit within the prison where he is confined. Second, statistics cannot tell us how many potential criminals have refrained from taking another's life through fear of the death penalty. He quotes Judge Hyman Barshay of New York: "The death penalty is a warning, just like a lighthouse throwing its beams out to sea. We hear about shipwrecks, but we do not hear about the ships the lighthouse guides safely on their way. We do not have proof of the number of ships it saves, but we do not tear the lighthouse down."

Some of the commonsense evidence is anecdotal, as the following quotation shows. British member of Parliament Arthur Lewis explains how he was converted from an abolitionist to a supporter of the death penalty:

> One reason that has stuck in my mind, and which has proved

[deterrence] to me beyond question, is that there was once a professional burglar in [my] constituency who consistently boasted of the fact that he had spent about one-third of his life in prison. . . . He said to me "I am a professional burglar. Before we go out on a job we plan it down to every detail. Before we go into the boozer to have a drink we say 'Don't forget, no shooters'— shooters being guns." He adds "We did our job and didn't have shooters because at that time there was capital punishment. Our wives, girlfriends and our mums said, 'Whatever you do, do not carry a shooter because if you are caught you might be topped [executed].' If you do away with capital punishment they will all be carrying shooters."

It is difficult to know how widespread this reasoning is. My own experience corroborates this testimony. Growing up in the infamous Cicero, Illinois, home of Al Capone and the Mafia, I had friends who went into crime, mainly burglary and larceny. It was common knowledge that one stopped short of killing in the act of robbery. A prison sentence could be dealt with—especially with a good lawyer—but being convicted of murder, which at that time included a reasonable chance of being electrocuted, was an altogether different matter. No doubt exists in my mind that the threat of the electric chair saved the lives of some of those who were robbed in my town. No doubt some crimes are committed in the heat of passion or by the temporally

(or permanently) insane, but some are committed through a process of risk assessment. Burglars, kidnappers, traitors and vindictive people will sometimes be restrained by the threat of death. We simply don't know how much capital punishment deters, but this sort of commonsense, anecdotal evidence must be taken into account in assessing the institution of capital punishment. . . .

Gernstein quotes the British Royal Commission on Capital Punishment (1949–53), which is one of the most thorough studies on the subject and which concluded that there was evidence that the death penalty has some deterrent effect on normal human beings. Some of its evidence in favor of the deterrence effect includes these points:

1. Criminals who have committed an offense punishable by life imprisonment, when faced with capture, refrained from killing their captor though by killing, escape seemed probable. When asked why they refrained from the homicide, quick responses indicated a willingness to serve life sentence, but not risk the death penalty.
2. Criminals about to commit certain offenses refrained from carrying deadly weapons. Upon apprehension, answers to questions concerning absence of such weapons indicated a desire to avoid more serious punishment by carrying a deadly weapon, and also to avoid use of the weapon which could result in imposition of the death penalty.

3. Victims have been removed from a capital punishment State to a non-capital punishment State to allow the murderer opportunity for homicide without threat to his own life. This in itself demonstrates that the death penalty is considered by some would-be-killers.

Gernstein then quotes former District Attorney of New York, Frank S. Hogan, representing himself and his associates:

We are satisfied from our experience that the deterrent effect is both real and substantial . . . for example, from time to time accomplices in felony murder state with apparent truthfulness that in the planning of the felony they strongly urged the killer not to resort to violence. From the context of these utterances, it is apparent that they were led to these warnings to the killer by fear of the death penalty which they realized might follow the taking of life. Moreover, victims of hold-ups have occasionally reported that one of the robbers expressed a desire to kill them and was dissuaded from so doing by a confederate. Once again, we think it not unreasonable to suggest that fear of the death penalty played a role in some of these intercessions.

On a number of occasions, defendants being questioned in connection with homicide have shown a striking terror of the death penalty. While these persons have in fact perpetrated homicide, we think that their terror of the death penalty must be symptomatic of the attitude of many others of their type, as a result of which many lives have been spared . . . .

Gernstein notes:

The commissioner of Police of London, England, in his evidence before the Royal Commission on Capital Punishment, told of a gang of armed robbers who continued operations after one of their members was sentenced to death and his sentence commuted to penal servitude, but the same gang disbanded and disappeared when, on a later occasion, two others were convicted of murder and hanged.

Gernstein sums up his data: "Surely it is a common sense argument, based on what is known of human nature, that the death penalty has a deterrent effect particularly for certain kinds of murderers. Furthermore, as the Royal Commission opined, the death penalty helps to educate the conscience of the whole community, and it arouses among many people a quasi-religious sense of awe. In the mind of the public there remains a strong association between murder and the penalty of death. Certainly one of the factors which restrains some people from murder is fear of punishment and surely, since people fear death more than anything else, the death penalty is the most effective deterrent."

I should also point out that *given the retributivist argument* for the death penalty, based on desert, the retentionist does not have to prove that the death penalty deters *better* than long prison sentences, but if the death penalty is deemed at least as effective as its major alternative, it would be justified. If evidence existed that life imprisonment were a *more effective* deterrent, the retentionist might be hard pressed to defend it on retributivist lines alone. My view is that the desert argument plus the common-sense evidence—being bolstered by the following argument, the Best Bet Argument, strongly supports retention of the death penalty.

The late Ernest van den Haag has set forth what he called the Best Bet Argument. He argued that even though we don't know for certain whether the death penalty deters or prevents other murders, we should bet that it does. Indeed, due to our ignorance, any social policy we take is a gamble. Not to choose capital punishment for first-degree murder is as much a bet that capital punishment doesn't deter as choosing the policy is a bet that it does. There is a significant difference in the betting, however, in that to bet against capital punishment is to bet against the innocent and for the murderer, while to bet for it is to bet against the murderer and for the innocent.

The point is this: We are accountable for what we let happen, as well as for what we actually do. If I fail to bring up my children properly so that they are a menace to society, I am to some extent responsible for their bad behavior. I could have caused it to be somewhat better. If I have good evidence that a bomb will blow up the building you are working in and fail to notify you (assuming I can), I am partly responsible for your death, if

and when the bomb explodes. So we are responsible for what we omit doing, as well as for what we do. Purposefully to refrain from a lesser evil which we know will allow a greater evil to occur is to be at least partially responsible for the greater evil. This responsibility for our omissions underlies van den Haag's argument, to which we now return.

Suppose that we choose a policy of capital punishment for capital crimes. In this case we are betting that the death of some murderers will be more than compensated for by the lives of some innocents not being murdered (either by these murderers or others who would have murdered). If we're right, we have saved the lives of the innocent. If we're wrong, unfortunately, we've sacrificed the lives of some murderers. But say we choose not to have a social policy of capital punishment. If capital punishment doesn't work as a deterrent, we've come out ahead, but if it does work, then we've missed an opportunity to save innocent lives. If we value the saving of innocent lives more highly than the loss of the guilty, then to bet on a policy of capital punishment turns out to be rational. Since the innocent have a greater right to life than the guilty, it is our moral duty to adopt a policy that has a chance of protecting them from potential murderers. . . .

If the Best Bet Argument is sound, or if the death penalty does deter would-be murderers, as common sense suggests, then we should support some uses of the death penalty. It should be used for those who commit first-degree murder, for whom no mitigating factors are present, and especially for those who murder police officers, prison guards, and political leaders. Many states rightly favor it for those who murder while committing another crime, such as burglary or rape. It should be used in cases of treason and terrorist bombings. It should also be considered for the perpetrators of egregious white collar crimes such as bank managers embezzling the savings of the public. The savings and loan scandals of the 1980s, involving wealthy bank officials absconding with the investments of elderly pensioners and others, ruined the lives of many people. This gross violation of the public trust warrants the electric chair. Such punishment would meet the two conditions set forth in this paper. The punishment would be deserved and it would likely deter future crimes by people in the public trust. It would also make the death penalty more egalitarian, applicable to the rich as well as the poor.

Let me consider two objections often made to the implementation of the death penalty: that it sometimes leads to the death of innocents and that it discriminates against blacks.

Objection 1: Miscarriages of justice occur. Capital punishment is to be rejected because of human fallibility in convicting innocent parties and sentencing them to death. In a survey done in 1985 Hugo Adam Bedau and Michael Radelet found that of the 7,000 persons executed in the United States between 1900 and 1985, 25 were innocent of capital crimes. While some compensation is available to those unjustly imprisoned, the death sentence is irrevocable. We can't compensate the dead. As John Maxton, a member of the British Parliament puts it, "If we allow one innocent person to be executed, morally we are committing the same, or, in some ways, a worse crime than the person who committed the murder."

Response: Mr. Maxton is incorrect in saying that mistaken judicial execution is morally the same as or worse than murder, for a deliberate intention to kill the innocent occurs in a murder, whereas no such intention occurs in wrongful capital punishment.

Sometimes the objection is framed this way: It is better to let ten criminals go free than to execute one innocent person. If this dictum is a call for safeguards, then it is well taken; but somewhere there seems to be a limit on the tolerance of society toward capital offenses. Would these abolitionists argue that it is better that 50 or 100 or 1,000 murderers go free than that one innocent person be executed? Society has a right to protect itself from capital offenses even if this means taking a finite chance of executing an innocent person. If the basic activity or process is justified, then it is regrettable, but morally acceptable, that some mistakes are made. Fire trucks occasionally kill innocent pedestrians while racing to fires, but we accept these losses as justified by the greater good of the activity of using fire trucks. We judge the use of automobiles to be acceptable even though such use causes an average of 50,000 traffic fatalities each year. We accept the morality of a defensive war even though it will result in our troops accidentally or mistakenly killing innocent people.

The fact that we can err in applying the death penalty should give us pause and cause us to build a better appeals process into the judicial system. Such a process is already in most places in the American and British legal systems. That an occasional error may be made, regrettable though this is, is not a sufficient reason for us to refuse to use the death penalty, if on balance it serves a just and useful function.

Furthermore, abolitionists are simply misguided in thinking that prison sentences are a satisfactory alternative here. It's not clear that we can always or typically compensate innocent parties who waste away in prison. . . .

The abolitionist is incorrect in arguing that death is different from long-term prison sentences because it is irrevocable. Imprisonment also takes good things away from us that may never be returned. We cannot restore to the inmate the freedom or opportunities he or she lost. Suppose an innocent 25-year-old man is given a life sentence for murder. Thirty years later the error is discovered and he is set free. Suppose he values three years of freedom to every one year of life. That is, he would rather live 10 years as a free man than 30 as a prisoner. Given this man's values, the criminal justice system has taken the equivalent of 10 years of life from him. If he lives until he is 65, he has, as far as his estimation is concerned, lost 10 years, so that he may be said to have lived only 55 years.

The numbers in this example are arbitrary, but the basic point is sound. Most of us would prefer a shorter life of higher quality to a longer one of low quality. Death prevents all subsequent quality, but imprisonment also irrevocably harms one by diminishing the quality of life of the prisoner.

Objection 2: The second objection made against the death penalty is that it is unjust because it discriminates against the poor and minorities, particularly African Americans, over rich people and whites. Stephen B. Bright makes this objection. Former Supreme Court Justice William Douglas wrote that "a law which reaches that [discriminatory] result in practice has no more sanctity than a law, which in terms provides the same." . . .

Response: First of all, it is not true that a law that is applied in a discriminatory manner is unjust. Unequal justice is no less justice, however uneven its application. The discriminatory application, not the law itself, is unjust. A just law is still just even if it is not applied consistently. For example, a friend once got two speeding tickets during a 100-mile trip (having borrowed my car). He complained to the police officer who gave him his second ticket that many drivers were driving faster than he was at the time. They had escaped detection, he argued, so it wasn't fair for him to get two tickets on one trip. The officer acknowledged the imperfections of the system but, justifiably, had no qualms about giving him the second ticket. Unequal justice is still justice, however regrettable. So Justice Douglas is wrong in asserting that discriminatory results invalidate the law itself. Discriminatory practices should be reformed, and in many cases they can be. But imperfect practices in themselves do not entail that the laws engendering these practices themselves are unjust. . . .

If we concluded that we should abolish a rule or practice, unless we treated everyone exactly by the same rules all the time, we would have to abolish, for example, traffic laws and laws against imprisonment for rape, theft, and even murder. Carried to its logical limits, we would also have to refrain from saving drowning victims if a number of people were drowning but we could only save a few of them. Imperfect justice is the best that we humans can attain. We should reform our practices as much as possible to eradicate unjust discrimination wherever we can, but if we are not allowed to have a law without perfect application, we will be forced to have no laws at all.

Nathanson argues that the case of death is different. "Because of its finality and extreme severity of the death penalty, we need to be more scrupulous in applying it as punishment than is necessary with any other punishment." The retentionist agrees that the death penalty is a severe punishment and that we need to be scrupulous in applying it. The difference between the abolitionist and the retentionist seems to lie in whether we are wise and committed enough as a nation to reform our institutions so that they approximate fairness. Apparently, Nathanson is pessimistic here, whereas I have faith in our ability to learn from our mistakes and reform our systems. If we can't reform our legal system, what hope is there for us?

More specifically, the charge that a higher percentage of blacks than whites are executed was once true but is no longer so. Many states have made significant changes in sentencing procedures, with the result that currently whites convicted of first-degree murder are sentenced to death at a higher rate than blacks.

One must be careful in reading too much into these statistics. While great disparities in statistics should cause us to examine our judicial procedures, they do not in themselves prove injustice. For example, more males than females are convicted of violent crimes (almost 90% of those convicted of violent crimes are males—a virtually universal statistic), but this is not strong evidence that the law is unfair, for there are biological/psychological explanations for the disparity in convictions. Males are on average and by nature more aggressive (usually tied to testosterone) than females. Simply having a Y chromosome predisposes them to greater violence. Nevertheless, we hold male criminals responsible for their violence and expect them to control themselves. Likewise, there may be good explanations why people of one ethnic group commit more crimes than those of other groups, explanations that do not impugn the processes of the judicial system nor absolve rational people of their moral responsibility.

Recently, Governor George Ryan of Illinois, the state of my childhood and youth, commuted the sentences of over 150 death row inmates. Apparently, some of those convicted were convicted on insufficient evidence. If so, their sentences should have been commuted and the prisoners compensated. Such decisions should be done on a case-by-case basis. If capital punishment is justified, its application should be confined to clear cases in which the guilt of the criminal is "beyond reasonable doubt." But to overthrow the whole system because of a few possible miscarriages is as unwarranted as it is a loss of faith in our system of criminal justice. No one would abolish the use of fire engines and ambulances because occasionally they kill innocent pedestrians while carrying out their mission.

Abolitionists often make the complaint that only the poor get death sentences for murder. If their trials are fair, then they deserve the death penalty, but rich murderers may be equally deserving. At the moment only first-degree murder and treason are crimes deemed worthy of the death penalty. Perhaps our notion of treason should be expanded to include those who betray the trust of the public: corporation executives who have the trust of ordinary people, but who, through selfish and dishonest practices, ruin their lives. As noted above, my proposal is to consider broadening, not narrowing, the scope of capital punishment, to include business personnel who unfairly harm the public. The executives in the recent corporation scandals who bailed out of sinking corporations with golden, million-dollar lifeboats while the pension plans of thousands of employees went to the bottom of the economic ocean, may deserve severe punishment, and if convicted, they should receive what they deserve. My guess is that the threat of the death sentence would have a deterrent effect here. Whether it is feasible to apply the death penalty for horrendous white-collar crimes is debatable. But there is something to be said in its favor. It would remove the impression that only the poor get executed.

Conclusion

. . . A cogent case can be made for retaining the death penalty for serious crimes, such as first-degree murder and treason. The case primarily rests on a notion of justice as desert but is strengthened by utilitarian arguments involving deterrence. It is not because retentionists disvalue life that we defend the use of the death penalty. Rather, it is because we value human life as highly as we do that we support its continued use. The combined argument based on both backward-looking and forward-looking considerations justifies use of the death penalty. I have suggested that the application of the death penalty include not only first-degree murder but also treason (willful betrayal of one's country), including the treasonous behavior of business executives who violate the public trust.

The abolitionists point out the problems in applying the death penalty. We can concede that there are problems and reform is constantly needed, but since the death penalty is justified in principle, we should seek to improve its application rather than abolish a just institution. We ought not throw out the baby with the dirty bathwater. ■

Why the United States Will Join the Rest of the World in Abandoning Capital Punishment

Stephen B. Bright

The United States will inevitably join other industrialized nations in abandoning the death penalty, just as it has abandoned whipping, the stocks, branding, cutting off appendages, maiming, and other primitive forms of punishment. It remains to be seen how long it will be until the use of the death penalty becomes so infrequent as to be pointless, and it is eventually abandoned. In the meantime, capital punishment is arbitrarily and unfairly imposed, undermines the standing and moral authority of the United States in the community of nations, and diminishes the credibility and legitimacy of the courts within the United States.

Although death may intuitively seem to be an appropriate punishment for a person who kills another person and polls show strong support for the death penalty, most Americans know little about realities of capital punishment, past and present. As Bryan Stevenson describes, the death penalty is a direct descendant of the darkest aspects of American history—slavery, lynching, racial oppression, and perfunctory capital trials known as "legal lynchings"—and racial discrimination remains a prominent feature of capital punishment. The death penalty is not imposed to avenge every killing and—as some contend—to bring "closure" to the family of every victim, but is inflicted in less than 1 percent of all murder cases. Of more than 20,000 murders in the United States annually, an average of fewer than 300 people are sentenced to death, and only 55 are executed each year. Only 19 states actually carried out executions between 1976, when the U.S. Supreme Court authorized the resumption of capital punishment after declaring it unconstitutional in 1972, and the end of 2002. Eighty-six percent of those executions were in the South. Just two states—Texas and Virginia—carried out 45 percent of them.

Any assessment of the death penalty must not be based on abstract theories about how it should work in

Stephen B. Bright, "Why the United States Will Join the Rest of the World in Abandoning Capital Punishment," from *Debating the Death Penalty: Should America Have Capital Punishment?* edited by Hugo Adam Bedau and Paul G. Cassell (New York: Oxford University Press, 2005): 152–182. Reprinted by permission of Oxford University Press, Inc.

practice or the experiences of states like Oregon, which seldom impose the death penalty and carry it out even less. To understand the realities of the death penalty, one must look to the states that sentence people to death by the hundreds and have carried out scores of executions. In those states, innocent people have been sentenced to die based on such things as mistaken eyewitness identifications, false confessions, the testimony of partisan experts who render opinions that are not supported by science, failure of police and prosecutors to turn over evidence of innocence, and testimony of prisoners who get their own charges dismissed by testifying that the accused admitted the crime to them. Even the guilty are sentenced to death as opposed to life imprisonment without the possibility of parole not because they committed the worst crimes but because of where they happen to be prosecuted, the incompetence of their court-appointed lawyers, their race, or the race of their victim.

Former Illinois Governor George Ryan is a prominent example of a supporter of capital punishment who, upon close examination of the system, found that it "is haunted by the demon of error—error in determining guilt, and error in determining who among the guilty deserves to die." As a member of the legislature in 1977, Ryan voted to adopt Illinois's death penalty law and he described himself as a "staunch supporter" of capital punishment until as governor 23 years later, he saw that during that period the state had carried out 12 executions and released from its death row 13 people who had been

exonerated. In 2003, Governor Ryan pardoned four people who had been tortured by police until they confessed to crimes they did not commit and commuted the sentences of the remaining 167 people on Illinois's death row. . . .

Further experimentation with lethal punishment after centuries of failure has no place in a conservative society that is wary of too much government power and skeptical of the government's ability to do things well. Further experimentation might be justified if it served some purpose. But capital punishment is not needed to protect society or to punish offenders, as shown by over 100 countries around the world that do not have the death penalty and states such as Michigan and Wisconsin, neither of which have had the death penalty since the mid-1800s. It can be argued that capital punishment was necessary when America was a frontier society and had no prisons. But today the United States has not only maximum security prisons, but "super maximum" prisons where serial killers, mass murderers, and sadistic murderers can be severely punished and completely isolated from guards and other inmates.

Nor is crime deterred by the executions in fewer than half the states of an arbitrarily selected 1 percent of those who commit murders, many of whom are mentally ill or have limited intellectual functioning. The South, which has carried out 85 percent of the nation's executions since 1976, has the highest murder rate of any region of the country. The Northeast, which has the fewest executions by far—only 3 executions between 1976 and the end of 2002—has the lowest murder rate.

The United States does not need to keep this relic of the past to show its abhorrence of murder. As previously noted, 99 percent of the murders in the United States are not punished by death. Even at war crimes trials in The Hague, genocide and other crimes against humanity are not punished with the death penalty. The societies that do not have capital punishment surely abhor murder as much as any other, but they do not find it necessary to engage in killing in order to punish, protect, or show their abhorrence with killing.

Finally, capital punishment has no place in a decent society that places some practices, such as torture, off limits—not because some individuals have not done things so bad that they arguably deserved to be tortured, but because a civilized society simply does not engage in such acts. It can be argued that rapists deserve to be raped, that mutilators deserve to be mutilated. Most societies, however, refrain from responding in this way because the punishment is not only degrading to those on whom it is imposed, but it is also degrading to the society that engages in the same behavior as the criminals. When death sentences are carried out, small groups of people gather in execution chambers and watch as a human being is tied down and put down. Some make no effort to suppress their glee when the sentence is carried out and celebrations occur inside and outside the prison. These celebrations of death reflect the dark side of the human spirit—an arrogant,

vengeful, unforgiving, uncaring side that either does not admit the possibility of innocence or redemption or is willing to kill people despite those possibilities.

A Human Rights Violation that Undermines the Standing and Moral Authority of the United States

If people were asked 50 years ago which one of the following three countries—Russia, South Africa, or the United States—would be most likely to have the death penalty at the turn of the century, few people would have answered the United States. And yet, the United States was one of four countries that accounted for 90 percent of all the executions in the world in 2001 (the others were China, Iran, and Saudi Arabia), while Russia and South Africa are among the nations that no longer practice capital punishment. Since 1985, over 40 countries have abandoned capital punishment whereas only four countries that did not have it have adopted it. One of those, Nepal, has since abolished it. Turkey abolished the death penalty in 2001 in its efforts to join the European Union, leaving the United States the only NATO country that still has the death penalty.

The United States is also part of a very small minority of nations that allow the execution of children. Twenty-two of the 38 states with death penalty statues allow the execution of people who were under 18 at the time of their crimes. Between 1990 and the end of 2001, these states put 15 children to death, with Texas carrying out over 60 percent of those executions. The only other countries that executed children during this time were the Congo, Iran, Nigeria, Pakistan, Saudi Arabia, and Yemen. The United States and Somalia are the only two countries that have not ratified the International Covenant on the Rights of the Child, which, among other things, prohibits the execution of people who were children at the time of their crimes.

Being among the world leaders in executions and the leader in execution of children is incompatible with asserting leadership on human rights issues in the world. As Frederick Douglass said over a century ago, "Life is the great primary and most precious and comprehensive of all human rights— [and] whether it be coupled with virtue, honor, and happiness, or with sin, disgrace and misery, . . . [it is not] to be deliberately or voluntarily destroyed, either by individuals separately, or combined in what is called Government."

The retention of capital punishment in the United States draws harsh criticism from throughout the world. . . .

Just as the United States could not assert moral leadership in the world as long as it allowed segregation, it will not be a leader on human rights as long as it allows capital punishment.

Arbitrary and Unfair Infliction

Regardless of the practices of the rest of the world or the morality of capital punishment, the process leading to a death sentence is so unfair and influenced by so many improper factors and the infliction of death sentences is so inconsistent that this punishment should be abandoned.

The exoneration of many people who spent years of their lives in prisons for crimes they did not commit— many of them on death rows—has dramatically brought to light defects in the criminal justice system that have surprised and appalled people who do not observe the system every day and assumed that it was working properly. The average person has little or no contact with the criminal courts, which deal primarily with crimes committed against and by poor people and members of racial minorities. It is a system that is overworked and underfunded, and particularly underfunded when it comes to protecting the rights of those accused.

Law enforcement officers, usually overworked and often under tremendous public pressure to solve terrible crimes, make mistakes, fail to pursue all lines of investigation, and, on occasion, overreach or take shortcuts in pursuing arrests. Prosecutors exercise vast and unchecked discretion in deciding which cases are to be prosecuted as capital cases. The race of the victim and the defendant, political considerations, and other extraneous factors influence whether prosecutors seek the death penalty and whether juries or judges impose it.

A person facing the death penalty usually cannot afford to hire an attorney and is at the mercy of the system to provide a court-appointed lawyer. While many receive adequate representation (and often are not sentenced to death as a result), many others are assigned lawyers who lack the knowledge, skill, resources—and sometimes even the inclination—to handle a serious criminal case. People who would not be sentenced to death if properly represented are sentenced to death because of incompetent court-appointed lawyers. In many communities, racial minorities are still excluded from participation as jurors, judges, prosecutors, and lawyers in the system. In too many cases, defendants are convicted on flimsy evidence, such as eyewitness identifications, which are notoriously unreliable but are seen as very credible by juries; the testimony of convicts who, in exchange for lenient treatment in their own cases, testify that the accused admitted to them that he or she committed the crime; and confessions obtained from people of limited intellect through lengthy and overbearing interrogations. . . .

These are not minor, isolated incidents; they are long-standing, pervasive, systemic deficiencies in the criminal justice system that are not being corrected and, in some places, are even becoming worse. . . . Law enforcement agencies have been unwilling to videotape interrogations and use identification procedures that are more reliable than those presently employed. People who support capital punishment as a concept are unwilling to spend millions of tax dollars to provide competent legal representation for those accused of crimes. And courts have yet to find ways to overcome centuries of racial discrimination that often influence, consciously or subconsciously, the decisions of prosecutors, judges, and juries.

A Warning That Something Is Terribly Wrong: Innocent People Condemned to Death

Over 100 people condemned to death in the last 30 years have been exonerated and released after new evidence established their innocence or cast such doubt on their guilt that they could not be convicted. The 100th of those people, Ray Krone, was convicted and sentenced to death in Arizona based on the testimony of an expert witness that his teeth matched bite marks on the victim. During the ten years that Krone spent on death row, scientists developed the ability to compare biological evidence recovered at crime scenes with the DNA of suspects. DNA testing established that Krone was innocent. On Krone's release, the prosecutor said, "[Krone] deserves an apology from us, that's for sure. A mistake was made here. . . . What do you say to him? An injustice was done and we will try to do better. And we're sorry." Although unfortunate to be wrongfully convicted, Krone was very fortunate that there was DNA evidence in his case. In most cases, there is no biological evidence for DNA testing.

Other defendants had their death sentences commuted to life imprisonment without the possibility of parole because of questions about their innocence. For example, in 1994, the governor of Virginia commuted the death sentence of a mentally retarded man, Earl Washington, to life imprisonment without parole because of questions regarding his guilt. Washington, an easily persuaded, somewhat childlike special-education dropout, had been convicted of murder and rape based on a confession he gave to police, even though it was full of inconsistencies. For example, at one point in the confession Washington said that the victim was white and at another that the victim was black. Six years later, DNA evidence—not available at the time of Washington's trial or the commutation—established that Washington was innocent and he was released.

Although DNA testing has been available only in cases where there was biological evidence and the evidence has been preserved, it has established the innocence of many people who were not sentenced to death—more than 100 by the end of 2002. A Michigan judge in 1984 lamented the fact that the state did not have the death penalty, saying that life imprisonment was inadequate for Eddie Joe Lloyd for the rape and murder of a 16-year-old girl. Police had obtained a confession from Lloyd while he was in a mental hospital. Seventeen years later, DNA evidence established that Lloyd did not commit the crime. On his release, Lloyd commented, "If Michigan had the death penalty, I would have been through, the angels would have sung a long time ago."

Sometimes evidence of innocence has surfaced only at the last minute. Anthony Porter, sentenced to death in Illinois, went through all the appeals and review that are available for one so sentenced. Every court upheld his conviction and sentence. As Illinois prepared to put him to death, a question arose as to whether Porter, who was brain damaged and mentally retarded, understood what

was happening to him. A person who lacks the mental ability to understand that he is being put to death in punishment for a crime cannot be executed unless he is treated and becomes capable of understanding why he is being executed. Just two days before Porter was to be executed, a court stayed his execution in order to examine his mental condition. After the stay was granted, a journalism class at Northwestern University and a private investigator examined the case and proved that Anthony Porter was innocent. They obtained a confession from the person who committed the crime. Anthony Porter was released, becoming the third person released from Illinois's death row after being proven innocent by a journalism class at Northwestern....

Some proponents of capital punishment argue that the exoneration of Porter and others shows that the system works and that no innocent people have been executed. However, someone spending years on death row for a crime he did not commit is not an example of the system working. When journalism students prove that police, prosecutors, judges, defense lawyers, and the entire legal system failed to discover the perpetrator of a crime and instead condemned the wrong person to die, the system is not working. Porter and others were spared, as Chief Justice Moses Harrison of the Illinois Supreme Court observed, "only because of luck and the dedication of the attorneys, reporters, family members and volunteers who labored to win their release. They survived despite the criminal justice system, not because of it. The truth is that left to the devices of the court system, they would probably have all ended up dead at the hands of the state for crimes they did not commit. One must wonder how many others have not been so fortunate." . . .

Gerald W. Heaney announced, after 30 years of reviewing capital cases as a federal appellate judge, that he was "compelled . . . to conclude that the imposition of the death penalty is arbitrary and capricious." He found that "the decision of who shall live and who shall die for his crime turns less on the nature of the offense and the incorrigibility of the offender and more on inappropriate and indefensible considerations: the political and personal inclinations of prosecutors; the defendant's wealth, race, and intellect; the race and economic status of the victim; the quality of the defendant's counsel; and the resources allocated to defense lawyers." . . .

Even if every single reform were adopted, it would not eliminate the posibility of executing innocent people. As the Canadian Supreme Court recognized in holding that it would not allow the extradition of people to the United States if the death penalty could be imposed, courts will always be fallible and reversible, while death will always be final and irreversible.

The Two Most Important Decisions—Made by Prosecutors

The two most important decisions in every death penalty case are made not by juries or judges, but by prosecutors. No state or federal law ever requires prosecutors to seek the death penalty or take a capital case to trial. A prosecutor has complete discretion in deciding whether to seek the death penalty and, even if death is sought, whether to offer a sentence less than death in exchange for the defendant's guilty plea. The overwhelming majority of all criminal cases, including capital cases, are resolved not by trials but by plea bargains. Whether death is sought or imposed is based on the discretion and proclivities of the thousands of people who occupy the offices of prosecutor in judicial districts throughout the nation. (Texas, for example, has 155 elected prosecutors, Virginia 120, Missouri 115, Illinois 102, Georgia 49, and Alabama 40.) Some prosecutors seek the death penalty at every opportunity, and others never seek it; some seldom seek it; some frequently seek it. There is no requirement that individual prosecutors—who, in most states, are elected by districts—be consistent in their practices in seeking the death penalty.

As a result of this discretion, there are great geographical disparities in where death is imposed within states. Prosecutors in Houston and Philadelphia have sought the death penalty in virtually every case in which it can be imposed. As a result of aggressive prosecutors and inept court-appointed lawyers, Houston and Philadelphia have each condemned over 100 people to death—more than most states. Harris Country, which includes Houston, has had more executions in the last 30 years than any *state* except Texas and Virginia. A case is much more likely to be prosecuted capitally in Houston and

Philadelphia than in Dallas, Ft. Worth, or Pittsburgh....

Thus, whether the death sentence is imposed may depend more on the personal predilections and politics of local prosecutors than the heinousness of the crime or the incorrigibility of the defendant.

The Role of Racial Bias

The complete discretion given to prosecutors in deciding whether to seek the death penalty and whether to drop the death penalty in exchange for guilty pleas also contributes to racial disparities in the infliction of the death penalty. In the 38 states that have the death penalty, 97.5 percent of the chief prosecutors are white. In 18 of the states, all of the chief prosecutors are white. Even the most conscientious prosecutors who have had little experience with people of other races may be influenced in their decisions by racial stereotypes and attitudes they have developed over their lives.

But the rest of the criminal justice system is almost as unrepresentative of American's racial diversity as prosecutors' offices. In the South, where the death penalty is most often imposed and carried out, over half the victims of crime are people of color, well over 60 percent of the prison population is made up of people of color, and half of those sentenced to death are members of racial minorities. Yet people of color are seldom involved as judges, jurors, prosecutors, and lawyers in the courts.

For example, there is not one African American or Hispanic judge on the nine-member Texas Court of Criminal Appeals, the court of last resort for all criminal cases in that state, even though 43 percent of the population of Texas is nonwhite, over 65 percent of the homicide victims are people of color, and nearly 70 percent of the prison population is black, Hispanic, or other nonwhite. This court handles over 10,000 cases each year, most of them involving the lives and liberty of people of color. In Alabama, no African American sits among the nine members of the Alabama Supreme Court or the five members of the Alabama Court of Criminal Appeals—the two courts that review capital cases— even though 26 percent of the population of Alabama is African American, 59 percent of the victims of homicide are African American, and over half those on death row are black. In many court-houses, everything looks the same as it did during the period of Jim Crow justice. The judges are white, the prosecutors are white, the lawyers are white and, even in communities with substantial African American populations, the jury may be all white. In many cases, the only person of color who sits in front of the bar in the courtroom is the person on trial. The legal system remains the institution that has been least affected by the civil rights movement.

Although African Americans constitute only 12 percent of the national population, they are victims of half the murders that are committed in the United States. Yet 80 percent of those on death row were convicted of crimes against white people. The discrepancy is even greater in the Death Belt states of the

South. In Georgia and Alabama, for example, African Americans are the victims of 65 percent of the homicides, yet 80 percent of those on death rows are there for crimes against white persons. Studies of capital sentencing have consistently revealed such disparities. . . .

Study after study has confirmed what lawyers practicing in the criminal courts observe every day: People of color are treated more harshly than white people. A person of color is more likely than a white person to be stopped by the police, to be abused by the police during that stop, to be arrested, to be denied bail when taken to court, to be charged with a serious crime as opposed to a less serious one that could be charged, to be convicted, and to receive a harsher sentence. But a person of color is much *less* likely to be a participant in the criminal justice system as a judge, juror, prosecutor, or lawyer.

It would be quite remarkable if race affected every aspect of the criminal justice system except with regard to the death penalty—the area in which decision makers have the broadest discretion and base their decisions on evidence with tremendous emotional impact. The sad reality is that race continues to influence who is sentenced to death as it has throughout American history.

The Death Sentence for Being Assigned the Worst Lawyer

Capital cases—complex cases with the highest stakes of any in the legal system—should be handled by the most capable lawyers, with the

resources to conduct thorough investigations and consult with various experts on everything from the prosecution's scientific evidence to psychologists and psychiatrists to investigate the defendant's mental health. The right to counsel is the most fundamental constitutional right of a person charged with a crime. A person accused of a crime depends on a lawyer to investigate the prosecution's case; to present any facts that may be helpful to the accused and necessary for a fair and reliable determination of guilt or innocence and, if guilty, a proper sentence; and to protect every other right of the accused. However, U.S. Supreme Court Justice Ruth Bader Ginsburg observed in 2001 that she had "yet to see a death case among the dozens coming to the Supreme Court . . . in which the defendant was well represented at trial. People who are well-represented at trial do not get the death penalty."

Those receiving the death penalty are not well represented because many states do not provide the structure, resources, independence, and accountability that is required to insure competent representation in an area of such specialization. . . .

Justice Hugo Black wrote for the U.S. Supreme Court in 1956 that "[t]here can be no equal justice where the kind of trial a [person] gets depends on the amount of money he [or she] has." But today, no one seriously doubts that the kind of trial, and the kind of justice, a person receives depends very much on the amount of money he or she has. The quality of legal representation tolerated by some courts shocks the conscience of a person of average sensibilities. But poor representation resulting from lack of funding and structure has been accepted as the best that can be done with the limited resources available. The commitment of many states to providing lawyers for those who cannot afford them was aptly described by a Chief Justice of the Georgia Supreme Court: "[W]e set our sights on the embarrassing target of mediocrity. I guess that means about halfway. And that raises a question. Are we willing to put up with halfway justice? To my way of thinking, one-half justice must mean one-half injustice, and one-half injustice is no justice at all."

The proponents of capital punishment are always quick to say that people facing the death penalty *should* receive better legal representation. But they do not explain how this is going to be accomplished—whether by a sudden burst of altruism on the part of members of the legal profession, who are going to suddenly start taking capital cases for a fraction of what they can make doing other work; a massive infusion of funding from state legislatures that are searching for revenue for education, transportation, and other areas that have a constituency; or some other miracle. The right to competent representation is celebrated in the abstract, but most states—and most supporters of capital punishment—are unwilling to pay for it. As a result the death penalty will continue to be imposed not upon those who commit the worst crimes, but upon those who have the misfortune to be assigned the worst lawyers.

Death for the Disadvantaged

Capital punishment is inflicted on the weakest and most troubled members of our society such as children, the delusional, the paranoid, the brain-damaged, the chemically imbalanced, those who were abused and neglected as children, and people who endured the most terrible trauma imaginable in military service during war, who came back with post-traumatic stress syndrome, addicted to drugs, with various mental and emotional problems.

Charles Rumbaugh is one of many examples of the execution of the mentally ill. He was only 17 at the time of his crime and suffered from schizophrenia and depression to the point that he repeatedly mutilated himself and attempted suicide. Rumbaugh's parents tried to convince a court not to let him withdraw his appeals. During a hearing, Rumbaugh advanced on a marshal and provoked the marshal to shoot him in the courtroom. He was taken to the hospital while the hearing continued. He was allowed to withdraw his appeals and was executed by Texas.

Another example is Pernell Ford, who was allowed to discharge his lawyers and represent himself at his capital trial in Alabama in 1984. Ford wore only a sheet to the penalty phase of the trial. He tried to call as witnesses people who were no longer alive. After lawyers appealed his conviction to a federal court, Ford wrote to the court and asked that the petition be dismissed. During a hearing, Ford said that he wanted to die because he was a member of the Holy Trinity, he had supernatural powers that would be enhanced when he died, and he would be able to transfer his soul to people outside the prison. He said that when he died, his 400 thousand wives would receive the millions of dollars he had put in Swiss bank accounts. One psychiatrist who evaluated Ford said that these statements were reflective of Ford's religious beliefs—not evidence of mental illness. Another psychiatrist found that Ford suffered from depression and personality disorder but was still capable of making rational choices. A third psychiatrist found that Ford was incapable of thinking rationally. The court concluded that Ford could give up his appeals because he understood the "bottom line" of his legal situation. Like Charles Rumbaugh, he was allowed to withdraw his appeals. Alabama executed him. . . .

The execution of such severely mentally ill people and treating mentally ill people so that they can be executed should be beneath the American people. Unfortunately, many mentally ill people are left on their own without support and supervision. Society would be better served by providing some care to insure that they take their medications and receive proper treatment to prevent episodes of violence than by executing people who are out of touch with reality. And once a severely mentally ill person has committed a serious crime the appropriate response is to place them in secure mental health facilities, not in execution chambers. . . .

Abandoning fairness, reliability, the quest for racial equality, the rule of law, and the independence and integrity of the judiciary are enormous prices to pay to bring about executions. Some are willing to sacrifice even more—the lives of innocent people. They argue that we are fighting a "war on crime," and, as in any war, there are going to be some innocent casualties. The American notion of justice was once that it was better for ten guilty people to go free than for an innocent person to be convicted. Now, proponents of the death penalty argue it is acceptable to sacrifice more than a few innocent people to wage a war on crime.

Conclusion

Courts should not be war zones, but halls of justice. It is time to reexamine the "war of crime"—a war the United States is fighting against its own people, its own children, and the poorest and the most powerless people in society. The American people must ask what kind of society they want to have and what kind of people they want to be. Whether they want a hateful, vengeful society that turns its back on its children and then executes them, that denies its mentally ill the treatment and the medicine they need and then puts them to death when their demons are no longer kept at bay, that gives nothing to the survivors of the victims of the crime except a chance to ask for the maximum sentence and watch an execution.

We should have the humility to admit that the legal system is not infallible and that mistakes are made. We should have the honesty to admit that our society is unwilling to pay the price of providing every poor person with competent legal representation, even in capital cases. We should have the courage to acknowledge the role that race plays in the criminal justice system and make a commitment to do something about it instead of pretending that racial prejudice no longer exists. And we should have the compassion and decency to recognize the dignity of every person, even those who have offended us most grievously. The Constitutional Court of South Africa addressed many of these issues in deciding whether the death penalty violated that country's constitution. Despite a staggering crime rate and a long history of racial violence and oppression, the Court unanimously concluded that in a society in transition from hatred to understanding, from vengeance to reconciliation, there was no place for the death penalty. The American people will ultimately reach the same conclusion, deciding that, like slavery and segregation, the death penalty is a relic of another era, and that this society of such vast wealth is capable of more constructive approaches to crime. And the United States will join the rest of the civilized world in abandoning capital punishment. ∎

⁝ The Continuing Debate

What Is New

Perhaps the biggest impact on the contemporary capital punishment debate has been that of the development of DNA testing, and the use of DNA evidence to establish the innocence of many persons wrongly convicted and sentenced to death. Illinois governor George Ryan had been a steadfast supporter of capital punishment; but after 13 Illinois death row inmates were proved innocent through DNA testing, in 2000 he called for a moratorium on capital punishment in Illinois. The Death Penalty Information Center, using DNA studies, has uncovered over 100 cases of innocent prisoners wrongly sentenced to death, and many more who were wrongly convicted of lesser crimes have been exonerated by DNA evidence. Since DNA evidence is available for review only in the case of a small proportion of those who have been convicted, the question arises of how many current death row prisoners were wrongly convicted.

Where to Find More

Full transcripts of all U.S. Supreme Court cases dealing with capital punishment can be found at www.Oyez.org. For further study of key Supreme Court death penalty cases, a good source is Barry Latzer, *Death Penalty Cases: Leading U.S. Supreme Court Cases on Capital Punishment* (Woburn, MA: Butterworth-Heinemann, 1997).

Franklin E. Zimring and Gordon Hawkins, *Capital Punishment and the American Agenda* (Cambridge: Cambridge University Press, 1986), place capital punishment within a world setting and draw the historical and sociological background for use of capital punishment in the United States. A recent issue of *The Journal of Criminal Law & Criminology*, Volume 95, Number 2 (2005), is devoted to articles discussing the death penalty.

Michael A. Mello, *Dead Wrong: A Death Row Lawyer Speaks out Against Capital Punishment* (Madison: The University of Wisconsin Press, 1997), is very readable. A recent book by David R. Dow, *Executed on a Technicality: Lethal Injustice on America's Death Row* (Boston: Beacon Press, 2005), uncovers basic injustices committed in the prosecution of many now on death row.

Three books offer interesting debates on the subject: E. Van den Haag and J. P. Conrad, *The Death Penalty: A Debate* (New York: Plenum, 1983); Louis P. Pojman and Jeffrey Reiman, *The Death Penalty: For and Against* (Rowman & Littlefield, 1998); and (in a much larger context) Jean Hampton and Jeffrie Murphy, *Forgiveness and Mercy* (Cambridge: Cambridge University Press, 1988).

Among the many anthologies are Hugo Adam Bedau and Paul G. Cassell, *Debating the Death Penalty: Should America Have Capital Punishment?* (New York: Oxford University Press, 2005); Carol Wekesser, *The Death Penalty: Opposing Viewpoints* (San Diego, CA: Greenhaven Press, 1991); Robert M. Baird and Stuart E. Rosenbaum, *Punishment and the Death Penalty: The Current Debate* (Amherst, NY: Prometheus Books, 1995); James R. Acker, Robert M. Bohm, and Charles S. Lanier, *America's Experiment with Capital Punishment* (Durham, NC: Carolina Academic Press, 1998); Austin Sarat, *The Killing State: Capital Punishment in Law, Politics, and Culture* (New York: Oxford University Press, 1999); and Austin Sarat, *The Death Penalty, Volume 1: Influences and Outcomes* (Aldershot, UK: Ashgate, 2005).

For arguments opposing capital punishment, see Stephen Nathanson, "The Death Penalty as a Symbolic Issue," Chapter 11 of his book *An Eye for an Eye? The Morality of Punishing by Death* (Totowa, NJ: Rowman & Littlefield, 1987): 131–146; Charles Black, *Capital Punishment: The Inevitability of Caprice and Mistake*, 2nd Edition (New York: W.W. Norton, 1976); and Thomas W. Clark, "Crime and Causality: Do Killers Deserve to Die?" *Free Inquiry* (February/ March 2005): 34–37. The pro–capital punishment view can be found in Walter Berns, *For Capital Punishment: Crime and the Morality of the Death Penalty* (New York: Basic Books, 1979); and Ernest van den Haag, "In Defense of the Death Penalty: A Legal-Practical-Moral Analysis," *Criminal Law Bulletin*, Volume 14 (1978): 51–68.

For more information on wrongful convictions of death row inmates and other prisoners, and on the DNA evidence that has freed some innocent prisoners, see Sandra D. Westervelt and John A. Humphrey, editors, *Wrongly Convicted: Perspectives on Failed Justice* (New Brunswick, NJ: Rutgers University Press,

2001); and Barry Scheck, Peter Neufeld, and Jim Dwyer, *Actual Innocence* (New York: Doubleday, 2000).

The Ethics Updates website has links to other sites, full-text online articles, video discussions, and audio recordings of relevant radio programs; check particularly the link to excellent resources provided by the documentary series *Frontline*. Go to www.ethics.sandiego.edu/Applied/Death Penalty.

16

Are Boot Camps a Good Way to Deal with Youthful Offenders?

Juvenile Boot Camps Can Be Promising Programs
> Advocate: Cheryl L. Clark, Director of Shock Development, New York
> State Department of Correctional Services; Ronald Moscicki,
> Superintendent of Lakeview Shock Incarceration Facility; and Joshua
> Perry, formerly Training Specialist at U.S. Army Military Police School.
> Source: "To March or Not to March: Is That the Question?" *Juvenile
> and Adult Boot Camps*, edited by American Correctional Association
> staff (Lanham, MD: American Correctional Association, 1996).

Juvenile Boot Camps Raise Serious Questions
> Advocates: Francis T. Cullen, Distinguished Research Professor of
> Criminal Justice and Sociology at the University of Cincinnati,
> President of the American Society of Criminology, and Past
> President of the Academy of Criminal Justice Sciences; Kristie R.
> Blevins (Ph.D., University of Cincinnati), Assistant Professor in the
> Department of Criminal Justice, University of North Carolina at
> Charlotte; Jennifer S. Trager, Doctoral student in criminal justice,
> University of Cincinnati; and Paul Gendreau, University Research
> Professor of Psychology and Director of the Center for Criminal
> Justice Studies at the University of New Brunswick, and Past
> President of the Canadian Psychological Association.
> Source: "The Rise and Fall of Boot Camps: A Case Study in Common-
> Sense Corrections," in Brent B. Benda and Nathaniel J. Pallone,
> editors, *Rehabilitation Issues, Problems, and Prospects in Boot Camp*
> (New York: The Haworth Press, 2005), which was also published as
> Volume 40, Number 3/4 (2005) of *Journal of Offender Rehabilitation*.

In the United States, prison policy has traditionally been guided by two goals: punishment and rehabilitation/reform. Juvenile facilities were often called "reformatories," while adult prisons were known as "penitentiaries," where adults might become *penitent* and sorry for their wrongdoing and thus reform themselves. The strong punishment element is even more obvious: The United States is almost the only Western country to practice capital punishment, and the conditions of many U.S. prisons—particularly the maximum security prisons—are notoriously cruel. The goals of punishment and rehabilitation are not easy to reconcile: capital punishment dispenses with even the pretense of rehabilitation, and it is obvious that the U.S. prison system (including juvenile facilities), with its extremely high recidivism rate, is more likely to harden criminals than reform them. Thus it is not surprising that the "boot camp" movement, with its promise of harsh punishment combined with effective reform, should have widespread appeal. On the harsh punishment measure, it has certainly been successful; for rehabilitation, the results are not so positive.

One question that has constantly surrounded boot camp programs is the level of physical violence and demeaning treatment used against the prisoners in the camps. While Clark, Moscicki, and Perry insist that "discipline is not abuse, nor is it humiliation," they also emphasize the importance of tough disciplinary measures: "these are 'in your face' programs, there is no getting around it." Whether such "get tough" programs are too harsh and too open to abuse, and whether they are effective, are questions that this debate examines.

▙▙▙ Points to Ponder

- Suppose that instead of "boot camps" we tried "beach camps": youthful offenders are sent for an eight-week crash program of rehabilitation at a beautiful sandy beach resort, where they would sip cool beverages, frolic in the surf, go sailing and scuba diving, live in luxury hotels, and do pleasant lessons on finding alternatives to criminal behavior. And we discover that not only are these "beach camps" less expensive than the harsh boot camps, but they are also incredibly effective in turning youthful offenders away from lives of crime (while the more expensive boot camps report marginal effectiveness, at best). Would you then be in favor of replacing boot camps with beach camps?

- In "To March or not to March," Joshua Perry is quoted as saying—in defense of the stern discipline practiced—that discipline is required for the jobs young offenders will hold: "Unless you're Bill Gates, you're going to work for someone else. You aren't going to last long at McDonald's if you don't understand that basic fact." But of course jobs at McDonald's are the symbol of dead-end jobs; indeed, dictionaries have recently added "Mcjob" to their word list, a word that is in common usage to mean a boring dead-end low-paying job. Joshua Perry insists that instilling the *discipline* to be "at the appointed place at the appointed time, in the proper uniform, doing what you're told, when you're told and how you're told" is a vital part of the boot camp training. Is that type of mindless unquestioning obedience a proper goal for citizens in a democratic society? While it may make for excellent McDonald's employees or for low-wage workers on some assembly lines, is it actually in the long-term interests of the boot camp inmates? Would they be better served by developing some alternative set of abilities?

- Boot camps were highly popular (among politicians and the public) as promising ways of dealing with the criminal behavior of youthful offenders. They combined a number of elements that many people found very attractive: tough drill instructors dishing out harsh treatment to the "young toughs" who had posed a threat to society; a quick, painful, and lasting change in the character of the offenders (almost like a conversion experience); the assumption that harsh punitive measures against offenders could solve crime problems, without the costly and difficult task of dealing with poor educational systems, bad home environments, lack of promising job opportunities, and racism. Of these factors, which do you think were the greatest contributors to the popular enthusiasm for boot camp programs? Were there other significant factors contributing to their political popularity?

To March or Not to March
Is That the Question?

Cheryl L. Clark, Ronald Moscicki, and Joshua Perry

The Birth of Boot Camps

Soon after the first modern boot camps were established in Georgia and Oklahoma in 1983, the military model of corrections was touted as the answer to the problems of systems bursting at the seams because of escalating prison populations. Mandatory drug sentencing laws of the 1970s resulted in prisons increasingly overcrowded with offenders committed for nonviolent offenses and drug-related crimes. In the ten year period between 1973 and 1983, with the "war on drugs" accelerating, the prison population doubled; in the next ten years, it doubled again. By October 1994, more than one million men and women were incarcerated in the United States. Six million others swelled the ranks of probation and parole.

Criminal justice officials, the public and legislators were desperately

---

Cheryl L. Clark, Ronald Moscicki, and Joshua Perry, "To March or Not to March: Is that the Question," *Juvenile and Adult Boot Camps*. Reprinted by permission of American Correctional Association, Alexandria, VA.

attempting to find solutions. Everyone was worried; criminal justice because overcrowding was straining scarce resources to the limit, fraying tempers and fanning the fears of the incarcerated and staff alike. Increasingly, gang activity, in and out of prisons, erupted in fights, tension, and deaths. The public was afraid to take a walk in neighborhoods where once they did not have to lock doors. Senior citizens, locking themselves into their homes at dusk, were afraid to answer their doors because of their fear of young predators, ready to steal welfare and social security checks for drug money. Legislators and government officials struggled, because the demand to punish even more offenders is a costly undertaking. How does one satisfy constituents by making them feel safe but keep taxes down? As a nation, the "drug wars" were on everyone's mind. What was the solution?

In 1983, two states simultaneously led the way into the future of corrections with correctional "boot camps." Oklahoma and Georgia were the first to experiment with this innovative idea. The belief was that a highly intensive, brief incarceration period might be a more effective means of dealing with this increasingly young, nonviolent population. Early intervention, a "scared straight" approach that lasted for longer than an afternoon, coupled with teaching self-discipline, became the leading edge of incarceration programs. Legislators saw boot camps as a means of having an impact on crime, while at the same time conserving scarce tax dollars, because of the shorter duration of the programs. Those who had served in the military remembered with fondness how

the military "made a man" out of them. The public liked the "get tough on crime" message from media presentations featuring "in your face" drill instructors yelling at young offenders blamed for the lack of safety in their communities. Conservatives appreciated the "tough, no nonsense" approach to the problem of drugs in the community. Liberals liked the idea that young, nonviolent offenders were released early. Everyone breathed a collective sigh of relief. The boot camp phenomenon in prison was born.

By the beginning of 1987, there were eight states with "boot camp" programs. In August of 1987, the New York State Department of Correctional Services became the ninth state to implement the phenomenon, but with a new twist. Rather than solely emphasize military components, hard labor, physical training, drill and ceremony, the New York Shock Incarceration program focused on intensive substance abuse treatment, academic education, decision making and life skills, for a full six months, rather than the average 90 to 120 days for most boot camps, and it included an intensified aftercare program. A few other states, notably Louisiana, had included some optional education and treatment components by this time, but New York was the first to make "intensive substance abuse treatment and education" mandatory for all participants. Another key addition was a requirement for an intensive, one month period of training for all staff who worked in the program. Soon, this "second generation" of boot camps became a model for others to follow. . . .

But Do Boot Camps Work?

If boot camps are harsh, it may be because correctional policy responds to what society appears to want. The National Institute of Justice report on boot camps said, "... there is little evidence that the getting tough element of shock incarceration by itself, will lead to behavioral change." Most heard, "Boot camps don't work!" (A.P. headline) but still want inmates punished. In the race for federal funding, it appeared that the only programs with a chance of acquiring scarce resources were those which appeared to "get tough on crime" and assured that violent offenders would be locked up for longer and longer periods of time. The public however, does not always distinguish between violent and nonviolent criminals. Purse snatching feels violent to the person who has been violated.

The general public equates prison with murderers, rapists, and child molesters. When the nightly news opens with five stories of gang violence, drive-by shootings, and alarming features of increasing violence in cities, it is obvious that "they" belong behind bars. Elected officials who get votes are those who vow to "lock them up and throw away the key." They are bowing to the mandate of their constituents. For all the different perspective and experience, the corrections professional is still a member of a community, influenced by the larger society and cultural norms. It is up to correctional professionals to set the tone and articulate standards and goals of effective corrections practice. It is up to those who endorse the concept of boot camp programs to ensure that the programs are founded in principles of integrity and support the success of all involved, both staff and inmates. Punishment does not reduce violence, evidence suggests it increases it.

The demand for discipline and adherence to rules characterized by the military model is seen by critics as rigid, dehumanizing, humiliating, and as breaking the spirit. They ask, "Why can't they talk at meals? Shouldn't they be learning how to have dinner conversation?" When trying to keep the mess hall running on time, this is the last question the sergeant wants to hear. However, it is a valid question for which a reasoned response clearly is necessary. . . .

Meals are one of the few times in a day when offenders in these highly structured programs do not have to actively perform. Once they get used to eating in silence, inmates experience the quiet at meals as an opportunity to reflect on their day. When the mess hall is full and those seated at the tables can be members of rival gangs from the old neighborhood, silence helps maintain order. The last thing a correctional officer needs is a problem erupting between Crips, Bloods, Latin Kings, Néta or other rival gang members seated at the same table. There is little opportunity for privacy in prison. The luxury of a private thought relieves tension. . . .

Form Follows Function

Those who come for tours from outside the correctional experience frequently raise questions about why boot camps operate the way they do. It is important for administrators and staff of programs to know the reasons for their methods and present the rationale in a way that makes sense to those unfamiliar with correctional practice. Even more important, administrators and staff have to understand and clearly articulate the reasons for policies and practice. . . .

"Why do they have to say 'Ma'am and Sir?' Why can't they say 'I, me, my?' Why do you cut the women's hair? Aren't learning experiences harsh? Why do you need the military piece? Why not just do treatment? Why do they have to stand so rigidly at attention? What is the point of drill and ceremony?" These questions worry the sensitive, compassionate, and inexperienced who come for two- or three-hour tours. We have been told by visitors that they have been brushed off by some to whom they posed these questions, or told, "Because that's how we do it." Responses like that do not help those who support a military model in these programs. The following is offered as a response to the questions posed above from the authors' perspective, to stimulate discussion and ideas. They are not intended to be perceived as the answers.

Graduates of Shock Incarceration, working for aftercare service providers, know how hard it is for those with criminal records to get decent jobs. Their advice: "Sir" and "Ma'am" go a long way to getting you a job. Politeness and respect count. You are competing in a tough job market, stand out from the crowd. Mothers, fathers, and other relatives are touched by the respect from children over whom they had despaired. "I didn't recognize him/her. S/he called me 'Ma'am.' That never happened before. . . . I had to wait to come to prison to go to my child's graduation," they say with tears in their eyes. Those who are younger and will be returning to school after graduation from Shock frequently have been excluded from schools as behavior problems. They were considered troublemakers by teachers in the past and need to convince them that they deserve another chance. How they speak, act, and handle their feelings is critical to overcoming their past.

It is easy to say "I, me," or "mine" without thinking. A key reason many young offenders end up in prison is because acting without thinking is a bad habit of theirs. While this may be true for other than those who go to prison, offenders have not had the resources to avoid a prison sentence when they have legal problems. They need as many tools they can get to help them overcome obstacles to employment or educational opportunities. Good programs teach offenders how to make autonomous choices by increasing expectations for personal responsibility. One simple way to help them to learn to control impulsive behavior is to have them consciously hesitate the two-to-four seconds it takes the brain to integrate feelings and thoughts. That is why they are expected to stop, state their name, then, make their request. When participants refer to themselves by name, this slows them down and gives them time to think. In large programs, it also helps staff to learn their names faster. On the other hand, detaching from one's feelings is not appropriate in group processes designed to have them fully experience a wide range of feelings, so referring to themselves in the third person is not a functional strategy for those sessions.

Women's hair is cut short for many reasons in Shock Incarceration. First and most importantly, for ease of cleanliness and convenience. The day moves quickly from 5:30 A.M. until 9:30 P.M. It is packed with events. There are as many as ninety women in a single dormitory, sharing sinks, showers, living space and trying to get to program activities on time. They do not have time for hair styling. Another reason for this practice is because both the men and women have been so attached to their negative "operating image" that they are challenged to let go of their limiting beliefs about who they are and what makes them unique, to shed the old, negative image, and give themselves six months to redefine who they are and where they are going with their lives.

The women have frequently defined themselves and their self-worth in the past by their power to attract a man. Many, often because of abusive relationships, alcohol and drugs, are co-dependent, giving up their sense of self to others who use and abuse them. Their past relationships have failed. The goal of Shock Incarceration in New York is to have them focus on themselves and on what they need. They also learn skills to help them be good mothers to their children when they return home. The last thing they need to worry about is how attractive they look to the guy, another convicted felon, in their platoon. Co-dependency is one of the principal contributing factors to criminal behavior and addiction in women. The women's hair is not cut to degrade

or humiliate them, nor is that appropriate. It has a function in a program with large numbers of women. It may not be as necessary or functional in programs where there are very few women. They may need the advantage of people remembering that they are women and not "one of the boys."

Learning experiences should be designed to interrupt a pattern of repeated negative behavior when people continue to take the same self-defeating actions over and over again. One state, which has since closed down its program, used the term "thrashing" to describe corrective actions and interventions. Terms like that are asking for trouble. Inmates who are learning to replace negative behaviors with positive ones need to be supported in their learning, not punished. One of the slogans on the walls in Shock Incarceration says "Most people change, not because they see the light, but because they feel the heat." This is vitally important with a population where "the heat" has been guns, police, pressure from "friends," crack, cocaine, and other addictive drugs. With this group, the desire to change has to outweigh the attraction of the "old life" and because of the short duration of these programs, it has to happen quickly. Learning experiences turn up "the heat," making them uncomfortable with self-defeating habits and receptive to new behaviors.

Military bearing teaches people to listen, to control their bodies, and to pay attention. This is critical for a population raised on Ritalin, with Attention Deficit Disorder (ADD), and other learning dysfunctions, who are addicted to crack cocaine and other drugs which change the chemistry of their brains and impair their healthy functioning. In both the six-month Shock Incarceration program and the new ninety-day Drug Treatment Center modeled after Shock, average academic grade level improvements are two-to-three years for all participants. Many achieve as much as five-to-seven or eight-grade level improvements.

Inmates in Shock attend academic classes twelve hours a week and treatment sessions twenty-eight hours a week. In the drug treatment program, participants attend academic classes twelve hours each week and are in treatment an additional thirty-four hours weekly. Staff who have worked in other correctional settings are impressed with the responsiveness of Shock participants, their commitment to and active involvement in recovery-oriented treatment sessions. Teachers (who also work in public schools) remark about the eagerness to learn of the students in these programs. They enjoy teaching and are relieved at not having to function as security guards, hall monitors, and police. Service providers who continue substance abuse treatment with this population after release are pleased with the "treatment readiness" of program graduates. Follow-up research indicates that while limited employment opportunities for offenders may not result in any greater employment for Shock graduates than for other parolees, they are much more likely to be involved in personal growth and recovery-related activities. They are far less likely to violate parole or return to new crimes than comparison groups (annual reports).

Research in accelerated learning and "whole brain" learning techniques cite the body–mind connection in learning. The rhythm and movement of drill and ceremony in time with cadences has a direct, positive effect on the brain and learning. The movements duplicate "cross-crawling" methods developed to improve hand-eye coordination, reading and thinking skills in those with learning disabilities or emotional disorders. Most of those who enter the program have learning or emotional difficulties. Brain research encourages rhythmic movement and breathing techniques as important interventions for emotional and psychological difficulties, and for improving general learning ability in anyone. Brain chemistry is positively affected by the physical movement of drill and ceremony. It is severely damaged by addiction. Structured environments, with clearly established rules, controls and expectations are highly recommended by therapists working with those who suffer from attention deficit disorder....

Boot Camps: Purpose and Goals

The term "boot camp" was coined by the military, to identify a six-to-eight week period of intensive training designed to turn young recruits into disciplined, effective soldiers. The "boot" is the newest member of the armed forces. Like the boots they wear, they are on the lowest rung of the ladder. They spend their time in boot camp learning how to be "all that you can be," "one of the few," "the brave, the proud," and "to aim high." Basic training is designed to teach "boots" military bearing and discipline, how to take care of body and mind, personal hygiene, to learn problem solving skills, teamwork, and respect for authority. In addition, it teaches recruits how to march in step in formation, pay attention to those around them, and to develop pride, esprit de corps, physical fitness, knowledge, skills and abilities. In brief, boot camps were designed to teach new soldiers how to survive in combat conditions. After the initial period of instruction, advanced training focuses on skill development including leadership skills, and other specialized training.

The "war on drugs" was a natural for borrowing the terminology and methods of a boot camp program, originally designed to help young, raw recruits survive in combat, by incorporating the methods into a similar program for offenders. The inner cities, from where most of these young offenders come, are referred to as "combat zones" where weapons abound. The guilty and the innocent, children and senior citizens alike, are killed along with young people engaged in the "turf wars" in the struggle for power the drug trade feeds.

Corrections, like the military, is an authority-based, hierarchical model. Jobs are designated by the same terms as those of the military. Rank, structure, and chain of command are all from a military model. As Vietnam War era veterans have come of age and begun to influence public policy, it is a logical outgrowth to look back at one's own experience for solutions to problems. What was it that helped that callow, naive, young high school graduate or dropout learn how to "be a man"? For that matter, some of those who will admit it say that the military was what saved them from going to prison themselves. Since the end of the draft in 1972, the prison population has quadrupled in the United States. Many cite the end of the draft as the beginning of the escalation of crime and prison crowding. Boot camps for offenders are a logical response to this paradigm. . . .

When planning a boot camp, its leaders should take responsibility for the development of a program that is designed to teach offenders skills that will help them to be successful in society and reject criminal behavior as a lifestyle. Self-discipline is an essential component of success.

Discipline is not punishment. Discipline is setting standards, establishing clear expectations of behavior, and living up to those standards. Discipline leads to strength, to the development of personal integrity. Command Sergeant Major Joshua Perry's definition of discipline is, "Being at the appointed place at the appointed time, in the proper uniform, doing what you're told, when you're told and how you're told." He goes on to say that, "Unless you're Bill Gates, you're going to work for someone else. You aren't going to last long at McDonald's if you don't understand that basic fact." Most of the offenders in boot camps are going to be working for someone; even as they did in their street dealing days. They need to learn discipline to get and keep jobs, study and earn diplomas, pay the rent, buy groceries and raise their children.

Discipline is not abuse, nor is it humiliation. Director Clark and Superintendent Moscicki were asked to review a script for a training video on boot camps. It had been written by someone who never worked in a prison. One planned voice-over line read "Punishment and humiliation play an important role in the boot camp experience." They do not! There is no place for punishment or humiliation in these programs. Those behaviors are dangerous. The script included one scene in a mess hall where the drill instructor was supposed to throw water in an inmate's face, while the inmate, looking "upset," stood rigidly at attention. This was intended to show how boot camps instill discipline in inmates; certainly not in staff if this scene had played. At Lakeview, there are more than 250 inmates in each mess hall at one sitting. The two mess halls are only separated by an open kitchen. Imagine that! The writers of the video script obviously had never been in a mess hall when there was a fight, if they had ever been in one at all.

As Command Sergeant Major Joshua Perry says, "Violence begets violence." There is no excuse for abuse, or for harassing inmates in the name of the "military model." Superintendent Moscicki discussed the issue of the backlash of antimilitary sentiment from boot camp critics:

I am concerned that critics of the boot camp program almost always associate screaming drill instructors, cursing, brutalizing and humiliating the inmate with military discipline, the "Full Metal Jacket" approach to corrections. . . . Bad boot camp programs . . . provide our critics with all the ammunition they need to shoot us down.

[They] rely on compliance and teaching inmates to follow orders. Compliance alone is not enough. Compliance only works when you're being watched. The compliance model supports our critics' claims that boot camp programs produce robots who just know how to follow orders and do pushups. These programs rarely work and have no lasting effect on inmates. Push-ups will not make you smarter.

Military discipline is not just following orders. Military discipline is not punishment. Military discipline is the ability to perform a task to specifications with exacting attention to detail. Military discipline teaches inmates to listen, controlling their minds and bodies. Once that is accomplished, the academic and treatment components of the program can take hold and inmates can learn pride and dignity. The combination of discipline and treatment is what works. This combined approach is what can make the difference in the lives of the inmates in boot camp programs.

The Importance of Consistency

The balance between treatment and discipline is important. Both are necessary in order to be effective. Staff must respect and reinforce each other's discipline. They must set appropriate limits. In the old therapeutic community days, such discipline was called "finger in the chest." At the same time, it is important to have the sensitivity to be able to "pat them on the back," to encourage and support them when that is necessary. Some inmates have been so deprived that they do not know how to tie their shoes or bathe properly. Calling them "stupid" does not teach them anything and is cruel and cowardly. There is no excuse for cruelty in any program, especially boot camps. As a leader, you are responsible for everything that happens in the boot camp program. If you see abuse, stop it. Insist on standards of performance and then monitor and supervise to ensure that staff are doing what is expected. Be clear about what you expect.

All staff have to be trained alike. They have to be "on the same sheet of music" for the program to be effective. An inmate cannot think that alcohol and substance abuse treatment is only important to the counselor and military bearing only the concern of the drill instructor. That kind of thinking drives wedges between staff and inmates. An African proverb says, "It takes a whole village to raise a child." Similarly, in the boot camp environment, everyone is responsible for every aspect of the program. It takes everyone in the program, working together, to produce a high quality program.

Command Sergeant Major Joshua Perry says, "A leader must be competent, consistently firm, fair and impartial, and practice honesty in word, deed and signature." Competent leaders command respect. They do not have to demand it. Firmness is commitment, not harsh or tyrannical behavior. If leaders demonstrate those principles of integrity, subordinates will respect them and follow them

anywhere. They may not like "the boss," but they will respect him or her. When subordinates respect their leaders, they will do the job expected of them. Critics may not like the program, but they too will respect the job you do. . . .

One of the goals of Shock Incarceration in New York is to teach the idea and practice of "shared responsibility" to the inmates in the program. This is the essence of the community living component of the program for which drill instructors, teachers, counselors, cooks, supervisors, and administrators are responsible. Inmates can learn this principle only from the staff who work with them. Staff learn how to teach these principles from their leaders. In setting the direction for a boot camp program, leaders have to be clear about the course they set "in word, deed and signature." Thankfully, this does not require that leaders always be at their best, just that they do the best they can. Murphy's Law says, "Only a mediocre person is always at his best." Leaders do have to demonstrate how to deal with failure, even their own, to admit their mistakes, correct them and move on. We learn from mistakes, our own and others. We need to teach inmates how to learn from their mistakes, as well. Staff learn how to be effective from leaders " . . . who cleanse, who teach, who convince—in short, who do whatever is necessary to give us a chance." To be such a leader, one has to be willing to set the pace, not just to follow the tide.

Dostoyevsky said in *Crime and Punishment,* "A society can be judged by entering its prisons." In the United States, one in three black men is either incarcerated or on parole. One and a half million children in the United States have a parent in prison; that is one out of fifty. More than two-thirds of all offenders are in prison for nonviolent crimes, usually related to drug and alcohol abuse. This is the collective failure of society. As a society, we must work together for solutions. As corrections professionals, we are responsible for the quality of treatment of offenders entrusted to our care. The question is then, do our programs "give us . . . a chance to survive both as individuals and as a community?" Whatever the correctional program, it must provide the opportunity for growth. If a boot camp model is what you choose, then it is even more important to focus on goals, because of the limited time offenders spend in these programs.

Boot Camps Are Not an Easy Answer

There are some people in boot camp programs who do not understand the responsibility of power. There are always people who will abuse power if they have it. Abuse of power has occurred at every level in every organization throughout history. That does not excuse abuses of power in any system. Being vigilant, monitoring, training, and supervising guard against that. Ensuring that clearly articulated goals and standards are followed is another way to maintain a quality program. Do not fall into the trap of believing that you will ever be "finished" once you start a program like this. This is a commitment. If you accept the responsibility, then you must follow through. It takes continual

maintenance to ensure a quality program.

The results in New York have shown that consistent policy, training of all staff, monitoring and ensuring that policies are followed, with all staff working together toward the same goals, has produced impressive results. As of the end of November 1995, the Shock Incarceration program had graduated more than 13,500 inmates and had saved the State of New York more than $439.5 million dollars in cost of confinement and capital construction, since the first inmates began being released in March of 1988. The fact that there has been a strong aftercare program postrelease in most of the state is important as well. Just as the military does not put soldiers into war zones without followup and further training after boot camp, corrections cannot expect that a boot camp program will have a lasting effect without followup.

Aftercare is important in boot camp programs. Drug abuse is a life-threatening disease. Relapse prevention does not happen in a vacuum. It takes time and commitment of resources. Even with good aftercare programs though, it is still ultimately the offender who decides its success or failure, not the program. John Zachariah cautions that hospitals are not blamed if patients relapse after they are discharged when they no longer need hospital care. If a patient does not follow the recommendations of the doctor and refuses to take prescriptions, hospitals are not blamed if the patient gets sick again. Corrections is not forgiven in the same way if parolees refuse to follow the programs prescribed for them while they were in the system. In the course of educating society, legislators, and critics of the system, it is important to remind them that continuing treatment and resources in the community are as important as the institutional phase.

Boot camps can be very effective with the right people in charge, with committed, well trained staff, good supervision, and for a select population of inmates. These programs have powerful tools. They can be misused to become terrible weapons. Boot camps are not for the faint-hearted.

These are "in your face" programs, there is no getting around it. If you are a gentle soul, with a tendency to fall for the "sad, sad tales" that are often real, then you need to be very clear that "tough love" is critical to the boot camp model. If you are uncomfortable with confrontation, do something else. Do not do this program. There are many excellent models for change. Boot camps are not for everyone, neither inmates nor staff. Boot camps may not be the answer, despite how much you may want them to be.... ■

The Rise and Fall of Boot Camps: A Case Study in Common-Sense Corrections

Francis T. Cullen, Kristie R. Blevins, Jennifer S. Trager, and Paul Gendreau

The most enduring, seemingly intractable reality facing American corrections—a reality from which there has, for some time, appeared to be "no escape"—is the steady replenishment of large numbers of offenders in prison and under state legal supervision. The statistics, of course, are familiar: On any given day, in excess of 1.4 million offenders are housed in state and federal prisons, a count that climbs to over 2 million when jail inmates are indexed:

approximately 4 million people are on probation and another 750,000 are on parole; and, when all the figures are added up, more than 6.5 million offenders are supervised daily by the correctional system. Although there are some signs that the growth in prison populations may be slowing few commentaries on the status of U.S. corrections can avoid discussing the sheer number of offenders that must be managed day in and day out.

Francis T. Cullen, Kristie R. Blevins, Jennifer S. Trager, and Paul Gendreau, "The Rise and Fall of Boot Camps: A Case Study in Common-Sense Corrections," from *Rehabilitation Issues, Problems, and Prospects in Boot Camp*, edited by Brent B. Benda and Nathaniel J. Pallone (New York: The Haworth Press, 2005). Also published in Volume 40 (2005) of *Journal of Offender Rehabilitation*.

By contrast, an equally remarkable reality—but one that less frequently captures media headlines or scholarly notice—is the persistent commitment by correctional leaders and among the public to the goal of changing the criminally wayward for the better. Good intentions have permeated the often dark history of corrections and have surfaced even in recent years when corrections has been characterized as being in the grips of the "penal harm movement" and the "imprisonment binge." To be sure, this hope that offenders might be saved usually does not extend to the most heinous criminals and does not ensure the allocation of resources needed for the task of reforming criminals. Nonetheless, Americans believe that the correctional system should do more than warehouse and control; the system should, as its name implies, also "correct."

But realizing this goal of correcting offenders is hardly uncomplicated. Beyond incapacitation or the mere infliction of pain, the daunting puzzle confronted by corrections is *how to intervene* in such a way as to transform the lawless into the law-abiding. One answer increasingly being proposed is to base interventions "on the evidence"—that is, on what works to reduce recidivism. This approach, which is becoming known as "evidence-based corrections," draws its rationale from a similar movement within medicine. In both cases, the logic is persuasive: Not to use scientific evidence to direct interventions is to risk subjecting people to procedures that are either harmful or ineffective. Of course, an evidence-based approach is not without its own demands. Thus, to have a salutary effect, knowledge of "what works" must be

accumulated, transferred, and then implemented in the "real world." Still, the alternative to taking on these challenges is to engage in interventions that can rightly be called "quackery."

Unfortunately, corrections is a field in which quackery is pervasive. Undoubtedly, the reasons why so many ineffective interventions are invented, implemented, defended, and sustained are complex. Criminologists, for example, must share part of the blame for not generating, until recently, a body of research-based knowledge that could direct the selection of effective treatment modalities. Correctional employees similarly have failed to define their work as a profession organized, like other professions, around expertise rooted in science and training. It is safe to suggest that the current state of affairs also can be traced to a lack of resources, bureaucratic inertia, and politics. Nonetheless, another factor that richly deserves to be cited is the willingness of policy-makers, practitioners, and the public to embrace interventions on the basis of *common sense*.

Let us hasten to say that common sense is not inherently a recipe for failure in corrections. At times, the collective wisdom in a field can be just that: wisdom well worth consulting. The difficulty, however, is that common sense is often accorded a privileged status in which, as a basis of knowledge, it is allowed to trump science and more systematic ways of determining a course of intervention. In this scenario, common sense can be boldly cited both to preclude undertaking evaluation research "which will only prove what everyone already knows" or to reject contrary empirical evidence because "the study must be wrong since statistics can show anything you want them to show." Common sense thus becomes a socially constructed reality that is resistant to falsification. It is true virtually by definition.

In the current analysis, we propose that common sense was a key ingredient that facilitated the growth of "boot camps" as a correctional intervention. Boot camps were not rooted in empirical research and showed considerable resilience even when unfavorable research results mounted. Even so, the boot camp saga has had an ending that, for the positivists among us, has been happier rather than disappointing. Although boot camps persist as an intervention, the reputation of this intervention has been significantly tarnished. In this case, it appears that scientific research may be winning the battle with common sense.

The Appeal of Boot Camps

Although their origins can be traced back to at least 1971 in Idaho, correctional boot camps emerged as a significant initiative in the 1980s, with Oklahoma and Georgia developing such camps in 1983. In the decade following the inception of these initial programs, over 40 boot camps were implemented, with camps found in over half the states. The sudden emergence and spread of boot camps thus raised the question of why the 1980s and the 1990s provided a receptive context for this particular correctional intervention. Why were boot camps appealing at this historical juncture?

"Getting Tough" Through Intermediate Sanctions

The answer to this query starts with the observation that boot camps were not an isolated venture but rather part of a broader movement called "intermediate sanctions" or "intermediate punishments." The term "intermediate" refers to a place somewhere in between "prison" and "probation." Commentators often decried that, when sentencing offenders, judges had only two main options: life-altering placement behind bars versus a mere "slap on the wrist" with probation. This would be tantamount to a doctor having to choose between hospitalizing patients or prescribing "two aspirins in the morning." For liberals, these disparate options inevitably prevented judges from allocating sentences that were more finely calibrated to the seriousness of the offense. Injustice thus was always on the horizon because, in their view, many offenders were sent to prison who did not truly deserve to be there—or did not deserve to be there more than others released into the community. If only judges had more options—something less stringent than prison but harsher than probation—then many of these individuals might well escape incarceration. In short, intermediate sanctions might allow for more justice in sentencing.

In the end, however, "justice" was only a subsidiary reason—one mostly trumpeted by progressives—why intermediate sanctions captured the imagination of policymakers. As DiIulio pointed out, officials were concerned that there was no escape from rising prison populations and the concomitant institutional crowding. Many conservatives were searching for a solution to the financial costs associated with housing burgeoning numbers of inmates. One option might have been the greater use of community "corrections," justified by the rationale that prisons were harmful places and the community was a location where rehabilitation services could be delivered more efficaciously. But in the context of the Reagan era and the movement of the United States toward the political right, such talk would have been—indeed was—dismissed as the empty rhetoric of bleeding hearts clinging to the therapeutic logic of the now-discredited welfare state. Instead, crime must be confronted with the iron fist, not the velvet glove, of the state, and criminals must be disciplined and scared into submission.

The genius of intermediate *sanctions* or *punishments* was that they ostensibly rejected the tradition of earlier community sanctions, which were assembled under the label of *corrections*. Instead, they pushed thinking in a dramatically different direction: What if interventions could be created that, though administered largely in the community, were oriented not toward social welfare for undeserving criminals but toward the control of, and the infliction of discomfort on, offenders? What if it were possible to "get tough" in the community? If so, then it would be feasible to lessen the prison crowding problem in a way that was both fiscally prudent and politically defensible.

Intermediate sanctions/punishments, of course, offered this seemingly perfect solution. Offenders would no longer be "reintegrated" and counseled by probation and parole officers schooled in social work. Instead, community supervision would be transformed mainly into a policing function—what one observer called a "pee 'em and see 'em" style of corrections. In this new paradigm, offenders placed in the community would now be *controlled*; they would be subjected to random drug tests, intensive supervision, home incarceration, and/or electronic monitoring. They would experience these sanctions as unpleasant and would fear that stepping out of line would be quickly detected, with the threat of imprisonment looming for the uncooperative. It was assumed that only the irrational—the undeterrable—would dare trifle with such a newly vigilant state.

Boot camps had some unique features, but largely "fit" with this intermediate sanctions movement and the larger "get tough" context in which they were enmeshed. Unlike the other sanctions, boot camps involved a stay in behind bars—albeit one that lasted only a few months (typically three to six months). Boot camps also promised not just to watch offenders but also to change them for the better—albeit through means (military discipline) that would not be mistaken for lenient, bleeding-heart corrections.

This last point is crucial. Although offering to exchange long prison stays for short prison stays—harshness for leniency—boot camps were acceptable precisely because they promised to be, well, boot camps! That is, they were prepared to subject offenders to a

Spartan lifestyle, to exhausting physical demands, to planned and repeated humiliation, and to authoritarian (if secretly well-intentioned) drill sergeants who would be unrelenting in their discipline. As Tonry notes, "images of offenders participating in military drill and hard physical labor make boot camps look demanding and unpleasant, characteristics that crime-conscious officials and voters find satisfying." Underneath it all, offenders might be "loved," but it was a love that would always be tough. Indeed, it is instructive that boot camps were sold not just as an intermediate sanction but as a "tough" intermediate sanction. Equally illuminating, they were often given the alias of "shock incarceration."

In short, boot camps—like other intermediate sanctions—used a language and promised a toughness that resonated with the prevailing political climate. The task now was to randomly test, intensively supervise, electronically monitor, and discipline the wayward. With such an array of weapons, it would be safe—and much cheaper than paying for their prolonged imprisonment—to control offenders in the community, especially after the shock of life in a boot camp. The logic was certainly persuasive. However, for specific interventions to be enthusiastically accepted, something more than toughness and promised costs savings had to be present. One other ingredient would seal their popularity: There had to be some reason to believe that these intermediate sanctions actually would "work."

Consult the Evidence or Consult Common Sense?

One option might have been to review the extant empirical evidence and to develop the case that criminological scholarship, however limited, was on the side of the proposed intervention. Such an evidence-based approach would have required a professional orientation, a belief that libraries contain valuable information, and a willingness to expend the effort to sit and read for a bit. But if this approach had been embraced, it would have revealed troubling facts. For example, there has never been any consistent evidence that smaller probation caseloads that allow for more intensive supervision reduce recidivism. We will return shortly to this point as it relates to boot camps.

There was no need, however, for boot-camp advocates to worry about the data. Another standard could be applied to justify the allocation of millions of dollars and untested interventions into the lives of thousands of offenders: common sense! Again, part of what made intermediate sanctions—including boot camps—sensible was that they rejected doing something *for* the offender and promised to do something *to* the offender. But "get tough" rhetoric aside, the common sense underlying most intermediate sanctions was the "parable of the hot stove." This means, of course, that we all grow up and learn—either firsthand or through cringing observation—that touching a hot stove immediately yields the pain of a burn. In the same way, intermediate sanctions were portrayed as making the state into a hot stove: As soon as the offender did something wrong, the drug test, the electronic monitor, and the intensively supervising probation officer would zap them with the burn of a sanction. How could it not work?

Boot camps, however, were different, but the influence of common sense was, if anything, far more powerful. There was a widespread belief that the discipline of military experience would transform the immature and wayward into mature and contributing citizens. We can ask once again for the basis of this view. An evidence-based approach would have urged caution. If advocates of boot camps had taken the time to inspect research on military service, they would have discovered that the impact of such service is complex and often contradictory, and that the special effects of boot camps have not been disentangled from those of other experiences related to the military (e.g., job training and guaranteed employment while in the service, educational benefits after release, time spent in combat).

Sampson and Laub's reanalysis of the Glueck and Glueck's longitudinal data set is instructive. The Gluecks' study was initiated in 1939 with boys ages 10 to 17; two-thirds of the sample would eventually enter the military, including many who had histories of delinquency. Sampson and Laub recognize that being in the service might benefit some men and even help to "surmount childhood disadvantage." But they also note that "it is not inconsistent that the military can serve to turn some men's lives around, even as it disrupts other men's lives . . . or provides yet another setting for some men to continue their deviant behavior." Indeed, in their empirical analysis, they report that length of military service had an insignificant effect on later criminal behavior during adulthood. Equally salient, they show that, *despite the experience of being in a boot camp*, the military was not particularly successful in blunting the criminal predispositions of those with a past history of delinquency. For example, when compared with a matched sample of non-delinquents, individuals with an official record of delinquency (i.e., a prior placement in a juvenile correctional school) were three times more likely to commit crime in the military (64% versus 20%), and seven times more likely to be a frequent offender, to be a serious offender, and to be dishonorably discharged. Similar results were found for men who scored high on prior measures of unofficial or reported delinquency. Not surprisingly, the United States military no longer recruits men or women with criminal records.

Although more positive in her assessment, Bouffard's examination of two longitudinal data sets of individuals in the Vietnam War era (born in 1945 and 1949, respectively) also shows the complexities of asserting that boot camps are panaceas for crime. In one data set drawn from Racine, Wisconsin, military service reduced offending. However, in the other data set drawn from Philadelphia, military service limited the likelihood of criminal involvement for those with no past record of delinquency, but had no effect on those with a delinquent record—precisely the group held to benefit from correctional boot camps. In neither study, we should note, did military service affect future violent offending.

Findings such as these, however, never surfaced in the rush to establish boot camps. As Tonry points out, correctional boot camps garnered instant legitimacy from the supposedly *transforming personal experiences* that many citizens believed they had had in the military. "Many Americans," observes Tonry, "have experienced life in military boot camps and remember the experience as not necessarily pleasant but as an effective way to learn self-discipline and to learn to work as part of a team." Thus, if they had been changed for the better by boot camps, it was only common sense that camps could save other wayward souls. Moreover, this common-sense commitment to boot camps could insulate its holders—at least for a time—from countervailing critical analysis and empirical data. Thus, when state officials in Georgia were presented with evaluation research revealing the ineffectiveness of boot camps, they responded in this illuminating way:

> Reacting to the study, a spokesman for Governor Zell Miller said that "we don't care what the study thinks"—Georgia will continue to use its boot camps. Governor Miller is an ex-Marine, and says that the Marine boot camps he attended changed his life for the better; he believes that the boot camp experience can do the same for wayward Georgia youth.... Georgia's Commissioner of Corrections ... also joined the chorus of condemnation, saying that academics were too quick to ignore the experiential knowledge of people "working in the system" and rely on research findings.

The common-sense appeal of correctional boot camps drew strength from another factor: the unchallenged, almost hegemonic cultural belief that military boot camps "break a person down" and then "build 'em back up." When probed, most people have no specific idea what this means—that is, they cannot articulate what is being broken down and what is being built back up. Rather, they harbor only some vague notion that boot camps strip away a recruit's youthful immaturity, slovenliness, and general disrespect for authority and "turn them into a man." This break-'em-down/build-'em-up theory comes to life in uplifting, if not heartwarming, television shows and movies, such as *An Officer and a Gentleman*. A familiar and comforting theme is repeated: We see the slightly delinquent, confused, perhaps self-centered, youthful rebel saved from personal and social failure by the demanding but ultimately caring drill sergeant who pulls the recruit back from the brink of going AWOL. The ending of these films is particularly revealing. They invariably show the group that had survived boot camp proudly marching out in their pristine dress uniforms just as a new group of recruits sporting long hair and ill-fitting clothes staggers off the bus to the inhospitable greetings of the drill sergeant. We all know what awaits them!

In a dialectical way, these images both reflect and reinforce the notion that boot camps are imbued with special, transforming powers. It thus becomes merely a matter of common sense to make the leap in logic—or, perhaps more accurately, the leap in faith—that *correctional* boot camps can break offenders down and build them back up. These notions obscure the dual reality that the causes of crime are complex and that the effects of military service are complex. Where caution should reign, common sense rushes us to the judgement that boot camps are a cure for crime that should be implemented without delay. . . .

The Fall of Boot Camps

Two decades after the inception of the correctional boot camp movement, the bloom is off the rose: Boot camps no longer are seen as unproblematic and certain to work. To be sure, they continue to exist and have not lost all their popularity. But critics have succeeded in making them "controversial." Common sense, which was an important fuel to the movement, is no longer able to insulate boot camps against scrutiny and serious doubts.

Part of the decline in boot camps' appeal is due to the efforts of critics to deconstruct the image of boot camps as providing tough love that would instill much-needed character in wayward adolescents and younger adults. Instead they offer a different construction of reality: "Camp Fear." Thus, boot camps are portrayed as places where youths are humiliated and potentially abused; as places where adult bullies are given unfettered power over vulnerable charges; and as places where aggression is celebrated and likely modeled. These characterizations have taken on meaning when investigations have uncovered instances in which youths experienced psychological deterioration, physical abuse, and callous neglect of illnesses and injuries that resulted in deaths.

But the most devastating blow to the boot camp movement has come from another source: evidence-based corrections. Over time, studies from diverse sources have accumulated that have reached the same discouraging conclusion: Contrary to optimistic claims rooted in common sense, boot camps have not proven effective in reducing recidivism. These findings do not mean that some bright spots might not be detected. Thus, boot camps likely are no worse than traditional sanctions and correctional settings; some offenders do better in these camps than do others; they tend to induce short-term positive attitude change; when coupled with treatment and aftercare, they may provide a vehicle to provide effective treatment in a politically palatable way; a program here and there may modestly reduce recidivism; and so on. Even so, the consensus in the criminological community is that the evidence is persuasive that boot camps are largely a failed enterprise. They have not lived up to expectations, and there is little reason to expose offenders to "shock incarceration" when more effective alternative interventions are available.

Again, contrary evidence does not mean that a correctional intervention—in this case, boot camps—will vanish or lose all of their supporters. But advocates of boot camps now face the daunting prospect of facing critics equipped not simply with their dislike of "camp fear" but also with negative evaluation studies. In the battle against common sense, they are no longer defenseless.

Conclusion: Beyond Common-Sense Corrections

Correctional officials and their agencies will be confronted repeatedly with the challenge of how best to invest public monies in the pursuit of public safety. In the past, they have too often made choices based on common sense—on what resonated with their understandings of the world and thus what struck them as most likely to reduce offender recidivism. To a degree, their choices in earlier days were excusable. More often than not, criminologists had provided only the vague admonition that "nothing works" in corrections. Left to their own devices, officials had little direction on what might be the "best bets" in reforming the offenders under their charge.

Fortunately, criminologists no longer are silent regarding what works, what might be promising, and what is irresponsible, if not harmful, to attempt. We are now entering an era of "evidence-based corrections" in which research is accumulating that can guide programmatic choices. Scholars have developed principles of effective intervention that, if followed, produce meaningful reduction in re-offending. The decision not to consult this research and allow it to help inform which interventions are initiated is to remain in a "field of ignorance."

In fact, all of us should continue to be wary of common sense. It is dangerous precisely because it seems so correct, leaves our biases unchallenged, and requires virtually no effort to activate. As we have seen, boot camps are a case study in what

can occur when common sense is celebrated and allowed to shape our policy decisions. Countless offenders—many of them youths—have been subjected to military-style corrections. Should it not disturb us that these individuals have likely lost an important opportunity to turn their lives around? Should it not bother us that scarce agency funds have been ill spent when more effective interventions might have been employed? Should it not bother us that citizens have subsequently been victimized and public safety sacrificed because common sense blinded us to the inherent criminological defects in boot camps?

The temptation, of course, will be to find value in boot camps—to see how they might be tweaked and used to do some good, such as by grafting on treatment modalities and offering aftercare. We see this strategy as "throwing good money after bad," of ignoring the mounting evidence that boot camps are limited in their effectiveness and are not the best that we can do. Instead, we suggest an alternative vision: We urge officials to start over—to enter the marketplace of interventions, to survey the available correctional options, and then to select for implementation programs for which the research evidence is the most convincing. This approach requires a professional perspective and does not guarantee success. But it does offer the prospect of moving beyond common sense to a point where the most scientifically valid evidence at our disposal guides our correctional future. We have done—and could do—worse. ∎

▪▪▪ The Continuing Debate

What Is New

The effectiveness of boot camps is very difficult to study. The most obvious problem is that those sent to boot camps are not a representative sample of offenders, and so there is no "control" or comparison group with which to make comparisons. For example, in some cases those who are sent to boot camps may be those who are considered most likely candidates for reform, or those who have not committed violent crimes, or who have stronger family ties (with perhaps a parent who advocates that the youthful offender be sent to boot camp rather than a regular prison). As Brent Benda has noted, "Often offenders sent to boot camp programs would not have been incarcerated if these programs had not existed," and that raises obvious problems for comparing the subsequent behavior of boot camp inmates with the later behavior of prison inmates. If a group of primarily nonviolent young prisoners are sent to a boot camp, and a year or two later they are compared with violent offenders who spent time in traditional prisons, then it would not be surprising if after their release the boot camp residents were committing fewer crimes (and graduating from high school and finding jobs more often) than those released from traditional prisons. But that would certainly not establish the effectiveness of boot camps.

While boot camps still exist, the initial enthusiasm for such camps has been dampened by two sources: first, several widely reported cases of abuse, injury, and even death of prisoners. Second, criminological research strongly indicates that boot camps are generally not successful programs. As Cullen, Blevins, Trager, and Gendreau note, "the consensus in the criminological community is that the evidence is persuasive that boot camps are largely a failed enterprise." However, the political and public popularity of harsh treatment for offenders (especially youthful offenders) means that boot camps are not likely to disappear soon.

Where to Find More

A book of essays published by the American Correctional Association paints a very positive picture of boot camp programs: *Juvenile and Adult Boot Camps*, edited by American Correctional Association staff (Lanham, MD: American Correctional Association, 1996). A much more critical assessment, published a year later, is Michael Peters, David Thomas, and Christopher Zamberlan, "Boot Camps for Juvenile Offenders: Program Summary" (Washington, DC: OJJDP, September, 1997). A somewhat more positive assessment (though with significant reservations) of boot camp programs can be found in Doris Layton MacKenzie and Gaylene Styve Armstrong, editors, *Correctional Boot Camps: Military Basic Training or a Model for Corrections?* (Thousand Oaks, CA: Sage Publications, 2004); though it is an edited work, the book primarily presents the views of Doris Layton MacKenzie, who authored or co-authored 20 of the 21 articles in the book.

A superb examination of boot camps—including articles on boot camp programs for women, reports of follow-up studies on boot camps, and extensive coverage of the research on boot camps—is Brent B. Benda and Nathaniel J. Pallone, editors, *Rehabilitation Issues, Problems, and Prospects in Boot Camp* (New York: The Haworth Press, 2005). It was also published as Volume 40, Number 3/4 (2005) of *Journal of Offender Rehabilitation*.

Among many recent articles on boot camps are Faith E. Lutze and David C. Brody, "Mental Abuse as Cruel and Unusual Punishment: Do Boot Camp Prisons Violate the Eighth Amendment?" *Crime & Delinquency*, Volume 45, Number 2 (April 1999): 242–255; Jerry Tyler, Ray Darville, and Kathy Stalnaker, "Juvenile Boot Camps: A Descriptive Analysis of Program Diversity and Effectiveness," *The Social Science Journal*, Volume 38 (2001): 445–460; Michael P. Arena, "Is that the Sound of 'Taps' Playing in the Distance for Correctional Boot Camps?" *Journal of Forensic Psychology Practice*, Volume 2, Number 4 (2002): 59–70; and (one of the most careful empirical studies of boot camp programs) Jean Bottcher and Michael E. Ezell, "Examining the Effectiveness of Boot Camps: A Randomized Experiment with a Long-Term Follow Up," *Journal of Research in Crime and Delinquency*, Volume 42, Number 3 (August 2005): 309–332.

The "scared straight" program planted the seeds for the more extensive boot camp programs; James O. Finckenauer and Patricia W. Gavin offer a detailed critique in *Scared Straight: The Panacea Phenomenon Revisited* (Prospect Heights, IL: Waveland Press, 1999).

17

Should We Eliminate the Special System of Juvenile Justice?

The Distinct Juvenile Justice System Should Be Eliminated
    Advocate: Jeffrey A. Butts, Research Fellow at Chapin Hall, Center for
    Children at the University of Chicago; formerly senior research
    associate in the Program on Law & Behavior at the Urban Institute,
    Washington, DC.
    Source: "Can We Do Without Juvenile Justice?" *Criminal Justice
    Magazine*, Volume 15, Number 1 (Spring 2000).

The Juvenile Justice System Must Be improved and Preserved
    Advocate: Hon. Arthur L. Burnett, Sr., Senior Justice of the Court of
    the District of Columbia; also serves as "judge-in-residence" with the
    Black Community Crusade for Children of the Children's Defense
    Fund.
    Source: "What of the Future? Envisioning an Effective Juvenile
    Court," *Criminal Justice Magazine*, Volume 15, Number 1
    (Spring 2000).

As the United States has moved toward a more punitive and retributive model of criminal justice, with less emphasis on rehabilitation and more on severe punishment, the treatment of juvenile offenders has undergone a similar change. More and more juveniles are transferred to regular adult criminal court, and more juveniles are sentenced to adult prisons. The minimum age for transfer in most states is 14, and in some states even younger children can be transferred from juvenile to criminal court; and several states have made 15 the maximum age to be tried in juvenile court. In some juvenile systems the emphasis has moved more toward blame and punishment rather than rehabilitation.

This "get tough" approach to juvenile justice was in large part motivated by media accounts of extremely violent youthful "superpredators," young people who were supposedly much more brutal and violent and dangerous than in past years. This "urban myth" of a wave of terrifying superpredator youth was debunked by a report by the U.S. Surgeon General, whose research revealed "no evidence that the young people involved in violence during the peak years of the early 1990s were more frequent or more vicious offenders than youth in early years." But the false perception proved more influential than the less sensational facts.

The move away from juvenile systems, and toward greater (or even exclusive) use of the adult criminal system for juvenile offenders, has two distinct motivations. On the one hand, there are those who push a "get tough" policy with juveniles in the belief that meting out the severe punishments of the adult criminal system will deter juveniles from committing crimes. On the other hand, there are also those who believe that the rights of accused juveniles are inadequately protected by the looser procedures of juvenile justice, and that, therefore, transferring them into the criminal court system will better protect their basic legal rights.

⊥⊥⊥ Points to Ponder

- Under the current juvenile court system, a juvenile charged with a felony is tried before a juvenile court judge, and cannot choose a jury trial. Should a juvenile accused of a serious crime have the right to a jury trial, just as adult defendants have the right to a trial by jury? If the basic right to a trial by jury is a right to be tried by a "jury of one's peers," should the jury trial of a juvenile defendant include other juveniles on the jury?

- Thirteen-year-old children are generally a year away from entering high school; but if a 13-year-old child borrows a readily available gun from his dad's car and robs a pizza stand, then in Georgia that 13-year-old is automatically tried in criminal court for armed robbery, and is likely to receive a long mandatory sentence in a harsh adult prison environment. Is such a policy consistent with the American concept of justice? Does it matter that such a policy violates international policy standards for the treatment of juveniles?

- The juvenile court system is *supposed* to be distinctly different from the criminal court system. What are some of the differences that are *supposed* to characterize the different systems? Are those differences still there? Are the differences still worth promoting?

- Jeffrey Butts suggests that new specialized criminal courts might replace the juvenile court system; if you favor that alternative, what are some of the features that you would want such a specialized youth court to have? Would *all* youthful offenders—including those who are 10 or 11—be tried in such courts?

- Justice Burnett notes that "much delinquent behavior can be traced to the [dysfunctional] family dynamics," and he contends that "Judges should be authorized to order family members into counseling and treatment along with the juvenile." This is a somewhat radical suggestion: that when a youthful family member gets into trouble, a judge should have the power to order other family members (who have not been charged with any crime) to undergo specific treatment programs. Is this a good idea?

- Though Butts and Burnett are arguing for very different conclusions, on what key points would they *agree*?

Can We Do Without Juvenile Justice?

Jeffrey A. Butts

To satisfy constituent demands for stronger crime policies, elected officials throughout the U.S. are gradually dismantling the juvenile justice system and replacing it with a pseudocriminal system, one that emphasizes mandatory sentences and formal, adversarial procedures. Large portions of the juvenile court's original caseload have already been re-assigned to the criminal court. Is the separate, juvenile justice system still feasible? If not, what can replace it? Policymakers need to confront these questions, and they need innovative answers. New policies should aim for more than simply abolishing the juvenile court's delinquency jurisdiction and sending all young offenders to conventional criminal courts.

A compelling argument can be made for abolishing the juvenile justice system, or more specifically, abolishing delinquency, the idea that young offenders aren't fully responsible for their behavior and should be handled in a separate court system. Abolishing delinquency is not the same thing as abolishing the entire juvenile court. Even if lawmakers ended the juvenile court's jurisdiction over criminal law violations, the juvenile court could continue to handle other types of cases (e.g., abused and neglected children, truants, curfew violations). In fact, youthful offenders could continue to be handled by the same judges in the same courtrooms that handle them now, but the courts would operate as youth divisions of a criminal court using criminal procedures under the criminal code.

Neither would abolishing delinquency require that all young offenders be sent to adult correctional programs or adult probation agencies. Many

Jeffrey A. Butts, "Can We Do Without Juvenile Justice?" *Criminal Justice Magazine*, Volume 15, Number 1 (Spring 2000). Copyright © 2000 by the American Bar Association. Reprinted with permission.

states already operate separate correctional facilities for young adults. The decision to handle all young offenders in the criminal court would not prevent correctional specialization. States would still be free to separate offenders by age when incarcerating or otherwise supervising convicted offenders, and the federal government would still be free to require such separation as a condition of financial support for state corrections agencies.

Debate over abolition of the juvenile justice system refers only to the court's responsibility for delinquency cases. Policymakers must decide what type of court should have legal jurisdiction over young people who violate the law. The debate centers on whether to continue defining law violations by young people as delinquent acts, or to classify them simply as crimes and refer them to criminal court.

Are Juvenile Courts Still Different?

Juvenile courts today bear only a passing similarity to the original concept of juvenile justice formulated a century ago. State lawmakers built the first juvenile courts around an informal, quasi-civil process. Juvenile court judges had broad discretion with which they could intervene quickly and decisively, even in cases involving hard-to-prove charges. Juvenile offenders received minimal procedural protections in juvenile court, but in return they were promised a court that would focus on their best interests. The mission of the juvenile court was to help young law violators get back on the right track, not simply to punish their illegal behavior.

Long before the first juvenile court reached its 100th birthday in 1999, this original notion of juvenile justice had been largely abandoned by state courts. According to Professor Barry Feld of the University of Minnesota, America's juvenile courts became "scaled-down, second-class criminal courts." In his view and that of other abolitionists, the court's responsibility for young offenders should be ended. The juvenile court no longer lives up to its part of the initial bargain. Prosecutors in juvenile court openly promote dispositions that amount to proportional retribution. Judicial decisions are based explicitly on the severity of each juvenile's crime rather than the complexity of his or her problems.

The juvenile justice system has strayed too far from its original mission, according to Feld. Policymakers should cancel the nation's juvenile justice experiment. Today's juvenile court retains much of the terminology of juvenile law, but it functions as a pseudocriminal court. Worse, it fails to provide complete due process protections for accused youth. Juvenile courts are still not required to provide bail, jury trials, or the right to a speedy trial for youthful offenders.

Feld recommends that all law violations be handled in criminal court, although he hopes the system will continue to recognize the lessened culpability of the very young by imposing sentences with a "youth discount"—a 17-year-old defendant would get 75 percent of the sentence length due an 18-year-old, a 16-year-old would get 50 percent, etc. Even if Feld's "youth discount" is ultimately rejected by policymakers, the insights and observations on which he bases his proposal cannot be ignored. Lawmakers will soon have to confront the basic question, "Can we do without the juvenile justice system?"

Juvenile Justice Politics

The juvenile justice system provokes strong opinions, and not all of them fit into neat categories like "liberal" or "conservative." It would be wrong to assume that all critics of the juvenile court are heartless, law-and-order types who feel little compassion for the poor, disproportionately minority youth who comprise the bulk of the juvenile court's clients. The critics most in favor of abolishing the juvenile justice system (Professor Feld, for example) are often motivated by a concern for youth. In their view, the juvenile court has never lived up to its rehabilitative promise and it never will. More importantly, the juvenile court's lower standards of due process are no longer tolerable given its modern emphasis on just deserts and retribution. Courts were meant to handle law violations, the abolitionists say, not social welfare problems.

It would also be wrong to characterize all defenders of the juvenile court as "soft on crime" or unconcerned with victim rights. Some of those who defend the juvenile justice system do so because they believe despite its flaws, the juvenile court offers a unique opportunity for broad, early intervention and effective crime prevention. In fact, the juvenile court was originally conceived as an informal, quasi-civil court precisely in order to free it of the procedural complexities that prevent the criminal court from acting too aggressively. The juvenile court was deliberately designed to be flexible and quick to intervene.

Both extremes in the battle over juvenile justice can go too far in pursuing their agenda. The traditionalists support a strict demarcation between juvenile and adult court and would like to save the original concept of an informal, nonstigmatizing, juvenile justice system. This position is completely unrealistic, however, given the legislative changes already implemented across the country. Contemporary juvenile courts operate much like criminal courts with strict rules of evidence, adversarial procedures, and official goals that include incapacitation and retribution. Moreover, nearly every state has enacted laws to send greater numbers of youth to adult court. It is too late to save the traditional system because the traditional system is already gone.

Abolitionists, however, can be just as impractical. Many would simply eliminate the juvenile court's responsibility for young offenders. If juveniles are going to be punished according to the severity of their crimes, the abolitionists argue, they should be tried in real courts with full due process rights. The abolitionists contend it is no longer possible to maintain the fiction that juvenile courts are fundamentally different. Yet, without significant reform of the criminal courts, the abolition of juvenile justice would require sending all youth—even the youngest and most vulnerable—to the same general trial courts criticized by policymakers as ineffective and overwhelmed. If the traditionalists appear naïve, the abolitionists seem reckless.

Policymakers have tried to find middle ground in this conflict. Unfortunately, their compromise solution was to slowly criminalize the juvenile court. Especially since the U.S.

Supreme Court's Gault decision in 1967, lawmakers across the country have encouraged juvenile courts to embrace the goals and operational style of criminal courts. Juvenile courts today pursue many of the objectives once unique to criminal courts, including incapacitation and retribution. Both juvenile courts and criminal courts rely on plea bargaining for case outcomes. Both are forced by growing caseloads to adopt assembly-line tactics and they often have difficulty providing individualized dispositions. The day-to-day atmosphere in modern juvenile courts (especially in urban areas) is increasingly indistinguishable from that of criminal courts.

Although these reforms may have been enacted for good reason, they raise serious questions about the continuing need for a separate, juvenile court system. As lawmakers continue to increase the similarity of juvenile and criminal court sanctions, it becomes harder to rationalize the separation of the process that imposes them. As judicial discretion is restricted, the juvenile court's once sweeping authority becomes diluted, making the court more bureaucratic and inflexible. Decades of reform increased the severity of the juvenile court process, but they also curtailed the court's ability to provide individualized and comprehensive interventions for young offenders.

Sacrificing Some to Save Others

Do we still need a separate, juvenile justice system? Throughout most of the juvenile court's 100-year history, there was little doubt that we did. Juvenile courts allowed society to intervene early in the lives of troubled youth and they prevented a variety of horrors that occurred whenever young defendants were thrown in with adult criminals. Defending the juvenile court was instinctive among youth advocates, social workers, family therapists, clergy, educators, defense attorneys, judges, and even many prosecutors.

If there were no costs to be paid for maintaining a separate juvenile court, there would be no need to debate its existence now. All conscientious and well-intentioned people would support the juvenile court without question. In recent years, however, it has become clear that efforts to retain the separate, juvenile court entail significant costs, for the justice system and for youth.

Juvenile justice as currently practiced imposes two significant costs on American youth. First, the juvenile court itself no longer delivers on its promise (rehabilitation and low stigma in exchange for less due process). Second, the continuing existence of the juvenile justice system (even if in name only) allows courts, corrections, and other youth-serving agencies to ignore the inherent youthfulness of many offenders now defined as adults. Thousands of 14-year-old and 15-year-old "adults" are removed to criminal courts every year to be treated just like any other adult. They are no longer a concern to youth-serving professionals. Of course, neither are the many more thousands of youths ages 18 and 19 who are viewed through the same either—or prism, either juvenile or adult.

The growing use of criminal court transfer (or waiver) has been very damaging to the institutional integrity of the juvenile court. Public safety proponents are unduly focused on increasing the use of transfer, despite research casting doubt on its effectiveness. At the same time, youth advocates have painted themselves into a corner. They are compelled to relinquish large portions of the juvenile court's original caseload in exchange for whatever remnants of the juvenile system policymakers might agree to preserve. In recent years, there have been few voices of opposition willing to challenge state lawmakers each time they designate another group of juveniles for transfer to adult court. Few complained when New Hampshire and Wisconsin lowered the age of criminal court jurisdiction in 1996, effectively transferring all 17-year-olds in those states to the adult court system.

Growing numbers of youth as young as age 13 are tried and sentenced in criminal courts that are often not prepared to create specialized procedures and programs for developing adolescents. The juvenile justice professionals who would be most qualified to design such programs are not interested in (or welcomed by) the adult system. In effect, the juvenile justice system sacrifices one group of youth (legally defined as adults) in an effort to save its programs for a second group (legal juveniles).

Undoing Traditional Juvenile Justice

Today's juvenile system is vulnerable to abolition because it attracts intense criticism from the public. Some of this criticism stems from ignorance of juvenile law and its purpose, but not all of it comes from lack of information. Many people simply no longer accept the concept of delinquency, or diminished legal responsibility due to age. To them, a juvenile drug dealer is still a drug dealer. When a 13-year-old Oklahoma boy fired a gun at his school striking several classmates in December 1999, the local prosecutor was asked on national television why he was seeking to handle the case in adult court. "This type of crime," he replied, "requires a serious response." He elaborated that according to Oklahoma law, a juvenile offender cannot be held in secure confinement beyond age 19.

Equating seriousness with the length of confinement conflicts with the traditional concept of juvenile justice, but support for traditional juvenile justice is wearing thin. Federal and state lawmakers have enacted sweeping changes in the nation's juvenile justice systems and the pace of change continued even when juvenile violence began to plummet in the mid-1990s. Nearly all states have passed laws to send far more juveniles to criminal court and some jurisdictions have introduced formal sentencing guidelines that limit the discretion of juvenile court judges. Together, these efforts have begun to unravel the juvenile court's reason for being.

Transfers to Criminal Court

No issue in juvenile justice captures the attention of the public or of policymakers like criminal court transfer. Many policymakers believe that serious juvenile offenders should be tried in criminal court in order to achieve more certain and more severe punishment. Does this, in fact, happen? Does the public get more punishment for its money when juveniles are tried as adults? Researchers who examine this question tend to find that the use of transfer does increase the certainty and severity of legal sanctions, but only for the most serious cases, perhaps 30 percent of transferred juveniles.

In about half of all transfers, the offenders receive sentences comparable to what they might have received in juvenile court. Some (about one-fifth) actually receive more lenient treatment in criminal court. Some may be convicted of lesser offenses or the charges against them may be dismissed due to the greater evidentiary scrutiny in criminal court. The bottom line is that criminal court transfer does not ensure incarceration, and it does not always increase sentence lengths even in cases that do result in incarceration. Yet, few policies are as popular with the public or with elected officials.

During the 1980s and 1990s, lawmakers enacted new transfer laws on an almost annual basis. Moreover, there was an increase in laws that moved entire classes of young offenders into criminal court without the involvement of juvenile court judges. Judicial authority in transfer decisions was diminished while the role of prosecutors and legislatures increased. Nonjudicial mechanisms now account for the vast majority of juvenile transfers.

For instance, many states enacted policies that made judicial waiver presumptive, shifting the burden of proof from the prosecution to the defense. Presumptive waiver provisions typically require a defense attorney to show proof that a youth is amenable to juvenile court handling. Otherwise, the juvenile is transferred to criminal court....

Another increasingly popular strategy for moving juveniles into the criminal courts is mandatory waiver. While presumptive waiver allows juveniles to rebut the presumption of nonamenability, mandatory waiver provides no such escape. If a juvenile meets the criteria for mandatory waiver, a juvenile court judge is left with no choice but to transfer jurisdiction. Mandatory transfers became very common during the 1990s after being quite rare as recently as the 1970s....

Other mechanisms have contributed even more to the deterioration of the juvenile justice system. One mechanism that became widespread during the 1980s and 1990s was statutory exclusion, known in some states as automatic transfer. Statutory exclusion laws mandate that some young offenders are transferred automatically to criminal court as soon as they are charged with certain offenses. Judicial consent is unnecessary. If a youth is at least a certain age and charged with a certain offense, state law places the case directly in criminal court. Georgia, for example, excludes all juveniles age 13 and older from juvenile court if they are charged with one of several violent offenses such as murder, voluntary manslaughter, rape, or armed robbery with a firearm. Arizona automatically excludes juveniles charged with any felony if the youth was adjudicated for two or more prior felony offenses. As of 1997, 28 states had legislation to exclude at least some juveniles from the juvenile court.

Direct file, also known as concurrent jurisdiction or prosecutor discretion, is another increasingly prominent form of criminal court transfer. Direct file laws give prosecutors the discretion to prosecute juveniles either in juvenile or adult court. . . .

Blended Sentencing

Transferring juveniles to the adult court system is the most widely recognized method of increasing the severity of sanctions for young offenders, but it is not the only method. During the 1990s, some states gave judges the power to blend criminal court sentences with juvenile court dispositions. Instead of choosing between sentencing a youth in juvenile or adult court, judges can draw upon both systems. A youth might begin a period of confinement in a juvenile facility before being sent to an adult prison at age 18.

Blended sentencing policies were devised primarily to provide longer terms of incarceration for juveniles, but they also helped to blur the distinction between juvenile justice and adult justice. Increasing the variety of sentencing options may reduce the resistance of courts to handle very young offenders in the adult system since juveniles may not be subject to immediate confinement with adults. Blended sentencing policies may also allow judges to draw upon the traditionally richer treatment and supervision resources available in the juvenile justice system without having to sacrifice the lengthy periods of incarceration once available only in the criminal court system. . . .

Mandatory Minimums and Sentencing Guidelines

Sentencing guidelines and mandatory minimum policies for juveniles also began to proliferate during the 1980s

and 1990s. As of 1997, 17 states and the District of Columbia had enacted some type of mandatory minimum sentencing provisions for at least some juvenile offenders. Some jurisdictions applied sentencing guidelines to juveniles by first requiring that they be tried in criminal court, but others (e.g., Arizona, Utah, and Wyoming) enacted formal sentencing guidelines that applied to juvenile delinquency cases handled by juvenile court judges. These laws required juvenile court dispositions to be consistent with a pre-defined sentencing menu based upon the youth's most recent offense and prior record.

The use of structured sentencing fundamentally contradicts the basic premise of juvenile justice by making sentence length proportional to the severity of an offense rather than basing court outcomes on the characteristics and life problems of offenders. As the popularity of these policies increases, it becomes very difficult to justify the continuation of a juvenile justice system that fails to provide complete due process protections for the youth it handles.

Reduced Confidentiality

Almost all juvenile court proceedings and records were confidential as recently as the 1960s. Confidentiality was an integral part of the traditional juvenile justice model, based upon the theory that publicly designating a juvenile as a law violator would stigmatize a young person. This stigma would then encourage the juvenile to adopt a deviant self-image and reduce the potential for rehabilitation.

As juvenile justice policy became more contentious during the 1980s and

1990s, support for confidentiality protections began to erode. Practical issues such as jurisdictional information sharing and greater media interest in juvenile court proceedings began to win out over confidentiality. Most states opened their juvenile court proceedings or records to the public and to the media. By 1997, 30 states had enacted provisions to allow open hearings in at least some juvenile cases. Forty-two states had enacted legislation authorizing the release and publication of the names and addresses of alleged juvenile offenders in some cases. States also began to allow more juveniles to be fingerprinted and photographed. Nearly all states now allow juvenile fingerprints to be included in criminal history records, and nearly all states authorize juveniles to be photographed for later identification.

In addition, many states enacted laws that required juvenile records to remain open longer or prevented the sealing or destruction of juvenile records altogether, typically those involving violent or serious offenses. Florida, for example, requires records about juveniles considered habitual offenders to be retained until the offender reaches age 26. North Carolina prevents authorities from expunging records altogether for certain serious offenses. By 1997, half the states had enacted laws restricting the sealing and/or expunging of juvenile records.

Using Juvenile Records in Criminal Court

Finally, some states have even passed laws enabling juvenile court records to affect criminal court sentences. Enhancing criminal court sentences

with juvenile court adjudications abrogates the agreement that allowed the juvenile court to exist in the first place. Adjudication in juvenile court begins to involve potentially serious jeopardy for youth.

As of 1997, according to research by Joseph Sanborn, all 50 states and the District of Columbia had enacted statutes or court rules allowing this practice or they had case law that sanctioned it. For example, Illinois and Indiana allow juvenile offense histories to serve as sufficient grounds for increasing sentence length or imposing consecutive sentences. Three states (California, Louisiana, and Texas) allow juvenile adjudications to serve as the first and second "strikes" against an adult offender. Thus, an offender with two prior juvenile court adjudications could face life in prison for a first appearance in criminal court.

Chronic Frustration

These changes were implemented in response to public demands for tougher juvenile crime policies. Yet, the public still views the juvenile court as a weak and inadequate response to juvenile crime. As always, the most popular response to this perception is to send more juveniles to criminal court. Not because criminal courts have been found to be more effective than juvenile courts, but because the adult system offers a more potent symbol of crime control than does the juvenile court. Professor Franklin Zimring of U.C. Berkeley points out that the impetus to enact new crime legislation is nearly always its symbolic value rather than its operational impact.

This is why one wave of reform is inevitably followed by another.

Perhaps the public's frustration with the juvenile justice system is perpetuated by the fact that juvenile courts are a distinct and highly visible component of the criminal justice system. Individual, criminal acts by 25-year-olds, or divorced people, or computer programmers do not often provoke calls for sweeping reforms of the criminal law. There is no system set aside for these groups. Every shocking crime by a young person, on the other hand, calls attention to possible problems in the court system especially designed to deal with juveniles. The juvenile justice system acts like a magnet, attracting the public's frustrations about the crime problem, even if juveniles are only a small part of the problem.

Every time juvenile crime appears in the headlines, Americans wonder why the police refer to the youth involved as a delinquent and not simply as a criminal. Why does the juvenile court have its own, unique process and vocabulary? Why do officials avoid using words like "verdict" and "conviction" and instead describe the juvenile court as "establishing facts" and "reaching adjudication"? If a long prison term is warranted, why can't it be imposed by a juvenile court? Why do prosecutors first have to transfer the case to adult court? Juvenile court begins to sound like a synonym for weak and lenient.

Even professionals who work in the juvenile justice system can be confused by juvenile law and procedure. This author recently participated in a workshop for administrators and judges representing every juvenile court jurisdiction in one western state.

During the workshop, an experienced juvenile court clerk observed that juvenile court terminology seems mainly intended to obscure the court process and to keep the public from understanding it completely. Of those attending the workshop, only half seemed to fully support the continued use of the juvenile court's unique terminology.

The words used in the juvenile court, of course, are intended to symbolize the unique mission and legal philosophy of the juvenile justice system. Youths adjudicated in juvenile court are technically not guilty of criminal offenses. Instead, they are "found to be delinquent" which authorizes the juvenile court to intervene in their behalf, even if the court's intervention includes locked confinement. This legal distinction supposedly spares youth the stigma of a "guilty" verdict and preserves the chances that one day they can again be productive citizens without the taint of a criminal conviction.

A century of juvenile court jurisprudence has established that the juvenile justice system is supposed to be different from the criminal justice system. Increasingly, however, it is not different in the ways that once counted the most. The juvenile court's existence inflames political rhetoric but it fails to deliver quality justice for all youth.

Beyond Dichotomy: A New "Youth Justice" System

Youth advocates may need to reconsider their position on the juvenile court. Instead of concerning themselves only with youth who still happen to be legal juveniles, they may want to shift their focus and work to ensure fair and timely justice for all youth—even those processed in the criminal court system. This work could be done from either side of the juvenile-criminal border, by making youth-oriented improvements from within the criminal justice system, or by helping juvenile justice professionals to get involved in programs for young adult offenders. It may be even more effective, however, if the border no longer existed.

Criminal courts are not as evil and juvenile courts are not as virtuous as some might suggest. The justice system as a whole might benefit if lawmakers, judges, and practitioners were able to stop fighting over the politically hobbled delinquency jurisdiction of the juvenile court. If delinquency laws were abolished and all offenders young and old were handled in an integrated criminal court system, youth advocates could begin to focus on ensuring the quality of the process used for all youth.

The question is how to get from here to there. How can we build a new justice system that protects the public safety and the rights of youth while ensuring that youthful offenders get every chance they deserve to mend their ways and rejoin society? One way to begin may be to take advantage of the growing diversity of specialized courts.

The public generally assumes there are only two types of courts—criminal or juvenile. Consequently, any effort to increase the symbolic strength of juvenile crime policy necessarily favors making greater use of criminal courts. American courts, however, are far more diverse than this. Innovative, specialized courts such as drug courts, gun courts, and community-based courts are bringing new ideas and a wider range of choices to the criminal justice system. Some of these new courts actually resemble the traditional juvenile court in their philosophy of human behavior, their approach to processing cases, and their efforts to monitor offender compliance with court orders by close, judicial supervision.

For the past two decades, state and federal officials have been slowly dismantling the juvenile justice system without much thought as to what will replace it. The emergence of innovative, specialized courts within the adult system presents an unprecedented opportunity to create a new "youth justice system." Ideally, this new system would retain the best features of the juvenile court while gradually incorporating new ideas and procedures developed by the specialized courts now spreading across the country.

Eventually, every state could begin to implement a wide assortment of court models and establish individualized intake procedures for routing young offenders to the most appropriate forum. Once such a system was fully in place, the old dichotomy of juvenile court versus adult court may no longer seem as important. Lawmakers may be able to consider abolishing the juvenile court's delinquency jurisdiction and improve the coherence of criminal justice policy for all youth. Most importantly, the juvenile court would no longer be such an easy target when politicians go looking for symbolic victories over crime.

After all, the central issue is not whether young offenders are called delinquents. The real issue is what happens when young people are arrested and when they appear in court. What process is used to determine their culpability? Who chooses the most appropriate response for each case? How quickly does the process occur, and does it ensure the safety of the public while guarding the rights of offenders? Is the process designed to maximize each person's chances of rejoining the law-abiding community?

Satisfactory answers to these questions will be possible only when every community has an effective, understandable intake process, a fair and efficient system of fact finding and adjudication, and a diverse menu of services and sanctions that are suitable for a wide range of offenders. Maintaining the juvenile court and its separate delinquency jurisdiction may have once guaranteed such a system for young people. The benefits are far less certain today.

Conclusion

Recent decreases in juvenile violence offer the nation's policymakers an opportunity to pause and reflect upon how they have changed the juvenile court and what its future should be. This is a good time to ask whether a separate system of juvenile justice is in fact sustainable, either legally or politically. If not, how can state and local officials design a new system that will meet the needs of youth and their communities during the next century? There may be just enough time to fashion a new youth justice system before the next violent crime wave comes along. . . . ■

What of the Future? Envisioning an Effective Juvenile Court

Hon. Arthur L. Burnett, Sr.

It is not uncommon to hear that "our children are our future" and "it takes a whole village to raise a child," but society has a long way to go to substantively implement these concepts. As we enter the 21st century there must be a commitment to a stronger, reinvigorated, and more innovative juvenile court system. In the past decade, the emphasis has turned from rehabilitation and treatment to punishment, as state legislators pass statutes that remove juveniles from the jurisdiction of the juvenile court in order to treat many more of them as adults. In fact, the public perception of extremely violent youth is based on the acts of a small number of juveniles with ready access to guns. The age of transfer has been lowered in many jurisdictions, and a broader range of felonies can lead to adjudication as an adult. Fully 90 percent of all states have toughened their juvenile justice laws in recent years, and some states have no minimum age of transfer. But the conduct of the violent few should not govern the policies as to the role of juvenile courts in the 21st century. What legislators and executive officials should do is provide the juvenile courts with greater resources to deal effectively with children, revitalizing the courts in the context of contemporary society and giving them the capacity to achieve the purpose for which they were originally created. With such resources, juvenile judges and administrators must be more creative and effective in utilizing them to achieve the maximum results desired. Policymakers, such as legislators and executive branch officials, can no longer afford to treat the juvenile court as the stepchild in the overall court system. Some would argue that given the importance of reaching troubled youth in the most formative time in their lives, juvenile courts should be placed at the head of the line for sufficient financial funding and proper staffing with committed judges, social workers, psychologists, psychiatrists, and other personnel necessary to meet the demand. For many courts, the problem is finding appropriate programs in which to place troubled children. This is especially true for indigent youth.

Choosing the Court's Mission

As we begin the 21st century, what should be the mission of the juvenile court? Should its role be limited only to cases involving the first-time, non-violent offender, who offers the optimum opportunity for success, where it can devote more of its resources and energies to prevent recidivism? Is this approach too limited? Or should the juvenile court have an expansive jurisdiction that includes repeaters and those charged with violent offenses, giving discretion to judges to determine, based on an adequate factual record after a due process hearing, when a juvenile warrants waiver to adult criminal court because he or she can no longer be handled in the juvenile court system? Instead, for the child in the margins, where the judgment call may be difficult, why not try the "blended sentencing" approach enacted into laws in New Mexico and Minnesota. Blended sentencing, which permits juvenile court judges to impose juvenile and adult sentences at the same time, is designed to reduce reliance upon automatic and discretionary transfer, allowing the "transfer" decision to be made after a child's experience with juvenile court interventions can be evaluated. The effect of a latent adult sentence provides a powerful incentive for the juvenile to respond to services provided by the juvenile court and protects society if the child does not respond in a positive manner. Blended sentencing schemes impose substantial punishment, provide incentives for rehabilitation, and where rehabilitation works, eliminate the economic and social costs of long-term incarceration in adult prisons. In this connection, note that in 1996 only 9 percent of the juveniles charged were for the violent offenses of criminal homicide, forcible rape, robbery, and aggravated assault.

Half of those charged were for property offenses. Some 10 percent of the juvenile arrests were for drug law violations, and 19 percent were for public order offenses. Juvenile justice policy affecting 100 percent of the American youth should not be predicated upon the alleged violence of 9 percent or less of those arrested. Policy must be guided by consideration for the greatest good for the greatest number of youth while remembering that each child is important as an individual. It is essential that the first time a youngster is brought before the juvenile court, the maximum resources necessary be made available to change his or her attitudes and values so that child does not become a repeater in the juvenile justice system and, ultimately, an adult criminal offender. From this perspective, it is more important that legislators and the executive branch spend more resources on the juvenile court to ensure its maximum efficiency and provision of services than on the adult criminal court. If the juvenile justice system is to be saved from becoming the "farm system" for adult criminal offenders, we must focus more of our resources and attention on early and effective intervention during a child's first contact with the juvenile courts. If successful, this could significantly reduce the number of adult criminal cases in the future. We must start with the quality of the judges and judicial officers serving in our juvenile courts. They must have not only a knowledge of the law applicable to juvenile delinquency cases, but they must recognize one of the fundamental truths upon which the juvenile court is based: Children, by virtue of their age and

inexperience, require special protections under the law. They must fully understand and appreciate the stages of child development, the educational needs of children at various stages in their development, and child behavioral issues. To that purpose, the juvenile court judge and judicial officer must be sufficiently immersed and gain a depth of understanding that equals the substantive knowledge expected of social workers and psychologists who deal with children and their behaviors. They should receive specialized training, which is comprehensive and multidisciplinary. They must also become culturally sensitive so as to appropriately evaluate each child who comes before the juvenile court on the basis of his or her own character and individual value system, without being influenced by stereotypes and assumptions based on race, national origin, and poverty circumstances. This also applies to social workers, psychiatrists, psychologists, probation officers, and others in order to make accurate risk assessments in evaluating each individual child. This is necessary so that the recommendations they make to the judge or judicial officer will reflect the true inner core of that child. Such recommendations then provide the basis for an intelligent decision as to what services will assist that child to become a positive functional youngster who will not offend again. Judges and their staff, with community support, should design and implement effective alternatives to detention that will achieve this objective while keeping the youngster in the community. When a youngster fails to conform to conditions of probation or release in the community, there should be meaningful, graduated sanctions appropriate to the conduct. Detention should be the ultimate sanction when necessary to protect the safety of others and the community. Judges and judicial officers should have a sufficient commitment and dedication to serve in the juvenile court for at least two years to acquire the needed knowledge and expertise. In this manner, the juvenile court can become a highly functioning special court for children—the Children's Court—which can accomplish its mission, provided legislators give it the highest priority along with adequate financial and human resources.

Intake Screening Process

A progressive juvenile court must have an effective intake screening process to evaluate the risk and behavior factors of each child brought before the court. For instance, when the youngster is a first offender for a property offense, a minor assault, or a minor drug offense, an adult from a faith-based organization might come forward to serve as a mentor to that child and as a helper to the parent. The trial on the juvenile petition or complaint could be stayed or deferred for a period of four to six months to determine if the child will improve under the watchful eye of a concerned mentor operating much like a favorite uncle or aunt. If at the end of the deferred prosecution period the child is well adjusted in school and has made positive adjustments in the community, the prosecutor could then drop the charge without jeopardizing the safety of the community or worrying about whether the child felt he or she

had merely received a "slap on the wrist" with no appreciable consequences. Indeed, during this period, 25 or more hours of community service could be required of the youngster—a giving back to the community. In this manner, these mentors could become like Thomas Calhoun Walker of Virginia who served as the "children's lawyer" for African American youth in Virginia in the first half of the last century. According to juvenile justice scholar Professor Robert E. Shepherd of the University of Richmond's T.C. Williams School of Law, Walker persuaded local judges to bond boys who had been jailed into his custody. He would then place them among families of his acquaintance or take them home to his wife. Many of these youths were adopted by these families and went on to college or into a trade without further difficulties. The utilization of church-based or faith-based mentors who are truly committed and dedicated could greatly increase the number of juveniles who correct their ways and become responsible and productive adult citizens in our communities. The only requirement, in order to maintain the church/state separation, is that the court make clear that religious instruction or church attendance must not be required of the child in order to participate in such a program.

Teen Courts

Another alternative available to the juvenile court is the use of "teen courts," also known as "youth courts." In the past decade they have become a popular intervention for young and first-time offenders. The number of teen courts nationwide grew from an estimated 50 programs in 1991 to 400–500 programs in 1998. According to the Office of Juvenile Justice and Delinquency Prevention, survey findings indicated that teen courts nationwide handled approximately 65,000 cases in 1998. Most teen courts do not determine the guilt or innocence of juveniles, rather they serve as diversion alternatives. Although individuals must admit to the charges against them in order to qualify for teen court, no formal adjudication is made nor judgment entered. The types of offenses include theft, misdemeanor assault, disorderly conduct, and possession of alcohol. The most popular teen court model involves the use of an adult judge with juvenile "lawyers." These courts utilize youths in various roles, including prosecutors, defense counsel, and as members of juries that determine factual guilt or as advisory juries to fashion appropriate dispositions. Community service is the most common disposition used in teen court cases. Other dispositions include victim apology letters, apology essays, teen court jury duty, drug/alcohol classes, and monetary restitution. The proponents of such teen or youth courts hope to achieve reduced recidivism, increased pro-social attitudes, and improved perceptions of justice.

In November 1999, the District of Columbia Coalition Against Drugs and Violence voted to support the expansion of the youth court program and to use its influence and outreach efforts to involve more community collaborators in providing the services these youngsters need to ensure that they make a positive social adjustment and do not commit further juvenile offenses. In this way we can expand the availability of services to each individual youngster in a manner expressly designed to treat the problems and behaviors of that individual.

Many youngsters referred to the juvenile justice system are alcohol or drug dependent, or on their way to becoming such. More services need to be provided to the juvenile justice system for addressing these problems in an effective and meaningful fashion. In the Superior Court of the District of Columbia in 1999 a juvenile drug court was established as a 12-month substance abuse treatment program aimed at promoting abstinence and healthy living choices for juveniles and their families. This program is comprehensive in scope and is directed at the nonviolent substance abusing juvenile population. Treatment is designed using a strengths-based model that focuses on the individual's and the family's most positive characteristics. The program is intensive and includes structured supervision, regular court appearances, mandatory drug/alcohol testing, ongoing assessment, group and individual counseling, drug education, family counseling, education and support, recreational therapy, and a myriad of wraparound services designed to support healthy and responsible living. In developing these strengths, the juvenile and his or her family will be empowered to develop a drug-free lifestyle and accomplish goals for responsible living. Upon successful completion of the program, the judge has the authority and power to dismiss the charges that brought the juvenile before the court.

When Cases Go to Trial

When pretrial diversion programs or other approaches do not result in the dismissal of the juvenile delinquency charges, the case must be tried. At this stage it is essential that the juvenile be represented by defense counsel as knowledgeable and competent as any lawyer who would represent a criminal accused in adult criminal court. Young lawyers right out of law school should not merely view juvenile court as a training ground to prepare them to represent adults in criminal court. Rather, they should view the role of defense counsel in juvenile court as being even more demanding than adult court because there are serious questions as to a child's ability and capacity to understand the proceedings and to assist counsel.

Counsel must also fully appreciate the implications of In re Gault, 387 U.S. 1 (1967) and its progeny and be fully competent to protect the constitutional due process rights of the juvenile in the trial process. Further, counsel in juvenile delinquency cases may make a far greater contribution by assisting in designing a disposition plan that may change a child's life, rerouting a juvenile's path from repeat offender to a productive and useful citizen, making significant contributions to the community in which he or she will live as an adult. Effective, committed, and knowledgeable lawyers for juveniles should come forward to advocate for each child at every stage of the proceeding.

It is also important that a substantial number of minority lawyers come forward to handle juvenile delinquency cases. . . . With the disproportionate minority confinement statistics that now exist in this country, minority lawyers must accept the challenge of educating judges, psychologists, social workers, and others in the juvenile justice system on how better to assess and evaluate all minority youths—their inner values, mores, cultural and family traditions—so as to design effective rehabilitation programs in connection with proposed dispositions, which lead to probation and a change of attitudes and values that result in a child becoming a responsible, productive, and law abiding individual.

Effective representation requires counsel to meet the juvenile client immediately in order to understand what brings the child to court. Counsel should then gather critical information from the family, schools, and social service agencies and conduct at least a preliminary inquiry into the nature of the charges. This will enable the lawyer to present the client in the best light. If pretrial release is not obtained on the initial presentment, counsel should endeavor to obtain a review proceeding as to release, gather additional information, and make the best case possible for the release of the client to the community. Obtaining a strong potential mentor, setting up a program of regular school attendance that will be monitored, and an after-school program to ensure that the child is engaged in positive activities should be ingredients of any release plan. If there is indication of drug use, drug testing and counseling should enable counsel to obtain the release of the juvenile, unless the offense is an exceptionally violent one or the youth has a serious history of prior offenses. In this way, counsel can assist in reducing the disproportionate confinement of minority youth held in pretrial detention. Such an approach by defense counsel at the very beginning of the case is absolutely necessary to ensure that juveniles are not held in secure detention when they pose no significant danger to themselves or others. Once the juvenile has been released from pretrial detention, or if the child continues to be held, counsel should be just as diligent in the investigation of the case and preparation for trial as if it were an adult criminal trial.

Effective Probation

If the charges against the juvenile are sustained, the juvenile will need continued representation to ensure that the disposition-sentencing-order is fair and appropriate. Putting a youngster on probation must be more than imposing conditions that tell the youngster "to go and sin no more." There must be more than the hortatory "thou shall not" with reference to engaging in future delinquent or criminal conduct. Effective probation programs for a youth must provide for giving the offender the required literacy skills and education necessary to function in society in the 21st century. Probation conditions should be established to achieve giving the probationer the basic life skills and the job training to be employable and self-sustaining once the probation period is successfully completed. Juvenile court judges should seek to tap all available community resources as options for meaningful probation conditions that will change values and really rehabilitate. Indeed, the juvenile court may seek to establish a collaborative working relationship with community groups that work with youths to give them positive direction

and to provide the youth probationer with the wherewithal to change his or her life. Such an example is Project Soar, which ran from fall 1995 to summer 1997. Offenders in that program ran a pizza delivery restaurant, participated in after-school tutoring, and learned computer-base skills. This program was designed to create a special place for young offenders who were committed to leaving criminal behavior behind and working hard to improve their academic skills, gain employment experience, and enhance their own ability to make good decisions. In the spring of 1997 this program was expanded into a model comprehensive youth development program and renamed "See Forever," an innovative program integrating academics, the world of work, and life skills. "See Forever" opened its doors in September 1997 as a tuition-free, alternative school and real-world employment training program. In May 1998 the founders created an affiliate, a second student-based business, the "See Forever Student Tech Shop," at which students use their technical skills to produce technology/graphics design products and to teach parents and siblings computer skills. In the summer of 1998 the founders of these entities separately incorporated the school to establish it as a public charter school and named it "The Maya Angelou Public Charter School" as a sole member nonprofit subsidiary of "See Forever." The school held its first graduation in July 1999 and all three of its graduates entered college this past fall. During the past summer two of its graduates taught a six-week computer course to seven students participating in the Superior Court Juvenile Drug Court/Probation program in Washington, D.C. In September 1999, the school started with 52 students and opened its fourth "See Forever" residence. Thirteen students now live in small "homes" around the school, each staffed by a "See Forever" adult; it is also planning to open another girls' residence in the near future. Such a resource for referral of offenders placed on probation by juvenile court judges of the Superior Court of the District of Columbia could serve as a model for changing lives and achieving the optimum success with juvenile probationers.

Another example of an exciting resource for offenders in the Washington, D.C., court system is the ARCH program—Action to Rehabilitate Community Housing. Its YouthBuild Program was recently funded by a $650,000 grant from the U.S. Department of Housing and Urban Development. This program will provide vocational training and education to 40 District of Columbia youths, aged 16 to 24, who are under the control of the superior court. This pilot program will combine academic instruction, vocational training in construction, leadership development, community service, life and employability skills training, social services and job placement, and follow-up. This will be the first YouthBuild program in the country that will serve only adjudicated youth. It is contemplated that the average stay in the program will be nine to 14 months and that every effort will be made to place a youth who completes the program with an employer. This is a program with a real pragmatic promise of changing lives.

Another program with much realistic promise is the Urban Services Program, also operated by the Superior Court of the District of Columbia. This is a year-long intensive probation supervision program for nonviolent youthful offenders between the ages of 14 and 26. It is a special emphasis program, the purpose of which is to interrupt and reduce criminal activities by providing a highly structured, community-based, intensely supervised program conducted in three phases. The first stage is a residential boot camp to build structure and discipline in a probationer's life. During the first 30 days, emphasis is placed on physical conditioning, ropes course, drills, bonding, survival skills, nutrition, and therapeutic groups, focused on anger management, conflict resolution, value clarification, and goal setting. The second stage lasts six months during which time the emphasis is on life preparation. Probation officers are charged with developing an individualized treatment plan that addresses the needs of the offender based on an educational assessment, drug abuse assessment, and goals set by the offender during the first stage. Included in this intensive community supervision are electronic monitoring, home visits, twice weekly urine tests, referrals for employment readiness, job placements, GED preparation or school advocacy, therapeutic recreation, and other specific referrals deemed appropriate to assist the offender with becoming a productive law-abiding citizen. During the final phase, which runs five months, based on positive progress, office visits are reduced and probation officers continue to monitor the individual's compliance with the individualized treatment plans and probation conditions.

When, after adjudication, it becomes necessary for a juvenile court judge to decide on a disposition of probation or detention for a child, the judge should by statute be given the authority to fashion a probation program that is holistic in nature and that includes the entire family. Many youths before a juvenile court come from dysfunctional families where a multitude of legal, social, and economic issues are intertwined. Much delinquent behavior can be traced to the family dynamics. Judges should be authorized to order family members into counseling and treatment along with the juvenile. When the parent or guardian refuses to comply, the court by statute should have the authority to impose sanctions, including contempt.

There must be effective monitoring of compliance with even regular conditions of probation by the youth by the assigned probation officer or social worker. One such creative example is the school-based probation officer program in Pennsylvania. Truancy is frequently at the foundation of a child becoming a juvenile delinquent; by putting probation officers physically in the school they can monitor their probationers' school attendance and they can also meet with them, provide them counseling, and even tutor them in meeting their educational requirements. Pennsylvania has placed more than 150 probation officers in schools full-time. The probation officer's primary role is to provide the probationers who attend the school with daily intensive supervision. Further, this school-based model allows the probation officers to maintain close contact with the juveniles under their supervision, verify their attendance, and monitor their academic progress and general behavior.

When Detention Is Needed

Not all youngsters who are adjudicated juvenile offenders are suitable candidates, however, for probation. We recognize that there must be due consideration given to factors of accountability and protection of individuals in the community. Indeed, in some circumstances involving youngsters who are incorrigible or so committed to engaging in antisocial and juvenile offenses, it may become necessary to detain them even in pretrial custody. Thus, juvenile court judges and judicial officers must develop the keen insight and judgment to identify those individual juveniles where detention is necessary for the protection of individuals in our communities and to achieve their rehabilitation to the extent possible. In such situations, concerns for accountability and punishment must also play a role in the disposition. Such detention must not be in adult facilities, to ensure that these children are not abused and harmed nor educated in the ways of becoming hardened criminals, but should rather be in separate juvenile detention facilities where their behaviors can be addressed and hopefully corrected. Of the highest priority is the development and utilization of risk assessment tools to determine who should be detained. These tools must be carefully designed and applied as not to sweep too broadly to include in the net for detention those youngsters who can be released into the community with suitable monitoring and supervision so as not to be a threat to the safety of any individual in the community.

Further, a prudent legislative policy should leave in the hands of experienced juvenile court judges the decision as to which juveniles should be prosecuted as adults. In some exceptional cases involving violent, habitual, and older offenders, public safety considerations may mandate handling that child in the adult criminal justice system. Such an approach continues our cherished tradition of permitting individualized justice based on the conduct involved in the incident and the personal history of the individual youngster. A juvenile should be dealt with through individualized justice considerations based on his or her own conduct and particular needs, rather than a process solely dictated by the offense. These considerations are ill-served when the prosecutor is given the authority to file charges directly against a juvenile at a specific age and the offense involves multiple offenders, some of whom are adults and others juveniles, but who may be prosecuted as adults solely because the prosecution wishes to try the case only one time and not to expose the government's witnesses to multiple cases in different courts. It is also frequently the case that it is not clear at the beginning whether a juvenile was merely present, and thus perhaps only a material witness, or whether the juvenile was an aider and abettor in the particular incident that is the subject of the criminal charges. Further, it appears that far more juveniles are prosecuted as adults in criminal court when a prosecutor is given the authority to file directly against a youth, and thus the net pulls far more

youths into adult criminal court then may be in the interest of a sound criminal justice system or a sound juvenile justice system. With the benefit of specific knowledge and information about the offender and the offense, experienced juvenile court judges are best able to select the most serious, violent, and chronic juvenile offenders to be transferred after due process hearings in open court to an adult court for criminal prosecution. In all cases, it's important to remember that a 14-year-old sentenced to 10 years in adult prison for unarmed robbery in a purse snatching will return as a 24-year-old who has spent the formative years without affection or guidance and often the subject of prison abuse.

Furthermore, it has been suggested that judges serving on juvenile courts should not be isolated from the community in which they serve, merely sitting on the bench and going to and from home and otherwise leading a very private existence. Rather, they have a duty to reach out to the community and tap community resources on behalf of children. Further, they can urge the creation of community resources and programs for children. They can also talk to civic clubs and community organizations to obtain better services for children and youth. They can encourage broader opportunities and exposures for our youths through internships, work-study experiences, and community involvement. Such activities could help mold their values and attitudes in a way to decrease the likelihood that they will engage in conduct detrimental to their own advancement and achievement. Simultaneously, this improved behavior would promote the safety and protection of all citizens in the community. Such activities would advance the administration of justice, especially in our juvenile courts, and could well reduce the number of juvenile delinquency cases and criminal cases in adult court that would thereafter come into the court system.

In conclusion, a revitalized and reinvigorated juvenile court in this century, adequately financed by the legislature, and staffed with dedicated and committed judges and support staff, can significantly reverse the crime trends in America. However, no court system by itself can solve the delinquency or crime problem. The circumstances of poverty and other socioeconomic factors in our society, along with cultural and diversity issues and personality of individuals, will continue to have a significant role on delinquency and crime in the United States. But to the extent that sufficient funding and adequate human resources are made available to the juvenile courts, they can function effectively to achieve the mission of rehabilitating many juvenile offenders, reducing recidivism in those who come before the court, and, to a significant degree, reduce the number of individuals who go on to become adult criminal offenders. In this way, the juvenile courts of the future can make a significant contribution to improving the quality of lives of the individuals who come before them and to a significant degree improve the quality of life in the communities they serve, including some incremental increase in the protection and safety of the citizens living in those communities. . . . ∎

▚ The Continuing Debate

What Is New

"Blended sentencing," in which the juvenile or the criminal court can impose sentences to either juvenile or adult facilities and programs (or to both), is becoming increasingly common. It is designed to allow courts to sentence juveniles more harshly: under some juvenile court procedures, juveniles cannot be confined to juvenile facilities beyond a certain age, when they must be released. With blended sentences, judges can sentence juveniles to juvenile facilities until they reach 18, and sentence them to then be transferred to an adult prison. However, such blended sentences may still be less harsh than transferring a child to the adult criminal court, where—following conviction—the child will be sent immediately to an adult prison. Furthermore, with blended sentencing, the judge would sometimes have the option of suspending the adult prison sentence if juvenile rehabilitation has gone well.

Where to Find More

Jeffrey A. Butts (with Daniel P. Mears) explores innovations to make a rehabilitative juvenile justice system effective in "Reviving Juvenile Justice in a Get-Tough Era," *Youth and Society*, Volume 33, Number 2 (December 2001): 169–198. See also a book he wrote with A. V. Harrell, *Delinquents or Criminals? Policy Options for Juvenile Offenders* (Washington, DC: The Urban Institute, 1998). Gary S. Katzmann, editor, *Securing Our Children's Future: New Approaches to Juvenile Justice and Youth Violence* (Washington, DC: Brookings Institute Press, 2002), contains a number of interesting proposals concerning juvenile justice.

Barry C. Feld, "Abolish the Juvenile Court: Youthfulness, Criminal Responsibility, and Sentencing Policy," *Journal of Criminal Law and Criminology*, Volume 88 (Fall 1997): 68–136, advocates doing away altogether with the juvenile court system, which he describes as "a punitive juvenile court whose only remaining distinctions are its persisting procedural deficiencies." See also Feld's "Juvenile (In)justice and the Criminal Court Alternative," *Crime and Delinquency*, Volume 39 (1993): 403–424.

The debunking of the sensationalist "superpredator" accounts of juvenile crime can be found in *Youth Violence: A Report of the Surgeon General* 5 (2001); and V. E. Kappeler, M. Blumberg, and G. W. Potter, *The Mythology of Crime and Criminal Justice*, 3rd Edition (Prospect Heights, IL: Waveland, 2000).

There is an excellent review of the policy of transferring juveniles to adult criminal courts in Richard E. Redding, "The Effects of Adjudicating and Sentencing Juveniles as Adults: Research and Policy Implications," *Youth Violence and Justice*, Volume 1, Number 2 (April 2003): 128–155. The psychological and social effects of transferring juveniles to criminal courts, and of placing them in adult prisons, are examined in R. J. Sampson and J. H. Laub, *Crime in the Making: Pathways and Turning Points in Life* (Cambridge, MA: Harvard University Press, 1993). The brutal conditions of existence for juveniles in adult prisons—the high rates of suicide, sexual and physical assault, the conditioning for violence—are described in M. Beyer, "Experts for Juveniles at Risk of Adult Sentences," in P. Puritz, A. Capozello, and W. Shang, editors, *More than Meets the Eye: Rethinking Assessment, Competency and Sentencing for a Harsher Era of Juvenile Justice* (Washington, DC: American Bar Association, Juvenile Justice Center, 1997): 1–22.

There are some indications of a movement back toward rehabilitation and special treatment for juveniles; see Alida V. Merlo, "Juvenile Justice at the Crossroads: Presidential Address to the Academy of Criminal Justice Sciences," *Justice Quarterly*, Volume 17 (2000): 639–661; and Alida V. Merlo and Peter J. Benekos, "Defining Juvenile Justice in the 21st Century," *Youth Violence and Juvenile Justice*, Volume 1, Number 3 (July 2003): 276–288. A strong supporter of a rehabilitative model of juvenile justice is Dan Macallair, in "Reaffirming Rehabilitation in Juvenile Justice," *Youth and Society*, Volume 25, Number 1 (September 1993): 104–125.

Many regard the restorative justice model as particularly promising when dealing with juvenile offenders; see Lynn S. Urban, Jenna L. St. Cyr, and Scott H. Decker, "Goal Conflict in the Juvenile Court: The Evolution of Sentencing Practices in the United States," *Journal of Contemporary Criminal Justice*, Volume 19, Number 4 (November 2003): 454–479, for discussion of restorative justice in juvenile settings; see also the suggested readings for Chapter 8.

"Blended sentencing" is discussed by R. E. Redding and J. C. Howell, in "Blended Sentencing in American Juvenile Courts," in J. Fagan and R. E. Redding, editors, *The Changing Borders of Juvenile Justice: Transfer of Adolescents to the Criminal Court* (Chicago: University of Chicago Press, 2000): 75–96; the book contains a number of excellent articles on the implications of trying adolescents in criminal courts and punishing them in adult prisons. F. E. Zimring, *American Youth Violence* (New York: Oxford University Press, 1998), raises grave concerns about blended sentencing and its implications for juvenile rehabilitation.

The PBS Frontline documentary series produced an excellent study of the juvenile justice system, and the web page accompanying the program can be found at www.pbs.org/wgbh/pages/frontline/shows/juvenile/bench.html.

18

Should We Continue the "War on Drugs"?

The War on Illegal Drugs Must Continue

Advocate: Theodore Dalrymple, a physician and psychiatrist who works in a British prison. A contributing editor of *City Journal*, he recently wrote *Life at the Bottom: The Worldview that Makes the Underclass* (Chicago: Ivan R. Dee, 2001).

Source: "Don't Legalize Drugs," *City Journal*, Volume 7, Number 2 (Spring 1997).

The War on Drugs Is Counterproductive

Advocates: Eric L. Jensen, Professor of Sociology at the University of Idaho; Jurg Gerber, Professor in the College of Criminal Justice, Sam Houston State University; and Clayton Mosher, Associate Professor of Sociology, Washington State University, Vancouver.

Source: "Social Consequences of the War on Drugs: The Legacy of Failed Policy," *Criminal Justice Policy Review*, Volume 15, Number 1 (March 2004): 100–121.

The debate over whether marijuana (and perhaps other illegal drugs) should be decriminalized is not a debate over whether elementary school children should be able to buy marijuana at the candy store or smoke a joint in the school cafeteria after lunch. The question is instead whether to decriminalize possession or sale of illegal drugs (such as marijuana, cocaine, and opium), which is currently punishable by criminal sanctions, and regulate their sale and use much as we now regulate alcohol and tobacco: perhaps *more* strictly, but that is a point of detail, and not the fundamental issue.

Though most conservatives are vehemently against drug decriminalization, there are many leading conservatives—Ethan Nadelmann, for example, but also Nobel Prize economist Milton Friedman, conservative columnist William Buckley, and others—who view the U.S. drug policy not only as a disastrous and expensive failure but also as a fundamental infringement on our rights as adult citizens to make our own decisions about things that affect only ourselves and do not harm others. While those who favor decriminalization are more likely to fall on the liberal side, many liberals also adamantly oppose the decriminalization of drugs.

While currently the U.S. "war on drugs" is being pursued fervently, complete with a "drug czar" and an enormous prison population, other countries—the Netherlands is a noteworthy example—take a very different approach to the problem of drugs. In the Netherlands, marijuana is legally available on a "coffee shop" model, in which shops selling small quantities of marijuana are regulated by local ordinance (and those that prove troublesome are shut down, analogous to the shutting down of U.S. taverns that lose their liquor licenses). While there is dispute concerning the level of drug addiction in the Netherlands, most studies indicate that the rate of adult addiction and teenage drug use is lower than in the United States, and there is no dispute that the violent crime rate there is only a fraction of ours. While other European countries do not have as liberal a policy as the Netherlands, neither do they have policies as harsh as those of the United States, particularly toward the use of marijuana.

There are two major lines of argument concerning drug decriminalization. One is that the current criminal policy is and will remain a costly failure, so we are better off trying a new policy to deal with this ineradicable problem. In this argument, the sociological question of what effect decriminalization would have—on drug addiction, violence, law enforcement—looms large. The other argument is that even if the current criminal program worked, it should still be rejected as a paternalistic program that violates our right of free choice (including the right to make bad choices that harm only ourselves). In the second argument the key question is what are the rights of individuals to make their own decisions (including harmful ones) as opposed to the right of the state to regulate behavior that might harm the individual and perhaps indirectly damage the state?

⁝⁝⁝ Points to Ponder

- Dalrymple acknowledges the importance of freedom, but he opposes the "freedom"of butterflies and children. What concept of freedom does Dalrymple favor? Which concept of "freedom" seems more plausible? Are there other models for "freedom" than the two discussed by Dalrymple?
- Dalrymple rejects the "pragmatic" argument for legalization: the argument that legalizing drugs would have good practical effects in reducing crime. He claims that legalizing drugs would *possibly* produce another effect, which would possibly lead to *increased* crime. What is the possible effect on which his argument hinges, and how plausible is his supposition?
- Dalrymple claims that "Amsterdam, where access to drugs is relatively unproblematic, is among the most violent and squalid cities in Europe." In fact, Amsterdam in 2001 had a homicide rate of 3.1 for each 100,000 of population, which is comparable to other European cities, and far lower

than in U.S. cities (the 2001 homicide rate in New York City was 6.6, in LA it was 12.6, in Chicago 15.6, and in Detroit 39.3). The Netherlands has significantly less heroin addiction and drug addiction, and significantly fewer drug-related deaths, than in France, Germany, and England, and the rate is far lower than in the United States. And rather than "squalid," it is generally regarded as a particularly clean and beautiful city, and a wonderful place for walking or biking. If Dalrymple is wrong in this claim, does it undercut any key elements of his argument?

- Jensen, Gerber, and Mosher argue that long prison terms for drug offenders ultimately lead to an increase in criminal behavior. In their analysis, what are the steps from higher rates of imprisonment to higher rates of crime?

Don't Legalize Drugs

Theodore Dalrymple

There is a progression in the minds of men: first the unthinkable becomes thinkable, and then it becomes an orthodoxy whose truth seems so obvious that no one remembers that anyone ever thought differently. This is just what is happening with the idea of legalizing drugs: it has reached the stage when millions of thinking men are agreed that allowing people to take whatever they like is the obvious, indeed only, solution to the social problems that arise from the consumption of drugs.

Man's desire to take mind-altering substances is as old as society itself— as are attempts to regulate their consumption. If intoxication in one form or another is inevitable, then so is customary or legal restraint upon that intoxication. But no society until our own has had to contend with the ready availability of so many different mind-altering drugs, combined with a citizenry jealous of its right to pursue its own pleasures in its own way.

The arguments in favor of legalizing the use of all narcotic and stimulant drugs are twofold: philosophical and pragmatic. Neither argument is negligible, but both are mistaken, I believe, and both miss the point.

The philosophic argument is that, in a free society, adults should be permitted to do whatever they please, always provided that they are prepared to take the consequences of their own choices and that they cause no direct harm to others. The locus classicus for this point of view is John Stuart Mill's famous essay On Liberty: "The only purpose for which power

Theodore Dalrymple, "Don't Legalize Drugs," *City Journal*, Volume 7, No. 2 (Spring 1997). Reprinted with permission from *City Journal*.

can be rightfully exercised over any member of the community, against his will, is to prevent harm to others," Mill wrote. "His own good, either physical or moral, is not a sufficient warrant." This radical individualism allows society no part whatever in shaping, determining, or enforcing a moral code: in short, we have nothing in common but our contractual agreement not to interfere with one another as we go about seeking our private pleasures.

In practice, of course, it is exceedingly difficult to make people take all the consequences of their own actions—as they must, if Mill's great principle is to serve as a philosophical guide to policy. Addiction to, or regular use of, most currently prohibited drugs cannot affect only the person who takes them—and not his spouse, children, neighbors, or employers. No man, except possibly a hermit, is an island; and so it is virtually impossible for Mill's principle to apply to any human action whatever, let alone shooting up heroin or smoking crack. Such a principle is virtually useless in determining what should or should not be permitted.

Perhaps we ought not be too harsh on Mill's principle: it's not clear that anyone has ever thought of a better one. But that is precisely the point. Human affairs cannot be decided by an appeal to an infallible rule, expressible in a few words, whose simple application can decide all cases, including whether drugs should be freely available to the entire adult population. Philosophical fundamentalism is not preferable to the religious variety; and because the desiderata of human life are many, and often in conflict with one another, mere philosophical inconsistency in policy—such as permitting the consumption of alcohol while outlawing cocaine—is not a sufficient argument against that policy. We all value freedom, and we all value order; sometimes we sacrifice freedom for order, and sometimes order for freedom. But once a prohibition has been removed, it is hard to restore, even when the new-found freedom proves to have been ill-conceived and socially disastrous.

Even Mill came to see the limitations of his own principle as a guide for policy and to deny that all pleasures were of equal significance for human existence. It was better, he said, to be Socrates discontented than a fool satisfied. Mill acknowledged that some goals were intrinsically worthier of pursuit than others.

This being the case, not all freedoms are equal, and neither are all limitations of freedom: some are serious and some trivial. The freedom we cherish—or should cherish—is not merely that of satisfying our appetites, whatever they happen to be. We are not Dickensian Harold Skimpoles, exclaiming in protest that "Even the butterflies are free!" We are not children who chafe at restrictions because they are restrictions. And we even recognize the apparent paradox that some limitations to our freedoms have the consequence of making us freer overall. The freest man is not the one who slavishly follows his appetites and desires throughout his life—as all too many of my patients have discovered to their cost.

We are prepared to accept limitations to our freedoms for many reasons, not just that of public order. Take an extreme hypothetical case: public exhibitions of necrophilia are quite rightly not permitted, though on Mill's principle they should be. A corpse has no interests and cannot be harmed, because it is no longer a person; and no member of the public is harmed if he has agreed to attend such an exhibition.

Our resolve to prohibit such exhibitions would not be altered if we discovered that millions of people wished to attend them or even if we discovered that millions already were attending them illicitly. Our objection is not based upon pragmatic considerations or upon a head count: it is based upon the wrongness of the would-be exhibitions themselves. The fact that the prohibition represents a genuine restriction of our freedom is of no account.

It might be argued that the freedom to choose among a variety of intoxicating substances is a much more important freedom and that millions of people have derived innocent fun from taking stimulants and narcotics. But the consumption of drugs has the effect of reducing men's freedom by circumscribing the range of their interests. It impairs their ability to pursue more important human aims, such as raising a family and fulfilling civic obligations. Very often it impairs their ability to pursue gainful employment and promotes parasitism. Moreover, far from being expanders of consciousness, most drugs severely limit it. One of the most striking characteristics of drug takers is their intense and tedious self-absorption; and their journeys into inner space are generally forays into inner vacuums. Drug taking is a lazy man's way of pursuing happiness and wisdom, and the

shortcut turns out to be the deadest of dead ends. We lose remarkably little by not being permitted to take drugs.

The idea that freedom is merely the ability to act upon one's whims is surely very thin and hardly begins to capture the complexities of human existence; a man whose appetite is his law strikes us not as liberated but enslaved. And when such a narrowly conceived freedom is made the touchstone of public policy, a dissolution of society is bound to follow. No culture that makes publicly sanctioned self-indulgence its highest good can long survive: a radical egotism is bound to ensue, in which any limitations upon personal behavior are experienced as infringements of basic rights. Distinctions between the important and the trivial, between the freedom to criticize received ideas and the freedom to take LSD, are precisely the standards that keep societies from barbarism.

So the legalization of drugs cannot be supported by philosophical principle. But if the pragmatic argument in favor of legalization were strong enough, it might overwhelm other objections. It is upon this argument that proponents of legalization rest the larger part of their case.

The argument is that the overwhelming majority of the harm done to society by the consumption of currently illicit drugs is caused not by their pharmacological properties but by their prohibition and the resultant criminal activity that prohibition always calls into being. Simple reflection tells us that a supply invariably grows up to meet a demand; and when the demand is widespread, suppression is useless. Indeed, it is harmful, since—by raising the price of the commodity in question—it raises the profits of middlemen, which gives them an even more powerful incentive to stimulate demand further. The vast profits to be made from cocaine and heroin—which, were it not for their illegality, would be cheap and easily affordable even by the poorest in affluent societies—exert a deeply corrupting effect on producers, distributors, consumers, and law enforcers alike. Besides, it is well known that illegality in itself has attractions for youth already inclined to disaffection. Even many of the harmful physical effects of illicit drugs stem from their illegal status: for example, fluctuations in the purity of heroin bought on the street are responsible for many of the deaths by overdose. If the sale and consumption of such drugs were legalized, consumers would know how much they were taking and thus avoid overdoses.

Moreover, since society already permits the use of some mind-altering substances known to be both addictive and harmful, such as alcohol and nicotine, in prohibiting others it appears hypocritical, arbitrary, and dictatorial. Its hypocrisy, as well as its patent failure to enforce its prohibitions successfully, leads inevitably to a decline in respect for the law as a whole. Thus things fall apart, and the center cannot hold.

It stands to reason, therefore, that all these problems would be resolved at a stroke if everyone were permitted to smoke, swallow, or inject anything he chose. The corruption of the police, the luring of children of 11 and 12 into illegal activities, the making of such vast sums of money by drug dealing that legitimate work seems pointless and silly by comparison, and the turf wars that make poor neighborhoods so exceedingly violent and dangerous, would all cease at once were drug taking to be decriminalized and the supply regulated in the same way as alcohol.

But a certain modesty in the face of an inherently unknowable future is surely advisable. That is why prudence is a political virtue. What stands to reason should happen does not necessarily happen in practice. As Goethe said, all theory (even of the monetarist or free-market variety) is gray, but green springs the golden tree of life. If drugs were legalized, I suspect that the golden tree of life might spring some unpleasant surprises.

It is of course true, but only trivially so, that the present illegality of drugs is the cause of the criminality surrounding their distribution. Likewise, it is the illegality of stealing cars that creates car thieves. In fact, the ultimate cause of all criminality is law. As far as I am aware, no one has ever suggested that law should therefore be abandoned. Moreover, the impossibility of winning the "war" against theft, burglary, robbery, and fraud has never been used as an argument that these categories of crime should be abandoned. And so long as the demand for material goods outstrips supply, people will be tempted to commit criminal acts against the owners of property. This is not an argument, in my view, against private property or in favor of the common ownership of all goods. It does suggest, however, that we shall need a police force for a long time to come.

In any case, there are reasons to doubt whether the crime rate would fall quite as dramatically as advocates of legalization have suggested. Amsterdam, where access to drugs is relatively unproblematic, is among the most violent and squalid cities in Europe. The idea behind crime—of getting rich, or at least richer, quickly and without much effort—is unlikely to disappear once drugs are freely available to all who want them. And it may be that officially sanctioned antisocial behavior—the official lifting of taboos—breeds yet more antisocial behavior, as the "broken windows" theory would suggest.

Having met large numbers of drug dealers in prison, I doubt that they would return to respectable life if the principal article of their commerce were to be legalized. Far from evincing a desire to be reincorporated into the world of regular work, they express a deep contempt for it and regard those who accept the bargain of a fair day's work for a fair day's pay as cowards and fools. A life of crime has its attractions for many who would otherwise lead a mundane existence. So long as there is the possibility of a lucrative racket or illegal traffic, such people will find it and extend its scope. Therefore, since even legalizers would hesitate to allow children to take drugs, decriminalization might easily result in dealers turning their attentions to younger and younger children, who—in the permissive atmosphere that even now prevails—have already been inducted into the drug subculture in alarmingly high numbers.

Those who do not deal in drugs but commit crimes to fund their consumption of them are, of course, more numerous than large-scale dealers. And it is true that once opiate addicts,

for example, enter a treatment program, which often includes maintenance doses of methadone, the rate at which they commit crimes falls markedly. The drug clinic in my hospital claims an 80 percent reduction in criminal convictions among heroin addicts once they have been stabilized on methadone.

This is impressive, but it is not certain that the results should be generalized. First, the patients are self-selected: they have some motivation to change, otherwise they would not have attended the clinic in the first place. Only a minority of addicts attend, and therefore it is not safe to conclude that, if other addicts were to receive methadone, their criminal activity would similarly diminish.

Second, a decline in convictions is not necessarily the same as a decline in criminal acts. If methadone stabilizes an addict's life, he may become a more efficient, harder-to-catch criminal. Moreover, when the police in our city do catch an addict, they are less likely to prosecute him if he can prove that he is undergoing anything remotely resembling psychiatric treatment. They return him directly to his doctor. Having once had a psychiatric consultation is an all-purpose alibi for a robber or a burglar; the police, who do not want to fill in the 40-plus forms it now takes to charge anyone with anything in England, consider a single contact with a psychiatrist sufficient to deprive anyone of legal responsibility for crime forever.

Third, the rate of criminal activity among those drug addicts who receive methadone from the clinic, though reduced, remains very high. The deputy director of the clinic estimates that the number of criminal acts committed by his average patient (as judged by self-report) was 250 per year before entering treatment and 50 afterward. It may well be that the real difference is considerably less than this, because the patients have an incentive to exaggerate it to secure the continuation of their methadone. But clearly, opiate addicts who receive their drugs legally and free of charge continue to commit large numbers of crimes. In my clinics in prison, I see numerous prisoners who were on methadone when they committed the crime for which they are incarcerated.

Why do addicts given their drug free of charge continue to commit crimes? Some addicts, of course, continue to take drugs other than those prescribed and have to fund their consumption of them. So long as any restriction whatever regulates the consumption of drugs, many addicts will seek them illicitly, regardless of what they receive legally. In addition, the drugs themselves exert a long-term effect on a person's ability to earn a living and severely limit rather than expand his horizons and mental repertoire. They sap the will or the ability of an addict to make long-term plans. While drugs are the focus of an addict's life, they are not all he needs to live, and many addicts thus continue to procure the rest of what they need by criminal means.

For the proposed legalization of drugs to have its much vaunted beneficial effect on the rate of criminality, such drugs would have to be both cheap and readily available. The legalizers assume that there is a natural limit to the demand for these drugs, and that if their consumption were legalized, the demand would not increase substantially. Those psychologically unstable persons currently taking drugs would continue to do so, with the necessity to commit crimes removed, while psychologically stabler people (such as you and I and our children) would not be enticed to take drugs by their new legal status and cheapness. But price and availability, I need hardly say, exert a profound effect on consumption: the cheaper alcohol becomes, for example, the more of it is consumed, at least within quite wide limits.

I have personal experience of this effect. I once worked as a doctor on a British government aid project to Africa. We were building a road through remote African bush. The contract stipulated that the construction company could import, free of all taxes, alcoholic drinks from the United Kingdom. These drinks the company then sold to its British workers at cost, in the local currency at the official exchange rate, which was approximately one-sixth the black-market rate. A liter bottle of gin thus cost less than a dollar and could be sold on the open market for almost ten dollars. So it was theoretically possible to remain dead drunk for several years for an initial outlay of less than a dollar.

Of course, the necessity to go to work somewhat limited the workers' consumption of alcohol. Nevertheless, drunkenness among them far outstripped anything I have ever seen, before or since. I discovered that, when alcohol is effectively free of charge, a fifth of British construction workers will regularly go to bed so drunk that they are incontinent both of urine and feces. I remember one man who very rarely got as far as his bed at night: he fell asleep in the lavatory, where he was usually found the next morning. Half the men shook in the mornings and resorted to the hair of the dog to steady their hands before they drove their bulldozers and other heavy machines (which they frequently wrecked, at enormous expense to the British taxpayer); hangovers were universal. The men were either drunk or hung over for months on end.

Sure, construction workers are notoriously liable to drink heavily, but in these circumstances even formerly moderate drinkers turned alcoholic and eventually suffered from delirium tremens. The heavy drinking occurred not because of the isolation of the African bush: not only did the company provide sports facilities for its workers, but there were many other ways to occupy oneself there. Other groups of workers in the bush whom I visited, who did not have the same rights of importation of alcoholic drink but had to purchase it at normal prices, were not nearly as drunk. And when the company asked its workers what it could do to improve their conditions, they unanimously asked for a further reduction in the price of alcohol, because they could think of nothing else to ask for.

The conclusion was inescapable: that a susceptible population had responded to the low price of alcohol, and the lack of other effective restraints upon its consumption, by drinking destructively large quantities of it. The health of many men suffered as a consequence, as did their capacity for work; and they gained a well-deserved local reputation for reprehensible, violent, antisocial behavior.

It is therefore perfectly possible that the demand for drugs, including opiates, would rise dramatically were their price to fall and their availability to increase. And if it is true that the consumption of these drugs in itself predisposes to criminal behavior (as data from our clinic suggest), it is also possible that the effect on the rate of criminality of this rise in consumption would swamp the decrease that resulted from decriminalization. We would have just as much crime in aggregate as before, but many more addicts.

The intermediate position on drug legalization, such as that espoused by Ethan Nadelmann, director of the Lindesmith Center, a drug policy research institute sponsored by financier George Soros, is emphatically not the answer to drug-related crime. This view holds that it should be easy for addicts to receive opiate drugs from doctors, either free or at cost, and that they should receive them in municipal injecting rooms, such as now exist in Zurich. But just look at Liverpool, where 2,000 people of a population of 600,000 receive official prescriptions for methadone: this once proud and prosperous city is still the world capital of drug-motivated burglary, according to the police and independent researchers.

Of course, many addicts in Liverpool are not yet on methadone, because the clinics are insufficient in number to deal with the demand. If the city expended more money on clinics, perhaps the number of addicts in treatment could be increased five- or tenfold. But would that solve the problem of burglary in Liverpool? No, because the profits to be made from selling illicit opiates would still be large: dealers would therefore make efforts to expand into parts of the population hitherto relatively untouched, in order to protect their profits. The new addicts would still burgle to feed their habits. Yet more clinics dispensing yet more methadone would then be needed. In fact Britain, which has had a relatively liberal approach to the prescribing of opiate drugs to addicts since 1928 (I myself have prescribed heroin to addicts), has seen an explosive increase in addiction to opiates and all the evils associated with it since the 1960s, despite that liberal policy. A few hundred have become more than a hundred thousand.

At the heart of Nadelmann's position, then, is an evasion. The legal and liberal provision of drugs for people who are already addicted to them will not reduce the economic benefits to dealers of pushing these drugs, at least until the entire susceptible population is addicted and in a treatment program. So long as there are addicts who have to resort to the black market for their drugs, there will be drug-associated crime. Nadelmann assumes that the number of potential addicts wouldn't soar under considerably more liberal drug laws. I can't muster such Panglossian optimism.

The problem of reducing the amount of crime committed by individual addicts is emphatically not the same as the problem of reducing the amount of crime committed by addicts as a whole. I can illustrate what I mean by an analogy: it is often claimed that prison does not work because many prisoners are recidivists who, by definition, failed to be deterred from further wrongdoing by their last prison

sentence. But does any sensible person believe that the abolition of prisons in their entirety would not reduce the numbers of the law-abiding? The murder rate in New York and the rate of drunken driving in Britain have not been reduced by a sudden upsurge in the love of humanity, but by the effective threat of punishment. An institution such as prison can work for society even if it does not work for an individual.

The situation could be very much worse than I have suggested hitherto, however, if we legalized the consumption of drugs other than opiates. So far, I have considered only opiates, which exert a generally tranquilizing effect. If opiate addicts commit crimes even when they receive their drugs free of charge, it is because they are unable to meet their other needs any other way; but there are, unfortunately, drugs whose consumption directly leads to violence because of their psychopharmacological properties and not merely because of the criminality associated with their distribution. Stimulant drugs such as crack cocaine provoke paranoia, increase aggression, and promote violence. Much of this violence takes place in the home, as the relatives of crack takers will testify. It is something I know from personal acquaintance by working in the emergency room and in the wards of our hospital. Only someone who has not been assaulted by drug takers rendered psychotic by their drug could view with equanimity the prospect of the further spread of the abuse of stimulants.

And no one should underestimate the possibility that the use of stimulant drugs could spread very much wider, and become far more general, than it is now, if restraints on their use were relaxed. The importation of the mildly stimulant khat is legal in Britain, and a large proportion of the community of Somali refugees there devotes its entire life to chewing the leaves that contain the stimulant, miring these refugees in far worse poverty than they would otherwise experience. The reason that the khat habit has not spread to the rest of the population is that it takes an entire day's chewing of disgustingly bitter leaves to gain the comparatively mild pharmacological effect. The point is, however, that once the use of a stimulant becomes culturally acceptable and normal, it can easily become so general as to exert devastating social effects. And the kinds of stimulants on offer in Western cities—cocaine, crack, amphetamines—are vastly more attractive than khat.

In claiming that prohibition, not the drugs themselves, is the problem, Nadelmann and many others—even policemen—have said that "the war on drugs is lost." But to demand a yes or no answer to the question "Is the war against drugs being won?" is like demanding a yes or no answer to the question "Have you stopped beating your wife yet?" Never can an unimaginative and fundamentally stupid metaphor have exerted a more baleful effect upon proper thought.

Let us ask whether medicine is winning the war against death. The answer is obviously no, it isn't winning: the one fundamental rule of human existence remains, unfortunately, one man one death. And this is despite the fact that 14 percent of the gross domestic product of the United States (to say nothing of the efforts of other countries) goes into the fight against death. Was ever a war more expensively lost? Let us then abolish medical schools, hospitals, and departments of public health. If every man has to die, it doesn't matter very much when he does so.

If the war against drugs is lost, then so are the wars against theft, speeding, incest, fraud, rape, murder, arson, and illegal parking. Few, if any, such wars are winnable. So let us all do anything we choose.

Even the legalizers' argument that permitting the purchase and use of drugs as freely as Milton Friedman suggests will necessarily result in less governmental and other official interference in our lives doesn't stand up. To the contrary, if the use of narcotics and stimulants were to become virtually universal, as is by no means impossible, the number of situations in which compulsory checks upon people would have to be carried out, for reasons of public safety, would increase enormously. Pharmacies, banks, schools, hospitals—indeed, all organizations dealing with the public—might feel obliged to check regularly and randomly on the drug consumption of their employees. The general use of such drugs would increase the locus standi of innumerable agencies, public and private, to interfere in our lives; and freedom from interference, far from having increased, would have drastically shrunk.

The present situation is bad, undoubtedly; but few are the situation so bad that they cannot be made worse by a wrong policy decision.

The extreme intellectual elegance of the proposal to legalize the distribution and consumption of drugs, touted as the solution to so many problems at once (AIDS, crime, overcrowding in the prisons, and even the attractiveness of drugs to foolish young people) should give rise to skepticism. Social problems are not usually like that. Analogies with the Prohibition era, often drawn by those who would legalize drugs, are false and inexact: it is one thing to attempt to ban a substance that has been in customary use for centuries by at least nine-tenths of the adult population, and quite another to retain a ban on substances that are still not in customary use, in an attempt to ensure that they never do become customary. Surely we have already slid down enough slippery slopes in the last 30 years without looking for more such slopes to slide down. ■

Social Consequences of the War on Drugs
The Legacy of Failed Policy

Eric L. Jensen, Jurg Gerber and Clayton Mosher

In a previous article, we argued that "the 1986 War on Drugs has resulted in some of the most extensive changes in criminal justice policy and the operations of the justice system in the United States since the due process revolution of the 1960s." This most recent in a series of drug wars in the United States has now lasted almost 17 years. Although huge amounts of economic resources, $18.8 billion by the federal government in fiscal year 2002 alone, personnel, and massive prison construction have been hurled at the problem, the drug war has failed to eliminate illegal drug use. In fact, the Household Survey of Drug Abuse shows that illegal drug use was declining substantially in the 6 to 7 years before the drug war was declared by President Reagan and continued this downturn for the next 6 years with fluctuations occurring since the early 1990s. Given this seemingly natural downturn—which was occurring in Canada also—the drug war seems to have had no effect on illegal drug use.

The war on drugs and its influences on the criminal justice system have received a great deal of attention

Eric L. Jensen, Jurg Gerber, and Clayton Mosher. "Social Consequences of the War on Drugs: The Legacy of Failed Policy," *Criminal Justice Policy Review,* Volume 15, Number 1 (March 2004): 100–121. Copyright © 2004 by Sage Publications. Reprinted by permission of Sage Publications.

from criminologists and other social scientists. Prison populations have exploded with persons convicted of drug offenses. Between 1980 and 2001, the number of persons in state and federal prisons for drug offenses increased by approximately 1,300%. Incarceration and prison construction have become major industries; in part replacing the old rust belt industries that were the economic backbone of America for decades. Law enforcement personnel are being redirected away from handling other types of crimes in favor of drug offenses. Criminal courts are so overloaded with drug cases that special drug courts have been created to more speedily handle the burdensome caseloads. For the first time in American history much harsher sentences are required for one form of an illegal drug (crack) than another form of the same substance (powder cocaine). Attempts have been made to criminalize the behavior of pregnant women by charging them with delivery of drugs to a minor. If these charges fail—as they most often do—child protection services have been used to remove the baby from its mother.

The drug war has also spread over into the civil arena. This pandemic spillover of state intrusion into the civil arena in the name of controlling crime represents a rapid and drastic slide down the slippery slope of reducing what heretofore were considered the due process rights of Americans. The most pervasive example of crime control absent due process is the civil forfeiture of assets in drug-related cases. Law enforcement agencies seized nearly $7 billion in allegedly drug-related assets from

fiscal year 1985 through 1999. When law enforcement is partially self-financed, it becomes less accountable to the public.

Public school students are required to take drug tests in an increasing number of schools even when drugs have not been shown to be a serious problem in the school. Drug-sniffing dogs are frequently used in schools and school parking lots to uncover illegal drugs without search warrants.

The U.S. drug war is becoming global. The federal government is attempting to influence the governments of other nations throughout the world to deal with drug issues as the U.S. government sees fit. This international arm twisting and cajoling interferes with the sovereignty of foreign governments.

Although criminologists are aware of this multitude of problematic justice system outcomes associated with the War on Drugs, we must now begin to consider the widespread social, economic, health, political, and human costs of the current antidrug crusade. The objective of this article is to bring attention to these broader societal costs of the drug war. Drug policy has become a major force in the lives of millions of persons caught in the justice system; the same holds true for millions of their family members, relatives, and friends; and the inner-city communities that suffer as a result of the policies emanating from this state-constructed moral panic.

What does the future hold for the millions of young men—disproportionately African American—who will come out of prison to face a new life stigmatized as ex-convicts and drug addicts? Will they find living-wage jobs and form stable families or return to the destructive lifestyles of their youth? How is the legitimate political influence of African Americans being influenced by the loss of the right to vote of millions of young, Black men who are convicted felons? How have repressive policies regarding syringes led to the spread of HIV/AIDS? The prison construction boom of the 1980s and 1990s may lead to the need for continued, expanded wars on crime when the cohorts of young men are smaller in the future—capacity causes utilization. Crime control is now a basic industry in the United States. The benefits of medical cannabis use for the chronically ill may not be realized due to the active federal intervention to stop state initiatives that allow it. These are the broader issues that we will begin to draw attention to in this article.

Prison Capacity: If you Build it, They must Come

It has been argued by some criminologists that the creation of prison capacity generates the prisoners to fill this capacity; others assert that limited prison capacity acts as a constraint on prison populations. In the late 1960s, criminologists and other analysts of criminal justice system trends, perhaps deluded by the increased use of alternative sanctions such as probation, predicted a leveling-off, or even declines in the overall level of imprisonment in the United States. The President's Commission on Law Enforcement and Administration of Justice predicted that the increased use of community programs would curtail institutional growth: "the population projection for the prison system shows the smallest aggregate increase of any of the correctional activities." In addition to the impact of alternative sanctions on prison populations, some held that judicial decisions on prison overcrowding in the 1970s, which prevented corrections officials in some states from receiving new inmates and even ordered some facilities closed, presaged a decline in the use of incarceration.

As early as 1971, however, the American Friends Service Committee argued that the result of providing new cell space was "inevitable: the coercive net of the justice system will be spread over a larger number of people, trapping them for longer periods of time." Similarly, a 1980 study sponsored by the National Institute of Justice, while indicating that the data were only "suggestive," asserted that

> as a matter of history, this study has found that state prison populations were more likely to increase in years immediately following construction than at any other time, and that increases in the numbers of inmates closely approximates the change in capacity.

Between 1990 and 1999, the total number of inmates in state and federal prisons increased 75%. State prisoners increased by 71% and federal prisoners by 127%. States with the largest increases in prison populations during this time were Texas (173%), Idaho (147%), West Virginia (126%), and Hawaii (124%). California has built 21 new prisons in the last 20 years and increased its inmate population eightfold. As Schlosser has noted, the number of drug offenders imprisoned in California in 1997 was more than twice the number imprisoned for *all* crimes in 1978.

During the mid-1990s, an average of three 500-bed prison facilities have opened *each week* in the United States. Christie in his provocatively titled book *Crime Control as Industry*, refers to low-level offenders as the "raw material" for prison expansion. He suggests that the prison industry needs inmates just as the paper industry needs trees—the key difference, however, is that trees may well turn out to be a finite resource.

And of course, the war on drugs has led to unprecedented racial disproportions in our prison population. Donzinger estimated that if current growth rates continue for the next 10 years, by the year 2020 more than 6 in 10 African American males between the ages of 18 and 34 will be incarcerated, with the total prison population topping 10 million. And once built at an average cost of $100,000 per cell, these prison beds must be occupied.

Significant developments in the 1980s and into the 1990s would appear to indicate that the incredible recent growth rates in incarcerated populations will not soon abate; although the rate of growth in prison populations slowed somewhat from 1999 through 2001. Consider, in this context, the rising rates of juvenile incarceration and the continual calls for transferring more juveniles to adult court. There is also the issue of the increasing involvement of private companies in the imprisonment business; the globalization of the economy, whereby companies that are unwilling or unable to obtain cheap labor in Third World countries are making increased use of prison labor, and the growing interest of rural communities in securing prisons as a means of economic development. As a prison liaison group chair in a rural Michigan jurisdiction noted, "this is going to mean more jobs and more money to the community... there's no possible way for those guys to get out, so we just reap the benefits."

There is of course a very cruel irony in all these developments. As state governments take funds from education and social programs to expand their prison systems, citizens are less able to compete in an increasingly competitive marketplace. Skills will be low, employment opportunities limited, and more people will live in poverty. Such conditions are criminogenic, but instead of investing in programs to prevent criminal activity, "the government spends dollars on the final result of the poverty circle."

As Schlosser recently pointed out, there are several similarities between the emergent prison-industrial complex and the military-industrial complex that it appears to have superseded. Although crime has replaced communism as the external evil that can be exploited by politicians, the most striking similarity between the two is the need to create policies that are more concerned with the economic imperatives of the industry than the needs of the public it allegedly serves. In addition, the policies allegedly create significant employment opportunities in the communities where prisons locate, thereby tying the economic prosperity of literally millions of people to the growth of the crime control industry. Finally, both the military and prison industries have an internal logic that allows them to benefit regardless of whether their policies succeed or fail. As Donzinger notes,

if we lose a war, we need more weapons to win the next one; if we win a war, we need more weapons so we can keep on winning; if crime is up, we need more prisons to lower crime, if crime is down, we need more prisons so it stays down.

The importance of labor market conditions was also emphasized by Sellin who argued that "the demands of the labor market shape(d) the penal system and determined its transformation over the years, more or less unaffected by the theories of punishment in vogue." Similarly, Rusche and Kirchheimer in their classic historical-comparative study of prisons, noted that compared to European countries, the United States was characterized by a shortage of labor in the early industrial period, with the result that convict labor needed to be productive. However, this position has been critiqued for its tendency to economic reductionism. In a recent comparative study of the influences on rates of imprisonment from 1955 to 1985, Sutton found that significant predictors of growth in prison populations in the United States were higher rates of unemployment, the right-party (Republican) domination of the cabinet, and declines in welfare spending.

Diminished Life Chances: Incarceration, Joblessness, and Weak Social Bonds

Between 1980 and 2001, the number of persons incarcerated in state prisons in the United States grew by 316%. Furthermore, the number of incarcerated persons per 100,000 population rose from 139 in 1980 to 470 in 2001. Interestingly, "tough on crime" policies implemented during the Clinton administration resulted in the largest increases in federal and state prison populations of any president in American history.

Incarceration is concentrated among young, uneducated males; particularly African Americans. In 1999, over 44% of the number of inmates in state and federal prisons and local jails were Black, and 11% of Black males in their 20s and early 30s were either in prison or jail in 1999. In the mid-1990s, one out of every three young Black males was under some form of state supervision.

A growing proportion of prison inmates has been convicted of nonviolent drug offenses. In 1979, 6% of state prison inmates were convicted of nonviolent drug offenses, whereas in 1998 the proportion had increased to nearly 21%, nearly a fourfold increase. In 1985, before the declaration of a new war on drugs and the passage of harsh federal antidrug legislation, 34% of federal prisoners were incarcerated for drug offenses. By 1998, 58% of federal prisoners had been sentenced for drug offenses.

Furthermore, sentences for drug offenses are long in comparison to other crimes. In 2000, mean times served for selected federal offenses were as follows: drug offenses 41 months, violent crimes 54 months, fraudulent property crimes 15 months, and other property crimes 19 months. Thus, average times served for drug offenses were closer to those for violent crimes than for property offenses.

It has also been found that African Americans are more likely than Whites to be in prison for drug offenses. This disproportionality of incarceration by race is exacerbated by the infamous 100:1 sentencing ratio for crack offenses. In 1996, 86% of federal convictions for crack offenses were Black whereas only 5% were White. In addition, the median sentence for Blacks convicted of a federal drug offense was 84 months—2 years longer than the average sentence for a violent crime—whereas it was 46 months for Whites. Thus, Blacks experience the brunt of these extremely harsh crack sanctions.

In sum, the end result of these changes in penalties and prosecution of drug offenses is a large number of young, Black males in prison for such offenses. Additionally, they are serving long prison terms in comparison to many other inmates. Although the effects of this change in patterns of imprisonment for the criminal justice system are intuitively obvious, we must turn our attention to the long-term effects on society, specifically the unemployment and further marginalization of these men once they are released from prison.

Research has clearly shown that the likelihood of unemployment increases as a result of incarceration. Western and Beckett found that incarceration has large negative effects on the employment of ex-prisoners, which decay 3 to 4 years after release. Changes in public policies since the Reagan Administration years have exacerbated this problem. As Petersilia has recently pointed out, "dozens of laws were passed restricting the kinds of jobs for which ex-prisoners can be hired, easing the requirements for their parental rights to be terminated, restricting their access to welfare benefits and public housing, disqualifying them from a host of job training programs." In addition, the ability to find and retain employment are key factors in forming bonds to the conventional society and desistance from criminal behavior.

Employment, and the lack thereof, is related to marriage. Studies cited by Wilson found that 20% to 25% of the decline in marriage rates of African Americans is due to the joblessness of Black males. This is particularly problematic for young Black males. In addition, these studies were of general samples of African Americans and not specific to the low-income communities from which most drug prisoners are sentenced. The effect of the explosion in joblessness in inner cities combined with the obstacles faced by ex-prisoners finding employment can be expected to produce larger negative outcomes in these communities.

Research by Sampson found that both the total sex ratios and the employment prospects of Black men had independent effects on the structure of Black families in cities in the United States: "this race-specific interaction clearly supports Wilson's hypothesis regarding the structural sources of black family disruption." In this earlier work, Wilson proposed that the ratio of employed men per 100 women of the same age and race influenced marital stability. With the decline in the number of economically stable Black men, Black female-headed households increased. More specifically, Sampson also found strong independent effects of sex ratios and employment on family disruption among those families in poverty. That is, "the lower the sex ratio and the lower the male employment rate, the higher the rate of female-headed families with children in poverty."

Furthermore, one of the strongest predictors of urban violence is family structure. With other factors controlled, "in cities where family disruption is high the rate of violence is also high." Based on his earlier work, the author states that this causal connection appears to be based in patterns of community social ties and informal networks of social control.

The causal chain between incarceration, joblessness, and weak social bonds is therefore long and complex. As stated by Sampson and Laub,

> job stability and marital attachment in adulthood were significantly related to changes in adult crime—the stronger the adult ties to work and family, the less the crime . . . We even found that strong marital attachment inhibits crime and deviance regardless of the spouse's own deviant behavior, and that job instability fosters crime regardless of heavy drinking. Moreover, social bonds to employment were directly influenced by State sanctions—incarceration as a juvenile and as an adult had negative effects on later job stability, which in turn was negatively related to continued involvement in crime over the life course.

Thus, the binge of imprisonment for drug offenses has substantial negative outcomes for society and inner-city African American communities in particular. The incarceration of large numbers of young Black men for drug offenses has created an artificially low unemployment rate in the United States in recent years.

In 2002 alone, nearly 600,000 people were released from prison. This puts hundreds of thousands of young Black men with the stigma of ex-convict back into primarily low-income urban communities each year. The obstacles they face in finding employment that provides a living wage and related marital stability should be focal points of public concern and social policy in the immediate future. As they currently exist, the punitive justice policies so popular in the United States today simply continue to fuel the social disorganization and decline of the most disadvantaged segments of our society. . . .

The War on Drugs and Disenfranchisement

One of the unanticipated consequences of the war on drugs is the disenfranchisement of a particular segment of society. Although most Americans will not be unduly disturbed by the prospect of convicted felons being unable to vote, the disproportionate impact of felony disenfranchisement on African Americans should be cause for concern.

Historically, the United States limited the right to vote to relatively few, primarily affluent White males, and excluded women, African Americans, and the poor. One other category, convicted felons, were unable to vote as a result of the United States's adopting the European practice of declaring convicted offenders "civilly dead" on conviction. The felony disenfranchisement laws gained some additional currency after the Civil War when White Southerners sought to limit Black suffrage with the aid of supposedly race-neutral laws (e.g., grandfather clauses).

Depending on state legislation, convicted felons may not lose the right to vote; or lose it while in prison, on probation, on parole, or even *for life*. The numbers of disenfranchised people are exceptionally large, but the proportions of certain categories of people are even more disturbing:

- 3.9 million adults are currently or permanently disenfranchised as a result of a felony conviction;
- Florida and Texas have each disenfranchised more than 600,000 people;
- 73% of the disenfranchised are not in prison but are on probation, on parole, or have completed their sentences;
- In Alabama and Florida, 31% of all Black men are permanently disenfranchised;
- 13% of all adult Black men are currently disenfranchised;
- 1.4 million Black men are disenfranchised compared to 4.6 million Black men who voted in 1996. . . .

Unfortunately, if current trends continue, the situation will become worse. Mandatory minimum sentence laws, "three strikes" laws, and the war on drugs will increase the number of disenfranchised people and, most likely, increase the racial disparity in this practice. The long-term consequence of this will be the further attenuation of African American political power. More than a decade ago, Wilson spoke of *The Truly Disadvantaged*. Not only is work disappearing, what little political clout existed has eroded. Urban areas have traditionally been strongholds of minority politicians and politicians sympathetic to minority issues. The disenfranchisement of some of their supporters will lead to a political restructuring of the city. In turn, this will lead to even fewer programs for these populations. Instead, politicians will likely heed the calls for more "law and order" emanating from the remaining electorate. And the vicious spiral will continue.

Conclusions

Few scholars who study the war on drugs are not aware of some of the problems this war entails for the criminal justice system. In fact, even professionals in the field echo some of the concerns of academicians. Former federal drug czar Barry McCaffrey spoke of "America's internal gulag" when referring to the seemingly ever-growing number of drug offenders in prisons. The irony of such a development must be overwhelming for Christie, should he be aware of McCaffrey's label.

Some positive developments are occurring at the state level, however. Since late 2000, Republican governors in at least seven states, including George Pataki in New York, Gary Johnson in New Mexico, and Dirk

Kempthorne in Idaho, have called for placing more drug offenders into treatment and fewer in prison— although the previous year Governor Kempthorne advocated and passed longer sentences for methamphetamine offenses. Although these developments can be viewed in a positive light, it is important not to lose sight of the opposition of many criminal justice officials in the states where these changes have been suggested and of recent developments at the federal level.

In Arizona and California, citizen initiatives have passed that provide drug treatment instead of prison for persons convicted of first- and second-time drug possession offenses when no violent crime is present. Although these laws have faced criticism by prosecutors, police, and judges who assert that the law does not give criminal justice authorities enough power to force offenders into treatment, the research shows that these laws are diverting tens of thousands of persons convicted of possession from incarceration into treatment.

In the November 2002 elections, the voters of the District of Columbia passed a measure similar to those in Arizona and California. This initiative requires that persons convicted of drug possession for a nonviolent offense receive treatment instead of incarceration. The law contains no funding for implementation of this policy, however.

Recent appointments to key positions in the federal government by President George W. Bush indicate that the war may not yet be over. Former Senator John Ashcroft, appointed U.S. Attorney General, has supported revoking the driver's license of anyone arrested for marijuana possession, even if they were not driving at the time. He also supported evicting entire families from public housing if one of their members was suspected of using or selling drugs, even when the other family members were not involved. Ashcroft also opposes devoting funds to demand-side programs believing that a government that shifts resources to drug treatment and prevention programs instead of police and prisons "is a government that accommodates us at our lowest and least." President Bush also appointed John Walters to the position of federal drug czar, leading Smith to comment "Walters' appointment is the clearest sign yet that the Bush administration is committed to a punishment approach to the problems caused by illegal drugs." In 1996, Walters indicated that he opposed needle exchange programs on moral grounds; he also fervently opposes the decriminalization of marijuana. Walters actively campaigned against a marijuana initiative in the state of Nevada and in response to a proposal for decriminalization of marijuana in Canada, stated "If Canada wants to become the locus for that kind of activity, they're likely to pay a heavy price." As Stroup and Armentano suggest, "many of Mr. Walters more egregious claims about cannabis appear to have been lifted straight from the 1936 propaganda film [Reefer Madness]."

The rhetoric in recent federal documents might lead one to believe that there have been some changes, however. Witness, for example, the relative prominence that the prevention and treatment of drug abuse received in the 2001 Annual Report of the National Drug Control Policy,

Preventing drug abuse in the first place is preferable to addressing the problem later through treatment and law enforcement. . . . There are approximately five million drug abusers who need immediate treatment and who constitute a major portion of domestic demand. . . . Accordingly, the *Strategy* focuses on treatment. Research clearly demonstrates that treatment works. . . . Providing access to treatment for America's chronic drug abusers is a worthwhile endeavor. It is both compassionate public policy and sound investment.

Unfortunately for the harm reduction effort, such rhetoric is offset by the reality of budgetary appropriations. An overview of the proportions of the budgets devoted to law enforcement and drug treatment during the decade of the 1990s indicates that there have not been major redistributions. Although there have been some increases in the percentage devoted to treatment, any declarations that the drug war is over are clearly premature.

However, it might be interesting to speculate how the end of the war on drugs would affect the consequences that we identified in this article. Although it seems highly improbable that we will witness such an event, it is theoretically possible that the war will be ended with the stroke of a few legislative, judicial, and executive pens. Even if this were

to occur, such an event would not fundamentally change the adverse long-term consequences that have cumulated during the last 17 years. Only a comprehensive and vigorously enforced affirmative action–like program aimed at overcoming the negative consequences of the war would do so.

Incarceration provides one example. The mean time served for a federal drug sentence for a drug offense is 41 months. Even if the war ended today, the most recently admitted convicts would remain in prison an average of well over 3 years. The only escape from this situation would be large-scale pardons for drug offenders. Obviously this will not happen. Furthermore, the internal logic of prison expansion would also necessitate new "raw material" for the cell space that exists. If nothing else, states must pay off the long-term debts that have been encumbered for this unprecedented wave of prison construction. A new war on some other outlawed, or yet to be outlawed, behavior would likely be the end result.

Postconviction employment would continue to be problematic for exoffenders. Given that the average time served is over 3 years and that employment difficulties are most pronounced for the first 3 to 4 years after release, employment difficulties would be with us for almost a decade after the end of the war on drugs. The problems associated with unemployment, such as marital instability and family violence would also exist, and their effects would be passed on to yet another generation. . . . ■

⁞⁞⁞ The Continuing Debate

What Is New

A number of states have passed laws making drug penalties less severe, and in many states a first offense possession of a small amount of marijuana is treated as a misdemeanor with no incarceration; in addition, a number of states have passed medical marijuana laws allowing some patients legal access to marijuana to prevent nausea. The U.S. federal government, however, continues to pursue a very stern policy toward drugs: the federal Higher Education Act prohibits student loans to students convicted of any drug offense (including marijuana possession), and federal authorities vigorously pursue the prosecution of those who seek to supply and use medical marijuana.

The issue of medical marijuana has pitted several states against the federal government. Under the 1996 Federal Controlled Substances Act, no patients are allowed to use marijuana, though many patients and physicians have affirmed its value in relieving nausea and suffering (and ten states, including California, have approved the use of medical marijuana). In 2003, Ed Rosenthal—who was growing marijuana under a state contract for distribution to cancer patients—was charged with a violation of federal law, and tried in a federal court. Rosenthal was convicted; the jury, on learning all the facts of the case, appealed to the judge to reverse the verdict. The judge did not reverse the verdict, but sentenced Rosenthal to a single day in prison. Recently, the Ninth U.S. Circuit Court of Appeals ruled that medical marijuana usage is noncommercial and therefore its regulation is exclusively up to the states; the U.S. Supreme Court, in 2005, overruled the Ninth Circuit Court, concluding that Congress does have the power to regulate or forbid the growing and use of medical marijuana.

Where to Find More

Searching for Alternatives: Drug-Control Policy in the United States, edited by Melvyn B. Krauss and Edward P. Lazear (Stanford, CA: Hoover Institution Press, 1991), offers competing views on drug policies. Another good collection, arranged as opposing positions on different aspects of the drug controversy, is Rod L. Evans and Irwin M. Berent, editors, *Drug Legalization: For and Against* (La Salle, IL: Open Court, 1992). Another good collection, containing both pro and con views, is James A. Inciardi, *The Drug Legalization Debate* (Newbury Park, CA: Sage Publications, 1991). The journal *Criminal Justice Ethics* devoted its Winter/Spring 2003 issue to a symposium on Drug Legalization. Arnold S. Trebach and James Inciardi debate U.S. drug policy in *Legalize It? Debating American Drug Policy* (Washington, DC: American University Press, 1993).

The Cato Institute generally supports minimizing the role of government, and thus opposes government interference in the choices of adults, and so favors drug legalization. A major paper by James Ostrowski, "Thinking about Drug Legalization," argues in favor of drug legalization, and can be found at www.cato.org/pubs/pas/pa121.html. Ostrowski's paper, along with papers by Kurt L. Schmoke and several others, is followed by a number of brief essays (primarily but not exclusively by conservatives) that criticize drug prohibition, in David Boaz, editor, *The Crisis in Drug Prohibition* (Washington, DC: The Cato Institute, 1991).

The Netherlands has adopted very liberal drug laws concerning marijuana, and is often regarded as a test of marijuana decriminalization. For a more detailed examination of the Dutch experience, see Craig Reinarman, "The Dutch Example Shows that Liberal Drug Laws Can Be Beneficial," which can be found at www.cedri-uva.org/lib/reinarman.dutch.pdf, or in Scott Barbour, editor, *Drug Legalization: Current Controversies* (San Diego: Greenhaven Press, 1999, 2000): 102–108.

On June 16, 1999, the U.S. Congress Criminal Justice, Drug Policy, and Human Resources Subcommittee (chaired by Representative John L. Mica), of the House Government Reform Committee, held a hearing on "Drug Legalization, Criminalization, and Harm Reduction." A number of papers were read into the record, both pro and con. Not surprisingly, the committee members were heavily against legalization: Representative Barr (R-GA) favored pursuing criminal charges against those who advocate decriminalization of marijuana, and Representative Souder (R-IN) compared them to rapists and child abusers. A transcript of the hearing and the papers can be found at the Federal News Service.

An essay by Joseph E. Kennedy, "Drug Wars in Black and White," *Law and Contemporary Problems*, Volume 66 (Summer 2003): 153–181, is a very insightful examination of the history of "drug wars" and drug use in the United States.

The conservative journal *National Review* favors drug legalization; their editorial statement, along with the views of several other writers, can be found at www.nationalreview.com/12feb96/drug.html. A good website on the use of marijuana for medical purposes is http://www.medicalmarijuanaprocon.org/.

19

Is the Patriot Act a Necessary Protection Against Terrorism Or a Threat to Our Civil Liberties?

The Patriot Act Is a Necessary Protection Against Terrorism
  Advocate: Andrew C. McCarthy, consultant at the Investigative
    Project; he was the lead prosecutor in the case against Sheik Omar
    Abdel Rahman and 11 others charged with the 1993 World Trade
    Center bombing.
  Source: "The Patriot Act Without Tears," *National Review* (June 14,
    2004): 32–35.

The Patriot Act Is a Threat to Our Civil Liberties
  Advocate: Stephen J. Schulhofer, Robert B. McKay Professor of Law at
    New York University Law School; author of several books, including
    *The Enemy Within: Intelligence Gathering, Law Enforcement and
    Civil Liberties in the Wake of September 11.*
  Source: "The Patriot Act and the Surveillance Society," in Richard C.
    Leone and Greg Anrig, Jr., editors, *Liberty Under Attack:
    Reclaiming Our Freedoms in an Age of Terror* (New York: Public
    Affairs, 2007).

The Patriot Act passed through the U.S. Congress in an almost hysterical rush and with little dissent (only one senator voted against it) following the infamous 9/11 attacks. The complex and wide-ranging act, 342 pages long, was passed without either a conference or a committee report. Few who voted to approve

367

the bill had any comprehensive understanding of what they had passed; indeed, very few had even read it.

There is little question that the Patriot Act places significant limitations on civil liberties; the debate is whether such limitations are actually useful in combating terrorism, and whether the limitations on our liberties have gone too far. This is an issue that cuts directly across traditional controversies between "liberals" and "conservatives." Obviously many conservatives supported the Patriot Act, as did many more liberal legislators. On the other side, the "Goldwater conservatives"—who fear enlarging and expanding the power of government over individuals—opposed many of the provisions of the act: Conservative Republican Larry Craig stated in a Judiciary Committee hearing, "I find it very difficult to believe that the federal government can enter my home, strip my hard drive, go through my records and then exit out the back door without telling me they were there." And they were joined in their opposition by such "liberal" groups as the American Civil Liberties Union. So in drawing your own conclusions concerning the Patriot Act, you cannot rely on easy "conservative" or "liberal" labels.

There are several very controversial elements of the Patriot Act. One is section 215, the "business records" provision, which grants the government power to obtain a court order (without requiring a search warrant or probable cause) to obtain your library, bookstore, medical, university, Internet, and various other records; and it prohibits the business or organization releasing the records from informing you that your records were released. A second controversial provision gives the government the right to deport any alien (including those legally in residence who are seeking citizenship) for associational activity with organizations listed as Terrorist Organizations by the Secretary of State— including associations that occurred before the organization was so designated. If an alien from Ireland supported a hunger relief fund for children in Northern Ireland, and the organization administering the relief program was later found to have some ties to the Irish Republican Army and was ultimately declared a terrorist organization, then that Irish immigrant could be detained indefinitely and deported—with no hearings and no appeal. A third controversial section is section 802, which criminalizes a very broad and rather vague category of "domestic terrorism," which includes dangerous acts that violate the criminal law and "appear to be intended . . . to influence the policy of a government by intimidation or coercion." This might be interpreted to include any vigorous protest in which the protesters are charged with failure to disperse or resisting arrest. Fourth, section 411 denies U.S. entry to any member of a political or social group "whose public endorsement of acts of terrorist activity the Secretary of Sate has determined undermines United States efforts to reduce or eliminate terrorist activities." Had a similar law been in effect in England in 1775, anyone voicing support for the Boston Tea Party (an illegal act which destroyed property) would have been denied entry into Great Britain. Finally, the Patriot Act endorses "sneak and peek" searches, in which government officials can carry out searches of the property of American citizens, without notifying them either during or after the search and without establishing probable cause to justify the search.

Andrew C. McCarthy concentrates on defending two elements of the Patriot Act that are widely accepted and rarely attacked: the provision to allow national security organizations and local criminal investigators to share information; and the provision to allow court-supervised subpoenas, with the establishment of reasonable grounds, for e-mail records (in a manner similar to the process for getting court-approved access to telephone lines). On more controversial issues (which McCarthy classifies as "red herrings"), he claims that section 215 (which allows federal investigators to check library, Internet, and university records, with little or no oversight) is rarely used; that the restrictions on funding for humanitarian purposes (and potential criminal charges based on such contributions) are beneficial; and that the "sneak and peek" search procedures simply give systematic organization to a practice that has long been in place. Stephen J. Schulhofer acknowledges that the Patriot Act has some positive sections, but contends that the Patriot Act broadens surveillance powers far beyond what is necessary for national security, and severely erodes oversight of surveillance practices and thus leaves them open to governmental abuse.

⚌ Points to Ponder

- Andrew McCarthy claims that the issue of government examination of library records—without the knowledge of library patrons, and without showing sufficient cause—is a "red herring" or a distorted issue. His key support for that claim is that library records "are not even mentioned in the statute." Does the fact that library records are not explicitly mentioned in the statute show that government surveillance of library records is a "nonissue"?
- McCarthy notes that the Patriot Act "provides that the attorney general must, twice a year, 'fully inform' Congress" of national security investigations into the reading habits and Internet usage of U.S. citizens. Schulhofer considers such a report an inadequate level of supervision, and no substitute for judicial oversight. *Is* the required attorney general's congressional report an adequate safeguard against governmental abuse of surveillance?
- You are not a terrorist, and you have no fear of criminal prosecution as a result of surveillance of your Internet usage. Would you nonetheless be troubled to discover that government agents had been monitoring your e-mails and Internet usage over the past year?
- Schulhofer suggests that excessive surveillance of immigrants to the United States may be counterproductive in combating terrorism; what grounds or justification could be given for that claim?

The Patriot Act Without Tears
Understanding a Mythologized Law

Andrew C. McCarthy

It was mid-August 2001, the last desperate days before the 9/11 terrorist attacks. Desperate, that is, for an alert agent of the FBI's Foreign Counterintelligence Division (FCI); much of the rest of America, and certainly much of the rest of its government, blithely carried on, content to assume, despite the number and increasing ferocity of terrorist attacks dating back nearly nine years, that national security was little more than an everyday criminal-justice issue.

Since 1995, a "wall" had been erected, presumptively barring communications between FCI agents and their counterparts in law enforcement—the FBI's criminal agents and the assistant U.S. attorneys who collectively, after a string of successful prosecutions through the 1990s, had become the government's best resource for information about the threat of militant Islam. This wall was not required by law; it was imposed as policy. Justice Department lawyers, elevating litigation risk over national security, designed it to forestall accusations that the federal government had used its intelligence-eavesdropping authority to build criminal cases.

This FCI agent collided, head-on, with the wall; and strewn in the wreckage was the last, best hope of stopping 9/11. Putting disconnected clues together, the agent had deduced that two Qaeda operatives, Khalid al-Midhar and Nawaf al-Hazmi, had probably gotten into the U.S. Alarmed, he pleaded with the FBI's criminal division to help him hunt down the terrorists—but they refused: For agents to fuse their information and efforts would be a transgression against the wall. The prescient agent rued that, one day soon, people would die in the face of this paralyzing roadblock. Al-Midhar and al-Hazmi remained undetected until they plunged Flight 77 into the Pentagon on 9/11.

Facing Reality

By October 2001, the world had changed—and the USA Patriot Act was passed. So patent was the need for this law that it racked up massive support: 357-66 in the House, 98-1 in the Senate. In the nearly three years since, however, it has been distorted beyond recognition by a coalition of anti-Bush leftists and libertarian extremists, such that it is now perhaps the most broadly maligned—and misunderstood—piece of meaningful legislation in U.S. history. If our nation is serious about national security, the Patriot Act must be made permanent; instead, it could soon be gone—and the disastrous "intelligence wall" rebuilt.

Andrew C. McCarthy, "The Patriot Act Without Tears," *National Review*, June 14, 2004: 32–35. Reprinted with permission.

Contrary to widespread calumny, Patriot is not an assault on the Bill of Rights. It is, basically, an overhaul of the government's antiquated counter-terror arsenal, which had been haplessly fighting a 21st-century war with 20th-century weapons. Indeed, Patriot's only obvious flaw is its cloying acronym, short for "The Uniting and Strengthening America by Providing Appropriate Tools to Intercept and Obstruct Terrorism Act of 2001." But once you get past the title, Patriot is all substance, and crucial to national security.

The most essential improvement wrought by Patriot has been the dismantling of the intelligence wall. The bill expressly amended the government's national-security eavesdropping-and-search authority (under the Foreign Intelligence Surveillance Act or FISA) to clarify that intelligence agents, criminal investigators, and prosecutors not only may but should be pooling information and connecting dots. This is common sense: Along the way toward mass murder, terrorists inevitably commit numerous ordinary crimes, everything from identity theft to immigration fraud to bombing. One could not surveil them as agents of a foreign power (as FISA permits) without necessarily uncovering such crimes, and this, far from being a problem, is a bonus since these lay the groundwork for prosecutions that can both stop terrorists before they strike and pressure them to turn state's evidence.

Yet, as has been detailed in a decisive 2002 opinion by the Foreign Intelligence Surveillance Court of Review, FISA had for decades been misinterpreted by the government and the courts, which, owing to their obsession over the "rights" of enemy operatives, erroneously presumed that national-security intelligence was somehow separate and severable from criminal evidence. This false dichotomy culminated in the wall built by the Clinton Justice Department (and substantially maintained by Bush's DOJ), with awful consequences.

Tearing down the wall—as well as repealing legislation that had barred criminal investigators from sharing with intelligence agents the fruits of grand-jury proceedings and criminal wiretaps—has paid instant dividends. For example, while the wall once caused intelligence and criminal agents in Buffalo to believe they could not be in the same room together during briefings to discuss their parallel investigations of an apparent sleeper cell in Lackawanna, N.Y., the Patriot Act allowed the criminal investigators to learn that a theretofore anonymous letter to one of their subjects had, as intelligence agents knew, been penned by a Qaeda operative. This and other fact-sharing broke an investigative logjam, revealing a history of paramilitary training at al-Qaeda's Afghan proving grounds, and directly resulted in guilty pleas and lengthy sentences for six men who had provided material support to the terror network.

In a similar way, in 2002 law-enforcement agents in Oregon learned through an informant that Jeffrey Battle was actively scoping out Jewish schools and synagogues for a terrorist attack. It later emerged that Battle was among a group that set out to train with al-Qaeda in Afghanistan (they never made it). Battle was plainly a time bomb, but his confederates had not yet been fully revealed—and there naturally was fear that if Battle were arrested and removed from the scene the investigators would lose their best hope of identifying other terrorists. Because the wall was down, the criminal investigators had the confidence to delay the arrest and continue the investigation, knowing the intelligence agents using FISA were now free to share what they were learning. As a result, not only Battle but six others, collectively known as the "Portland 7," were identified, convicted on terrorism-support charges, and sentenced to between three and 18 years in prison.

Thanks to Patriot's removal of the blinders, action—sometimes long overdue—has been taken against many other accused and convicted terrorists. Criminal investigators won access to a historic trove of intelligence demonstrating that Prof. Sami al-Arian had been using his University of South Florida redoubt as an annex of the deadly Palestinian Islamic Jihad group responsible for over 100 murders, including that of Alisa Flatow, a young American woman killed in an Israeli bus bombing. The sharing provisions also ensured the convictions of nine other defendants in Virginia, on charges ranging from support of the Qaeda-affiliated Lashkar-e-Taiba to conspiracy to levy war against the U.S.; the conviction in Chicago of bin Laden intimate Enaam Arnaout for using his Benevolence International Foundation as a conduit to fund terrorist cells in Bosnia and Chechnya, and of Khaled Abdel-Latif Dumeisi for working in the U.S. for Saddam Hussein's brutal Iraqi Intelligence Service; the indictment of a University of Idaho graduate student, Sami Omar al-Hussayen, for using his computer skills to support the recruiting and fundraising of Hamas and Chechnyan terror groups; the

indictment in Brooklyn of two Yemeni nationals who bragged about having raised millions of dollars for bin Laden; and the smashing of a drugs-for-weapons plot in San Diego that solicited Stinger anti-aircraft missiles for the Taliban in exchange for heroin and hashish. Moreover, while much information provided by criminal investigators to the intelligence community must remain classified, the Justice Department also credits the sharing provisions with the revocation of visas for suspected terrorists, tracking and choking off of terrorist funding channels, and identifying of terrorists operating overseas.

21st-Century Tactics

Besides paving the way for agents to pool critical information, Patriot has been invaluable in modernizing investigative tools to ensure that more information is actually captured. While the critics' persistent caviling misleadingly suggests that these tools are a novel assault on privacy rights, for the most part they merely extend to national-security intelligence investigations the same methods that have long been available to law-enforcement agents probing the vast array of federal crimes, including those as comparatively innocuous as health-care fraud.

Among the best examples is the so-called "roving" (or multipoint) wiretap. As the telephony revolution unfolded, criminals naturally took advantage, avoiding wiretap surveillance by the simple tactic of constantly switching phones—which became especially easy to do once cellphones became ubiquitous. Congress reacted nearly 20 years ago with a law that authorized criminal agents to obtain wiretaps that, rather than aim at a specific telephone, targeted *persons*, thus allowing monitoring to continue without significant delay as criminals ditched one phone for the next. Inexplicably, this same authority was not available to intelligence agents investigating terrorists under FISA. Patriot rectifies this anomaly.

On the law-enforcement side, Patriot expands the substance of the wiretap statute to account for the realities of terrorism. Most Americans would probably be surprised to learn that while the relatively trivial offense of gambling, for example, was a lawful predicate for a criminal wiretap investigation, chemical-weapons offenses, the use of weapons of mass destruction, the killing of Americans abroad, terrorist financing, and computer fraud were not. Thanks to Patriot, that is no longer the case.

Analogously, Patriot revamped other telecommunications-related techniques. Prior law, for example, had been written in the bygone era when cable service meant television programming. Owing to privacy concerns about viewing habits, which the government rarely has a legitimate reason to probe, federal law made access to cable-usage records practically impossible—creating in service providers a fear of being sued by customers if they complied with government information requests. Now, of course, millions of cable subscribers—including no small number of terrorists—use the service not only for entertainment viewing but for e-mail services.

While e-mail-usage records from dial-up providers have long been available by subpoena, court order, or search warrant (depending on the sensitivity of the information sought), cable providers for years delayed complying with such processes, arguing that their services fell under the restrictive umbrella of prior cable law. This was not only a potentially disastrous state of affairs in terrorism cases, where delay can cost lives, but in many other contexts as well—including one reported case in which a cable company declined to comply with an order to disclose the name of a suspected pedophile who was distributing child pornography on the Internet even as he bragged online about sexually abusing a young girl. (Investigators, forced to pursue other leads, needed two extra weeks to identify and apprehend the suspect.) Recognizing that it made no sense to have radically different standards for acquiring the same information, Patriot made cable e-mail available on the same terms as dial-up.

Patriot also closed other gaping e-mail loopholes. Under prior law, for example, investigators trying to identify the source of incriminating e-mail were severely handicapped in that their readiest tool, the grand-jury subpoena, could be used only to compel the service provider to produce customers' names, addresses, and lengths of service—information often of little value in ferreting out wrongdoers who routinely use false names and temporary e-mail addresses. Patriot solved this problem by empowering grand juries to compel payment information, which can be used to trace the bank and credit-card records by which investigators ultimately establish identity. This not only makes it possible to identify potential terrorists far more quickly—and thus, it is hoped, before they can strike—but also to thwart other criminals who must be apprehended with all due speed. Such subpoenas, for example, have been employed repeatedly to identify and arrest molesters who were actively abusing children. The Justice Department reports that, only a few weeks ago, the new authority prevented a Columbine-like attack by allowing agents to identify a suspect, and obtain his confession, before the attack could take place.

Further, Patriot clarified such investigative matters as the methods for lawful access by investigators to stored e-mail held by third parties (such as AOL and other service providers). And it cured the incongruity that allowed agents to access voice messages stored in a suspect's own home answering machine by a simple search warrant but anomalously forced them to obtain a far more cumbersome wiretap order if the messages were in the form of voicemail stored with a third-party provider.

A Library of Red Herrings

One Patriot reform that has been irresponsibly maligned is Section 215 of the act, which merely extends to national-security investigations conducted under FISA the same authority to subpoena business records that criminal investigators have exercised unremarkably for years. Indeed, even under Section 215, intelligence agents remain at a comparative disadvantage since they must get the approval of a FISA court before compelling records production while prosecutors in criminal cases simply issue grand-jury

subpoenas. Nonetheless, this common-sense provision came under blistering, disingenuous assault last year when the ACLU and others raised the red herring of library records—which are not even mentioned in the statute. In 2002, for example, the *Hartford Courant* was compelled to retract in full a story that falsely accused the FBI of installing software on computers in the Hartford Public Library to monitor the public's use of the Internet. (In fact, the FBI had obtained a court-ordered search warrant to copy the hard drive of a single computer that had been used criminally to hack into a business computer system in California.)

In 2003, the ACLU issued a warning that Section 215 would allow federal "thought police" to "target us for what we choose to read or what Websites we visit." In reality, Section 215 (unlike criminal-grand-jury subpoena authority) expressly contains safeguards protecting First Amendment rights, and further provides that the attorney general must, twice a year, "fully inform" Congress about how the provision has been implemented. As of September 2003, the provision had not been used a single time—neither for library records nor, indeed, for records of any kind.

Unlike reading habits, financing—the lifeblood of terrorist networks—actually is a Patriot target. The act has significantly crimped the ability of overseas terrorists to use foreign banks and nominees to avoid seizures of their funds; it cracked down on the so-called "hawalas" (that is, unlicensed money-transmitting businesses) that have been used to funnel millions of dollars to terror groups; it extended the reach of civil money-laundering penalties—which loom large in the minds of financial institutions—against those who engage in transactions involving the proceeds of crime. And it further choked the funding channels by making currency smuggling itself (rather than the mere failure to file a report about the movement of currency) a crime, an initiative that bolsters the legal basis for seizing all, rather than a portion, of the smuggled funds. These and other Patriot finance provisions have enabled the government to obtain over 20 convictions to date and freeze over $130 million in assets worldwide.

Mention should also be made of another Patriot improvement that has been speciously challenged: the codification of uniform procedures for so-called sneak-and-peek warrants, which allow agents to conduct a search without seizing items, and delay notification to the person whose premises have been searched—thus ensuring that an investigation can proceed and agents can continue identifying other conspirators. Such warrants have been used for many years, and delayed notification has been a commonplace—just as it is in other areas, such as wiretap law, where alerting the subject would prematurely end the investigation.

Sneak-and-peek delayed notification, however, evolved through federal case law rather than by statute, and consequently there was a jumble of varying requirements depending on which federal circuit the investigation happened to be in. All Patriot did in this regard was impose a uniform national standard that permits delay if notification could cause endangerment to life, facilitation of flight, destruction of evidence, intimidation

of witnesses, or similar substantial jeopardizing of investigations. Yet critics drummed up outrage by portraying sneak-and-peek as if it were a novel encroachment on privacy rather than a well-established tool that requires prior court approval. So effective was this campaign that the House of Representatives responded by voting to deny funding for the delayed notification warrants. Inability to delay notification, of course, would defeat the purpose of using sneak-and-peek in the first place. The Senate has not seemed inclined to follow suit, but that so prudent a provision could become the subject of controversy illustrates how effectively the opposition has discredited the Patriot Act.

Palpably, the Patriot Act, far from imperiling the Constitution, went a long way toward shoring up the perilous state of national security that existed on the morning of 9/11. That is why it is so excruciating to note that, despite all we have been through, we will be transported right back to that precarious state if Congress fails to reauthorize Patriot. Because of intense lobbying by civil-liberties groups instinctively hostile to anything that makes government stronger—even in the arena of national defense, where we need it to be strong if we are to have liberties at all—Patriot's sponsors had to agree, to secure passage, that the act would effectively be experimental. That is, the information sharing, improved investigative techniques, and several other provisions were not permanently enacted into law but are scheduled to "sunset" on December 31, 2005. Dismayingly, far from grasping the eminent sense in making these improvements permanent, the alliance of Democratic Bush-bashers and crusading Republican libertarians is actually pushing a number of proposals to *extend* the sunset provision to parts of Patriot that were not originally covered.

At a time when the 9/11 Commission's public hearings highlight intelligence lapses and investigative backwardness—and when al-Qaeda publicly threatens larger-than-ever attacks while continuing to fight our forces and allies on the battlefield and in murderous attacks throughout the world—it is remarkable that elected officials would have *any* priority other than making the Patriot Act permanent. ■

The Patriot Act and the Surveillance Society

Stephen J. Schulhofer

On March 9, 2006, after much delay and heated accusations between Republicans and Democrats, Congress reauthorized the USA Patriot Act—the famous (or infamous) grab bag of law enforcement and intelligence-gathering powers originally approved by Congress immediately after the attacks of September 11, 2001. Despite the passage of five years and countless working hours of experience implementing its provisions, the bitter reauthorization debate unfolded in virtually complete darkness. The administration insisted that the new powers be preserved intact—indeed, that anything less would invite disaster. Yet the administration provided almost none of the concrete details necessary to assess the provisions or to understand their impact. In the end, the act's most controversial powers were approved with little or no change, and nearly all were made permanent.

The elections of November 2006, which shifted control of both the Senate and House of Representatives from the Republican Party to the Democrats, clearly signaled public dissatisfaction with the Iraq War but also a more general skepticism about unchecked executive authority and a hunger for responsible oversight. It remains to be seen whether Congress will accept that mandate or allow itself to be pushed back into the quiescent role it played during the past five years. Despite the meager results of the recent reauthorization debate, there is still time to correct some of the Patriot Act's worst flaws if Congress is willing to insist on obtaining essential information, make it

Stephen J. Schulhofer, "The Patriot Act and the Surveillance Society," from *Liberty Under Attack: Reclaiming Our Freedoms in an Age of Terror*, edited by Richard C. Leone and Greg Anrig, Jr. (New York: Public Affairs, 2007). Reprinted by permission of Public Affairs, a member of Perseus Books Group.

public where possible, and enact new legislation that reins in unnecessary powers and establishes effective safeguards against abuse.

As enacted on October 26, 2001, the original USA Patriot Act represented for many Americans the epitome of mindless overreaction, a tragically misguided grant of law enforcement power that will end by destroying our liberties in order to save them. Those reactions, though not baseless, are easy for the act's defenders to refute. As they accurately point out, the act is filled with innocuous technical correctives, well-justified responses to new communications technologies, and even a few provisions creating useful new safeguards for civil liberties. Of the act's 161 distinct provisions, most are in no way controversial or problematic. Among the provisions that really do enhance law enforcement power, many are narrow and carefully tailored, enough so that few experts see in them any legitimate basis for concern.

That said, the Patriot Act also includes provisions that seem technical but, once understood, have alarming implications. Many of its new surveillance powers are far broader than necessary. Some bear no relation to the terrorist threat at all. And even where a grant of new intelligence-gathering authority can be justified, the Patriot Act fails to ensure that executive branch officials remain accountable for the ways their broad new powers are used.

The absence of effective oversight is no minor detail. This deficiency is dangerous. It not only heightens the risk of over-reaching and abuse, but it also undermines the counterterrorism effort itself. As members of the 9/11 Commission unanimously warned: "The American public has vested enormous authority in the U.S. government. . . . This shift of power and authority to the government calls for an enhanced system of checks and balances to protect the precious liberties that are vital to our way of life." Yet the Patriot Act, as originally written, paid scant attention to this concern, and subsequent amendments have compounded the problem, expanding several of the act's most problematic provisions while doing little to require effective oversight.

Ultimately, therefore, the Patriot Act does deserve much of its dark reputation. Yet legitimate criticism and public uneasiness about the act have been swamped by skillfully manipulated fears of a new terrorist attack. And in some areas where the Patriot Act retains significant safeguards, the Bush administration has simply by-passed existing laws to engage in secret surveillance on its own terms, with no accountability whatsoever. These actions have generated criticism, to be sure, but much of the public has been favorable or indifferent to them, indicating again the absence of widespread appreciation that these unnecessary shortcuts are dangerous to both our civil liberties *and* our security.

Before focusing on the dangers, however, it is worthwhile first to acknowledge the places where the Patriot Act made constructive, well-justified changes in American surveillance law.

Legitimate, Uncontroversial Fixes

The laws that govern wiretapping and electronic surveillance are a dense web of technically detailed statutes enacted at different times and amended frequently, on an ad hoc basis, in response to particular problems. The resulting edifice, as it stood before September 11, 2001, was a largely workable framework that nonetheless suffered from important gaps, inconsistencies, and anachronisms.

So-called "roving" surveillance is one example. Ordinary warrants authorize tapping conversations from a particular phone, but occasionally an individual who fears surveillance will change phones frequently to defeat the government's surveillance efforts. As a result, domestic law enforcement statutes were amended to authorize surveillance of a suspect wherever he may be (rather than restricting surveillance to a particular telephone), although only when a judge finds that the suspect has taken evasive action that thwarts ordinary surveillance tactics. Such "roving" surveillance is broader, and potentially more subject to abuse, than wiretapping of a single phone, and it therefore has its critics. Nonetheless, when confined to suspects who switch phones frequently for purposes of evasion, the technique seems well justified on balance, and Congress has permitted it for many years in ordinary drug distribution and racketeering investigations. As a result of a quirk in the statutory structure, however, roving surveillance was not available in foreign intelligence investigations, an area where the government is ordinarily afforded more leeway. The Patriot Act justifiably fixed that illogical gap by authorizing roving surveillance, under the same conditions, in foreign intelligence investigations as well.

Technological change made some pre–9/11 statutory requirements obsolete or needlessly complicated. For example, the law required one kind of warrant to seize unopened e-mail messages stored on a server and a different, more cumbersome kind of warrant to seize unopened audio messages stored in a voice mail system. There was never a significant reason to treat the two types of messages differently, and recent innovations complicated the picture by blurring the differences between them. The Patriot Act dismantled this statutory obstacle course by eliminating the distinction and permitting a single type of warrant for both sorts of messages. In similar fashion, the Patriot Act justifiably eliminated the increasingly artificial lines that distinguished the legal rules applicable to customer records held by telephone companies from those held by Internet service providers and cable service providers.

Before 9/11, search warrants were, with rare exceptions, valid only within the judicial district where the judge who issued the order sat. In an investigation of national scope, agents had to prepare separate warrant applications for each district in which a search or surveillance was required. The process was cumbersome and to no purpose. Also, Internet technology was rapidly compounding the difficulties, because magistrates in Silicon Valley, where many Internet service providers are located, were swamped with large numbers of surveillance applications unrelated to any local criminal activity. The Patriot Act, again with ample justification, fixed this problem by authorizing a judge in any district connected to the investigation to issue warrants of nationwide scope.

Dangerous Powers

Mixed among these easily defended corrective measures are many provisions that are partially justifiable but dangerously overbroad.

Private Records

Prior to 9/11, investigators normally could gain access to personal documents and records only by serving a subpoena, a procedure that affords substantial judicial safeguards to the person affected. A person or institution that receives a subpoena can challenge it in court. Additional safeguards are in place to protect individuals whose private records are held by someone else, such as clients whose financial records are held by their banks and students whose educational records are held by their schools or colleges. In these situations, statutes require the bank or college to notify the affected individual so that this person also has an opportunity to challenge the subpoena in court. Exceptions to these requirements were allowed in foreign intelligence and national security investigations, but only under narrow, carefully guarded circumstances.

The Patriot Act dramatically expanded the scope of these foreign intelligence and national security exceptions, placing highly sensitive personal records at risk, with few significant safeguards. One technique used to accomplish that revolutionary change was the National Security Letter (NSL). This device, an order issued by an FBI official (not a judge), requires certain business firms to give government agents access to particular kinds of financial data and telephone records for customers under investigation. Before 9/11, the FBI could issue an NSL only when it had specific facts indicating that the customer was a foreign agent. But the Patriot Act relaxed this restriction, requiring the FBI official to certify only that the records were "sought for an authorized investigation [of] international terrorism." In addition, the Patriot Act broadened the kinds of records subject to this type of inspection without judicial review, so that the NSL can now reach the records of real estate agents, car dealers, and any other business "whose cash transactions have a high degree of usefulness in criminal, tax, or regulatory matters." And the law imposes a "gag order" that forbids the firm receiving the NSL from informing anyone that it was required to make disclosures to the FBI.

The privacy of personal records has also been attacked in a much more comprehensive manner through the document-disclosure authority available under the Foreign Intelligence Surveillance Act (FISA). A FISA demand for the disclosure of documents requires a court order, a safeguard unavailable for NSLs, but the scope of this authority and its potential for abuse is far greater. Prior to 9/11, a judge of the Foreign Intelligence Surveillance Court could issue an order giving investigators access to certain kinds of "business records." This FISA order was limited in two notable ways. First, to get such an order, investigators were required to certify that they had specific facts indicating that the records pertained to the agent of a foreign power or a member of an international terrorist group. Second, the only records available for inspection in this way were the records of specific travel-related businesses—for example, airlines, railroads, car rental companies, and hotels (but not restaurants).

Section 215 of the Patriot Act eliminated the requirement that the records pertain to a foreign agent; instead FBI investigators were only required to certify that the records were "sought for an authorized investigation." In other words, investigators were merely required to self-certify that they were acting in good faith. And Section 215 eliminated all restrictions on the kinds of records that could be obtained. As amended, FISA now allows investigators to obtain access to the records of any business, as well as all records, documents, and any other "tangible things" held by any person or entity, including libraries, bookstores, hospitals, HMOs, charities, political parties, and religious associations, including any church, synagogue, or mosque. And FISA directives, like the NSLs, carry a "gag order": the organization is prohibited from ever informing anyone that records and documents were disclosed.

These sweeping powers open our most personal records to unrestricted government scrutiny. They also strike at the heart of political and religious liberty, undermining the shelter of privacy required for the associational activities of minority groups and dissenters of all stripes. No legitimate investigative need can justify making these powers available against persons not suspected of potential terrorist activity and in the absence of any objective facts supporting such a concern. In fact, the Justice Department has defended these powers by claiming (incorrectly) that "the law only applies to agents of a foreign power or a member of a terrorist organization." As that defense inadvertently acknowledges,

there is no valid reason for granting these dangerous powers in other circumstances. A top priority for the new Congress should be an effort to rein in these powers of access to sensitive private information.

Foreign Intelligence Surveillance

Because wiretaps and other electronic surveillance can sweep up vast amounts of information, much of it irrelevant to any legitimate inquiry, this investigative technique is subject to special statutory restrictions and safeguards. The most important of these statutory regimes, generally known as "Title III," governs the gathering of evidence for criminal prosecutions, and it imposes strict limits on the initiation, duration, and subsequent use of electronic surveillance, all subject to close judicial oversight. In foreign intelligence surveillance, however, government agents focus not on gathering evidence for use in criminal cases but rather on gathering information for intelligence analysis and the prevention of attacks. For that reason, this type of surveillance traditionally has been allowed more leeway. FISA—the statutory regime that regulates it—permits surveillance on a less specific standard of suspicion, and it allows surveillance to continue for longer periods of time, with less judicial oversight. In addition, the persons targeted under FISA (unlike those targeted under Title III) normally are never notified that they have been subjected to surveillance. As a result, the government actions remain secret indefinitely, and the checks on potential overreaching and abuse are thus far weaker than they are in the case of surveillance conducted under the authority of Title III.

Those differences predated 9/11, but the Patriot Act included one amendment that greatly multiplied their importance. Before 9/11, the more flexible FISA regime was available only when foreign intelligence gathering was the primary purpose of the investigation. Criminal prosecutors were not permitted to invoke the loose FISA regime on their own initiative, and the possibility of later utilizing the results of FISA surveillance in a criminal case could be, at most, an incidental or subsidiary purpose of the investigation. The Patriot Act, however, made the FISA regime available whenever foreign intelligence gathering was merely "a significant purpose" of the inquiry, with the result that *criminal prosecution* could now be the primary purpose. And criminal prosecutors are now permitted even to "direct and control" the deployment of FISA tools when they are investigating any crimes that have a national security or foreign intelligence dimension.

To be sure, the Patriot Act amendment was prompted by a legitimate concern, because FISA had been interpreted, and indeed misinterpreted, to impose an overly rigid barrier (the so-called "wall") between intelligence analysts and criminal investigators. But in dismantling the wall, the Patriot Act went much too far in the other direction, leaving prosecutors free to make virtually unrestricted use of FISA's secret, relatively unsupervised procedures. Congress could easily, as a minimum first step, correct this situation by requiring that oversight committees be kept apprised of prosecutorial use of FISA and that, absent exceptional circumstances, prosecutors no longer be free to "direct and control" FISA surveillance.

Sneak and Peek

When police search a business or residence, they ordinarily must give the property owner a copy of the search warrant so that the owner knows the exact scope of the officer's authority and what, if anything, he is permitted to seize. Notification of this sort is essential for assuring that government officials remain within the law and remain accountable when they exercise the power to forcibly enter and search our homes. In rare situations where secrecy is essential to the law enforcement objective (for example, when officers have court approval to plant a microphone or video camera), courts can permit a completely surreptitious entry and search. The so-called "sneak and peek" is carried out when the owner is away from the premises, and no copy of the warrant is left behind; instead, courts permit the police to postpone giving the required notice of the search until some time (usually a week) has passed. Delayed notice prevents contemporaneous observation of how the search is carried out but at least permits a relatively prompt check on overreaching or abuse.

The Patriot Act relaxed the requirements for a sneak-and-peek search and permitted the required notice to be delayed for a longer period—indeed, for any "reasonable" period of time. The diluted safeguards surrounding the sneak and peek so alarmed many civil liberties groups and libertarian conservatives that a bill prohibiting all delayed-notice searches passed the House by a lopsided majority in 2003, and many believed that this overbroad Patriot Act provision would not survive. Adding to the unease about the sneak-and-peek power is the fact, rarely noticed, that this new law enforcement authority is not a counterterrorism measure at all. The Patriot Act provision expanding sneak-and-peek powers is available for investigation of *any* crime. Moreover, it is not needed for terrorism cases because, in that area, an even broader sneak-and-peek authority is available under FISA, which permits sneak and peeks not with *delayed* notice but with *no* notice, ever.

In fact, the Patriot Act expanded the foreign intelligence sneak and peek as well. It doubled (from forty-five to ninety days) the period of time during which a U.S. citizen can be subjected to repeated sneak and peeks under FISA, and it eliminated the requirement that these FISA searches be used only when foreign intelligence gathering is the investigator's primary purpose. As a result of the Patriot Act amendments, criminal prosecutors can now initiate and control the use of this loosely regulated, never-give-notice search.

Despite the broad sneak-and-peek power available in terrorism cases and intense criticism of the Patriot Act provision expanding sneak and peeks in the investigation of ordinary domestic crime, the domestic sneak-and-peek authority ultimately survived with only modest, cosmetic changes. The 2006 amendments to the Patriot Act (the "USA Patriot Act Improvement and Reauthorization Act") set the initial period of delayed notice at thirty days and allowed courts to authorize further delay for an unlimited number of additional periods of ninety days each. That sweeping, surreptitious law enforcement power is both dangerously broad and completely unnecessary as a tool to combat international terrorism. In ordinary criminal cases—those not connected to international terrorism—the maximum period of delay should be much more limited; for example, as was the practice prior to 9/11, the initial delay ordinarily should not exceed seven days, with further extensions only at fourteen day intervals.

Internet Surveillance

American surveillance laws set a very low standard for court orders that authorize law enforcement officials to monitor only the telephone numbers (but not the content) of a suspect's incoming and outgoing calls. Officials must certify that the information sought is considered relevant to an ongoing investigation, but they need not present any facts indicating an objective basis for suspicion, much less probable cause. Before 9/11, however, the law was unclear as to whether comparable surveillance of e-mail (monitoring origin and destination addresses) was subject to the same regime, was more strictly regulated, or was not regulated at all.

The Patriot Act solved this puzzle by providing that e-mail and Internet addresses (specifically, "routing, addressing, and signaling information") will be subject to surveillance under the same low standard applicable to phone numbers. Although this approach is superficially logical, it ignores the fact that routing identifiers for e-mail and

Internet browsing (such as Web site URLs) convey much more sensitive information than does the number of an incoming or outgoing phone call. The new Patriot Act authority therefore poses a serious threat to the privacy of online communication and research. And the threat is not one that the dangers of terrorism in any way require us to accept, because the new Patriot Act authority is available in the investigation of any crime, no matter how trivial.

The Erosion of Accountability

While granting dangerous, unnecessarily broad surveillance powers, the Patriot Act failed to put adequate oversight mechanisms in place, and in some instances it even took steps to dilute the oversight safeguards that were previously available.

The treatment of private records is one example. The expanded NSLs can be issued by an FBI official with no judicial approval or oversight at all. Although FISA document-production orders must be issued by a FISA judge, the Patriot Act eliminated the requirement that officials seeking the order certify that they are targeting a foreign agent or terrorism suspect and that they have specific, objective facts supporting their suspicions. Instead, they now are required to certify only that the records are "sought for an authorized investigation." As a result, the Patriot Act for all practical purposes eliminated any significant opportunity for a judicial role in restraining or overseeing the way that these orders are employed.

The Patriot Act did create a few additional possibilities for congressional oversight. It required the attorney general semiannually to inform the House and Senate Judiciary Committees of the number of FISA document-production orders sought, granted, and denied. It also preserved the longstanding requirement of an annual report on the number of FISA electronic surveillance orders sought, granted, and denied. But the act did not require disclosure of any of the details that would have made either of these reports useful, such as the kinds of locations where electronic surveillance occurred, the average duration of surveillance, the number of times document-production orders were sought from libraries, political groups, or religious organizations, and the number of times electronic surveillance and document searches produced relevant information rather than fruitless intrusions on presumably innocent individuals. With respect to NSLs, moreover, the Patriot Act did not require any reports at all.

Subsequent legislation has modestly enhanced the available oversight tools, but much more vigorous measures remain needed. The Intelligence Reform Act of 2004 requires the Justice Department to provide slightly more information about FISA electronic surveillance, but it still permits the department to withhold many details that are in no way sensitive and that are routinely disclosed with respect to criminal investigations under Title III. The 2004 act, responding to a recommendation of the 9/11 Commission, also created a Civil Liberties Oversight Board in the executive office of the president. But although the 9/11 Commission (and the Senate bill implementing its proposal) contemplated a board with features designed to guarantee its independence and ability to investigate, the final version of the legislation stripped away these features and created a board with no independence whatsoever and with only the most limited ability to gather information about matters within its responsibility.

Congress again made efforts to redress this imbalance in the 2006 legislation reauthorizing the Patriot Act. The reauthorization act requires somewhat more detail in the reports made available to Congress, including information on the number of electronic surveillance orders that produced evidence for criminal prosecutions and, for the first time, disclosure of the number of NSLs issued. The gag orders that apply to NSLs and FISA document demands have been relaxed to the modest extent of permitting the recipient of the order to consult an attorney. There are now limited possibilities for seeking judicial permission to lift the gag order entirely, but this judicial power is subject to a unilateral veto by the attorney general—a prime example of the kind of constraints on oversight that the new Congress should remove. With respect to FISA document demands, investigators are now required to show "reasonable grounds" to believe that the items sought are relevant to an authorized investigation, restoring at least a slender basis for some judicial oversight. In addition, the Justice Department is now required to disclose to Congress the number of document demands granted and denied that pertain to

library records, book sales, firearms sales, tax returns, educational records, and medical records—but *not* the number that pertain to political and religious organizations. Finally, the reauthorization act requires the inspector general of the Department of Justice to audit and report to Congress on the effectiveness and use of NSLs and FISA document demands.

These are unquestionably constructive—and long overdue—steps in the direction of meaningful accountability. They pose no risk of impeding legitimate national security measures; to the contrary, they can only serve to enhance the prospects for keeping our counterterrorism activity well focused, minimizing waste, misdirected effort, and abuse of individual rights. But there is a great deal more that urgently needs to be done—for example, requiring full disclosure of all the circumstances surrounding demands for sensitive private records, granting the courts discretion to lift document "gag orders" in situations no longer justifying secrecy, and creating a full-time Civil Liberties Oversight Board with subpoena power and protection against arbitrary removal by the president. Only with safeguards such as these can we ensure that judicial, congressional, and public oversight will be well informed and effective. It remains to be seen, moreover, whether Congress and the public will succeed in forcing the executive branch to comply even with the modest reporting and disclosure obligations now in effect. Prior to the 2006 reauthorization act, when disclosure requirements were even less significant than they are now, members of the Senate Judiciary Committee nonetheless were driven to complain repeatedly that "[r]eports required by statute to be filed are months late or we never get them at all." And administration resistance to oversight has taken far more serious forms as well.

Defiance of the Law

Shortly after 9/11, the National Security Agency (NSA) began conducting warrantless electronic surveillance of international calls in which one of the parties was inside the United States. President Bush formally authorized the program in October 2001, at about the same time that the Patriot Act, with its many proposed amendments to FISA, was working its way through Congress. Yet neither then nor later did the administration seek legislation authorizing the program, which became public only when news of its existence was anonymously leaked to reporters and published in the *New York Times*.

For more than a year after that disclosure, the administration insisted on its right to continue conducting such surveillance without the FISA court approval and without revealing any information about the requirements and limits of the program. Indeed, the administration insisted that its ability to proceed outside the FISA framework was an indispensable tool in the struggle against terrorism. Then in January 2007, in what was either an abrupt about-face or an astute tactical retreat, the administration announced that the original surveillance program would be terminated and that the kind of surveillance conducted under that program "will now be conducted subject to the

approval of the Foreign Intelligence Surveillance Court."

As described by Attorney General Gonzales in a letter to the Senate Judiciary Committee, the new approach permits surveillance only when there is "probable cause to believe that one of the communicants is a member or agent of al Qaeda or an associated terrorist organization"—a prerequisite that sounds identical to the prerequisite that had been in place under FISA all along. Yet the administration continues to withhold specifics about what this requirement means and whether in particular its "probable cause" determination is made wholesale for a broad group of cases or is delegated to Justice Department officials, rather than remaining a matter for a FISA judge to assess independently on a case-by-case basis. The secrecy that continues to surround the program, together with the administration's track record of pushing law enforcement powers far beyond the boundaries publicly revealed and its continued insistence that surveillance outside the FISA framework was and is perfectly legal, all suggest that concerns about the wisdom and legality of the program have yet to be met.

As in the case of the original NSA surveillance initiative, important information about the new program remains unknown, including the prerequisites for conducting surveillance; the degree of *individual* suspicion (if any) that must attach to persons targeted; whether, in addition to targeting individuals, the surveillance also sweeps in a wide range of data on a deliberately indiscriminate basis; what limits (if any) apply to the distribution and use of information collected; and what sort of checks and oversight (if any) are in place to guard against abuse. Congress should no longer be willing to tolerate continued secrecy in these matters. No one, of course, seeks public disclosure of operational details, such as the names of suspects targeted or the technical capabilities of the equipment used. But there is no legitimate national security justification for continuing to withhold from Congress and the public the broad outlines of the program's threshold requirements and limitations.

In addition to these concerns regarding the new framework, the controversy surrounding the original NSA surveillance program remains relevant and important because the administration insists that the president has the power to conduct surveillance outside the FISA system whenever he judges necessary. The original NSA program was carried out for more than five years without FISA court approval, other clandestine surveillance programs may still be operational, and the administration claims the legal authority to put new ones into place at will. Yet the original NSA program was unquestionably illegal. FISA states explicitly that its procedures and those of Title III are the "exclusive means" by which electronic surveillance may be conducted. And FISA does not overlook the need for flexibility in unusual situations. It permits the attorney general to conduct warrantless surveillance for up to seventy-two hours under emergency circumstances, provided that the FISA court is notified and that a warrant is subsequently sought. It permits warrantless surveillance for a period not to exceed fifteen days in the event of a formal congressional declaration of war. Obviously, the original NSA program did not qualify under either of these emergency provisions; the fact that it did not meet their requirements makes doubly clear that the NSA program was in conflict with FISA. Indeed, Attorney General Alberto Gonzales conceded, in briefing the press on the program, that "[t]he Foreign Intelligence Surveillance Act requires a court order before engaging in this kind of surveillance that I've just discussed."

To defend its position that the NSA program was not illegal, despite its admitted conflict with FISA, the administration has argued that the Authorization to Use Military Force (AUMF), a congressional resolution enacted a week after 9/11, overrides statutory restrictions in effect before its passage. The AUMF grants the president the authority "to use all necessary and appropriate force against those nations, organizations or persons he determines planned, authorized, committed, or aided the terrorist attacks that occurred on September 11, 2001, or harbored such organizations or persons, in order to prevent any future acts of international terrorism." The administration contends that this endorsement for the use of "force" was not limited to the deployment of military force in its conventional sense but rather gave the president discretion to ignore at will any laws that normally restrict specific governmental actions, even within the United States.

This strained argument was expressly rejected by the Supreme Court in June 2006 in *Hamdan v.*

Rumsfeld. The Supreme Court has long held that new legislation should be interpreted as repealing an earlier statute only when there is "overwhelming evidence" that Congress intended to do so. Applying this well-settled principle in the *Hamdan* case, the Court held that the broad general language of the AUMF cannot be read to override legislation regulating specific aspects of military operations. The *Hamdan* ruling rejected the administration's claim that AUMF allowed the president to bypass statutes governing the manner in which enemy fighters captured on a foreign battlefield can be tried. The notion that the vague terms of the AUMF permit the president to bypass FISA's rules governing surveillance of individuals within the United States is even more far-fetched. As the Court expressly held in *Hamdan*, "[T]here is nothing in the text or legislative history of the AUMF even hinting that Congress intended to expand or alter the authorization set forth in [a specific statute]. . . . 'Repeals by implication are not favored.'" It was reasonably clear before *Hamdan*, and is now clear beyond any possible doubt, that the original NSA program violated existing law.

The violation, moreover, was inexcusable. FISA has been amended many times since 9/11. The administration could have sought congressional approval for further legal changes if they are indeed justified by the circumstances.

The administration's remaining defense of the original NSA program is that existing law, no matter what it says, cannot restrict the president's actions in military matters because the Constitution designates the president as "commander-in-chief" of the armed forces. The first point to notice here is that, *if* the administration's arguments were valid, then the elasticity of concepts like "war," "battlefield," and "military affairs" would in effect give the president carte blanche to ignore thousands of pages of domestic legislation, along with most of the principles and safeguards that we identify with the rule of law.

Fortunately, the administration's argument is not plausible, even in theory. The Constitution does not give the president sole responsibility for managing military affairs. It makes this crucial point clear in Article I, Section 8, by giving explicitly to *Congress*, not to the president, the power to "make Rules for the Government and Regulation of the land and naval Forces." When President Truman, during the Korean War, seized the steel mills to end a labor dispute that threatened to block production of military supplies, the Court held that Truman's authority as commander-in-chief did not include a power to seize property needed for the war effort, in the absence of legislation affirmatively granting such power. This principle of course applies even more strongly when Congress has not merely remained silent on the subject but has expressly prohibited the executive action, as it has in the case of FISA. Thus, even if electronic surveillance is considered a tool of military operations, the Constitution makes clear that the president cannot deploy it however he pleases in the face of congressional legislation to the contrary. The "commander-in-chief" clause was intended to place the military under civilian control; it cannot be converted, by the administration's inverted logic, into a vehicle for placing civilians under military control.

Many intelligence specialists nonetheless argue that FISA's requirements are no longer suited to modern technology and the needs of an effective counterterrorism effort. And, they add, it matters little in the end whether those requirements are updated by executive order or by Congress. Much of the public seems sympathetic to this contention. Yet, the first point—that FISA might be outdated has never been demonstrated, or even explained with any specificity. And the second point—that updates can just as well be made by the president as by Congress—is wrong in the most fundamental and disturbing way.

The NSA initiative is a scandal not only because of its impact on privacy but, more importantly, because the original program and its still-mysterious successor both represent a direct assault on our constitutional structure and our commitment to the separation of powers. The framers of the Constitution deliberately chose *not* to give the president the power to rule by decree, even under emergency circumstances. Precisely because reasonable people can disagree about the kind of electronic surveillance that should be permissible and the kind of oversight safeguards that are necessary, the judgment about whether and how to change the law must be made through democratic deliberation in Congress, as our Constitution specifies. It should not be made though unilateral decisions taken in secret by the president and his inner circle of advisors. Even if one knew exactly what the original and new NSA programs entail (none of us in the general public does), and even if one thought those details were all perfectly appropriate, the programs' most dangerous feature would remain—the claim that, because we are "at war," the president can unilaterally change laws and disregard laws at will.

What We've Lost

For the American public, the 9/11 attacks triggered widespread and wholly understandable feelings of insecurity. Americans normally suspicious of government instinctively relaxed their ordinary impulse to limit official powers and ensure close control of their exercise. Political leaders, predictably, exploited the fear and fanned it for their own partisan purposes. Much of the public has been readily persuaded by insistent claims, from the president, vice president, and others, that the executive branch must have sweeping new powers and freedom from bothersome oversight if it is to prevent future attacks of even greater magnitude. The result, paradoxically, is that accountability has been dramatically reduced at the very moment when it is needed more than ever. Even in the face of repeated, irrefutable evidence of executive branch capacity for catastrophic mismanagement, ranging from the response to Hurricane Katrina to the planning and execution of the occupation in Iraq, many citizens remain all too ready to believe that legislative and judicial oversight of counterterrorism powers will somehow make them ineffective.

The truth is just the reverse. In law enforcement and intelligence gathering, as elsewhere, unchecked powers are dangerous and counterproductive, permitting "mission creep" and the squandering of scarce energy and resources. The challenge of international terrorism, far from diminishing the need for accountability, makes unchecked executive powers unusually dangerous. For many Americans, the absence of effective oversight may not arouse personal anxiety or objections, but for immigrants, minority groups, and others whose support is crucial to a successful counterterrorism strategy, secret powers provoke suspicion or animosity and undermine the perceived legitimacy and fairness of every step our officials seek to take. As surveillance powers grow, secrecy and lack of accountability diminish the trust of these outsiders and chill cooperation at the very points where law enforcement authorities need it most.

As Benjamin Franklin warned, those who would sacrifice their liberty for security will in the end find that they have lost both. Franklin could not have foreseen the challenges of the twenty-first century, but his insight remains applicable, perhaps more so now than before. Unless Americans can recover their ability to face danger with self-confidence and a willingness to match strong military and law enforcement powers with equally strong safeguards, our world is likely to become increasingly dangerous. The quest for security will be ceaseless but futile. . . . ■

⁚⁚⁚ The Continuing Debate

What Is New

The Patriot Act was renewed by Congress on March 9, 2006, with no significant changes; and most of its provisions were made permanent. Controversy continues, however, and there is increasing concern about giving the government enormous powers of surveillance and detention with few safeguards and little oversight: several state legislatures and well over 100 communities have passed resolutions opposing various elements of the act. There is also great concern about what intelligence agencies refer to as "blowback": the unintended negative consequences of some security policies and efforts. One obvious effect of photographs and descriptions of mistreatment of prisoners at Abu Ghraib and Guantanamo is a strong negative attitude toward the United States internationally, and particularly in predominantly Muslim countries. And there is fear that a pattern of aggressively treating Muslims and persons of Arabic and Middle Eastern descent as potential enemies and suspected terrorists may ultimately transform potential allies (who are just as eager to avoid terrorist attacks as anyone else would be) into real enemies.

Where to Find More

A brief account of opposition to the Patriot Act among conservatives can be found in David Sarasohn, "Patriots vs. the Patriot Act," *The Nation* (September 22, 2003).

A superb examination of many specific legal cases and of larger questions concerning the relation of the Patriot Act to the U.S. Constitution can be found in Richard M. Pious, *The War on Terrorism and the Rule of Law* (Los Angeles, CA: Roxbury Publishing Company, 2006).

Amitai Etzioni examines the Patriot Act (though that is not his primary focus) from a communitarian perspective, in *How Patriotic is the Patriot Act* (New York: Routledge, 2004).

An interesting set of relatively brief readings, from a wide variety of sources, is contained in *The Patriot Act: Opposing Viewpoints* (Farmington Hills, MI: Greenhaven Press, 2005).

Strong critical examinations of the Patriot Act can be found in Stephen J. Schulhofer, *Rethinking the Patriot Act* (New York: The Century Foundation, 2005); and Nancy Chang, *Silencing Political Dissent: How Post-September 11 Antiterrorism Measures Threaten Our Civil Liberties* (New York: Seven Stories Press, 2002). Another book critical of the impact of the Patriot Act on civil liberties is David Cole and James X. Dempsey, *Terrorism and the Constitution,* 3rd Edition (New York: The New Press, 2006). Cole and Dempsey (Chapter 14) describe the wide variety of charges that the U.S. government has brought against "suspected terrorists," and then been forced to drop when evidence showed that there was no grounds for such charges; and they describe the resulting distrust this has caused in the Arab and Muslim communities here and abroad, and its negative effects on efforts to apprehend genuine terrorists.

An interesting reader on various issues related to terrorism and the Patriot Act is Russell D. Howard, James J. F. Forest, and Joanne C. Moore, editors, *Homeland Security and Terrorism* (New York: McGraw-Hill, 2006); the readings primarily (but not exclusively) support the Patriot Act and similar security measures. An anthology that questions the effectiveness as well as examining the civil liberties threats of such security programs is Richard C. Leone and Greg Anrig, Jr., editors, *Liberty Under Attack: Reclaiming Our Freedoms in an Age of Terror* (New York: Public Affairs, 2007). An excellent selection of essays, including both strong defenders and critics of the Patriot Act, is Stewart A. Baker and John Kavanagh, editors, *Patriot Debates: Experts Debate the USA Patriot Act* (Chicago: ABA Publishing, 2005). A very interesting anthology which gives special attention to technological issues related to national security and civil liberties is Clayton Northouse, editor, *Protecting What Matters: Technology, Security, and Liberty Since 9/11* (Washington, DC: Brookings Institution Press, 2006).

The U.S. Department of Justice maintains a website in support of the Patriot Act, at http://www.lifeandliberty.gov/index.html. The American Civil Liberties Union raises questions regarding various elements of the Patriot Act, at http://www.aclu.org/safefree/resources/17343res20031114.html;   and   at http.aclu.org/reformthepatriotact.html; or simply go to the ACLU site and look for material on the Patriot Act.